The Exceptional Professional

THE EXCEPTIONAL PROFESSIONAL

WHAT YOU NEED TO KNOW TO GROW YOUR CAREER

Callista Gould

ISBN: 1945663200
ISBN-13: 9781945663208
e-book: 978-1-945663-21-5
Library of Congress Control Number: 2017919292

Keller, Burns and McGuirk Publishing Co.
2301 West 45th Street
Denver, CO 80211

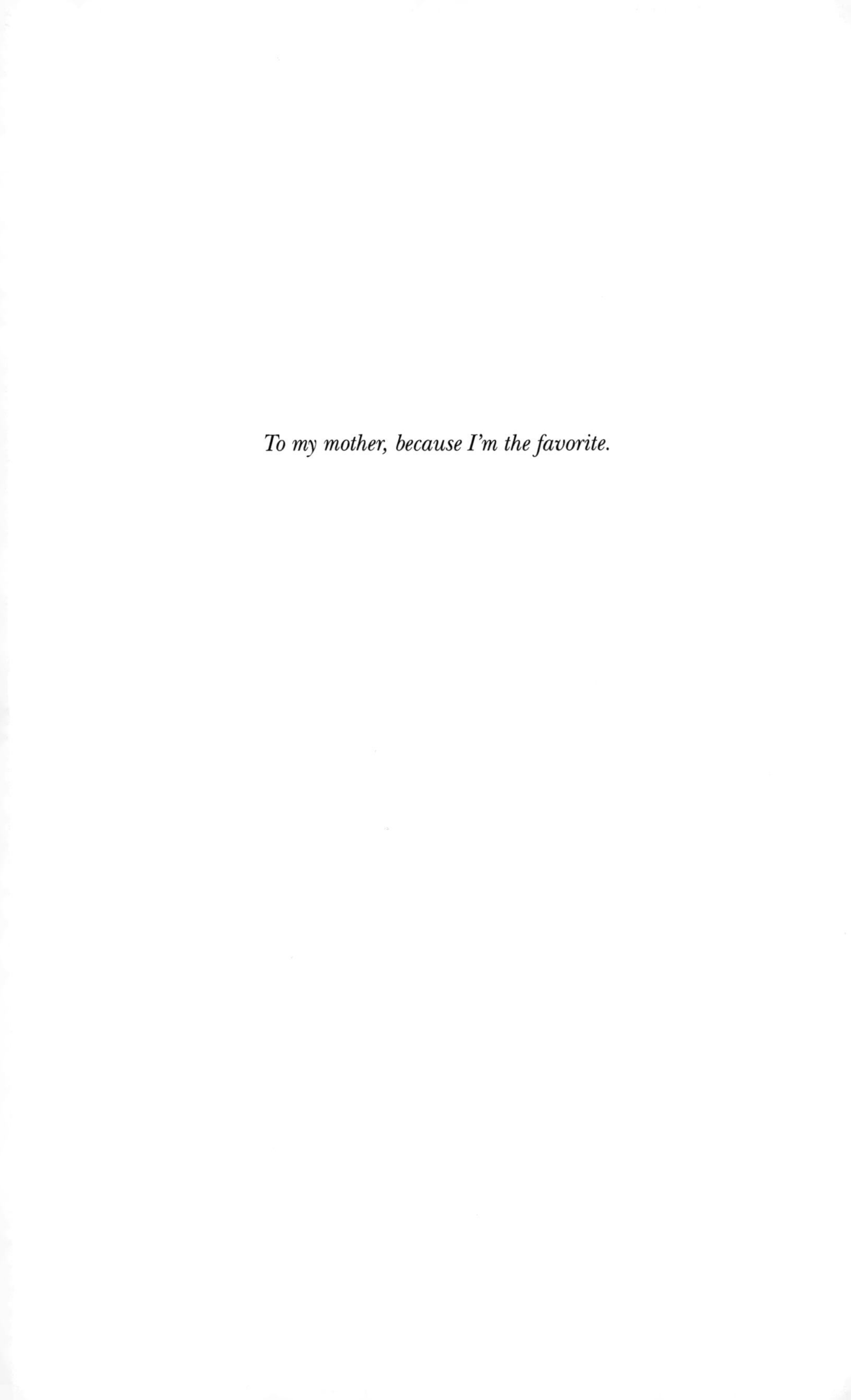

To my mother, because I'm the favorite.

CONTENTS

ACKNOWLEDGMENTS

I was waiting with my mother in the Des Moines Airport for a flight to Santa Fe, when my mother got up to stretch her legs. Five minutes later, she came back, with recommendations of what to see and where to eat in Santa Fe. She said when we return, we would be having lunch with a woman she just met, who was moving from Santa Fe to Des Moines.

I said, “How did all this come up in a five minute stretch of the legs?”

It then it occurred to me, that in my family of extroverts, my mother really is the most skilled networker. I am grateful for her example of openness to others, kindness, intelligence and always sunny disposition.

I am also thankful for my siblings, Jean, Fr. Jim, Patrick, Marie Therese, Catherine, Maureen, Michael and Mary. So much of your humor was incorporated into this book. I feel sorry for people who no longer speak to family members. Over email, the phone or in person, mine make me laugh every single day. To my late father, Dr. James P. Gould, we all miss your dry wit, routines and “Snoopy smile,” terribly.

Thank you to my clients and *Etiquette Tip of the Week* readers, for sharing your stories, many which are found in this book. To Steven Kravinsky, my first repeat client, and my only client to say, “You should charge more.” Thank you to Maria Everding of The Etiquette Institute, who put me on the path to professionalism and who continues to be my guide.

Much appreciation to Morgan McArthur, for the training at "Baraboot Camp," that helped me bring those stories to life in my presentations. Your coaching has been life-changing. Thank you, too, to speaking professional Mark Brown, for your inspiring example, advice and encouragement!

With gratitude to Dave Fisher, my Marketing Manager at Sony Music and Frank Murray, the CEO I worked for first at Goodman / Amana, then InterTech Media. The two of you gave me my creative wings in my career. Both had strategic vision that made my job interesting and challenging. But most of all, you made me look forward to coming to work every day.

To Dot Sparer, my first boss after college, who taught me how to be organized and doggedly persistent and when it seems like the place is burning to the ground around you, how to keep a cool head. To Ann Humbert, who in nine short months, prepared me for a lifetime in public relations.

Thank you to all the Sony Music alum: Carol Moy for your rock-solid friendship and for always being there; Genie Cesarotti and Jeanine Longeway for taking me under wing early on; and Erv Karwelis, Cynthia Johnson, Martha Nelson, Sally Spiegel and many others for your continued friendship over the years.

To lifelong friends Sarah Craig-Breuwet, Margaret Craig-Swack and Jen Schurman for your steadfast and unconditional friendship since we were in pigtails. Lisa Brink and Laura Foxall for your non-stop humor and Joe McAleer for your advice along the great adventure of writing this book.

Dave Makin and his team at Prometheus Indie Promotions did the cover design. I asked Dave for two designs: one, based on specific directions of what I wanted. And two, what he would do if left to his own creative instincts, with no direction from me. He hit it right down the middle and really captured the spirit of the book.

Teresa Magnus took on the Herculean challenge of editing the book under a tight deadline – I appreciated your insights and the younger, fresher perspective you brought to this book. Thank you to Kathleen DePhillips, for your prayers and prodding – without you, this book would have remained a work-in-progress indefinitely.

Lastly, to the late Dr. David Chamberlain, thanks for your wise direction at the University of Iowa. I want you to know I turned out well.

INTRODUCTION

If I were to ask, "What is the most outrageous, unprofessional behavior you have witnessed in a business setting?" Every person reading this would have a story.

One of the most shocking stories I have heard was told to me by two university professors who interviewed a PhD candidate over lunch at a restaurant. During the interview, the candidate planted a fork in the middle of a chicken breast, turned it upside down and began taking bites out of it—as if it were food on a stick at a state fair. The two interviewers sat, mouths agape. "I didn't know what to ask next," said one.

Sometimes it's the big things that cause us to not get the job or the potential client. But sometimes it is the little, quirky things. In my dining tutorial at another university, employers in the room revealed other behaviors that bounced interview candidates out of contention:

> *"She took butter and put it in her coffee. I was completely disgusted."*
> *"She blew a bubble with her chewing gum."*
> *"He licked his fingers. That was the hand I was supposed to shake at the end of meal."*

Why should it matter how we eat? Why can't we pick up the chicken breast with our hands and start gnawing on it?

The answer: because we are not just representing ourselves. We are representing our organization, our profession, maybe even our community. Our behavior reflects positively or poorly on others. Employers pay attention to our behavior, because each employee is the face of and future of the organization.

In relating the story of the PhD candidate, one professor said what I hear from many employers. "We didn't want anyone who would embarrass us." The person hired would represent the university at conferences, meetings at other universities and public events.

As a certified etiquette instructor for 10 years, I have noticed that my clients never say, "Teach our people etiquette." They say, "Teach our people to be more *professional*." When I dig deeper for specifics, there is a laundry list of challenges:

- Emails full of grammatical errors
- Sloppy or revealing clothing
- Disgusting table manners
- Texting during meetings
- Too casual with clients
- Lack of basic courtesy – greeting people, holding doors, etc.
- Cultural insensitivity
- Interrupting
- Failure to write thank you notes
- Poor hygiene
- Offensive language

What is a Professional?

Merriam-Webster's online dictionary (www.merriam-webster.com) defines "professional" as:

> (1) : *characterized by or conforming to the technical or ethical standards of a profession*
>
> (2) : *exhibiting a courteous, conscientious, and generally businesslike manner in the workplace*

This book will deal with the second part of that definition, also known as *business etiquette.* The word "etiquette" often intimidates. The biggest misconception is that etiquette is about perfection – a bunch of stuffy rules, designed to confine. But it's not about the rules. It's about being aware of and attentive to the people around us. My good friend and mentor, Maria Everding, founder of *The Etiquette Institute*, puts it this way: "The number one rule of etiquette is to break any rule to make the people around us more comfortable." Professionalism is not about *perfection*, it's about *connection*. A professional knows how to connect with people in a way that improves their own life and the lives of others.

Where Do We Learn Professionalism?

Everyone comes from a different experience. When I speak to middle or high school students, I ask, "Where did you learn your manners?" The majority will say, "My grandparents," rather than, "My parents." Is that because their overworked parents have no time to teach manners? Or are teens at that age, more receptive to their grandparents? I don't know.

Teachers, coaches or clergy can play a role. My nephew's middle school football coach instructed them to greet their teachers before each class and say, "Thank you," at the end of class. Others learn professionalism through mentors in their careers.

Some professional training comes from people like me. I have been a certified etiquette instructor for ten years, speaking at Fortune 500 companies, universities and associations across the United States and overseas. I come not as Little-Miss-Perfect, wound one notch too tight. I come as a flawed individual. In my extensive career before becoming an etiquette instructor, I have broken every single etiquette rule there is:

I have called people I have met dozens of times by the wrong name.

I have spilled beverages on myself and on others.

I have asked a woman if she was expecting—*and she wasn't.* (twice)

You can feel secure there is no etiquette mistake you can make that I have not already made. In this book, I put some of my most horrific mistakes out there, so others can benefit from what I learned the hard way.

Prior to being an etiquette instructor, I had more than 20 years of experience in a variety of corporate cultures, for global brands like Sony Music, Amana Appliances and web video pioneer, InterTech Media.

At Sony Music (Columbia and Epic recording labels), I helped plan special events for artists such as Celine Dion, Mariah Carey, Luther Vandross, Ozzy Osborne and Korn. I saw how artists behaved behind the scenes and the effect on their careers. There are musically-gifted artists, you will never know, because they were childish, demanding or aloof with people in radio or retail who could make or break their careers.

From there, I went to Amana Appliances, manufacturer of home appliances in rural Iowa. People at Amana would say, "The music industry must have been very different from Amana." I would reply, "Well, I noticed right away you did not have a *mimosa cart.*" At Amana, I witnessed the delicate relationships between union and management, offices and factory, client and vendors, consumers and customer service and how all the parts form the circle of life in any organization.

InterTech Media showed me the workings of a tech start-up and strategic thinking in unchartered territory. Start-ups teach teamwork and flexibility. People who say, "That's not in my job description," don't last. *The Exceptional Professional* also inspires entrepreneurs how to build relationships as they map out our future.

My etiquette training was with Maria Everding in St. Louis. Before that, I earned an MBA with a concentration in Accounting from Loyola University of Chicago and bachelors in English with a minor equivalent in Medieval Studies from the University of Iowa. For years, people counseled, "Lose the Medieval Studies from your resume." In Chapter 12.1: *Interviewing: Misfires, Inspires and Attire,* I will tell you why I didn't listen to them.

What Makes a Person *Exceptional?*

This book covers behaviors and habits that every professional should know. But it also goes deeper, exploring practices that distinguish a person. Sometimes it's as simple as repeating things back to another in conversation, to show you are tuned into that person. In this book, those practices that make a person exceptional are offset throughout the book, labeled, "BE EXCEPTIONAL."

Not everyone we encounter behaves like a professional and sometimes, quite the opposite. The incivility of a few can negatively impact an organization's profitability. *The Exceptional Professional* covers not only how to act, but how to *react* to people who behave badly.

What You Will Get from This Book

The Exceptional Professional gives you a fresh perspective to help move you forward in your career and in life, including:

- Simple, regular practices that make you more memorable
- How to determine the professional course of action by reason, rather than rules
- True stories of professional triumphs and disasters
- New ways of looking at your career and the people in it
- "Aha!" moments and valuable takeaways, for every experience level
- Inspiration to mentor the next generation

The Exceptional Professional aims to create life-long practices, with many happy returns. Ready to get started?

NETWORKING

1.1 *The Basics*

When I first moved to Chicago, I went to a networking event for young professionals. It was held at a beautiful venue – the top floor of a building where you could go out on a roof terrace and gaze upon the Chicago skyline, lit up at night like a giant holiday display window.

But in the "City of Big Shoulders," I got the big cold shoulder. No matter where I turned, no one would talk to me. Surprising, since the people who took my money at the door seemed so happy to see me. I had high hopes for that event and went home feeling like a beach ball with the air squeezed out of it.

I never want that to happen to anyone. I want you to be so comfortable going to events alone, you could crash someone else's family reunion and leave with valuable contacts. (That would not be a polite thing to do, but the idea is to have confidence in any situation.)

What I know now that I didn't know then, is there are certain skills we can practice, so we are not left standing alone. These skills will serve *The Exceptional Professional* well beyond the networking event and make it easier to deal with clients, vendors and co-workers.

In this chapter, you will learn:

- How to dive into a networking event, without knowing anyone
- How to introduce yourself in a memorable way
- How to follow up after a networking event.

Why We Network

Are you thinking, "Networking is torture. Why should I put myself through it?"

Some people love networking. They thrive on it. Others, not so much. They get nervous, they don't know what to say or who to approach. They retreat to a corner and pull out their phone.

Networking is like cold calling. When we cold call, we are calling up someone we don't know and have never met in order to make connections for business. With networking, we are also starting up conversations with people we don't know. It can be uncomfortable.

A friend of mine who is a realtor says, "The reason we cold call is we never know who needs us." It's the same for networking. We network because we never know who needs us.

Plus None

Wouldn't it be great, if at every event, someone took you by the arm and said, "I am so glad you are here! I can't wait to introduce you to all of these wonderful people." Ideally, a host or hostess of an event should do that. But we find ourselves many situations – large receptions, conventions, fundraisers or even social occasions like weddings – where the host or hostess may be too busy to introduce us around.

Networking is not hard, but it does take an effort on your part. The challenge of networking is you have to go it alone. Whether you are networking for a job, new clients or to meet people, you have to get into the mix and start pulling for yourself.

Does the thought of going to a networking event alone leave you as cold as a clammy handshake? Have you ever avoided a party because you didn't think you would know anyone? No one likes to go to events alone. Everyone has that fear of being in a room of strangers and having no one to talk to. It's like standing along the wall at a middle school dance.

Nothing pains me more than to hear someone say, "I did not go to that event because I did not have anyone to go with me."

Bringing a "wing-person," is like a dragging a security blanket – a comfortable guarantee you will always have someone to talk to. Being alone nudges you to seek out others and forge new friendships.

Bringing a friend to a networking event also makes you look dependent on others. Show you can hold your own. Cradling your cell phone for the entire evening is also a crutch. Ditto for the "helicopter mom" talking to employers for you at the career fair.

Networking Basics

Networking can be boiled down to three basics:

- Greet with enthusiasm
- Gather information
- Follow up

Step 1: Greet With Enthusiasm

If you don't know anyone at an event, who is the most logical person to start with? The person standing alone. That person is probably feeling awkward, just like you. You might be coming to the rescue.

Be proactive. Approach and introduce yourself. As my friend Maria Everding says, "The person who introduces himself or herself is more memorable than the one who hangs back and waits to be introduced."

If you see a group of people you would like to meet, stand outside their group, wait for a lull in the conversation, then step forward and introduce yourself.

Say, *"Hi, I'm* (first name, last name)*,"* as you extend your hand for a handshake. *"Hi, I'm Al Falfa."*

Speak up and enunciate. Say your name clearly and with confidence. Let your firm handshake match the enthusiasm in your voice.

In business, use your first name *and* your last name. When you give only your first name, it's like saying, "I'm not taking you too seriously as a potential contact." (Maybe you're not, but as a professional, your duty is make people feel important, not small.)

The other person should do the same. *"Hi Al, I'm Rhoda Dendron."* That's a very basic greeting. The "BE EXCEPTIONAL" feature will tell you how to kick it up a notch.

BE EXCEPTIONAL: *"How Do You Do?"*

Many will say, "I'm pleased to meet you," or "It's nice to meet you." That's okay. But *The Exceptional Professional*, says, *"How do you do?"*

And if you are really a star, you will repeat the person's name back to them, *"How do you do, Rhoda?"* This is what it might sound like:

"Hello, I'm Al Falfa."
"How do you do, Al? I'm Rhoda Dendron."
"How do you do, Rhoda?"

Why use, *"How do you do?"* It's a more sophisticated response. Listen for it in events or meetings and see who uses it.

Another reason is it makes the introduction about the other person instead of about you. ("It's nice to meet you" is like saying, "It's nice *for me* to meet you.") Remember, etiquette is about being attentive to the other person. "How do you do?" makes it about the other person.

Once, I had a young man in college protest, "I don't talk like that." And in his best mock-British voice: "I don't say, *'How dew yew dew?'*"

I told him, "I don't want you to say, *'How dew yew dew?'* like you're on *Masterpiece Theater*. I want you to say, 'How do you do?' in your normal voice."

Think about this. If a person is going through a room and hears, "It's nice to meet you... It's nice to meet you... It's nice to meet you..." then someone says, "How do you do?" That last person is going to stand out. That's really the goal here – to be memorable.

"How do you do?" is really a rhetorical question, but if you like, you may say, "I'm fine, thank you."

The response to "How do you do?" is not, *"Oh, my back is killing me and these bunions on my feet and my aching head..."* (We will cover how to deal with that person later.)

——

Some articles on networking give advice like, "When you walk in, scan the room and stake out the power players." I think these articles are written by people who never leave their homes. People can tell when you are scanning the room like a wolf searching for a fat zebra. Have you ever had someone shake your hand while looking past you?

When I worked in Washington D.C., I found a lot of people shake your hand, then look over your shoulder to see if there is someone more important they should be talking to. A long-time resident of the area told me, "When you first meet people here, they look you up and down to try to decide if you will be useful to them." That's an accurate assessment. But when you look past people, they can see right through you.

Never underestimate anyone at a networking event. I can't tell you how many times I have met people who I would not have picked out as the power player, who helped my career or became valuable friends.

We have all been in a situation where we have been misjudged or we misjudged someone else. One who looked unimportant was more important than we thought or one we assumed was significant was posing as something they were not. Be open.

Step 2: Gather Information

Now you have a name. It's time to gather information. Don't look at a networking event as a room full of strangers – look at it as a room full of stories. Each of us has something special about us. Our job is to get those stories and uncover that something special in everyone we meet.

To get the conversation rolling, ask questions.

What do you do for a living?

Listen, then ask more questions based on the answers.

How long have you worked there?
What do you like best about your job?

Conversation Helpers
Here is a list of conversation helpers - even if you are shy, give it a try:

Location... Location...
Are you from this area?
(From somewhere else?) *What made you decide to live here?*
How do you like living here? or *Are you enjoying the area?*
Do you have any family close by?
Do you get back to visit where you are from?
I would like to visit the area you are from - can you recommend sites to see or places to eat?

Vocation... Vocation...
What do you do for a living?
How long have you been with that organization?
How did you become interested in that field?
How did you get started in that field?
What type of training did you need to develop your expertise?
What do you like best about your job?
What are the biggest challenges in your industry?
Do you know if your organization is currently hiring?
If I were to get into your line of work, can you recommend steps to take?

Vacation... Vacation...
What do you like to do outside of work... or in your spare time?

Do you have any hobbies?
How did you get interested in that?
Do you need special gear?
Where do you go to practice your hobby?

Think Like a Journalist

If you need help thinking of questions, think like a journalist. If you have ever written a news story, there are five questions you must answer: Who? What? When? Where? Why?

- **Who:** the person's name
- **What:** *What do you do for a living?*
- **When:** *How long have you lived in this area? How long have you been with your organization?*
- **Where:** *Where are you from? Where do you work?*
- **Why:** *What made you choose that career? What do you like best about your job? How do you like living in this area?*

In my presentations, I have a conversation skills exercise where I introduce a volunteer from the audience and have audience members ask questions and follow up questions. With interns at a large financial services organization, my young volunteer was an actuary intern.

Through the questions, the other interns found out he was also a jazz musician, who played at local clubs at night. No one would have ever guessed. Several of the interns expressed an interest in going to hear him play and new friendships were formed. If you ask enough questions, you can find something in common with almost anyone.

What's In It for Me?

Some of you might be thinking, "When can I talk about myself?" After you have asked several questions, if you see a segue, talk about your own experience or interests. But don't take over and dominate the conversation. Return to asking questions. People will appreciate you more when you take an interest in them.

Don't Convert the Introvert

I have a friend who is handsome, charming, successful, extremely intelligent, well read, well mannered… and terrified of social situations. Walk into a room and talk to strangers? He'd rather die.

Learning to network doesn't mean everyone has to transform into this outgoing, life-of-the-party person. If you are shy or introverted, leverage that natural shyness.

Have a few open-ended questions to ask people you meet. An open-ended question is one which invites the person to give more than a short or single word answer. This requires minimal talk on your part and endears you to others. When you are not a talker, the simplest question is, "Tell me about yourself." The best networkers are listeners.

The other thing you can do as a shy person is make introductions. That allows you to stand back while others talk but still score big points. So, if you are shy, don't go changing.

BE EXCEPTIONAL: Introduce People

The Exceptional Professional knows the most popular person at any party is not the person who tells the best jokes. It is the person who introduces people to each other.

The information you gather from asking questions is valuable. It helps identify future clients, employers, business partners or friends. It's also used to bridge the conversation when you introduce others with similar backgrounds or interests.*"Candice, I'd like you to meet, Harry Wolf. Like you, Harry enjoys off-road cycling on his mountain bike. Harry, this is Candice Lupus."*

Always look for common ground, that helps the people you introduce have a starting point for conversation. Once, I introduced a man and woman who both had season tickets to the New York Jets football team. They ended up getting married. Not sure whose seats they ended up sin.

You could stand in one place and introduce people all night. The next time people see you at an event, they will gravitate to you, because they know they will meet others through you.

Ending a Conversation

When your conversation has run its course, you have exchanged business cards (or decided in your head it is not worth exchanging business cards), how do you move on to the next person? Reach out your hand to give a parting handshake and say one of, or a combination of these:

I enjoyed speaking with you.
It was a pleasure to meet you.
Thank you for your time.
Thank you for taking the time to speak with me.
You have an impressive background and I enjoyed hearing about it.
Enjoy the rest of your evening.
Enjoy the rest of the convention (or other event).
Thank you for your card. May I follow up with you next week?
Good luck to you.
I wish you the best.

Step 3: Follow Up

College students sometimes walk away from a networking event disappointed. "No one offered me a job," they say. Networking is not about instant gratification. Networking is about building relationships. That first contact at a networking event is only the beginning of your relationship. Follow through is up to you.

It begins with a business card. After an event, don't just cast aside those business cards. Review them and determine how you might follow up with each one. Discard ones where you have no plans to follow up.

Following up is the most essential part of networking and there are so many avenues you can take:

- Send an email.
- Make a phone call.
- Mail a card or a letter.
- Connect on social media.
- Invite the person out for coffee.
- Schedule a follow up meeting.

Your message could be:

> *"I enjoyed meeting you at the alumni event. Let's stay in touch."*
> *"Your start-up sounds very exciting. I look forward to the Open House."*
> *"I liked what you said about your organization's diverse culture and wondered if we could meet for coffee to talk about the possibility of working together?"*
> *"Thank you for taking the time to tell me about the possible openings at your organization. As promised, enclosed is a copy of my resume..."*

BE EXCEPTIONAL: Personalize Your Social Media Invite

Social media makes it easy to connect. On sites like LinkedIn, you click a button and a generic message is filled in: "I'd like to add you to my professional network."

But *The Exceptional Professional* knows it's wise to personalize. Add a sentence about where you met or why you want to connect. "We sat at the same table at the hospital fundraiser and I would like to stay in touch. Please join my network on *LinkedIn*."

If someone sends me the generic invite and I don't recognize the person, I don't accept the offer to connect. A friend of mine learned the hard way. She agreed to connect with a stranger and he ended up sending all of her contacts a solicitation, claiming she recommended him. Her contacts started emailing her, "Why did you refer this pushy salesperson person to me?"

Personalizing the invite creates a stronger connection and makes it more likely the invite will be accepted.

How Not to Follow Up

A friend invited me out for coffee, then surprised me by putting a printout of all my *LinkedIn* connections on the table and saying, "Who of these connections can you refer me to?" That's a technique taught in sales seminars. But it was too aggressive and made me uncomfortable.

Can Spam: do not start sending e-newsletters without asking a person's permission. I usually make a deal with people, "I'll read your e-newsletter if you read my *Etiquette Tip of the Week* emails."

Honor Your Commitments

"They say they will call. Then I never hear from them again." Surprisingly, I keep hearing this from professional people who give their business cards to people who are seeking employment.

If you take someone's business card and say, "I will call you next week because I would like to learn more about your organization..." or "I'll email you about going out for coffee..." that's a commitment. Being a professional means when you make a commitment, you honor it.

Thank Event Hosts, Sponsors and Organizers

When you leave a networking event, thank the host/hostess, sponsors or organizers of the event. Then follow up with a fold-over thank you note through the postal mail, letting them know how much you enjoyed the event and appreciated all the work that went into it.

Practice Networking

I met a woman who said, "My husband says I talk to all cashiers like they are family." What a wonderful way to go about life.

Whenever you are out in public, practice networking. Make conversation with the clerk behind the counter, with other people in line, with others on the elevator, as you leave a theater or church or on the sidelines of kids' sporting events.

When I was in the music business, going to concerts all the time, I used to turn to the person next to me and say, "I always try to guess the opening song. What do you think it's going to be?" That's networking.

Those are the basics. Now it's time to get down to the nuts and bolts of networking – all the elements that will help you put some muscle in your mingle.

1.2 *Put Some Muscle In Your Mingle*

The professor gave us 15 minutes to mingle and introduce ourselves to each other. He said, "One of the questions on your final will be to name as many of your classmates as you can – first name, last name. This was the first day of a marketing class in my MBA program at Loyola University of Chicago.

Some of the 45-50 students groused that memorizing names had nothing to do with marketing. On the contrary, it had everything to do with marketing. It was a very smart exercise for anyone in business.

In the last chapter, we covered the basics. If you know that much, you can navigate any networking event by yourself. But *The Exceptional Professional*, wants to thrive, not just survive. Now it's time to put some muscle into your mingle.

In this chapter, you will learn:

- How to make a memorable first impression
- How to remember what's-her-name and what to do if you can't
- The best answer for, "What do you do?"
- Business card protocol and trends

No Fear: Enter with Confidence

It's a room full of strangers but don't let them see your fear. Enter with confidence, shoulders back, chin up. My friend Maria Everding says having your chin up is a more attractive look. When your chin is down, others can see additional chins and more visible lines under your eyes. If you don't believe it, look in the mirror and see for yourself – it's not pretty. If most people knew this, they would not be constantly glancing down at their cell phones.

Hold your beverage in your left hand, shake with your right. If you have a beverage in your right hand and have to suddenly shift it to your left hand, your right hand will be cold and clammy from your drink and that leaves a bad impression.

Know the dress code for any event. I often see women in cocktail dresses at events where the code is business dress or people underdressed for events that require cocktail or formal attire. (More about that in Chapter 7.2: *Suiting Up and More Formal Codes.*)

Picture This: Roaming Photographers

When the photographer comes around, put your beverage down. Don't be photographed with a beverage in hand.

There is a right way and a wrong way to pose for a group photo. Standing with two shoulders squared, facing the photographer makes you look like the wide side of a barn. For the "slimming pose," turn sideways, give your body a quarter twist and point your forward foot towards the photographer.

It's okay to bow out of photos, especially when someone is snapping shots with their cell phone. You never know whose *Facebook* or other social media account you are going to end up on or in what context.

Eye Contact

Your eyes should be alert but relaxed. A deer-in-the-headlights look is disconcerting to those whom you are trying to engage in conversation. You may divert your eyes away every few seconds, so your eye contact is not a hard, fixed stare. Some people use a fixed gaze to intimidate.

When someone avoids eye contact with you, what does that make you think about that person? Shy? Not interested? Or maybe they are *up to something.* It might be cultural differences. Some cultures practice intermittent eye contact, where they look away more often than make eye contact. In other cultures, men and women avoid eye contact.

In the United States, professionals make direct eye contact. It shows you are giving that person your attention.

Your Handshake Speaks

When we introduce ourselves, we offer our hand for a handshake. Your handshake speaks. It must be firm and it should say: *"I am confident. I am enthusiastic. And I am darn glad to meet you."* A firm handshake also says, *"I am sincere,"* and *"You can trust me."*

A limp handshake says: *"I'm not sure of myself. I am not sure about you. I am not sure why I got up this morning."* And let's be honest, when you are on the receiving end of the "fingers handshake," it's kind of a yucky feeling.

The opposite, is the "Knuckle Crusher," where it feels like the person is trying to fuse your fingers into one. The crushing handshake says, *"I'm angry. I am controlling. I'm stronger than you."* Sometimes people who don't have a lot of power, try to squeeze the life out of your hand to make it look like they do. Don't be fooled.

Technique

Your palm fits in the other person's palm. Seal the grasp by wrapping your fingers around the other person's hand with a firm grip. No need to pump up and down like it's crack-the-whip.

Some say, "You have to touch web-to-web," meaning the web of skin between your thumb and index finger should touch the same on the other person. I don't say that, because the thought of someone touching my web is disturbing. Just reach out and grasp.

Practice your handshake with friends and other professionals. If you don't have anyone to practice with, take a remote control from a TV, turn it sideways and grip it with your right hand. If someone could walk up and easily slip the remote out of your hand, your grip is too weak.

Shake hands coming and going. Shake hands to say, "Hello," and shake hands to say, "Goodbye." If you mean business, if you want the job, the sale or credibility, say it with a firm handshake.

The Equal Opportunity Handshake

Shake hands with a woman as firmly as a man. To give a woman a light handshake is condescending and not treating her as an equal in business.

At many universities, I speak to student-athletes. One thing I find is the male athletes will give me very weak handshakes, while the female athletes will crush my hand like an aluminum can. I have to tell the female athletes, "Lighten up," and the male athletes, "Toughen up."

I Don't Want to Break Them

What if the person you are shaking hands with seems frail or suffers from arthritis? If you think a firm handshake might cause a person pain, mirror the pressure that person puts on your hand.

If the person is disabled and does not have the use of their right hand, shake their left hand with your left hand. In college, I shook hands with Senator Bob Dole of Kansas, who does not have the use of his right hand, due to an injury he suffered in World War II. I extended my right hand by accident. He reached out with his left hand and shook my right hand a little awkwardly. It was clumsy on my part, finesse on his. He was trying to make me feel at ease when I goofed.

Clammy Hands

A high school student told me she didn't like shaking hands because she had clammy hands. That's when a person's hand feels cold and moist – it's actually a very common condition. If you have clammy hands, wipe them off on your clothing or on a handkerchief. Attempt to warm them up by rubbing them together or by using one of those hand air-dryers in the restroom. Some people warm their shaking hand by tucking it under their leg when they are sitting.

Be kind to the person with clammy hands – many people have them as a result of a medical condition.

Phony Power Moves

"The Politician" handshake is where the person shaking your hand grabs your upper right arm with his left hand. Men do this more than women.

In my business etiquette classes, I learned women don't like it when men grab their upper arm while shaking hands. They feel it's controlling.

Some people reach for your hand in a handshake, then rotate their own hand, so it is on top. This is a phony power move. No need to arm wrestle back to the upright position. Just ignore it. Another phony power move is when the person shaking your hand tries to pull you toward him or her. Maintain the grip while taking a step backward.

Listen Up

Two of my college roommates said, "Your sister, Catherine, is my favorite Gould." I have eight siblings, so that says a lot. Catherine is a felony attorney for the Public Defender's Office in Dallas, Texas. One reason she is so skilled an attorney and so popular with friends, is she is an intense listener.

Listening is a valuable skill for any career. Highly effective attorneys, sales people or managers are not just "good talkers," they are good listeners. Dr. P.M. Forni, author of *The New York Times* bestseller, *Choosing Civility* and co-founder of the Johns Hopkins Civility Project, reminds us that humans want validation and listening is a fundamental form of validation. Networking events are places to hone listening skills.

BE EXCEPTIONAL: The Elite Repeat

The Exceptional Professional is attentive to others and therefore, practices active listening. There are two kinds of listening:

1. **Passive Listening**
When we listen passively, we are there and someone else is speaking. We may even be nodding, "Uh-huh... uh-huh..." But the words may be washing right over us.
2. **Active Listening**
Active listening is listening more intently. Practice active listening by taking one little nugget of what the other person is saying to you and paraphrasing it back.
"So you grew up in Minneapolis but then your organization transferred you to San Diego."
"What you are saying is you are happy with your team, but they could use more training."

Don't repeat everything people say back to them, as if you are a human parrot. That would be annoying. Do it once in a while to let them know you are listening and tuned in to what they are saying.

Active listening makes people feel valued and heard. It is also essential to problem solving. Try active listening in your regular conversations. Listen and repeat back some of what you have heard.

Name Recall

Do you ever say, "I'm just not good at remembering names?" Many think name recall is something we are born with. We either have it or we don't. Not true! Name recall is a skill to develop like any other. Name recall does not require a photographic memory. It requires practice. How do you get to Carnegie Hall? PRACTICE.

Like grammar, name recall is a life-long practice. Anyone can become skilled at name recall, it just takes a little effort. Whether you are working for a large entity or an entrepreneur starting your own business, remembering people's names is a tremendous advantage.

Elements to Help You with Name Recall

1. **Repeat person's name back to them when you are introduced.**
   "How do you do, Leo?"
2. **Practice the person's name silently to yourself.**
   "Leo... Leo... Leo... Leo... Leo..."
3. **Quiz yourself.**
   Scan the room and try to remember names of people you have met.
   "That's Leo... that's Charmaine... that's Margaret..."
4. **Create rhymes or other words of association.**
   Leo is health conscious, so *Leo must use oleo*. Maybe you picture him with a big mane, like *Leo the Lion.* (Roar!) As a teenager of the 80s, I think of the song, "Jungle Love" by Morris Day and

the Time and in my head, I'm singing, "O-Leo-Leo…" (The lyrics are "Oh-we-oh-we-oh...") The great thing about word association? The people you are remembering never have to know how you are remembering them. Your rhyming doesn't have to be exact. Here are some other examples:

"Sharmaine is charming."

"Margaret is a brunette."

5. **Write it down.**

   My father kept a set of index cards to capture names and notes to help him remember people. Today, some people keep notes on their phones. Make notes when you have a moment alone – not in front of others.

BE EXCEPTIONAL: Post Event Review

The Exceptional Professional knows that to be really good at name recall, it takes a little homework.

Make notes on anything you can remember about the people you met: what they looked like or details from your conversation. Review the business cards you received and try to picture each person. Don't just do it once, do it a few times a week or before your next event.

Learn the Faces of Your Connections Online

Professional networks online, like *LinkedIn*, usually feature headshots of your connections. Cover up the names of your connections and see if you can identify their faces. Can you name everyone?

And You Are…?

Someone comes up to you and says, "It's nice to see you again." You are drawing a complete blank. Or they look so familiar—but from where— and when? It happens to all of us. Then someone joins you and you have to introduce the two. "I'd really like you to meet, uh..." What do you do?I was speaking to a group of bankers' wives and one said, "I just say, 'Do you two know each other?' and let them take over." Some people think they are clever by saying things like, "Pronounce your last name again for me." The person replies, "It's Smmmiiittthhh."

Don't finesse, just confess. When you can't remember someone's name, say, "Please tell me your name again." It's a little less chilly than, "I'm sorry, I forgot your name." Nobody likes to be forgettable. Preface it with anything you do recall. *"I enjoyed our conversation at the opening reception..." "I remember we met at that Super Bowl party... please tell me your name again."*

It's Complicated

In a Toastmasters meeting, a gentleman from India was giving his first speech: the "Icebreaker." The Toastmaster introducing him took one look at his last name, which looked like the alphabet had a train crash, and said, "Your last name is difficult and we will never be able to pronounce it, so we'll just call you, 'Mr. B.'"

I said, "Stop. We are all in business here, we will learn your name." The new member said, "It looks complicated, but it's actually quite simple. And he pronounced his name for everyone. He was right, it was simple, almost musical. From that day forward, everyone knew his name.

If someone has a complicated name:

- Ask them to repeat it – again and again, until you get it.
- Have them spell it, write it down phonetically.

Most people will be pleased you made the effort. I have had people I just met say, *"I'm sorry, I know I am not going to remember your name."* That makes me want to say, "Likewise!" It is the same thing as saying, *"You are not worth the effort."* To not learn someone's name is to marginalize them. Make the effort. People are worth it.

What If People Don't Get Your Name?

What if someone keeps mispronouncing your name? Should you correct that person? How many times?

Believe me, I get this. With the name Callista, I get called Alyssa, Clarissa, Colesta, Calleesta. In high school, a gym teacher always called me, "Castella." After a while I said, "Just call me Stella." Most times, I assist people by saying, "It sounds like 'ballistic."

I have to confess, there are times I am the perpetrator and not the victim. I was at a dinner where the woman across from me was introduced to me as "Judith." In the first question out of my mouth, I called her, "Ruth." What was I thinking? I guess they are both Biblical.

The worst thing people can do is make up a nickname that is convenient for them. "How 'bout if I just call you, Cal?" or "Callie?" Sometimes they don't even ask. Please don't assume Catherine is "Cathy" or Margaret is "Maggie" or Andrew is "Andy" or "Drew."

If someone forgets your name, help them out. *"I'm Lan Line. I occupied the cubicle next to you for five years."*

If someone keeps mispronouncing your name or calling you by the wrong name, correct them three times. After that, forget it. They will never get your name. There's a man I was in a breakfast club with for many years. Every time I saw him, he would call out, "Hi, Celeste!" I tried correcting him several times. Then I gave up. I'm "Celeste" to him.

Hello My Name Is...

Imagine circulating through an event. A tiny camera on the edge of your eyeglasses locks in on a face. The facial recognition software immediately identifies the name of the person and delivers it to the screen on your eyeglasses. You reach out your hand, "Nice to see you again (name)!" You are a social star.

Until then, we are all stuck trying to steal a sneak peek at the name badge of the person who looks vaguely familiar, but whose name completely escapes us. This is the side glance dance. It's a tricky business. The person is approaching. Eye contact is made. We are trying to glance at their name badge without giving ourselves up.

With peel and stick name badges, we can make it easier on others by placing our name badge on the right side of our chest, just below the shoulder. When we shake hands, our eye naturally follows the person's arm to their right shoulder. The name badge is easier to see on the right.

Traditionally, name badges were worn on the left, because men had breast-coat pockets there and the name badges were clipped on. Some people place their name badge on the left because they are right handed – they peel off the badge, put it in their right hand, then naturally slap it across the left side of their chest.

But it is better to have it on the right. Making sure your name badge is visible and easy to read assists others in learning your name. We thwart others in their efforts to read our name badge when:

- We have long hair hanging down over our name badge.
- The letters are so microscopic, it's like wearing a business card.
- Our handwriting is so bad, it might as well be in hieroglyphics. (Seriously, who is good at writing names with fat *Sharpie* markers?)
- The name badge is hanging on a lanyard near our stomach, where it's covered up with an info packet, handbag or man-bag.

Questions to Answer in Your Mind Before a Networking Event

At some point, a person may turn the conversation back to you. Before an event, think of answers to common questions people ask at any event.

- *What do you do for a living?*
- *What do you do with your time off?*
- *Tell me about yourself.*

How Should You Answer, "What Do You Do?"

Have you ever tried to have a conversation with someone who is giving you one word answers?

"How is your new project going?" Answer: *"Fine."*
"How is the food?" Answer: *"Good."*
"What do you do for a living?" Answer: *"Insurance."*

In insurance, are you an underwriter? Claims adjuster? Sales person? Attorney? Actuary? Customer service professional? Human resources professional? The shorter your answer, the harder you make the other person work to drag the conversation out of you.

The better way is to give your title and a little nugget about your area of expertise or interest.

"I am a claims adjuster for Drama-free Insurance – I investigate and negotiate terms for our clients who have been in an auto accident."
"I am a public relations consultant who specializes in crisis communication."
"I am a chemical engineer and I research bio-fuels."
Another example: *What do you do for a living?*
Too short: *"I'm a college student."* Or *"I go to State College."*
Better: *"I'm a senior, business and sociology major at State College. I am interested in real estate and affordable housing solutions."*

Too Much Information

When you answer, "What do you do?" don't give too much info.

"I'm a chemistry major, because when I was a little kid, my parents bought me a chemistry set for my birthday and so I have always liked to tinker around with chemicals. And in middle school, I took an honors chemistry class and I joined the Chemistry Club..."

Elevator Speech

Some preach the elevator speech – a 30-second inventory of your experience and career aspirations or a pitch for your business. The name comes from the idea that you might run into someone important in an elevator and be able to pitch yourself to that person in the length of an elevator trip between floors.

Elevator speeches are not deployed in regular networking events that much, but they are useful in "speed networking" events. Speed networking is where you have two or three minutes to make a pitch to someone and when time is up, someone blows a whistle or rings a bell and you switch to the next person and do your pitch all over again.

Speed networking is fun and a great opportunity to practice your elevator speech, because by the time you give it four times or more, you will have fine-tuned it. In an elevator speech, convey three things:

1. Where I have been (experience)
2. Where I am going (goals)
3. What I can do for you and your organization (qualifications)

Number three is key, because as I have mentioned before, being a professional means making it about the other person and not yourself. Here is an example of an elevator speech:

> *"I am an English major and recently interned in the Public Relations Department at Happy Hospital, creating web content and promotional videos on healthcare and wellness. I enjoyed the creative and the multi-media aspects of the job and felt like I was doing something important for the community. I would like to find a full-time position in health care communications and I know I could create a great multi-media campaign to expand your organization's reach."*

The elevator speech is also useful in interviews when someone says, "Tell me about yourself."

What Not to Do: Verbal Business Card

Sometimes at a networking event, when I ask someone, "What do you do for a living?" I get a response like this: *"I help people realize their financial aspirations by turning their business visualization into actionable strategy."*

Wha...? This is a tactic known as the "Verbal Business Card." The idea is to withhold your real title and give vague, yet intriguing statement to "hook" the listener, who is then supposed to say, "Oooh, that sounds interesting. Tell me more."

I heard about it at a seminar and I recommend you don't use it. It doesn't work. It's like talking to an advertisement. People don't want to talk to advertisements. They want to talk to living, breathing humans who are being honest. "What do you do?" *I'm a financial adviser. I'm a design engineer. I'm a real estate attorney. I'm a dog walker.* In networking, don't play games. Be yourself.

If you encounter the Verbal Business Card, just ask in a good natured way, "What does it say on your business card?"

Business Cards

Let's talk about the real business card. Present your business card with the words on the card facing the person so he or she can take it and read it. Do not cover the business name with your finger or thumb.

A business card is a representation of the person, so show it respect. Do not shove it immediately into your back pocket. Do not write on a business card in front of the person. Look at it for a moment. If you like the card, compliment the person on the design or appearance.

When working with people from other cultures, learn their business card protocol. In China, present and receive business cards with two hands. Show respect by looking at the card at least a minute or two.

Some people hand out business cards like they are shooting tennis balls out of a ball machine. Do not throw your business cards at everyone in the room. Doing so tells people their contact was not important.

When should you take out your business card and hand it to someone? The business card should be offered just before you part ways with the person or before that person gets involved in another discussion. Some people take out their business cards right after the introduction or when the conversation gets going and it looks like there is an interest in staying in touch.

When you are dealing with a senior level executive, wait for the executive to offer you a card. Do not ask for the executive's card.

Business Card Trends

Trends in business cards come and go. At one time, there were business cards that could be placed in a computer DVD drive to play a presentation.

For a while, the paperless zapping of your card from one phone or digital device to another was the rage at conferences. It kind of lost its sizzle as people returned to paper business cards. Then came scannable QR codes on business cards. But those take up a lot of space on a business card and it's not clear how many people take the time to scan them. Some people have business cards with Braille characters for the vision-impaired.

Should you have your photo on your business card? It depends. Are you easy on the eyes? Just kidding. The real question is will your face sell your product or service? Many realtors and insurance salespeople include their pictures to help establish a personal connection.

I don't have my photo on my business card, but I appreciate it when others do, because it helps with name recall, as long as the photo was taken in the same decade and the hair color is close. Scott Stratten, author of *UnMarketing*, speaking at a National Speaker's Association conference, said, "If you have a bio photo, please look like it."[1]

BE EXCEPTIONAL: Bi-Lingual Business Cards

The Exceptional Professional who does a lot of international business has double-sided business cards that are English on one side and the language of their client on the other side.

If you do not know the language, make sure you have a reputable translator, who knows all the nuances of the language, proofread your card before it goes to print.

At the beginning of this chapter, I told the story of my marketing professor at Loyola University of Chicago, who told us one of the questions on our final would be to name our classmates. Throughout the term, I devoted time to getting to know my fellow students. When the question came up on the final exam, I not only listed their names but also where they worked and where they were from.

No matter what the challenge, always work to exceed expectations.

Since we're on the subject of challenges, next, we'll cover awkward moments in networking.

1.3 *Awkward at the Networking Event*

I was speaking at a chamber of commerce event and I had a question from a woman who was stunningly gorgeous, like she fell out of a magazine, but also a respected member of the business community.

"I feel like whenever I am in a business situation, men are trying kiss me when they greet me," she said. "How do I prevent that?"

I said, "That never happens to me."

Into any networking, awkward moments must fall. This chapter is about strategies for *The Exceptional Professional* to survive the awkward moments and make the most of networking time.

In this chapter, you will learn:

- Defensive moves for offensive behavior
- What to do when cornered by a talker
- How to keep from bombing at banter
- How to juggle food and drink

Blocking the Pass

The serious answer to the question on what to do with the men who are puckering up at events, is there are two defensive moves.

The first comes from my brother, who was in the Marines for 20 years. Take your right hand, shaking the offender's hand and pull them to the right. It doesn't take a lot of power and pulls the person off balance. The other move is to block them with your left arm straight out. If the beverage in your left hand spills onto the offender, so be it.

Greeting with a Kiss in Some Industries

Hugging and kissing is usually frowned upon in business. However, a greeting with a kiss on the cheek is common in certain industries: the music industry, entertainment industry and also the advertising industry.

As manager of public relations at Amana Appliances out in rural Iowa, I was part of the brand revitalization team working on a multi-million dollar TV and print campaign with advertising giant DDB Needham's New York branch. Members of DDB Needham's account team frequently greeted me with a kiss on the cheek. Being an arms-length person from the Midwest, I slapped a few of them before I figured out that was the norm. If you are interested in advertising, pucker up.

The greeting with a kiss goes like this: shake hands, lean in and give a light kiss to the person's right cheek. Not an air kiss. And not a wet, sloppy, Labrador retriever kiss. In some cultures, you may be expected to kiss both cheeks. In others, any such contact might be grossly offensive.

Greeting people with a kiss on the cheek is more common on the East Coast. I started college at Chestnut Hill College in Philadelphia and was surprised when my friends' parents would kiss me on the cheek. Back in Iowa, my parents would kiss me but not my friends.

If someone invites you into an office, shuts the door, then tries to give you a hug and kiss, that's different. You need to get out of there.

Cornered By a Talker

Everyone has experienced this. Getting cornered by the "talker," a person who will talk nonstop, monopolizing your time and verbally blocking all means of escape. If talkers pause to ask you a question, they don't really care what you have to say, it's just a segue to what they want to say next and continued conversation incarceration. What can you do?

This might sound unkind but introduce that person to someone else. If you are at an event to network, whether you are representing your organization or representing yourself, you are there to do business. If someone is preventing you from meeting others and conducting business, you need to get away from that person.

If there is no one around to introduce (meaning, everyone else in the room has identified the talker before you), say, "Please excuse me, there is someone I need to talk to before the end of the evening."

Do not even try, "I need to get another drink," or "I have to use the restroom," because the talker might say, "Me too! I'll go with you," or "Great! I'll wait for you." Be polite but get away. Leave skid marks.

The Quiet Person

The opposite of the talker is the quiet person. My friend went on a date with a man she met on the Internet. "He was so quiet," she said, "I felt like Oprah, trying to pull information out of him."

Shy people need a little space and a little time. Ask questions, but don't interrogate. Be patient if it takes them a little longer to respond. They may be relieved to listen while others speak. Encourage them by showing appreciation for their answers or insights.

"You bring up a very interesting point... "
"I didn't know anything about that... I am glad you mentioned it. "

Measure how the conversation is going by how they are looking at you. Do they smile back? Do they look hopeful? Do they look bored or annoyed? If the conversation is not going well, politely disengage and move on. *"It was nice to meet you. Enjoy the rest of your evening. "*

The Cold Shoulder

What if someone shows no interest in speaking with you? What if someone refuses your handshake? This is getting "the cold shoulder."

Sometimes you approach someone and they turn away or seem aloof. Don't take it personally. People are unpredictable. Not everybody is friendly, some are just socially awkward. Keep moving, because the next person you meet might be an essential contact.

We never know what's going on in another person's life. They might be having an off-night. Maybe they are distracted by issues at work or at home. Maybe they are not feeling well. Give people the benefit of the doubt rather than assume they are snooty.

Groups can be cliquey and unwelcoming, too. You approach a group, they are not open to a new person. Tick tock, the game is locked, like child's play. Move on. There are others in the room worth meeting.

Cell Phony

I was introduced to a manager who had one of those earpiece cell phones. He said, "Hi, how are you doing?" I thought he was talking to me. He was talking to the earpiece. It was awkward. I never really got to meet him, because he was absorbed with the earpiece throughout the event.

What if someone you are trying to talk to keeps answering or checking their cell phone? What's on their phone is obviously more interesting than you. Walk away.

It's so easy to retreat to the edges of the room to the comfort of your cell phone, to check messages and look busy. If you do that, you are cutting yourself off. Be present with the people who are present.

What to Do When They... *Ah-choo!*

What if someone is sneezing into his or her hand, then puts it out to shake yours? What do you do? Shake the hand. Then go and wash yours off or use hand sanitizer. But don't whip out your hand sanitizer in front of the person. Try not to refuse a handshake.

Don't panic. Not all who are sneezing, coughing or blowing their nose are viral. Some have food allergies or sensitivities to dusty or dry conditions. The polite thing to do is to not recoil in horror.

If you are the one under the weather, it is acceptable to say, "I hope you don't mind if we forego the handshake, I am getting over a cold and I do not want to pass it along." Most people will happily oblige. Never say, *"I have a touch of the flu."* Nothing clears out a room faster.

Eating While Meeting

Mingling gets more awkward when food is thrown into the mix. When there is food served at a networking event, some people think, "Dinner!" But snarfing down an entire wheel of brie or tackling the wait staff to get that last coconut shrimp is never a good career move. Eat before you go to the event, so you are not starving. Keep in mind, you are there to do business first and to eat, second.

Maria Everding says if you have a plate, take two appetizers. If you do not have a plate, take one. No eating directly from the buffet as you go through it.

Most networking event food is finger food. If there is a server circulating with an appetizer tray, take a napkin, then take an appetizer. Some things can be eaten in one bite. For anything bigger, take multiple bites. If you have a plate and a fork to cut items in half, do it.

Juggling Food and Drink

If you have an appetizer plate and a stemmed glass, you can hold both. Take your index finger on your left hand and loop it around the left side of the stem of the glass. Place your other three fingers on the right side of the stem, with the fingers stretched out and upward. Place the plate on your three fingers and put your thumb on top of the plate to balance.

Getting Saucy

When choosing appetizers, keep in mind you might be shaking hands with people. Avoid appetizers that are sticky or dripping in sauce.

Never lick your fingers. Don't even excuse yourself to go somewhere else and lick your fingers. Wipe your fingers on your napkin or excuse yourself to the restroom to wash your hands.

Do not double dip. This seems painfully obvious but you would not believe how many adults do this. Double dipping is when someone dips their chip, vegetable or other item, takes a bite, then puts the bitten end back in the dip. Break your chip in half, then dip each piece separately. Better yet, put the dip on your plate and dip from your plate.

The Toothpick

Ah, the toothpick. The most misunderstood of tools. If you are served an appetizer on a toothpick, you may eat the item from the toothpick. Do not place the toothpick back on the tray with the food. And definitely do not reuse it to harpoon other food items on the buffet table.

To dispose of the toothpick, leave it on your plate or find a trash receptacle. Do not shove the toothpick between the cushions of a couch.

Toothpicks are not multi-taskers. A toothpick in an appetizer or holding up the fruit in your beverage is not a device for cleaning your teeth. Never use a toothpick in public to dislodge debris from in between your teeth—not even if you grab one while walking out of a restaurant. (Walking and toothpicking is unwise, like running with scissors.)

One more thing—if your client, interviewer or potential contact breaks any of the above guidelines, you are not supposed to notice.

BE EXCEPTIONAL: I Now Pronounce You

In the beginning... there was food on toast. And no one could pronounce it. Then came etiquette instructors.

Hors d'oeuvre does not rhyme with maneuver. Canape does not rhyme with escape.

The Exceptional Professional knows how to pronounce those little, snacky things at the beginning of a meal or at a networking event:

> **Hors d'oeuvre** (OR-durv): light appetizer served as a first course or with cocktails. From the French, "Outside work," meaning outside the main course.

Canape (CAN-app-AY): cracker, toast or puff pastry topped with a decorative garnish. From the French, "couch," because the topping sits on the cracker like a person on a couch.
Crudites (CROO-dee-TAY): raw vegetables, usually served with dip. From the French, "Rawness."
Crostini or singular-Crostino (Cross-TEE-nee): toasted bread with toppings or a spread. From the Italian, "Little toasts."
Bruschetta (broo-sket-tah): grilled bread, brushed with garlic and olive oil, topped with fresh tomato and other vegetables and spices. From the Italian, "To roast over the coals."
Starters (star-turs): appetizers served in sports bars and chain restaurants, sometimes ordered instead of a meal by picky eaters who won't touch anything else on the menu. From the Middle English, "To rush out or leap." (Which makes zero sense, since you feel like neither rushing nor leaping after eating these.)

Don't Make a Joke of a Name or Profession

A woman who is a dentist told me, "Whenever I meet people and tell them what I do, they say, 'I hate you' or 'I hate dentists.'" I told her to smile and say, "Then you probably have the wrong dentist."

If you are continually getting a flip response from different people, you need a clever comeback. When I tell people I am an etiquette instructor, I get, "Well, I better watch MY MANNERS around you." I just tell them, "I'm off duty." Or "I'm an etiquette instructor, not the etiquette police."

I counted myself lucky in grammar school, because my name didn't rhyme with anything or have any obvious puns. Sometimes parents are to blame. Other times, we marry into it. I went to school with a woman who became a doctor. Her last name was Berger and when she married and hyphenated her name, she became Dr. Berger-King.

A college student asked me: "How do I respond to people I meet who make fun of my last name?"

"What's your last name?" I asked.

"Failure," she said.

"You need a clever response," I said. Humor, done right, is effective at deflecting insensitive remarks. If this happens to you, try this:

"I can tell you are a person who makes friends easily."
"That's hilarious." (delivered with blank expression)

When you meet someone with an odd name, one that rhymes with something or has an obvious metaphor and you feel the urge to make a joke, STOP. Don't do it. They hear it all the time. It does nothing for your reputation to pile on. Don't joke at someone else's expense. Make fun of yourself instead.

It's Complicated

A chemical engineer asked, "When I tell people what I do for a living, the conversation dies. What can I do to keep the conversation going?"

"Why do you think the conversation dies?" I asked.

"They are intimidated by my intelligence," he said, "they think they won't be able to talk to me." (This statement might sound arrogant but this young man was anything but.)

Again, I counseled to use humor. Humor can relieve tension and make people more at ease. "I am a chemical engineer, but you can talk to me —I have been told I have a sparkling personality." (Read that back in a monotone voice. Delivery is everything.)

The challenge with a complicated profession is to turn it into a teachable moment. "I know that sounds technical but what I do is research ways to produce vitamin A-infused grain to eradicate eye disease in economically challenged countries."

Some people might give you sarcastic answers. You don't have to charm the socks off everyone but you can maintain your self-respect.

What To Say Next?

You ask someone, *"What do you do for a living?"*

The person says, *"I'm an actuary."*

You think, "What am I supposed to say next? An actuary–oh, that sounds like fun." There is always something to ask to show an interest:

"How did you become interested in being an actuary?"
"What kind of training did you have to become an actuary?"
"What do you like best about being an actuary?"

If you don't know what an actuary is, say, *"I know the term actuary, but can you tell me more about what that means?"*

Conversation Stoppers

What if someone gives you an answer that stops you dead in your tracks?

I asked a man at a networking event, "Are you a native of this area?" He said, "No, I am originally from Nevada." I said, "What brought you to Iowa?" He said, "My ex-wife."

I cringed, thinking, "What am I supposed to say to that?" Then he said, "I am here so I can spend time with my kids." That gave me a better opening, "How old are your kids?" He softened and talked enthusiastically about his kids.

"Are you married?" or "Do you have kids?" are personal questions you should avoid in business. But once the other person opens the door by mentioning a spouse or kids, you can ask more questions.

About Your Children

No one will ever be as impressed with your children's accomplishments as you. If you have pets, people would rather hear about your pets than your children. Unless, you are one of those people who recreates conversations with your pet. "Then I said to the cat, 'You can't tear up my new couch like that!' and Fluffy just looked at me like, 'Try and stop me!' Then I said, 'No more cat treats for you!'" When someone starts talking like that, I usually say, "Have you met…?"

Other Questions *Not To Ask*

Here are other questions you should not ask, at business or social events:

> *"How much do you make?"*
> *"How much did you pay for that?"*
> *"Is that your real hair color?"*
> *"When is your baby due?"* My friend Kris was eight months along and obviously pregnant. When strangers asked, "When is your baby due?"
> She replied, "What baby?"

Reacting to Inappropriate Comments

I know a sales professional who, during a presentation to a room full of colleagues, told a sexually explicit joke. He thought it was fine, because people laughed. But two women in the room complained to his manager.

Avoid crude language or humor involving bodily functions or sexual situations. It causes discomfort in others and leads to misunderstandings. In the world of stand-up comedy, it's easy to come up with "poop," "fart" and "sex" jokes. At most open-mic nights, that is what you hear. A more clever person can be funny without this type of lowbrow humor.

If someone asks a question that is personal or says something inappropriate, there are a few options:

- Be shocked. *"I am surprised you would ask me that."*
- Be tactful and show no emotion. *"That's not an appropriate question."* Or *"Let's keep this professional."*
- Be coy. Smile and say, *"That's not for you to know."*

I Swear! Avoid Crude Language

Avoid crude language and profanity, including: *that sucks, bite me, I screwed up, I'm so screwed, crap, I gotta go pee, or O-M-G.* Nothing drops years off your education faster than profanity.

An Outpouring of Boring

If you sense you are starting to bore someone—their eyes start to glaze over or their stare becomes fixed—turn the conversation back to them. "I have been doing all the talking. Tell me more about your line of work."

Avoid the hallmarks of a boring person: boasting, talking over people's heads, excessive detail, big words, jargon, complaining. We all know loud characters who want to be the center of attention. That gets boring, too.

VIPs

Never monopolize a VIP (very important person) at an event. Whether it's a book signing, a backstage "meet and greet" or a celebrity roaming around the room, get in and get out. Don't try to make a personal connection. Move on. Let others take their turn.

"Loved your movie."
"Your book inspired me."
"Your stage dive into the crowd was so unexpected."

In a restaurant in Connecticut, Vince and Linda McMahon, of World Wrestling Entertainment fame, were seated at a table next to mine. During their dinner, a man in a black t-shirt and long ponytail approached their table. He said, "Oh Mr. McMahon, my brother and I are such big fans, could I bother you for an autograph?"

Vince McMahon stood up. He's a large, imposing figure with broad shoulders. What happened next was something no one was prepared for.

Vince McMahon smiled and shook the man's hand. His wife stood up, took a pen and paper out of her purse and wrote down the man's information and said she would send an autographed picture for both the man and his brother. (A little disappointing, because part of me wanted to see Vince McMahon pick the guy up, spin him over his head and then body slam him to the restaurant floor.)

They chatted with the fan for a while. The McMahons could not have been more gracious. Finally, the maître d' intervened and led the man away, so the McMahons could finish their dinner. The man retreated to the bar, but positioned himself so he could stare at the McMahons for the rest of their dinner. (Stalk-ward!) Having worked with celebrities in the music business, I know they need space and time to be ordinary citizens.

Groupies

If you are in charge of the VIP at an event, keep an eye on the VIP throughout the event and make sure the VIP is not cornered by a new, unwanted friend who is hogging his or her time. If this happens, you must dive in and rescue the VIP… I mean, politely intervene.

Professional Advice

People may try to solicit free professional advice from you at networking and other events. You may offer free advice if you like. Your other option is to hand them your card and say, "Here is my office information, if you would like to make an appointment."

Everyone Has a Bad Night

There will always be good events and bad. I started this chapter with the story of the networking event in Chicago, where no one would talk to me. 10 years later, I was in the same situation in New York City. I walked into a networking event, not knowing anyone. When I tried to start a conversation, I was rebuffed.

Then I had an epiphany. I thought if I were hosting an event like this, I would introduce people to each other and make sure everyone was engaged and having a good time. That's what I did, I started behaving like it was my party. I saw a young woman by herself standing a few feet away. I said, "Hi, I am Callista Gould. What's your name?"

She smiled and introduced herself. Her friend who was supposed to meet her there was running late. I asked her a few questions about herself. There was another woman standing by herself. I motioned to her to join us. I introduced her to the first woman.

The circle grew, both men and women. We were all laughing and talking and exchanging business cards. We were having so much fun, people that wouldn't talk to us before started gravitating to us.

What I learned that night is, if you are throwing a party or event, you should assign one or two people to circulate and make sure people are engaged in conversation. If there isn't someone like that at the event, pretend you are that person (even if it's not your event.) Find a person standing alone and introduce yourself. Find another person standing alone. Introduce the first person to the second person.

With humans being human, there will always be awkward situations. Every event is an adventure. Now that we're a little more confident in networking, it's time to put a strategy together.

1.4 *Strategy: Turn Your Contacts Into Advocates*

We go to events, exchange business cards and accumulate contacts on social media. Sometimes we have a collection of connections and no direction. One of the main purposes of networking is to find people who will advocate for us – who will refer us to potential clients, help us find new opportunities and offer us professional advice.

As *The Exceptional Professional,* it's time to do a little roadwork on our network.

In this chapter you will learn:

- How to line up your contacts with your goals
- How to grow your contacts
- How to turn contacts into advocates
- Where to meet contacts in person

Setting Goals

First, we need to set some goals. Then we need to ask, "Do our contacts line up with our goals?"

Try this exercise: write down five professional or personal goals.

1. ____________________
2. ____________________
3. ____________________
4. ____________________
5. ____________________

Here are some possible goals:

Join a board of directors
Find a mentor
Get clients or sales
Meet for creative collaboration
Be promoted in your organization
Run for elected office
Find leads to new jobs
Start your own group
Find new employees or interns
Be an entrepreneur
Make friends in business
Research for business or hobbies
Make friends outside business
Increase your education
Earn awards / be recognized
Learn new skills
Grow your influence in the community
Find people who help you solve problems
Become expert source for the media
Travel
Find a volunteer group
Learn other languages
Lead a volunteer effort
Pursue athletic interests
Get feedback
Train for a 5K
Discover new interests

Gather a list of contacts. Maybe you have a list on social media. (*LinkedIn* allows you to download your contacts to an *Excel* spreadsheet.) Or you might have an email group list or holiday card list. If not, start a list.

Let's say your five goals are:

1. Join a board of directors
2. Meet others for creative collaboration
3. Make friends in business
4. Find leads to new jobs
5. Earn awards/be recognized for your accomplishments

Goals and Contacts				
Board	**Creative**	**Friends**	**Leads**	**Awards**

Create a keyword for each goal: "Board," "Creative," "Friends," "Leads" and "Awards." Identify each contact with the goal keywords. For example: if you would like to serve on a board, find your contacts who already sit on boards. Also identify contacts in the type of organizations in which you would like to serve.

Not all of your contacts will fit into your goals. Some contacts will just be friends. Other contacts will fall into no-man's land. Don't discard them, you may need them in the future. Find which goals have the fewest contacts. That's where you need to focus your networking efforts.

Create an Action Plan to Find New Contacts

1. Research and reach out on social media.
2. Attend events where you are likely to meet the contacts in person.
3. Ask current contacts for an introduction.
4. Cold call or send an email introducing yourself.
5. Send emails, make calls or "Like" what people are posting online.

BE EXCEPTIONAL: Reach Out to Those Beyond Your Reach

The Exceptional Professional reaches out to people, even if it seems like a long shot.

I saw an article about a well-known CEO who was part of a foundation that had a committee on a subject that was near to my heart. I emailed him, told him about my background and how I could be useful to his committee. (Always make it about the other person.)

My expectations were low for ever hearing back from someone so high-up with so many responsibilities. To my amazement, he not only contacted me, but said, "Yes" to having me on his committee. On that committee, I learned from some of the best movers and shakers in the community. It was a great experience that started with a simple email.

Identify Current Contacts You Would Like to Know Better

Do you have people already in your social media network, who you would like to know better? I had "Research" as a goal. Because one of the topics I cover is professional dress, I made an effort to grow my contacts in clothing retail and custom tailoring. Reach out to the contacts you would like to know better.

Stay In Touch

Foster relationships with all of your contacts by staying in touch.

- Send thank you notes for assistance, referrals, mentoring, etc.
- Congratulate them for birthdays, anniversaries and other events.
- "Like" their articles and social media posts.
- Check in by email or phone once in a while.
- Write recommendations on social media.

Years after I started my business, I wrote notes to some of my earliest clients and said, "Thank you for hiring me when I was just getting started."

Turn Your Contacts Into Advocates

You want to get something for yourself or your business from a networking event, but you will get the most out of your networking experience if you help others get what they want.

Don't just collect names and business cards. Find people to help you reach your goals – and return the favor by helping them reach their goals. When you do good things for others, good things come back to you. When you meet someone, ask yourself, "What can I give? What can I do for this person?" Ask the person, "Who is your ideal or target customer or client?" (If they can't answer that, then you say, "Let me introduce you to my friend, the marketing consultant.")

Think about your current connections – the ones who are already helping you meet your goals. If you had to pick your most valuable connections, who would they be? Write down five connections who are valuable to you and why.

Ask yourself, "What have I done for them lately?" Networking is a two-way street – not just about what they can do for you but also about what you can do for them.

Setting goals and a strategy for growing your contacts will help you build the relationships that will help you develop as a professional. Now that we have a plan, let's look at the best places to network.

Getting Out

Put down the remote, get off the couch. Shut down the computer. Put away the iPad or other digital device. Stop making excuses about all the other things you need to do. It's time to get out and meet people. Where do you begin? There are three guidelines for networking events:

1. **Stay away from singles events.** Why? Because singles events attract desperate characters. Are you a desperate character? Of course not. Avoid singles events like plutonium.
2. **Go to everything else.** There are limitless opportunities: charity events, business networking events, chamber of commerce events, breakfast clubs, professional associations, college alumni events. Inexpensive memberships to art museums and other

museums get you on their mailing lists for special events. Get more ideas from the Where to Network list that begins on the next page.

3. **Create a group where there is none.** Have a special interest? Start your own group. Maybe it is a book club or technology club where you meet in a local library or coffee house.

BE EXCEPTIONAL: Who You Know Before You Go

The Exceptional Professional prepares for an event. If you go to a chamber of commerce event, a chamber usually has executive staff, a board of directors and sometimes ambassadors. Their pictures are often on the chamber website. Don't they look like nice people? They are. That's how they got hired to work at a chamber. Read their bios, get to know their faces before the event. Don't try to do last minute cramming on your phone at the event.

Same for a charitable function or association: visit the organization's website, research the staff and board and read the latest releases. Does the event have sponsoring organizations? Research them.

College or alumni event: who is on the alumni board? Which alumni live in your area? *LinkedIn* is a great resource for this.

At the event, if you recognize sponsors, thank them for sponsoring. Before you leave, thank your hosts or organizers, if they are available. You may not get a chance to speak to any of these people. But if you do, it's good to be prepared. It's not just who you know, it's who you know before you go.

Where to Network

Here is a more complete list of places to network:

- **Alumni clubs:** don't wait a decade for a reunion – university alumni clubs have great events all year long. If you are moving to a new location, see if there is an active alumni club from your university in the area. Stay in touch with the university after you graduate.

- **Civic organizations:** Rotary Club, chamber of commerce, etc.
- **Business networking events:** various organizations sponsor business networking events. They may have a guest speaker or just social time. Find them advertised on local news websites, business-related publications or the Business section of your local newspaper.
- **Volunteer Events:** volunteering is a great way to meet other nice people, because nice people volunteer.
- **Charitable events/fundraisers:** with charitable fundraising events, you can attend as a donor or volunteer to work at the event.
- **Breakfast clubs:** people in business meeting regularly over breakfast and discussing what's going on in their business. They often feature guest speakers and sometimes field trips.
- **Toastmasters:** has clubs all over the world, where you practice speaking and leadership skills. Not all clubs are the same. Visit several before joining one. Find out more at: www.toastmasters.org
- **Lectures:** universities, hospitals, public libraries, churches and other organizations have lectures open to the public. They are a great way to expand your mind and meet like-minded people.
- **Career fairs:** ask questions of employers, network with other job seekers, too.
- **Book clubs/discussion groups:** advertised through libraries, book stores, coffee houses.
- **Museum memberships:** can be very inexpensive. Museum memberships land you on the list for openings and other special events.
- **Theater/opera/symphony/ballet memberships:** get access to special events before the events.
- **Art gallery openings:** are often free and they broaden your horizons.
- **Athletic groups:** running clubs, biking, hiking, walking, yoga, etc.

- **Competitive co-ed sports leagues:** volleyball, bowling, softball, kickball, flag football, etc.
- **Sports watching groups:** groups that gather to watch college or pro football, baseball, etc.
- **Political events:** meet a candidate event or "town meeting" with an elected official.
- **Church groups:** study groups, discussion groups, volunteer projects.
- **Trade organization events:** public relations, marketing, sales, engineering, nursing, banking, etc.
- **Lunch with co-workers:** if your organization has a cafeteria, use it. Do not eat alone at your desk.
- **After work happy hours:** with friends/co-workers.

Community education: take a cooking class, wine tasting class or learn a new language.

BE EXCEPTIONAL: Create Your Own Group

Can't find a group that fits you? *The Exceptional Professional* creates his or her own group.

1. Create a concept for the group.
2. Promote it: send press release to media, post on social media, invite friends, distribute/post flyers.
3. Make people feel welcome: always have at least one person at each event in charge of greeting new people and introducing them around.
4. Establish an email list and maintain regular communication.

Can I Network at a Wedding?

Have you ever been to a wedding where you said to yourself, "These two are not going to make it?" Or "I give them six months?" While it's bad form to exchange bets at a wedding, it is okay to exchange business cards, as long as we observe a few guidelines of decorum:

- This is someone's special day. Please do not treat it as a chamber of commerce networking event.
- Do not turn every conversation into a sales pitch or elevator speech.
- Do not hand out business cards in church or during the blessed event on the beach, underwater or wherever.
- Do not hand out business cards at a dinner table at any event.
- Be discreet. If one person asks for your card, that doesn't mean you foist them on every hapless bystander.
- Don't jump the gun. If someone just wants your name, don't automatically hand them your card.
- If you want to sell your services to the happy couple or their parents – this is not a good time.

It's always good to have a few business cards handy. Because at weddings, we meet people and part of the discovery process of meeting people involves the question, "What do you do for a living?"

Again, the blessed event takes priority. Practice conversation skills by speaking well of the happy couple. Relax and have a piece of cake.

When we network, we collect new contacts and then follow up on social media. So in the next chapter, we'll look at all things digital, including professionalism on cell phones, in email and on social media.

DIGITAL DEVOTION

2.1 Attached at the Phone and Other Devices

There is one story, when I tell it at a university, I can see the whites around the eyes of the students.

After a talk in Oklahoma, a woman said, "I am the receptionist in my office. The hiring manager has asked me to keep an eye on the job candidates in the waiting room and report back which ones were talking on their cell phones, checking messages or texting. *Those are the candidates we do not hire.*"

Some think this is harsh. You have a few minutes alone... why wouldn't you check your messages? The reason is simple. Recruiting and hiring new employees is expensive for employers. Letting go the ones who don't work out is costly too. Most employers are scared to death of hiring someone tethered to personal texts and tweets while on the clock. They want to hire people who will be dedicated to their work.

While digital devices have added simplicity to our lives, they have also added new complications. While we hear mostly about cell phone offenses, *The Exceptional Professional* recognizes that sometimes that little digital extension of our arm is used for good.

In this chapter, you will learn:

- The distinction between good and bad cell phone use
- When cell phone use is bad for business

- How to respond to rude cell phone behavior by others
- About corporate spying, safety and privacy

When waiting for an interview, it's best not to bring a cell phone. Bring a legal pad or notebook and go over potential interview questions in your head or read any of the organization's brochures left in the waiting room.

When I wrote about the Oklahoma receptionist and idea of bringing written notes as my *Etiquette Tip of the Week*, a friend forwarded a comment from a young, digital-devotee in her organization who said, "I wonder how current these tips are? My notes would be on my phone."

Touché.

But here is the issue: the person watching you on your cell phone in the waiting room doesn't know if you are reviewing your notes on the organization or looking at the price of flights to Cancun. Better to set it aside and dispel any doubts.

Avoid using your cell phone or texting when waiting for an interviewer or client to arrive to a restaurant, too. Show you are focused on the business at hand and not distracted by your digital devices.

People Behaving Badly

92 percent of us carry cell phones, according to a study by the Pew Research Center. 31 percent of us never turn them off.[2]

If we understand that professionalism is about being aware of the people around us, we realize that rude cell phone behavior happens when we don't see each other.

Have you been on an airplane lately? What happens as soon as you touch down? Everyone snaps their cell phone to their ear, as if part of a military drill. Everyone has the same conversation: *"I'm on the ground."* They are talking to someone on the other end, saying, "*Thanks, I'm in the terminal.*" Thank goodness they have that phone for emergencies.

Have you ever tried to communicate with a checkout counter attendant or sales person who is chatting on a cell phone? How do you think they feel when *you are the one on the cell phone?*

A woman who is a coffee roaster at a popular coffee house in my hometown told me people order coffee at the counter without ever looking up from their phone. "Whatever happened to please and thank you?" she asked. Being a professional means not treating people as if they are invisible.

Cell Phones Used for Good

Sometimes, cell phones are used for good. The Pew study mentions that while using a phone in a group "might seem rude or inconsiderate to an outside observer," 78 percent whip out the cell phone for "group contributing" reasons. These include getting information they thought would be interesting to the group or reaching out to someone known by the group.

Here is the distinction between good and bad cell phone behavior:

Good: when the cell phone is used to **collaborate.**
Bad: when the cell phone is used to **disengage.**

Collaborating is when you are in a meeting, you need a statistic relevant to the discussion and someone looks it up on a cell phone. Another example: you are out to dinner with a group of friends and decide to go to a movie and one person looks up the movie times on a phone. This is collecting info for the good of the group.

Disengaging is when people in a meeting sneak a peek at their messages or start texting under the table. Some people think it's less conspicuous if they hold their device under the table while they text. You are not fooling anyone. Knock it off. Who hasn't been out to dinner with a group where one or more people are talking to or texting someone outside the group? That is using the phone to disengage.

30 percent, according to the Pew study, admitted using cell phones to disengage from a group. It's easy to drift out of the physical world and into the digital world. The message you give to those present is that the person on your digital device is infinitely more interesting. A professional is present with the people in his or her presence.

When Cell Phone Use is Bad for Business

When can you use your cell phone? Maria Everding says, "Unless you are waiting for a kidney, your cell phone should be off."

Use your cell phone where you will not disturb others. If there are people sitting, standing or downward dogging within 10 feet of you, do not talk on your cell phone out of courtesy to them. Avoid texting and checking phone messages in meetings or seminars. Give presenters your full attention.

A restroom stall is not a phone booth. It's disgusting when you can hear the person next to you in a public restroom chatting away. Ick!

Cell phones have also changed the way we argue. Arguments are settled quickly – whip out the cell phone and check the facts. The winner, however, should not engage in an NFL-worthy, rump shaking, victory dance. Dale Carnegie's argument for not arguing is still valid.[3]

Whose Phone Belongs to That Ring Tone?

You meant to turn your cell phone off. What if you accidentally leave it on? Avoid goofy ringtones that would embarrass you when they start ringing during a key meeting. If you have multiple ringtones, the one for your boss should not be, "The Bitch is Back" by Elton John.

Better Way to Make a Second Impression

Apparently, there is a new way to return a call when you get a call back on a resume or client pitch. A woman who handles the incoming phone calls in her organization told me people call and say, "Did someone call me from here?" They have no idea who or where they are calling, because they just saw, "Missed message" and hit "redial."

"Shouldn't you know," she asks the caller, "since you called here?"

There is a better way to make a second impression. Listen to your messages, especially when you are on the hunt for a new job or new client. Before calling back, look at any notes you have on the organization and collect your thoughts.

When Texting is Vexing

Sometimes a text sends the wrong message. An operations manager for a plumbing contractor told me some of their clients were annoyed by the contractors reaching out to them by text message. Why? The clients felt the text messages were an intrusion because they felt text messaging was more personal, something they do only with family.

How should you contact your clients? It depends on the client. Some might prefer a text. The safest thing to do is ask them:

"How do you prefer to be contacted?"
"What's the best way to reach you?"
"Do you mind if I send you a text message?"

Finding out how your clients like to be contacted is good for business.

Emergencies

If you have an emergency and you need to keep your digital device on during a meeting, let people know: *"I hope you don't mind, but my father is in the hospital and I need to have my cell phone on."*

A family crisis is an emergency. Expecting a call from a hard-to-reach client can be an emergency. Coordinating with friends about dinner plans is not an emergency.

Reacting to Rude Cell Phone Behavior

I was taking the *Friendly Limousine Bus* shuttle between the Narita and Haneda Airports in Tokyo, Japan when the following announcement came over the intercom: *"Portable electronic devices are not allowed on the bus, as they annoy your neighbors."* If only we could have this message blasting everywhere in the U.S.

My sister, Maureen, was sitting in a waiting room, quietly reading a book during an oil change service on her car, when a man sat down next to her and started talking loudly on his cell phone. Maureen said, "It made me want to read my book out loud to him."

Sometimes we're in a situation where we just have to ignore it to keep the peace and avoid confrontation with a stranger.

BE EXCEPTIONAL: Rise Above It

When others are behaving badly with their digital devices, *The Exceptional Professional* rises above it.

I was waiting by myself in a glass atrium just outside a restaurant when a woman talking loudly on her cell phone walked in. She took one look at me, turned her back and continued to talk loudly. Minutes later, the friend I was meeting for lunch walked in and we started talking.

The woman on her cell phone turned around and shoots us an angry look that says, "Do you mind? I'm on A CALL." Then she storms out. I wanted to follow her outside and say, "I'm sorry, were we BOTHERING YOU?" I quashed the urge.

When we are around strangers who are talking loudly on their cell phones, it's tempting to throw the person an angry or annoyed glare to express displeasure. Or make a cutting remark. Don't do it.

When I worked for Sony Music and incidents or people caused anger or frustration (when talking about the music business, there are many incidents and people that cause anger and frustration), my boss, Marketing Manager Dave Fisher, used to counsel, "Rise above it." That meant remain calm and carry on. Look for solutions or sometimes do nothing but don't let your angry attitude stew. I always appreciated that advice.

The Digital Bore

Which brings me to a new dysfunctional character on the social scene: *the digital bore*. Those are the people out in public who are completely engrossed in their little digital device. You can't go to a restaurant without seeing a couple out to dinner, one of them constantly texting or talking on a cell phone, while the other sits and waits.

I once observed two teenagers dining at a nice Italian restaurant. She was a petite, attractive blonde. He was a dark-haired, brawny boyfriend. The boyfriend was texting and ignoring his attractive date. She looked bored. Eventually, she produced a pink cell phone and started looking at her own messages. They were sitting across from each other, not talking.

Then the wait staff brought a dessert with a candle in it. It was the boyfriend's birthday. The girlfriend reached under the table and produced a large, wrapped gift. The boyfriend unwrapped it. It was a football jersey. He admired it, gave her a kiss and was back to texting.

Who do you think picked up the check? Not the birthday boy. The girlfriend footed the bill for an evening where she was ignored. No one should ever let another treat them this way.

Where do the kids learn this behavior? Maybe from their parents. There's nothing more sad than watching a children's soccer game and seeing a child look over to the sidelines to see if the parent saw the great play he or she just made, but the parent is absorbed in their cell phone.

What kind of parent are you if you can't stop texting or checking messages for half an hour to watch your child play a team sport or perform "Three Blind Mice" poorly at a school concert?

I saw a family waiting for a table at a busy restaurant. Mom, Dad and two kids – boy and a girl – were all looking at their cell phones instead of talking to each other. Their family night out must be a rip-roaring riot.

Don't be a digital bore. Be attentive to the people around you, whether they are across the dinner table or next to you at t-ball.

When It's Your Workplace

A female executive told me she was contacted by a sales vendor for an appointment. During their meeting, the vendor's cell phone went off and he answered it. He started jabbering away with another client.

The executive said, "I ended up walking out of my own office, so he could have privacy on his call. What should I do in a situation like that?"

Here are the options:

a. Wait for the vendor to finish his call.
b. Leave your office to give the vendor his privacy.
c. Throw a paperweight at the vendor's head.
d. Interrupt the vendor and ask him to make another appointment when he has more time.

The best option is d. Interrupt the vendor. By suspending the meeting while he took the call, the vendor was wasting the executive's time. At that point, the executive should politely interject and say, "Please go out and make an appointment with my assistant to see me when you have more time." Be polite, but firm.

Similarly, the executive should avoid cell phone calls during a meeting. If you are the vendor and your client starts using the phone, you may be stuck.

Corporate Spying

I was sitting in a doctor's office when a woman on her cell phone recited her bank account number out loud. Let's think about this. Anyone within earshot can write down her bank account number. When it's her turn to see the doctor, the nurse or assistant calls out her name. Now anyone with ears has her name and bank account number. How hard would it be for one dishonest person to start calling banks in the area to find the bank with her name and account number?

Overheard cell phone conversations are used for corporate spying, too. People talking loudly on cell phones give out sensitive information, when they think no one else is listening on airplanes, in hotel lobbies, restaurants and other public areas. Almost every time I travel, I hear people talking too loudly on cell phones, giving out sensitive information. If you are talking on a cell phone outside on a hotel balcony, a lot of people can hear you, even though you can't see them.

Safety First

I shake my head when I see people – especially women – walking down the street alone, completely fixated by their phones. People distracted by digital devices are prime targets for attackers. Whatever the conversation is, it can wait.

Use technology responsibly: don't talk or text and drive. I was walking in a crosswalk near Michigan Avenue in downtown Chicago, when a woman in a giant SUV almost plowed over me, because she was flying around the corner while talking on her phone. The near miss was over in a moment but I couldn't help thinking her conversation would have gone a little differently, had I let out a blood-curdling scream.

Person on the other end: *"What was THAT?"*

Woman talking and driving in giant SUV: *"Some crazy woman just jumped out in front of me."*

Other Issues

Does an employer have the right to ask for your cell phone number if your cell phone is not owned by the organization?

If you do have a land line and your organization has that number, you may refuse to give out a personal cell phone number. If you do not have a land line, then the organization that employs you may need your cell phone number, so they can reach you in the event of an emergency. (*"Your project exploded and burned the warehouse down. Could you please report to work?"*)

An organization that is in constant contact with certain employees by cell phone should provide those employees with a cell phone or reimburse employees for their cell phone services.

The most important thing to remember is to use that little digital device for good, but be present with the ones who are present. In the next chapter, we'll tackle a closely related issue – digital devotion to email.

2.2 *How to Prevail on Email*

When Raytheon put Amana Appliances up for sale in the late 1990s, there were a lot of suitors. Amana's management sent out company-wide emails about organizations coming to visit. An Amana employee forwarded one of the emails to a friend, with a crude comment that included sexual innuendo. Only she didn't hit "forward." She accidentally hit "reply to all."

Luckily, it only went out to 4,000 or 5,000 people. She was suspended for four weeks without pay and shortly after, left Amana on her own.

It wouldn't be the last time a poor choice of words, wreaked havoc on a person's career. We see stories in the media all the time about people who sent emails they thought were for another's eyes only.

The Exceptional Professional realizes email is an extension of our image and uses it effectively and efficiently for the good of his or her career and for others.

In this chapter, you will learn:

- How to write emails that get read
- What makes an email professional (formal vs. informal)
- About angry email: how to diffuse it when people lose it
- What to remember before you hit "send"

Writing Emails That Get Read

We live in a hurry up world. Digital communication is rapid. We can get documents in front of people faster than ever, wherever. Even Antler, North Dakota has Wi-Fi. We fire off emails quickly. And that's how we read them. Keep this in mind when writing a professional emails.

I learned from my previous job at a tech company, people today take their information in small chunks. Do you read email newsletters or hit "delete?" Time and energy are wasted producing newsletters few people will read. In business, brevity wins. Let's break it down a little more. Digital communication is:

- **Fast and efficient:** we can deliver documents faster than ever.
- **Mobile:** we can email from anywhere.
- **Cost-efficient:** it's cheaper than postal mail and it's paperless.

Because of this, there are some snags:

- **Fast:** emails are written quickly, leaving more room for error. People are more likely to scan an email or text than read every word.
- **Mobile:** there are expectations of an immediate response. *"Why didn't you respond? I texted you two minutes ago."*
- **Cost-efficient:** time is money. Money saved on email communication can also be money lost in productivity if emails are long-winded, confusing, distracting or take a long time to write.

Email Writing from a Professional Perspective

The Exceptional Professional is attentive to others, so what does that mean for our emails? That means we craft emails with the other person in mind. In consideration for others, our emails should be:

- Easy to read quickly
- Clear and concise with excess words eliminated
- Edited for grammar and punctuation
- Targeted to the reader (make it about them)

Most people don't read every word in an email, they skim it. Write emails with that in mind.

The Higher the Position, The Shorter the Email

The higher a person is in an organization, the more emails that person must sift through. CEOs, CFOs and other C-level executives receive hundreds of emails a day.

To be respectful of their time, our emails should be brief and to the point. That means eliminating excess words and phrases. It also means, expect shorter responses. If you email your plan to a CEO and get a one-sentence response, instead of the paragraph-by-paragraph, thoughtful analysis you were craving, it's not personal. It's a time thing.

In my public relations job at Amana Appliances, I was so ambitious and full of ideas, I used to send the CEO or vice presidents emails that were 3-4 paragraphs long. I would get responses with one line, "Great idea. Run with it." I gave all these different options and they ignored all of them. Did they even read them? Probably not.

One thing that taught me was to be a decision maker and not look for consensus or validation on every little detail. When you are a manager, people want you to manage.

Three Easy Steps to a Professional Email

1. **State your purpose early.** *"This is to confirm our meeting today."*
2. **Mention attachments early.** (As soon as you type, "attached," attach the document so you don't forget.) *"Attached is the quarterly sales report that shows our progress with the new ad campaign."*
3. **After you draft it, half it.** Eliminate excess words. *"~~I am writing to let you know that~~ I will be taking a vacation in March."* (In Chapter 9.1 on *Better Business Writing*, there is a worthwhile exercise for eliminating excess words.)

Another great insight came from an executive recruiter who said, "If someone emails you a request, acknowledge it." *"I will get you those numbers by end of business Thursday."*

Clean It Up First

On Halloween Trick-or-Treat night, we had a lot of zombies come knocking. There was a zombie bride, zombie cheerleader, zombie doctor, zombie nurse.

In a sense, we all wake up looking like zombies. When we peer into the mirror first thing, our hair is a mess, we have one eye open, mouth slightly agape and our clothing looks like we slept in it. We would never show up to an interview or an important meeting like this. We would clean up first.

Why then, send a business-related email before it has been cleaned up? Our emails are part of our image. Sending an email full of errors to a client or employer is like showing up to a meeting in our pajamas. Failing to proofread your emails shows a lack of respect for the recipient. An email full of errors is like telling the recipient, "You weren't worth me taking a second look." If it were someone important, we would proofread the email. Proofread twice: read first, for grammar and read a second time, to make sure the words connect and make sense. (More about Proofreading in Chapter 9.1: *Better Business Writing.*)

Remember, our emails are part of our image. Don't send out emails looking like zombies.

Jargon Complicates

I was fixated on the license plate of the car in front of me that said, "10SNE1." Finally, I got it: tennis, anyone?

Ever find yourself driving behind a car with a personalized license plate, studying it for a long time, trying to decode what it says? This is how people read your emails when you use texting jargon. Avoid texting jargon or any other language the person you are emailing might not be familiar with. Not everyone knows what FOTFLMAO means. If they did, they would agree it's not appropriate for the workplace. Call me old and unhip, but when I get texting jargon, I usually have to look it up.

AVOID ALL CAPS

Some people hit the "caps lock" button and type, so they don't have to shift between upper case and lower case letters. Not only is your message shouting, but it is also more cumbersome for the reader. Punctuation assists the reader to read more quickly. Example: Which paragraph below is easier to read?

1. *IN CRISIS MANAGEMENT SITUATIONS, MANY EXECUTIVES HAVE SAID TO ME, "BUT I TOLD THE REPORTER, THAT WAS OFF THE RECORD," AFTER THE THING THEY SAID ENDED UP IN PRINT. PEOPLE THINK IF YOU SAY, "NOW THIS IS OFF THE RECORD," THE REPORTER WON'T USE IT. WHEN YOU SAY, "OFF THE RECORD," SOME REPORTERS HEAR, "LISTEN UP, HERE COMES THE MONEY QUOTE."*
2. *In crisis management situations, many executives have said to me, "But I told the reporter, that was off the record," after the thing they said ended up in print. People think if you say, "Now this is off the record," the reporter won't use it. When you say, "Off the record," some reporters hear, "Listen up, here comes the money quote."*

The second paragraph should be easier to read, because of the punctuation and differences in case.

Formal vs. Informal Language

"Sign me up for your manner thing." That was my favorite email request to get on my *Etiquette Tip of the Week* email list. It came from a law student. I thought, "This person can really use my *'manner thing.'*"

Hey guys! It's time to talk about informal language. That means not starting an email with "Hey" or using "guys" to refer to everyone. If someone says, "Thank you," our response should be, "You're (or You are) welcome" and not "No problem" or "No worries."

Why should we care? Because other people care about this... *totally* (or a great deal.) They tell me about it all the time. One of my university clients said, "Students often send me, and presumably potential employers, emails and text messages that have all caps, typos, slang, abbreviated words, etc."

The idea of professionalism is to make the people around us more comfortable. Some think being informal makes people more comfortable. But sometimes, informality creates discomfort.

Don't freak out. That doesn't mean they are old-fashioned, uncaring, unfeeling stiffs. You might be surprised to learn they are people who are pulling for you, professionally and personally. (If you argue that you don't want to be judged because of your informality, that train track runs both ways, Honey Bun.)

As you will read throughout this book, err on the side of formality, especially with people who are new to you. Once you get to know someone, you will know whether you can be more informal or if you need to keep being formal.

Not to say we should look unkindly upon the informals, if their intentions were honorable. Personally, it doesn't bother me to hear, "No worries," because I know the person meant well. I have been known to let slip a "No problem" myself. Chillax! I'm working on it. But don't say, "My bad." That's really irritating. Err on the side of formality.

What Makes an Email More Formal?

"When an email doesn't have a salutation, I don't know whether it is addressed to me or blind copied to a hundred others."

That was a great insight I received from a career services executive at a top law school. When using email for business, make it more, well... businesslike. That doesn't mean it has to be stiff and formal with all the charm of the National Spelling Bee word list. It means, personalize it.

As you would with any business letter, begin with a salutation *(Dear Ms. Nutt:* or *To Coco Nutt:*) and end with a closing (*Sincerely, All the best, Warm regards,*). Use a colon after the salutation in a formal business email, especially with someone you don't know. Use a comma with people who are more familiar to you.

Mirror the Salutation of the Sender

It's less formal to open an email with, *"Hello..."* or *"Hi..."* But if someone sends an email with that salutation, mimic the same in reply.

If a person writes: *"Hello Callista!"* I write back, *"Hello Mark!"* It just makes sense. If someone emails me, *"Hi Callista,"* I am not going to respond, *"Dear Mr. Thyme,"*.

Gender Unknown?

Once I had two meetings in Chicago on the same day with Chris, then Alex. There were no pictures on their websites, nothing that gave away their gender. And I could not tell from the emails I was exchanging with them. I walked into both meetings ready for anything.

When contacting someone for the first time and you are unsure of the person's gender, use the first and last name: *Dear Sam Tastic:*

Can You Drop the Salutation from Multiple Emails?

When emailing back and forth with someone, it's more like a conversation, so there's no need to use a salutation every time. Unless it has been several days between each communication, then add the salutation. If the topic in the email changes, change the subject line.

BE EXCEPTIONAL: Have a Compelling Subject Line

The Exceptional Professional strives to be more compelling. If you want your email to get read, make the subject line interesting.

When dealing with contracts, be more straightforward. But if it is a marketing or sales pitch, make it a little bit of a tease. What's going to make that reader open the email and not just hit "delete?"

One of my most-read *Etiquette Tips of the Week* had the subject line: "Thank You for Not Hiring Me." The Etiquette Tip was on writing a thank you note to your interviewers, even if they chose someone else for the job.

A little rhyming is pleasing to the ear. For a financial planner:

Do you aspire to retire?
Who will you inspire, when you retire?
Live well and give 'em hell. (Okay, maybe not that one.)

Certain buzz words are triggers that are more likely to get your email labeled as spam. Steer clear of words and phrases in your subject line like: *Buy, Earn $, Opportunity, Cash, Get Paid, Guaranteed, Unlimited, Winner,* etc.

—

Those Little Smiley Faces

I know they are cute, but emoticons (those little smiley faces) or keystroked smiley faces are not professional. :o(. It's like the girls in middle school who used to dot their i's with a heart.

Super Info Highway Rage: Never Email Angry

You are in your car on the way to work. All of the sudden, another car cuts you off. With a cell phone in one hand and large coffee in the other, the driver still manages to give you an extremely offensive gesture.

You certainly didn't deserve that, so what should you do? Lay on the horn? Tailgate menacingly? Change lanes, push the accelerator to the floor, pull up next to the person and give "*the look*" (aka, the evil eye)?

People who are normally non-confrontational in face-to-face encounters can be very aggressive in the protective cocoon of their car. The same is true for email. People lose their social inhibitors when they are not face-to-face.

Robert Sutton, a professor from Stamford, who wrote the book, *The No Asshole Rule* said, "People who work mostly through emails and conference calls fight more and trust each other less."

Has anyone ever sent you an email that, when you read it, you were incensed? It's so easy and so quick to fire back, *"Oh yeah? Well…"* and hit "reply." But don't do it. Because you might regret it and once you hit "send," you can't reach into that computer and get your email back.

Never send an email while you are angry. People put thoughts into emails they would never say to a person's face. Email does not have a tone like your voice, so it is open for misinterpretation. Sarcasm doesn't always transmit well. Innocent questions can cause offense.

How many times have you had someone show you an email from another person and say, "How would you interpret this?"

Responding to the Incendiary Email

If someone sends you an incendiary or insulting email, do not respond immediately. Do not dwell on it. Do not read it over and over, which will just make you angrier.

Get up, walk around and clear your head before responding. If you can, let it sit for a few hours or longer or until you calm down. Don't stew about it. Wait until you can respond in a calm, professional way.

When you do respond, keep your tone neutral and make it as brief as possible. Do not engage in point by point arguments. Sometimes the best response is, "Why don't we meet and talk this out?"

I once had a co-worker who would send me inflammatory emails that were five-plus paragraphs long. My strategy: sit on them for 24-hours, then respond with as few words as possible.

I knew she probably spent hours composing and re-editing these emails to choose the most provocative words. Then after she sent it, she was most likely going nuts hitting "refresh" every five seconds to see if I had responded. The wait gave her a chance to cool off.

What's funny, is this woman was in a cubicle in the next room. Whenever I said, "Why don't we meet and discuss this face-to-face," she never would. Instead of responding in anger, let cooler heads prevail.

Avoid "Reply to All" Debates

Someone sent you an email on a political issue. There are 50 other people you don't know copied on the email. You disagree so strongly with the message, you are certain it is your civic duty to hit "reply to all," because it's a matter of life and death that you let everyone you don't know, know exactly how you feel about this political issue.

Wrong. It's not about you. Do not engage in "reply to all" debates. Respond to the original sender if you must, but leave all the other unwilling participants out of it. Better yet, let it go.

Furthermore, do not email letters to the editor or your own political statements from your organization's email, which might be mistaken as your organization's official position.

Blindsided by Email

"CC" stands for the old copying jargon "carbon copy." "BCC," also known as "blind carbon copy," is a feature used to obscure certain recipients from the primary recipient(s) of the email.

BCC is the equivalent of talking behind someone's back. We are not showing respect for the primary person(s) we are emailing, if we are using BCC to hide others on the email.

BCC is useful when sending a message out to a group, to protect members of that group from having their emails skimmed and used for other communication or to prevent "reply to all" annoyances.

BE EXCEPTIONAL: When Email Just Won't Do

"What's the one thing you should never do? Quit? Depends on who you talk to. Steal? Cheat? Eat food from a dented can?" This is how Ethan Canin begins his short story, "Abe The Carnival Dog, the Buyer of Diamonds." Likewise, some things should never be done by email or text. Some messages are more suitable for face-to-face communication. Some messages are better in a handwritten note.

Never send an email, when a handwritten note is necessary. *The Exceptional Professional* handwrites thank you notes after being a guest in someone's home or for gifts. Sympathy notes should also be written by hand.

After an interview, send the interviewer a thank you note by email (in case the decision is being made in the next 24 hours). Also send a typed thank you letter through the mail.

If it is more efficient to have a face-to-face or a phone conversation, do it. Email takes time to compose. (My friend, Ben Harrington, who is a homebuilder, said, "If email had been discovered before the phone, do you think we would be communicating by email? No, we would all be talking on the phone.")

Email is Not Private

Do not put anything in an email you would not want to see on the front page of a newspaper. Email is not private and may be monitored by your employer. If your employer is the government, your emails can be subject to a Freedom of Information Act (FOIA) search by the media or any taxpayer. They can be laid bare to the public eye at any time. Anything you email can and will be used against you.

We can't open a newspaper or news site these days without reading about public figures who ruined their careers by sending inappropriate emails, texts or photos that they thought were private.

It doesn't take a FOIA search. If you trash someone in an email, it can always be forwarded. If your emails were an open book in your workplace, would anyone read something that would upset them? As long as there are IT departments, no emails are completely private. If you don't want others to see it, don't put it on email.

Do Not Conduct Personal Business on Your Work Email

Company time belongs to your employer. It is not the time to correspond with friends, make weekend plans or plan weddings or other parties that are not work-related. Sending email invites at work is never a good idea.

When Forwarded Emails Are Unwanted

We all know people who forward junk email: jokes, cartoons, chain letters, cat videos, poems, petitions, heartstrings-tugging stories (which may or may not be true), etc. What can we do? For some people, it is their way of reaching out to us. They just want to maintain a connection.

We need to stress to friends who do this that we value their friendship and we want to hear about them but we don't want the forwarded content. If that doesn't work, sometimes, we need new people.

Represent Your Organization Well

Email is quick and convenient. It can help you professionally or it can cause you a world of pain. It is very easy to tap something out and regret it later. Keep it short and simple, keep it professional.

Now that you know how to write a better business email, you can get back to clearing yours. But first, see the next chapter on social media.

2.3 *Showcase Your Best Face on Social Media*

I have a friend who is a professor at an Ivy League school. One day he overheard his students snickering amongst themselves about how he was into swing dancing. How did they know he was into swing dancing? He never told them.

They read it on his *Match.com* profile.

Whatever you put on the Internet – on dating sites, blogs, *Facebook*, *Twitter* or *YouTube* – is public information. It can be seen by anyone – employers, co-workers, clients, competitors – *anyone.* A privacy setting is no guarantee of privacy.

The Exceptional Professional recognizes that social media offers all kinds of positives to boost our professional life. Used in the right way, social media can help us advance our career, start a business or build a network of helpful connections.

In this chapter, you will learn:

- How to showcase your best face
- Your professional purpose on social media
- What employers are looking for
- About career killers on social media
- How to build your network online

Reach More People, Faster

I have a photo I like to put up on a screen when speaking to audiences about social media. It's a photo I captured of my nephew, Jimmy, age 22, at the top of the Alyeska Ski Resort in Girdwood, Alaska. There is this amazing backdrop with the surrounding mountains and what is Jimmy looking at? His cell phone.

The picture is a little misleading. It looks like he is ignoring the scenery. He was actually snapping photos and sending them to friends on *SnapChat* and posting them on *Facebook*. He did this the entire trip.

How do I do the same thing? I snap photos throughout the trip, then download them onto my computer. I go through each one and delete the crummy photos. By that time, I am too tired to send them out to anyone, so I save it for another day. A few of my photos make it onto *Twitter.*

Who is the efficient one here? Jimmy was getting it done on the run. Social media is amazing in the way it helps us reach more people, faster.

How to Showcase Your Best Face

Years ago, comedian Jerry Seinfeld did a routine on *Late Night with David Letterman* about the perils of riding in a New York City taxi. Looking at the taxi driver's photo posted on the hack license inside the taxi, he said, "I wonder what it takes to get one of those hack licenses? I think, all you need is a face." That's where it begins with your online professional profile – all you need is a face.

When we think of an online professional profile, most think of *LinkedIn,* a social media site which connects people in business. You can have a professional photo on any number of social media sites.

Whether you are a college student about to be launched into the working world or someone launched long ago, here are some guidelines for your professional photo:

1. **Don't overthink this**.
   Some people pass over profiles and invites if there is no photo. Don't fuss over the perfect photo, you will never have it. If you have a cell phone and a wall, take the photo yourself. Don't wear sunglasses.
2. **Lose the third cheek**.
   Sometimes you see a slice of a significant other, cropped (unsuccessfully) out of the photo. If this is your professional photo, there should not be another person in it.

   The worst I have ever seen was a *LinkedIn* photo of a young man and his girlfriend (or fiancé or wife?) He was standing facing the camera, like a normal professional photo. The girlfriend was facing him, her back to the camera with both her hands on his chest. She was looking over her shoulder, smiling at the camera. Question number one from employers: "Does she come attached?"

3. **Match your professional photo with your line of work.**
   Choose your props carefully. My niece worked for a charity that advocated for children with serious illnesses. The CEO's profile photo on *Twitter*, which she was using to promote the charity, showed her with two dogs.

   I have also seen a profile photo of an advocate for animals, holding a baby. If your charity is an animal rescue, wouldn't it make sense to hold an animal in your photo? Let your professional photo reflect who you are professionally and where you are going.
4. **Dress like you mean business.**
   You can wear a suit or go business casual. But save the swimsuit photos for *Facebook*. Ditto for the wedding dress. (The wedding dress says, "Join my professional network... but I'll be thinking about my wedding.") If your neckline falls below the bottom of the picture, then no one knows how low it goes. With professional attire, modest is hottest. (More on that in Chapter 7.1: *The Case for Dressing Better.*)
5. **Head shot or full body?**
   Some people look minuscule, in an effort to show a great background or set a scene. If you are a college student on a beautiful campus, why not? My friend, Kayoko Kimura, a veterinary specialist at Iowa State University, is pictured with cows in her *LinkedIn* photo. It's fabulous. And it matches her line of work.

What else does your photo say?

- Smiling = friendly, approachable
- Unsmiling = solemn, serious
- Big grin = a little sassy
- Posed = professional
- Selfie = on the move

- Black and white photos = retro-hip
- Tilted at a diagonal = confident, a little cocky
- Cartoon or avatar = not confident in your appearance

Professional Purpose on Social Media

Now that you have your professional photo, let's talk about where you are going with it. When you join social media, what is your purpose?

- **Professional:** networking for business, job searching, education and skills development, promoting yourself or your business
- **Personal:** sharing photos and news with family and friends, reconnecting with classmates or friends, genealogy research
- **Leisure:** networking with others who share the same interests
- **Combination of Professional, Personal and Leisure:** mixing career interests with personal and leisure activities on social media. Doing this can build your persona as part of your brand.

Many think of *LinkedIn* as strictly professional and *Facebook* for personal and leisure pursuits. But there are limitless possibilities. Some people use *Facebook* to promote their business or career. Others use *LinkedIn* to connect with old friends and fellow alumni.

Some people maintain two pages on the same social media platform, such as *Facebook*, *Instagram* or *Twitter* – one for personal and one for professional. That sounds like a lot of work to me.

You can combine professional, personal and leisure. People in both print and television media do this very successfully. Sometimes you get a little glimpse behind the scenes or some family pictures. Showing a little of their personal side can be good for business, as it promotes them as being down-to-earth and relatable. At the same time, public figures also have to be cautious that they don't reveal too much info that might compromise their safety or the safety of their families.

Can Your Boss Be Your Friend on *Facebook*?

The line between professional and personal is occasionally blurred on social media. It's nice when your boss feels like your friend. But what if your boss wants to be your "friend" on *Facebook*? What if you are the supervisor and the invite comes from your employee?

Some say, "No way. That's personal."

Others say, "That's okay. There's nothing to hide."

This is a big debate. If your superior sends you a friend request, should you say, "Yes?" I look back on my own career and think of some superiors I would have friended and others I would not have. But who wants to say to the boss, "I don't want to be your FRIEND?"

Studies push us in either direction. Marketing firm Russell Herder found a third of employees connected to their supervisor on *Facebook* felt the online relationship "enables them to perform more effectively on the job."[4] On the flip side, a survey sponsored by staffing agency OfficeTeam, found six in 10 managers said they were uncomfortable with friend requests from their bosses or employees that report to them.[5]

Connecting with your supervisor or reports makes sense on *LinkedIn*, which is for professional networking. It doesn't make sense for *Facebook*, if you are using it to connect with friends and family. If you say, "*Facebook* is for my friends," Your supervisor or employee might say, "I thought we were friends." Awkward. Try, *"Facebook is part of my personal life. I want to keep it separate from my professional life."*

What if a potential employer asks for your social media passwords as part of the vetting process for a job? Unless the job involves high security clearance, I can't imagine why you would do that. Would you hand over the keys to your house? It seems like an invasion of privacy.

If being friends with your boss on *Facebook* works for you and it can help your career, do it. If not, you have the right to set boundaries.

What Employers Are Looking For

What positive things can you do on social media while on the job hunt?

- Show you can communicate in complete sentences.
- Have pictures with friends who don't have beers in their hands.

- Avoid politics, unless you plan to spend your life in politics.
- Wear clothes, not swimsuits.
- Let activities on your resume be reflected in your social media.

Content That Makes Employers More Likely to Hire You

Some social media content increases your chances of getting hired. Surveys by *CareerBuilder.com* showed one third of employers who researched candidates online, found content that made them more likely to hire the candidate[6]. Below are the most common reasons:

- Background information supported their job qualifications
- Site conveyed a professional image
- Personality came across as a good fit with the company culture
- Was well-rounded, showed a wide range of interests
- Had great communication skills
- Was creative
- Received awards and accolades
- Other people posted great references about the job candidate
- Had interacted with my company's social media accounts
- Had a large amount of followers or subscribers

Career Killers on Social Media

An employer told me how his organization was getting ready to tender an offer to a new college graduate. The last step in the process was a quick check of his *Facebook* page. On the *Facebook* page, the young man boasted about his third arrest for DUI (driving under the influence). The offer was never offered. "Never" is not entirely accurate. The offer went to the next candidate, whose *Facebook* page checked out.

The aforementioned 2016 *CareerBuilder.com* surveys revealed, "49 percent of employers who research job candidates on social media said they've found content that caused them to not hire the candidate..." That number had increased from 34 percent just two years earlier.

Most Common Reasons Employers Rejected Job Candidates After Viewing Social Media[7]

- Posted provocative or inappropriate photographs or information
- Posted information about them drinking or using drugs
- Discriminatory comments related to race, gender, religion, etc.
- Bad-mouthed their previous company or fellow employees
- Poor communication skills
- Lied about qualifications
- Shared confidential information from previous employers
- Was linked to criminal behavior
- Screen name was unprofessional
- Lied about an absence

Other Social Media Content Employers Might be Considering

- Time stamps: think twice about *when* you post as well as what you post. Do you post during work hours, when you should be, say... *working?* Do you post at 2 a.m.? Nothing good happens on the Internet after midnight.
- Side businesses: making plans to start a new career or taking classes for a different profession.
- Are you ready to tell your employers you are pregnant? They may find out if friends are posting messages of congratulations.
- Political activism: don't post hostile or inflammatory messages about people who disagree with you.
- Boring content: a social media bore posts tiresome facts from potty training to vacation brags, that read like a Xeroxed Christmas letter.

Ponder the Permanent Image

Our online image is serious business. On social media, stupid mistakes are immortalized. If you drink too much and pass out in the hallway of a college dorm and someone shaves your eyebrows off, you won't just suffer a few weeks embarrassment, you may suffer a lifetime when it gets posted online. (A college friend told me about the guy in his dorm who had this happen. It took a month for his eyebrows to grow back.)

The Internet lets images of our younger lives linger. If you were the naughty French maid or drunken loincloth man at the college Halloween party, you are not so far removed from the adult world for potential employers not to notice. Even if you would never wear an inappropriate costume, don't get photographed standing next to the person wearing the inappropriate costume.

Bad images are not limited to college. Have you ever attended a seminar, with a zany, pumped up keynote speaker urging volunteers on stage to take part in some embarrassing skit? Or to don some wacky costume all in the name of "team building" or "creative thinking?"

I was presenting at a conference where there was a team building "treasure hunt." One of the challenges was to take "the most unusual team photo." One group's photo was in the men's restroom in front of the urinals. And women took part in that. Can you imagine a photo like that on the Internet, tagged with your name?

Picture Not Getting Hired

While this author's expertise is business and not wedding etiquette, she does have advice for those in business who attend weddings. Rethink the strategy of shoving everyone out of the way and putting your heels through the backs of the fallen in your conquest for the bridal bouquet. Or being too enthusiastic during the garter removal (which, if I did do wedding etiquette, I would tell people not to do, because it's crass.)

For better and for worse, cameras on phones and digital devices have changed everything. At weddings, I used to be the embarrassing aunt, tearing it up on the dance floor. Now as soon as I see someone's camera phone out, I can't get off the dance floor fast enough.

Are Your BFF's Postings Hurting Your Image?

It doesn't matter if you didn't want your co-workers to know you were undergoing tests for cancer. Your friends' messages of concern, prayers and well-wishes on your *Facebook* wall might give it away.

On *Facebook*, friends can also "tag" unflattering or embarrassing photos of you with your name, so it appears on your page and in search engines. You may block the photo to keep the person from doing it again, but the damage is done.

There is no rule that says you must be in group photos, when a person, notorious for posting unflattering pictures is snapping away. Remove yourself from the situation. Step aside and get out of the picture.

Be sensible about who you are allowing into your social media network. Don't connect with people who post reckless messages or images, that might reflect poorly on you.

How to Build Your Network on *LinkedIn*

LinkedIn is a great tool for networking in business, as well as for researching. So much so, universities are having students build their *LinkedIn* profile as a project for classes on post-graduation preparedness.

Many people post a photo and their work history, but don't know where to go from there. Here are some easy instructions on adding connections and posting content.

Adding Connections

- Connect first with your friends and family.
- Add alumni from universities or other institutions you have attended.
- Search for people you know through professional associations or other organizations.
- Whenever you go to events, collect business cards and send invites to connect to those people.

- Once you have a few connections, *LinkedIn* will start recommending other people you might want to connect with.

When you invite someone to connect on *LinkedIn*, don't just send the generic invite. ("I'd like to connect with you on *LinkedIn*.") In your invite, introduce yourself, mention whether you have met before and why you want to connect.

> *"We met at the chamber of commerce event..."*
> *"We have a mutual friend in ... "*
> *"I noticed you are also in LinkedIn's chemical engineers group and thought it might be good to connect... "*

Some people rack up 500+ connections and forget about it. Stay active on *LinkedIn* with current contacts and keep looking for new ones.

What to Post on *LinkedIn*

It doesn't take a lot of effort to keep your content fresh – post or add something once a week:

- Articles from the Internet you find interesting
- Photos of your activities or interests
- "Like" or comment on articles from your connections

Get creative: one college career professional told me students use *LinkedIn* to show their work experience, then add video to make a "living, breathing resume."

BE EXCEPTIONAL: Write Your Own Articles

Go bold. *The Exceptional Professional* writes his or her own articles about areas of interest or projects in progress, and posts it on *LinkedIn*, a blog or other social media. Try doing it once a week.

If you really want people to read it, make it 300 words or less. When readers see a long post, they might not think it is worth the effort and click on something else.

When I first started my *Etiquette Tip of the Week*, I wrote 52 Tips, so I would have a year's worth stocked up. That way, if I was on the road or too busy one week, I had a kitty of content to select from.

Can you take any of your school projects, papers, speeches, research, etc. and turn them into content?

After you have posted many articles on a similar subject, you might just have enough for a book.

Join Communities on *LinkedIn*

There are a multitude of special interest groups with online discussions, you can join on *LinkedIn*:

- Alumni from universities or other institutions you have attended
- Industry and professional associations
- Groups for certain hobbies or interests
- Your own groups that you create

Twitter and Why It's Neat to Tweet

If you haven't tried *Twitter*, you should. This app limits users to 280 characters and is great for learning how to edit and make things concise. I love the creative exchange and humor. In addition to business news and universities, I follow art galleries and cultural sites around the world.

Twitter is often compared to how people communicate at a networking event. That's a perfect parallel. Interesting bits that are tweet-worthy – news, humor, recommendations, etc. – are great fodder for networking banter. Before going to a networking event, check your *Twitter* feed for the latest news, sports and cultural happenings, so you have current topics to talk about in your networking.

I tweet my *Etiquette Tip of the Week,* comments about business etiquette, travel photos and sometimes my paintings. If you are serious about marketing yourself or a business on *Twitter,* pay attention to the feedback ("retweets" and "likes"). What posts attract more followers? Posting randomly and not getting a response, is a waste of time.

Do I Have To?

"Do I have to be on social media?" I had a high school student ask this question. You don't care if that forgettable classmate ate turkey pot pie for lunch. It's not your thing. I have friends who stay off social media. But they are secure in their careers and the idea of posting information about themselves just doesn't appeal to them.

For someone starting out in their career, it might be better to have some presence. A 2017 *CareerBuilder.com* study revealed 57 percent of employers are less likely to interview a candidate they can't find online.[8]

No Such Thing as Anonymous

One college career services professional told me, "College students are leaving *Facebook,* they are resisting *LinkedIn* and they are heading for more controversial social media platforms."

Then the bomb: "What students don't realize is that anonymity does not mean you can't be found." This is true. If you need proof, plug into any search engine, "Student arrested for social media threat." You could be reading for days. Most social media work with law enforcement.

There is no such thing as "anonymous" on social media or email. If you don't want a potential employer or current employer to find it, don't post it. Don't even think it. Don't post anything anonymously on a message board or in a comments section that you would not want attached to your name if your identity was revealed.

Another college career services professional said she downloaded a program that pulls up a person's *Facebook* page, every time she received an email from that person. One student was posting disparaging remarks about the college's career center on *Facebook*, while she was emailing the same career center, asking for help. She had no idea the woman she was appealing to could see her *Facebook* comments on the same screen.

The Private Setting

Even with a "private" setting on your social media, your content can still be cut and pasted, forwarded or printed off for others outside your network. Are you sure you want to "friend" your workplace gossip?

Although you paid a fee to be a member, there's no guarantee that your dating website profile will be viewed by only potential dates. Your snoopy supervisor and catty co-workers recognized your photo, "Mr. Likes to Laugh!" Now they also know you have a thing for redheads.

Be careful of what you post, wherever you post, because you may not have control over whether it comes down or stays. Even though you deleted it, it may not have gone away.

Big Data and Social Media...*It's a Cookbook*

Have you ever seen *The Twilight Zone* episode called, "To Serve Man?"[9] That's where the nine-foot tall alien comes from another planet with a big book labeled, *"To Serve Man."* All the world leaders swoon, because they believe the alien is there to serve mankind by solving all the world's problems. They later find out, *To Serve Man,* is a cookbook... and they are on the menu.

That is what social media is – *it's a cookbook.* You use it for free, because social media organizations collect all kinds of data on their users, then serve it up to advertisers. There is a loss of privacy. You have heard about the industry developing around collecting and analyzing "big data?" Big data is you.

BE EXCEPTIONAL: Retain a Little Mystery

The Exceptional Professional is shrewd and does not put everything about himself or herself out there.

When you meet people who tell you everything about themselves up front, they cease to be interesting. A little mystery makes a person interesting. In the same way, when you publish everything you do, think and feel on social media – your mystery is history.

Everyone should retain a little mystery in their social life and business life. But the higher you go in an organization, the more you should dial back your social media presence.

Respect Your Organization's Internet Policy

Follow your organization's rules for the Internet. Like email, your Internet usage can be tracked. Think of what you would not want published on the front page of a newspaper. Do not visit inappropriate websites (profanity, explicit photos, etc.). Your Internet surfing leaves a trail.

Internet Pornography

I can't cover the Internet without bringing up the ugly subject of pornography. There has been so much to normalize pornography in our culture. Movies and sitcoms aimed at teens and 20-somethings treat viewing porn with a lackadaisical, "everyone does it" attitude.

Pornography is addictive. Viewing porn leads to worse and worse images and behavior. The images are degrading to women, degrading to men, degrading to children.

I have worked with men viewing pornography at work in two organizations. In both places, these men acted out more aggressively towards female colleagues, with crude comments and even sexual propositions. In one workplace, the porn viewers were fired as a result.

The Cost to Digital Devotion

Take advantage of social media, without letting it control you. How easy it is to get on the Internet at home, sort work emails, get back in touch with old friends, make new friends and feast on instant news and gossip. Before you know it, three hours have elapsed.

There is an opportunity cost to digital devotion. Time online is time not spent meeting people in person or time away from family. Step away from social media and be present with the ones who are present.

Spring Cleaning for Your Social Media

Just as you do spring cleaning in your home, you should do spring cleaning on your social media.

- Freshen up your profile photos. Does your photo represent the professional, confident look you want?
- Clear out photos that don't mix with your professional image.
- Delete old posts that don't serve your current career aspirations.
- Clean up your language and grammar. How you communicate online reflects how you will communicate with co-workers or clients.
- Change any social media signed up for with your work email to your personal email, so you don't lose access to your account if laid off.
- And sometimes, you have to let a few people go. Delete connections that are not helpful to your professional and personal image.

Doesn't that feel better? Don't you just feel like a new person online? Now it's time to get offline and into the business of meeting with people in person.

MEETINGS

3.1 *Making Meetings More Effective*

The meeting is long. The room is stuffy. The presenter's PowerPoint is longer than a James Michener novel. It's so boring, a gallon of coffee could not keep you awake. You start to slide down in your chair until your stomach is sticking out further than your nose.

When you have to run the meeting, how do you keep the board room from becoming the "bored room?"

An efficient, well-run meeting can make you feel energized and ready to take on anything. A bad meeting can suck the life out of you. Whether you are the welcoming host or a gracious guest to a business meeting, *The Exceptional Professional* makes a lasting impression and gets things done.

In this chapter, you will learn:

- How to host a meeting
- Protocol for meetings outside your workplace
- The best ways to seat people at a meeting
- About conference calls and video conferencing
- How to benefit from conferences and big meetings

How to Host a Meeting

Hosting a meeting, whether it's a quick pow wow or a sustained strategic session, takes planning. The meeting host has two chief responsibilities:

1. Make the guests comfortable, including monitoring room temperature and providing refreshments.
2. Ensure the meeting runs smoothly, including refereeing disputes and reining in long-winded participants.

Make the Guests Comfortable

The number one rule of professionalism is being aware and attentive to the people around you. Ensuring the comfort of your guests is key to hosting a meeting. Make sure the room temperature is agreeable and there is suitable ventilation. The more people in the room, the more the temperature rises, so adjust accordingly. What might feel like perfect room temperature in a small conference room before anyone has arrived, can quickly turn into a sauna with 15-20 people in the room.

The seating should be comfortable. The most painful conference room chair I've ever suffered was at an advertising agency in New York. I was part of the search team reviewing advertising firms for Amana Appliance's multi-million dollar branding campaign. During the search, I sat in all sorts of groovy conference rooms, with different décor themes.

This global ad agency had a meeting room designed to look like an old farmhouse kitchen. Since Amana was headquartered in rural Iowa, they must have thought we would feel at home in a country kitchen.

The colonial style table had a lower board around the rim that was tight and uncomfortable, especially for most of the Amana executives, who were over six feet tall. The high backed wooden chairs felt like they were a few straps and an electric current short of capital punishment.

Other agencies we visited had cushy, swivel chairs. Ideal conference room chairs have some cushion and adjust to people of different heights or back support preferences. There should also be room for wheelchairs at the table and space to maneuver.

Best Time to Schedule Meetings

If you have to schedule a meeting, certain times are better than others:

- Early in the morning: people are more fresh, even though some people are not morning people.
- Just after lunch: people are more content after they eat. We all know people who become agitated when hungry. In meetings scheduled right before lunch, people will be more irritable and argumentative.

One drawback: the later the meeting is after lunch, the greater chance people will be sleepy.

When Your Meeting is Sleep-inducing

An *Etiquette Tip of the Week* reader emailed me to ask, "What if someone falls asleep in my meeting?" I fell asleep in my high school earth science class. The teacher slammed his hands on my desk and shouted, "Wake UP!" (I don't recommend that, as I had to be peeled off the ceiling.) Direct a question to the person in a slightly raised volume. Unless it's your supervisor – then provide a pillow.

If people are falling asleep or getting restless in the meeting you are hosting, call for a break. Let people get up, go to the restroom, check messages, get a beverage and return refreshed. If you are falling asleep, excuse yourself from the room. Outside the room, stretch, walk around to wake yourself up and get some coffee or water.

Feeding at Your Meeting

Negotiations can be a piece of cake. If you want to get your way, bring food. Why? Because one out of 10 Americans skips breakfast every day, according to a survey by market research firm NPD.[10] People are happy when they are fed and more likely to be agreeable. That's why people often make business deals during meals.

You don't have to break the bank. There are lots of options, depending on your budget.

Continental Breakfast
Pastries or donuts or bagels and cream cheese
Fresh fruit
Coffee - regular and decaf, orange juice, bottled water

Lunch or Dinner
Sandwiches: turkey, roast beef, ham and a vegetarian option
Healthy options: salad, fresh fruit
Chips
Bottled water, sodas/pop or juice
Dessert: cookies, brownies
Pre-made sandwiches are more convenient than sandwich trays, which require you to assemble your own sandwich. The fewer hands, the more sanitary it is. Big sub sandwiches are tasty, but messy.
And of course, there is the fastest and easiest order-in meal: pizza.

Before the Meeting
To ensure the meeting runs smoothly, send an agenda to participants, so they can prepare. Let any presenters know ahead of the meeting how much time they will have.

If you have presenters, know their audio/visual needs:

- Laptop or tablet?
- Mac or Windows? What version?
- What type of connections are available? USB, VHF or other?
- Need a projector?
- Need an Internet connection?
- Microphone: wired or wireless; fixed, handheld, lavalier or headset?

How many times have you been in a meeting where there are technical difficulties and the hosts are looking for troubleshooters in the audience to help fix it? (*Is there a tech-spert in the house?*) Do an audio-visual check before the meeting. Schedule mic checks with any speakers.

Provide paper pads and pens (though some may be taking notes on digital devices). Organizations use these as a branding opportunity.

Seating When Meeting

Designate where people will sit. Have a seating arrangement and name cards, if necessary. When you are seating others:

- The highest ranked executive should be seated at the end of the table facing the door (not with his or her back to door)
- In negotiations, put key negotiators next to each other, not opposite. Sitting opposite each other is an adversarial position. Sitting beside each other is a collaborating position.
- Put people who disagree on same side of table. Then, they are not opposite each other, staring each other down. On the same side of the table, it's harder for them to make eye contact and more calming. (But maybe seat them far enough apart that they can't land a punch.)

Start on Time

Start on time. If you hold up meetings for latecomers, you are treating the people who did show up on time as if their time is less valuable.

Making a habit of starting late conditions everyone to show up late. People will assume your 9:00 a.m. meeting really begins at 9:20 a.m. and at 9:00 a.m. they will all still be grabbing coffee and a bagel.

Jacket On or Jacket Off

"Can I take my jacket off during a business meeting?" If you have a suit jacket or blazer, wear it when you greet people arriving to the meeting. You can shuck the jacket later in the meeting if you feel too warm.

BE EXCEPTIONAL: Know the Jacket Rules

When the situation requires a jacket, *The Exceptional Professional* knows the rules for when you keep your jacket on or take it off:

- In a formal dinner: jacket on.
- In an interview or interview meal: jacket on.
- In a meeting, jacket on. Jacket off, if your host or the most senior person removes his or her jacket first.
- Greeting people as they enter the meeting: jacket on.
- Sitting in your workspace: jacket off, unless you are chilly.
- When seated, unbutton your jacket.

When standing, always leave the bottom button of your jacket unbuttoned for ease of movement. Unless you are wearing a double-breasted jacket, which according to the late Leticia Baldrige, "looks awkward hanging open, like a gate that needs closing."
These rules apply to women's jackets (blazers) as well as men's.

Introductions

Informal introductions and small talk take place before the meeting. At the start of the meeting, the host makes more formal introductions and welcomes any special guests. The next step is to summarize the purpose of the meeting and briefly go over the agenda.

The Efficiently Run Meeting

The London Zoo has an exhibit designed to look like a Bolivian rain forest that visitors walk through. A while back, the zoo had a problem with the exhibit's squirrel monkeys stealing visitors' cell phones. The monkeys were supposedly drawn to the phones' bright lights and ring tones. (They were really using them to text: "Get me out of here.")

In the business world, when too many people are checking messages or texting during a meeting, it's easy to say, "They are being rude." This leads to lecturing or monkeying around with silly games like, "everybody put their cell phone in a basket." But too many texting under the table might be a symptom of something else: an inefficient meeting.

When I worked at Sony Music, we had a problem with some staff members sitting idle through long, monthly marketing meetings, where lengthy segments were irrelevant to their job or department. To fix this, our branch manager staggered the meetings, scheduling certain staff for specific times. This upgrade brought a new energy to the meetings.

Lecturing or confiscating the phones is not a solution. Look for ways to modify meetings, so people want to pay attention.

Keep the Peace and Rein in Windbags

There are people who derail meetings – by talking too long, getting off topic, starting heated arguments or splitting hairs over administrative details that don't involve the higher-ups in the room. As the host, it is your job to intervene and get the meeting back on track.

We all know people who can talk the leg off a chair and divert a meeting onto the strangest, inane topics. Everyone else at the table gets that, "Oh no, not again!" look. In your mind, you may be tackling the windbags at the knees and throwing them to the conference room floor. In reality, a simple, *"We seem to have slipped off topic and need to return to our agenda."* will do. Other transitions to return to the agenda:

> *"We may not be able to solve those issues here. Let's have a side meeting with just those involved."*
> *"We need to keep things moving to respect the time of everyone here."*

End of the Meeting

Respect your audience: end on time. Have an agenda and stick to it. Recap the meeting, have a call to action and review any assignments.

When You are the Guest at a Meeting

Just because you are not running the meeting, does not mean you are free from responsibilities.

Attending a Meeting Outside Your Organization

Arrive for your meeting in a timely fashion, not fashionably late. Be at least 10 minutes early if you are attending the meeting. Arrive at least 30 minutes early if you are presenting. This allows time to check your audio-visual connections.

Map out your parking and parking alternatives. There is one university where I love the people but the place is a parking menace. My first time there, my meter ran out and I got a ticket. The second time, the designated parking garage was full, due to some big event, which I think was "Entire State Bring Your Kid on a Campus Tour Day."

I drove around for 45 minutes looking for on the street parking. Twice, cars appeared out of nowhere and slid into an open spot before I got there. I sweet-talked a person in a utility truck into giving up his space. In truth, my sweet-talking skills are not that strong – I think he saw desperation in my face and he was a kind and generous man.

Luckily, it was only a block and a half from the building where I was speaking. I ran as fast as a crazy person in low heels can run.

Dress Out of Respect for Your Hosts

At a university's vendor training, the tables were arranged in a u-shape. Across from me was another vendor, wearing flip flops, which displayed a tattoo on her foot—of the mascot of the university's biggest rival.

If you had to pick between two vendors, all things being equal, would you select the one that's just not that into you?

For meetings outside your workplace: dress up out of respect for the people you are visiting. Whether you show up in a suit, business casual or a uniform, wear clean, pressed clothing. Upgrade your footwear from flip-flops and cover up those painted toenails or hairy, Hobbit-like feet.

Where It Begins

Too many people think a meeting outside their organization begins when they reach the meeting room. Your meeting begins at the front door. Be attentive, kind and convivial to anyone you meet on the way in and on the way out. This includes security personnel, maintenance people and receptionists or administrative professionals, also called, "gatekeepers."

Gatekeepers can put your appointment or messages on top of the pile, the bottom of the pile or in the circular file. Give them your full attention. If they are on the phone, step back and wait until they are available. Don't stare them down like, "I'm waiting."

BE EXCEPTIONAL: Know the Names of the Gatekeepers

When returning to the same organization for meetings, *The Exceptional Professional* learns the names of the gatekeepers or the people he or she meets regularly on the way in. Introduce yourself and present your business card.

Make note of their names, so you can call them by name the next time you see or talk to them on the phone.

Where to Sit

Everyone wants the best seat. But in a business meeting, wait for the host to designate where you should sit. Remain standing by your chair, until the host takes his or her seat.

What happens when the host says, "Sit anywhere?" With a long conference room table, leaders are usually seated at the ends of the table.

Take a seat somewhere in the middle. If you are the highest ranked person, it shows humility. If you are not that person, you won't have to worry about being told to move.

How to Fit in When We Sit In

Are you sitting down? If you are, it's time to talk about sitting etiquette.

An article on Body Language in *Forbes* by Rachel Laneri[11] revealed that women tend to make themselves small at a conference room table, while men spread out. Women pile their materials neatly in front of them on the table and sit with legs and hands tucked under the table. Men will push away from the table, spread their legs or cross their ankle over their knee and stretch their arms over other chairs.

How do we fit in when we sit in? Sit up straight with your shoulders back. This shows you are alert and attentive. Check your posture throughout the day and during long meetings. Lean forward slightly in your chair to show you are listening. Your knees don't have to be glued together, but they should not be distant cousins. Keep your shoes on. No airing the dogs under the conference room table.

Crossing the Legs

Man or woman, if you must cross your legs, cross them at the ankle. Again, knees not glued together, but not distant cousins.

For women, if your skirts or dresses end at or above the knee, don't cross your legs at the knees. And watch the way you sit when you are on stage in a panel discussion or sitting across from people.

I remember a meeting, where the tables were facing each other and a woman in a short skirt was sitting across from me. Her legs were crossed at the ankles and her knees apart, so her underwear was visible. (Talk about an etiquette dilemma. How do you inform someone during a meeting, "Your underwear is showing?")

There is a way first ladies and royalty are taught to sit, with their legs crossed at the ankles with feet slightly to the side and knees together. It looks more sophisticated. Unless you're doing it wrong, then you look like a human pretzel.

Men should not sit with legs sprawled apart and arms outstretched like they have been dropped from the floor above. Stretch before the meeting. Then pull yourself together so you are not a space invader.

Be aware of cultural differences. Showing the bottom of your shoe, when your ankle is crossed over your knee is offensive in some cultures, as is pointing with your shoe, with your legs crossed at the knee.

Some say it is better to keep your legs uncrossed because crossed legs signal a closed mind. That may be a little over the top, as crossed legs can also be a position of comfort and a signal you are relaxed with the person to whom you are speaking or listening.

If someone is shifting around and using different leg positions, they might have a back problem. My father had back problems and could not stay seated for long periods of time. He would often get up and move around and sometimes stand up with his back against a wall.

BE EXCEPTIONAL: Memory Maneuvers in the Meeting

So many new names to learn and so little time. At a meeting around a conference room table where each person introduces himself or herself, *The Exceptional Professional* draws a map of the table in his or her notes with the names of each person, where they are sitting and any additional info: titles, where they are from, etc.

Try to find patterns that will help you remember the names:

- Two "M" names: "Mark" and "Mariah;"
- Rhyming names: Terry and Larry
- Alphabetical order: Nancy, Olivia, Peter.

Memorize the faces that go with each name. As you look around the room, quiz yourself silently on the names. As mentioned in Chapter 1.2: *Networking: Put Some Muscle in Your Mingle,* name recall does not require a photographic memory. It requires practice.

Be Prepared and Be Attentive

Prepare. Know the agenda ahead of time and be ready with any research or presentation assigned to you. Being unprepared wastes everyone's time. Be attentive to people who are presenting or speaking. No checking messages or texting under the table.

In some cases, much preparation goes into presentations and to tune people out is thoughtless and not a good career move. At Amana Appliances, during our major re-branding campaign, our advertising agency recommended a public relations agency.

To bring the public relations agency account team up to speed on our home appliance product lines, which included refrigerators, freezers, washers, dryers, ovens, cooktops, microwaves and dishwashers, I arranged for the product managers to present their lines at our headquarters in Amana, Iowa. The presentations involved significant preparation and the product managers did an excellent job – they were compelling, conversational and welcomed questions.

The agency's account team was made up of a man, who was a senior account manager and two young women, green out of college. Shortly after the presentations began, the senior account manager left the room and was roaming the hallways talking on his cell phone. The two young women took no notes, asked no questions and spent the entire time looking over their manicured nails.

We decided to cut them loose. They lost a multi-million dollar account on day one, because of their complete inattention. Why would we pay an agency that had zero interest in our products?

Cell Phone in the Meeting

It's best to keep your cell phone off during meetings. If you have long meetings, you can check your messages during breaks. If you have an emergency, such as a sick child or parent, let people in the meeting know why you need to leave your cell phone on.

Presenting

Rehearse your presentation and time it. Presenters who are not prepared wander in their speech and go over time. It's terrible when a speaker rambles on with no regard for people falling asleep in their chairs or walking out the doors. I have seen half the audience walk out of a large auditorium and the speaker kept going.

If the meeting is running late or if the speaker before you takes too long, you may find your own presentation time cut in half. Be prepared with a shorter presentation with half the slides ready to go.

Introducing a Speaker

If you are in charge of introducing a speaker, ask the speaker well in advance of the event for a prepared bio. Most speakers have one. Some speakers even have a video intro. If there is no prepared bio, ask the speaker for bullet points or a website or blog, to help you craft an intro.

The intro should be three minutes or less. Don't spend 20 minutes introducing a keynote speaker. It's fraudulent to advertise a speaker and think the audience is there to hear you.

Some introduce a guest speaker, then make a mad dash from the lectern. The speaker has not even reached the stage and the one who did the introduction flies by without shaking hands and dives off the stage. Where's the fire?

When introducing a speaker, wait at the lectern until the speaker gets there. Shake hands with the speaker, then walk – don't run – back to your seat. If you are the guest speaker, wait for the emcee to return to the lectern and shake hands before departing.

BE EXCEPTIONAL: Transitioning Between Speakers

The meeting host transitions from one presenter to the next. This means thanking one presenter and introducing the next presenter.

The Exceptional Professional goes a step further and finds something positive to say about the previous presenter and connects it to what the next presenter is about to cover. It's enjoyable to hear talented hosts with clever transitions between speakers that are humorous and sometimes heartfelt and moving. The main idea is to keep it about the speakers and not make it about yourself. Anytime a speaker can refer back to speakers before him or her, shows incredible presence of mind.

Transitioning between speakers is a skill practiced in Toastmasters. Most people associate Toastmasters with public speaking, but it is also a good place to practice running a meeting. (Find out more at www.toastmasters.org)

Know When to Fold 'Em

A keynote speaker leaves everyone on a high note. When the keynote speaker is done, the event should be over. If it's a fundraiser, there is a final "ask" for more donations. But it must be quick and entertaining.

Some emcees make the mistake of talking too long after the keynote. I have witnessed countless situations where an inspiring keynote speaker lifted the audience up, only to have an emcee or follow up person (whose job was to close the meeting or event and get off the stage), "Blah, blah, blah…" for 15 minutes or more.

In one disastrous event, the dinner ran late and after the keynote, the audience was exhausted and ready to leave. A woman, whose only job was to sing a closing song, decided to give a keynote of her own. She gushed for 20 minutes about how the keynote speaker inspired her. She went on about her life story and all she had been through. Now an otherwise lovely event had turned into a hostage situation.

She wasn't finished. She announced it was the birthday of her friend in the audience who came with her and asked if everyone could join her in singing, "Happy Birthday." Participation was spotty. At the end of it all, the audience, now ready to slip under the tables, had to wait out her inspirational song. Any goodwill from the original keynote was lost.

If you are not hired to be the keynote speaker, don't be the keynote speaker. Do your job, then get off the stage.

Attending Conferences

Conferences are a great way to re-charge your batteries and gain new knowledge and creative infusion. Often more wisdom is exchanged and more deals are made in the hallways between sessions. The next time you are in between sessions at a conference or meeting, don't retreat to a corner with your cell phone. Use that time for valuable networking.

But even if the conference is being held at a luxurious resort in a tropical climate, you have to remember you are representing yourself or your organization. Dress the code, not like you are on vacation.

Getting to Know You

Don't play games. There's nothing worse than "Get to Know You" games to help break the ice with others in the room. For example: having a word slapped on your back and you ask questions to find out what it is. In this situation, I say to everyone I meet, "Just tell me," and see how many people it takes before one caves and tells me what's on my back.

A better way is to assign a couple of people to make sure no one is standing around by themselves. Have them make introductions and make sure everyone is engaged in conversation and having a good time.

Conceit of The Feet

Have you ever sat down at a conference with 10 empty seats on all sides, then someone plunks down directly in front of you? Of course, that person has a head like a water tower. This happens to me all the time.

I was at a conference where a woman sitting in the row behind me turned the chair in front of her, took off her shoes and put her feet up. She flexed and wiggled her bright blue painted toenails the rest of the session. I couldn't help thinking of a person using that chair at the banquet that evening, placing his or her napkin where the feet were.

It doesn't matter how much is paid to pedicure and paint them, feet are really gross. Unless you are changing a light bulb, feet off the seat.

How Was The Conference?

Sometimes when people sign up for conferences, their organization foots the bill, then they don't show up for any of the conference. They go out touring or head for the beach instead.

It's fine to use your free time during a conference for leisure or even tack on a few days of fun at your own expense. But pretending to be at a conference is dishonest and it's stealing from your organization.

Conference Calls and Webinars

Conference calls are like regular meetings, except you need to adjust slightly when you are not seeing the other participants, unless you are on a video conference.

The host or call facilitator should let others know who is on the call.

If others can't see you, identify yourself when you speak. There should be no silent partners, who people on the call are not aware of.

Treat conference calls as if you were in a meeting in the same room. Don't multi-task. Digital microphones are very sensitive and will pick up sounds of shuffling papers, tapping pens, whispered side conversations and comments muttered under breath. Background noises make it hard for other participants to hear. If you are not speaking, mute your phone.

With a video conference, like a regular in-person meeting, it's fine to banter a little bit before the meeting begins. Introduce yourself to the people on screen and talk small talk.

Now that we have covered how to host a meeting and how to attend a meeting, we're going to complicate things by throwing food into the mix. Read on to find out more about meetings over meals.

3.2 *Meeting While Eating*

A woman who worked for a *Fortune 500* company, told me how she revered her supervisor and held him up on a pedestal as a great mentor. Until one day at lunch, she saw him use his finger to push peas onto his fork. "It completely exploded his image in my mind," she said. "I lost all respect for him." There are two lessons in this:

> **Lesson 1**: Never hire anyone who knows more about table manners than you. That's what interview meals are for – weeding these people out. Right? Actually, Lesson 1 is: Those above you are not the only ones noticing your table manners. It's also those reporting to you.
> **Lesson 2**: Never use your finger to push peas onto your fork. If you can't scoop up that last pea or grain of rice, don't chase it around your plate like your fork is a hockey stick. Let it go.

The Exceptional Professional is comfortable in all types of settings where business and food collide and knows how to see to the comfort of others in these situations, too.

In this chapter, you will learn:

- How to invite someone out for a business meal
- The rules of the restaurant
- Big banquet basics
- How to eat food ordered in

Let's Do Lunch: Inviting Someone Out for a Business Meal

Knowing how to host a business meal can help close more deals, enhance your organization's image and contribute to your success.

Offer your guest the choice of two restaurants. If you offer an open-ended, "Where would you like to eat?" You might be thinking "soup and sandwich" while your guest is thinking "steak and lobster."

"Would you like to go to Panera Bread or Applebees?"
"How about Maloney and Porcelli or Smith and Wollensky?"

If the person you are meeting has invited you out previously, choose the same type of restaurant when you reciprocate. Don't pick a flashy, more expensive restaurant to outdo the person.

If you have a guest you want to impress, see the maître d' the day before to make arrangements. Ask for a certain table, the best service and for the check to be delivered to you. Tip the maître d' after the meal for that assistance. ($10 or more, depending on your attitude of gratitude).

Breakfast or lunch meetings are best because they are the easiest to end. You have to get back to work. With dinner, you could be stuck there all night and the bill would be a lot bigger. Allow two hours for a breakfast or lunch meeting, longer for a dinner meeting.

The Best Seat

Arrive early, so your guest is not kept waiting. Offer your guest the best seat. Which is the best seat?

- The seat facing out into the dining room
- The seat with the best window view
- The seat that is away from the aisle traffic
- The seat that is the most comfortable (If one side of the table has a cushioned, couch-like banquette and the other side has a hard wooden chair, offer your guest the cushy banquette.)

If you are sitting at a four-top table, the location for negotiation is next to your client, rather than opposite him or her. As we learned in the previous chapter, sitting next to the person shows you are working with him or her. Sitting directly across from the person is more adversarial.

The Order of Business

The guest orders first, the host orders second. Pay attention to what your guest orders. If the wait staff makes a mistake and brings your guest the wrong thing, it is your job to ask the wait staff to correct it.

Do not talk business before ordering your food. This will make you seem pushy. And it also makes sense, because before you order, there are more interruptions – the specials, beverage orders, food orders. Better to start the business discussion after all this. Talk small talk for 10-15 minutes before a breakfast or lunch and 20-25 minutes before a dinner.

BE EXCEPTIONAL: Stand Tall by Talking Small

Small talk might seem a little awkward at first, but *The Exceptional Professional* knows that being skilled at small talk can open doors to bigger opportunities. Small talk is light, spontaneous conversation on non-critical subjects. It allows us to gage if people are shy or social, what kind of mood they are in and if they are open to conversation.

Small talk before a business meal is a warm-up exercise, a little test drive before a more involved conversation or negotiation. Here are some good small talk topics:

Weather: *How about this weather?*
Surroundings: *I've heard great things about this restaurant.*
Sports: *Who are you rooting for in the football playoffs?*
Pop Culture: *I saw a great movie over the weekend.*
Compliment: *You are looking well. Are you training for any more marathons or half-marathons?*

If you know the person and his or her family:

Where's your next family trip?
Are your kids playing soccer this spring?
How is your mother's health? (Okay, that might be a critical subject.)

There is a right way and wrong way to answer a stimulus to small talk:

> *Who are you rooting for in the football playoffs?*
> Wrong: *I hate football.*
> Better: *I don't follow football. Who do you say I should root for?*
>
> *How about this weather?*
> Wrong: *It's too cold. I don't know why I live here.*
> Better: *It's cold now but it's supposed to warm up by week's end.*

Keep it positive and keep it light. Honing your small talk skills can often lead to bigger things.

Breakfast Meetings

Have you ever seen an adult eat the toast insides and leave the crusts? For some reason, people get quirky with their food at breakfast more than any other meal. But during a breakfast meeting, avoid habits that may distract from the business at hand, such as the following:

- Mixing all the food on your plate into a pile of hash
- Putting ketchup on your eggs
- Dipping your toast into your over-easy egg yolks
- Dunking your doughnut, toast or Danish into your coffee
- Buttering a croissant, which are practically made of butter
- Add jelly or jam if you like, but not butter.
- Overloading your coffee with so much cream and sugar, it would be ice cream if you froze it
- Drinking the milk out of your cereal bowl
- Picking up the orange slice garnish or melon slice with your fingers and gnawing it off the rind
- Shaping your scrambled eggs into a butterfly body, with toast wings and bacon antennas (Okay, maybe just my mother that does that. But it's so cute!)

How many times have you tried to eat a cinnamon roll slathered in frosting with your fingers, then slyly wipe your fingers on your perspiring water glass, before trying to clean them off under the table on your napkin? Don't do it. If you are at a business meal, tackle the gooey cinnamon or pecan roll with a fork and knife. I will not even mention finger licking, because I know you would never ever do that.

Get the Most of Your Toast

When eating a roll or slice of bread served at a meal, tear off a bite-size piece, butter it, then eat it. The question comes up, "What about toast?"

There is a different approach to toast. Cut the toast in half (if it's not served that way) and butter each half on your bread plate, not cradled in the palm of your hand. Same with applying jelly, jam or nut spread, etc.

The reason is, toast is best enjoyed when the butter melts into it. Though we all know, most toast served in a restaurant arrives to the table at the same temperature before it went into the toaster.

Hold the toast by the edge and bring it to your lips. If any of the jelly slips onto your fingers, wipe your fingers on your napkin.

The Pace is Not a Race

Keep pace with your guest. Don't finish too far ahead, so the guest feels rushed or too far behind, so the guest feels delayed. When you, as the host, ask for the check and place your napkin on the left side of your place setting, that's the signal for the end of the meeting.

It Pays to Know

Whoever does the inviting in a business lunch, picks up the check. If a woman invites a man out to lunch, the woman pays. I was explaining this during a dining tutorial for a university and from the back of the room, a young man called out, "Oh, I like that rule! You should go over that again. Ladies, did you hear that? The ladies *HAVE to PAY.*"

I turned to him and said, "This weekend, you are going to find yourself alone."

Always review the check to make sure everything looks right. Question things that don't. Do not quibble over cents. Do not spend too much time reviewing the check or your guests will think there is trouble.

In some restaurants, the wait staff are trained not to offer or bring a check until you ask for it. In New York City, where table turnover is rapid, wait staff will hover and do everything but push the eject button or trap door to get you to leave.

Restaurant Manners

Men should remove their hats. Even in casual sports bars, once you enter, baseball caps come off. Women are allowed to leave their hats on.

Purses, pocketbooks, handbags or man-bags should be off the table during a meal. If it's small, place it on your lap, under your napkin. If it is one of those giant saddle bags that you are hauling around like a piece of luggage, place it on the floor either between or touching your feet.

Do not sling the purse over the back of your chair, where it might hinder traffic and it is an easy target for pickpockets. Well, that and it is really embarrassing when you stand up and the chair falls backwards.

The Flatware Bundle

What if your eating utensils come snugly tucked into a napkin bundle, like they are going off to summer camp? First, free the flatware and place the napkin in your lap. What goes where with the flatware? Here is an easy way to remember:

- The words "fork" and "left" have four letters, so forks go on the left side of your place setting.

- The words "spoon," "knife" and "right" have five letters, so spoons and knives go on the right. Knives are closest to the plate, blade in, and spoons are on the outside.

The Black Napkin

Some restaurants that cater to business people will offer a "black napkin." The idea is that people in business wear dark suits – navy, charcoal gray, black – and a white napkin is more likely to shed white lint on a dark suit. In some restaurants, you may request a black napkin. When I first heard about this, I thought, "Is this a big problem? Are business people walking around, plastered with unsightly white napkin lint and unbeknownst to them, causing others to give them wide berth?"

People plastered with cat hair and dog hair is a bigger issue. I get that. Growing up, we had an American Eskimo dog, a white fluffy hunk o' burning love that, as soon as you put on anything navy, would chase you around the house looking for affection. My brother Michael used to say, "We need a blue dog."

I saw a message board on the Internet where someone complained about not being offered a black napkin at an expensive steakhouse. That's pretentious. If the restaurant has black napkins, great. But please do not make a special request for a black napkin during a business meal. You never want to appear high maintenance.

The Menu: The Fixe Is In

What do the words "prix fixe" mean on a menu? Prix Fixe (rhymes with "bee cheeks" or "flea flicks") is French for "fixed price."

It does not mean the restaurant has it out for you. It means a predetermined meal, usually multiple courses, including dessert, is offered at a set price. The advantage is the chef, flexing his or her culinary expertise, may create a meal with foods that complement each other, that you might not have thought to put together.

Another term for prix fixe is "table d'hote" (rhymes with "hobbled goat" – sort of). Table d'hote is French for "host's table." It's the same idea: set meal, set price.

The opposite, is "ala carte" (rhymes with "wall apart"), French for "according to or by the menu." Ala carte means each item you select has a separate price. If you want roasted asparagus and garlic mashed potatoes with your filet, that's going to cost you.

I Now Pronounce You

There are worse things you can do at a business meal than order steak tartare medium rare. That's why it is helpful to know how to pronounce items on the menu correctly, so as not to look like a rube to co-workers, clients, interviewers or investors. Please forgive me, if the instruction on how to pronounce a few sauces is a little, well... saucy.

- Roux (roo): a mixture of flour and fat used to thicken sauces
- Bechamel (BAY-sha-mel): a white sauce with milk, butter, flour and onions
- Mornay (mohr NAY): a thick cheese sauce, a variation of bechamel
- Beurre blanc (burr-blahn): a butter sauce made with white wine or vinegar
- Demi-glace (dehm-ee-GLAHSS): a rich brown sauce reduced to a syrupy consistency
- Espagnole (es-puhn-YOL): a brown sauce made with veal stock, vegetables, herbs and tomatoes
- Veloute (veh loo TAY): a white sauce made with chicken, veal or fish stock and thickened with flour and butter
- Remoulade (ray moo LAHD or ray mah LAHD): a mixture of mayonnaise, seasonings and herbs, often served cold
- Hollandaise: (hol UHN days): a butter sauce made with egg yolks and lemon juice
- Bearnaise (BEHR-nays): a variation on hollandaise, with vinegar and tarragon or shallots
- Coulis (koo LEE): a sauce made with pureed vegetables or fruit
- Au Ju (OH zhoo): "with juice," natural juices extracted from the meat after cooking, sometimes with another liquid and seasonings

- Pesto (PEH stoh): an Italian sauce made by blending crushed garlic, basil, pine nuts, olive oil and parmesan cheese
- Pistou (PEES too): a cold sauce made of basil, garlic and olive oil

Now that you know the pronunciations and translations, try not to flaunt it with your dinner companions. That would be rude. Bon appetit!

No Prices on the Menu

A senior executive is treating you to a business dinner at an upscale restaurant or club. You know to order something moderately priced. To your chagrin, the menu has no prices. What should you order? Here is the hierarchy, in general, from least to most expensive entrees:

- Vegetable or pasta
- Chicken
- Fish or Pork
- Veal
- Steak or Lobster

There are numerous nuances:

- Wild caught seafood is always priced higher than farmed. Wild salmon is priced higher than farmed salmon. If the menu says, "Atlantic Salmon," it is most likely farmed.
- Catfish, trout and flounder are less expensive than whitefish or walleye. Any of these are less than halibut or swordfish. (Better deals might be had closer to where the fish came out of the water.)
- Sole can be inexpensive. Dover sole is one of the most expensive.
- Porterhouse is often the most costly steak (and hefty enough to feed a small town in Kansas).
- Sirloin is often least expensive. Flat iron or skirt steak is even more economical, but found in more casual eateries. Filet mignon, prime rib and strip steak are more pricey than sirloin.

- It's possible to order a lighter cut: an 8 oz. filet mignon vs. a 10 or 14 oz. Fish have lighter cuts, too.
- Shrimp or scallops are a toss-up: could be less but sometimes more.
- Specials tend to be more expensive (that's why they're so special).

These are good guidelines for interviews, because you never want to look like one who will run up the expense account.

Twist and Desist

Seasoning your food before tasting it gives the impression you are someone who does not think before you act. During a dining tutorial, I was explaining this, when someone asked, "What if the wait staff offers to put freshly ground pepper on your salad or fresh parmesan on your pasta? Do you taste it first?"

In this case, you would not taste it first. But keep in mind, when out on business, all things in moderation. Do not let the wait staff pile on the pepper or the fresh parm. It should be a couple of twists, not like the wait person is reeling in a big fish.

The Wait Staff

When placing your order, make eye contact with the wait staff. Say "please" when ordering and "thank you" when it arrives. Instead of *"Can I…"* say *"May I…" "May I have another Diet Coke, please?"* How do you get your wait person's attention?

1. Start by trying to make eye contact.
2. If that fails, raise your hand slightly when the person is near. Never grab anyone by the arm. Hands off.
3. Flag down a bus person or another wait person.
4. Stand up as a last resort.

If you have ever worked in a restaurant, you know it's a character building experience. In college, I worked at "Romeo's Pizza and Mexican Food." The manager was a screaming maniac. The other waitresses were snacking out of the bus tubs. Customers would steal my meager tips. I went home each night smelling like the menu. When I punched in (ka-chunk!), it was like clocking into Hell.

One Wednesday, I opened up the morning paper and screamed. The restaurant had a coupon in the newspaper. Coupon Night attracts diners who want five star restaurant service and leave one star restaurant tips. That night, the rest of the wait staff called in sick.

Instead of the usual four to six tables, I was covering 20. I wasn't that good at waiting on four tables. A lot of pennies were left that night. It was a great motivator for me to stay in college, but it also gave me a deep respect for people who wait tables.

When eating out, be good to your wait staff. In a high end restaurant, a wait person covers four tables at a time. In a lower or mid-priced restaurant, it might be five or six. If your wait person is covering more, he or she is carrying more than a normal workload. Have patience.

What to Tip

Tip 20 percent of the bill. Tip more, if you like. If you use a coupon, don't forget to tip based on the price of the meal before the coupon.

Eliminating Ambiguity About Auto Gratuity

An automatic gratuity or tip may be assessed to parties of a certain number (usually 8 or more). This is because a table with many people is a major pain in the backside to serve. Without the gratuity, large parties often walk away leaving little or no tip. ("*I thought YOU left the tip.*")

When I waited tables, I recall a table of 18 people, 8 of whom were toddlers. The kids were at one end of the table, flinging food all over the place. The parents had me constantly on the run for more drinks and petty requests. Taking their order took forever, because while some were ready, others said, "Mmmm... I don't know... I was thinking, this... but that looks tempting..." When I said, "Let me come back," they protested.

They left behind a huge mess. On the toddler side of the table as well as the adult side, there were food remnants and sticky spilled stuff all over the table, chairs and floor. The tip for a table of 18, who hogged the table for hours? Two dollars. That, is why restaurants assess automatic gratuity for large parties.

Some think if there is gratuity, there's no need to leave any more. But if gratuity is only 10 percent, leave enough to make it 20 percent.

Once in a while, you hear a great story about a generous customer who recognized their wait staff was having a bad day. One wait person told me a story how, due to a kitchen mix-up, her customers at a diner waited forever for their food. When it finally came, they were salivating as they watched her walking down the aisle with the huge tray of food on her shoulder. Just before she got there, she slipped.

Their dinner went crashing down on the floor before their horrified eyes. Despite the disaster, they left a $20 tip for a $40 meal.

Poor Service

At a restaurant, mistakes are made. Orders are misplaced. Errors are made in the kitchen. Some items take longer than expected. If you are receiving bad service, are there other mitigating factors? Is the restaurant short-staffed? Overbooked? Did a bus of seniors suddenly appear?

Sometimes the wait person is obnoxious, indifferent or downright rude. If you received bad service, do not leave zero tip or a penny to express your discontent. Leave a standard tip, then speak to the manager.

Poor Patron Performance

I was out at a restaurant with business colleagues. The service was fine but one of my co-workers became completely unglued, constantly berating our wait person and sending food back. (Her drink was not right, the appetizer was not hot enough, etc.) I wanted to crawl under the table. The guests we were entertaining that night were also mortified.

I couldn't do anything about my colleague's behavior. She didn't report to me. But I could help make it right with the wait person. I had to leave a little early, so on the way out, I apologized for my colleague's behavior and gave her extra money for the tip.

Waiting tables is hard work and there are a million things in a restaurant that can go wrong. It's cowardly to berate or humiliate any wait staff who cannot defend themselves without risking the loss of their own job. And it's embarrassing to those dining with you.

Makes You Want to Scream

What happens if, during your business lunch, a child at the next table starts screaming out of control? As the child's volume is increasing, you feel your blood pressure increasing. Stop and think before you react.

If you want to really mortify and embarrass the business person with whom you are dining, you can:

1. Wonder out loud, so the child's handlers can hear, "Why don't they take that kid out of here?!"
2. Stare angrily at the child and parent. You know, send a message.

Wondering out loud is the worst. And an angry stare is not a suitable way to communicate. (Unless it's your offspring – and even that can be futile. My brother Patrick, a retired Marine major, claimed he had a stare that could make Marines cry, that had no effect whatsoever on his four-year-old daughter.)

If you are the host of the business lunch, ask the wait staff to re-seat you away from the noisy disturbance, which might also be someone talking loudly on a cell phone or a group of people laughing like hyenas. If you are the guest, you can do one of the following:

- Nothing. This shows you are patient and not easily distracted.
- Treat it like the elephant in the room that it is and make it part of your conversation: express sympathy for the person trying to comfort the child, especially if you have kids.
- Make a light joke about it. "I wonder what that child ordered for lunch?" or "He must be a Cincinnati Bengals fan."
- Use it as a segue. "That reminds me to tell you about my experience marketing to families..."

Be merciful to parents trying to calm a screaming baby. If people could schedule their children's meltdowns like everything else, they would. We were all babies once. We all entered this world screaming. Hopefully we won't go out that way.

That said, be wary of restaurants that seat women dressed for business in the "women and children" section and men in business suits in a quieter part of the restaurant. My sister was lunching with a female supervisor who pointed this out. She said, "Groups of women are thought to be noisier and therefore seated away from business men." If you want to sit away from a noisier section, speak up.

Big Banquet Meals

It could be a convention, a chamber of commerce luncheon or an awards banquet. There's a ballroom full of round, ten-top tables and no seating assignment. Kill me now.

If you are by yourself and the first to sit at a table, you worry. Will anyone join me? Or will I sit here alone looking like a pariah? Worse, people come by your table, look you over and move on. You try that, but the person makes eye contact. Too late, now you have to sit there.

Have you ever sat at a big round table, opposite two people talking to each other and neither of them talks to you? Don't they get the concept of the round banquet table? It's about community. If you weren't supposed to talk to each other, the ballroom would be set up with desks.

Then there's the chair tippers. *"These seats are all saved."* I want to reply, "Your friends are using you. You need new people."

Here is the strategy when you are by yourself at the banquet:

1. Find the table with the married couple – the older, the better. Every banquet has them. They are usually charming, engaging and happy to talk to you, because they are used to talking to each other.
2. At the table, ask, "May I join you?" or "Is this seat taken?"
3. Don't put more than one chair between you and the next person.
4. Introduce yourself to each person at the table. Walk around the table and shake hands.
5. Introduce people who join the table to people you have already met.

First question for your new married couple friends: "How did you two meet?" You'll never be disappointed.

Can't Touch This

Do not touch the bread basket or cracker basket until the meal begins. Some people at business banquets dive into the bread and devour it before everyone is seated at their table. The bread and crackers are not a pre-meal snack. Before the meal, hands off.

When to Begin

If there is an invocation or grace being said before a big banquet (your program should tell you), wait until it is completed before placing your napkin in your lap. At a smaller occasion, such as a dinner party, if there is no invocation, place your napkin in your lap when your host does.

Shared platters of food or condiments are passed around the table counterclockwise – from your left to your right. Take the food item closest to you and keep the platter moving. Place the serving utensils toward the next person who will receive the platter.

May I Eat During The Keynote?

When the master of ceremonies introduces the after dinner speaker, all else ceases. There is no tittering, twittering, dithering or jittering. Finish eating and sipping coffee before the speaker begins, turn your chair toward the speaker and give the speaker your undivided attention.

If your dessert arrives after the speaker begins, finish it as quietly and unobtrusively as possible. A speaker can be distracted by clanking dishes, silverware and glasses or the uttering of "yummy noises."

You may not ask the banquet staff to box any part of the meal "to go" or put food into a plastic baggie in your purse, man-bag or pockets.

The Buffet Way

There's a lot of buffet dining in business. With buffets, comes food in slices, either in layered rows or fanned out, sometimes prettily displayed.

No matter what it is – deli meat, pancakes, egg foo young – take the slice at the front of the row. Don't sift through the pile looking for the slice with the most pleasing shape or the portion that seems a fraction of a millimeter thicker. It's a buffet – it's all pretty much the same. Your food play is everyone else's delay.

When dining buffet style, you may begin eating as soon as you are seated. But it's polite to wait until a few people join you. You never want to appear ravenously hungry in business.

Can't Feel My Face

Back in 1995, two enterprising young women came out with the book, *The Rules*, offering advice on how to land a man. One of the nuggets was, "When your hair falls in front of your face, you tilt your head back and comb back your hair with your hand from the top of your head in a slow, sweeping motion."

One place where that is not sexy: the dinner table. At a business lunch, banquet dinner or dinner in someone's home, keep your hands out of your hair and off your face.

In winter or dry climates, everybody's itchy. There's that pesky, persistent itch on the end of your nose. Resist the urge. Ditto for that beard you grew over vacation, that rivals anything seen in Major League Baseball. What's wrong with a little scratch or inconspicuous rub? It's unappetizing, especially when those same hands will be reaching into the bread basket or passing other food items.

Try not to scratch anything. Not even the back of the person next to you. I was at a dinner party where the couple seated next to me was petting and pawing each other the entire meal. I am not sure why they needed two chairs. It was awkward. (That kind of public display is not a sign of unbridled passion. It's the sign of an insecure relationship.)

As for the hair toss, if your hair keeps falling in front of your face, it might be time for a haircut.

Ordering In Food

Into business, a lot of sandwich trays must land. Sandwiches are ordered for long meetings or for visiting guests. Sometimes an ordered-in lunch is a nice treat for a hard working staff.

Sandwiches are a great convenience: a way to re-charge everyone's batteries while keeping everyone close to the conference room. Usually there are chips involved, sometimes a side salad and if you are lucky, cookies for dessert. Here are a few sandwich tray guidelines:

- If a toothpick is holding the sandwich together, remove the toothpick before you take a bite.
- Open mustard or mayonnaise packets with your fingers, not your teeth. If you can't open it, find a scissors or let it go. Don't struggle or you, or the person next to you, will be wearing the contents.

- Don't do anything quirky, like putting potato chips on your sandwich. Save that for dining with family and friends.
- Take small, manageable bites. This is not an eating contest.
- Have extra napkins available, especially with wrap sandwiches that split apart and spill their contents.
- Don't grouse about the selection or next time, you can buy lunch.
- Avoid seconds. No one at your meeting is impressed by how much
- food you can put away.
- When finished, go wash off your smelly "sandwich hands."

Remember to thank the person who ordered the sandwiches and the person who paid for them.

Now that you know about meetings over meals, we're going to take a deeper dive into the nuts and bolts of table manners.

TABLE MANNERS

4.1 *Eating in Front of Others*

"Do I really need to know all this?" said the frustrated the young man. "Who cares where I set down my knife and fork?"

The scene is an etiquette banquet for 150 college students in a high-ceilinged ballroom with oak-paneled walls at a major university. My job is to walk these students through dinner and teach the rules of the table. When to begin eating, American vs. Continental style, how to keep a cherry tomato from flying off the plate – it's all part of the program.

The students come from a wide-array of experiences. Some sit up straight with their elbows in and wield a knife and fork with dexterity. Others have a fork and knife in each fist and are planting the fork like a tent stake in the entrée, as if they are worried it might get away.

Whether speaking at a university, corporation or Rotary Club, my goal is not to impose more rules on a maxed out society. My goal is to persuade people to look outside themselves and focus on others. *The Exceptional Professional* does not go through the motions and follow rules, but thinks of table manners in terms of how they affect others.

In this chapter, you will learn:

- How to navigate your place setting
- What to do before you begin eating
- Continental vs. American style
- Finished vs. Resting positions
- How to eat soups and salads

Alcohol protocol is a separate chapter. If you avoid alcohol or don't have any interest in it, you can skip it.

The Place Setting

A friend of mine, who attends a lot of fundraising dinners in Chicago said, "What makes me crazy is when the person to my left takes my bread plate and the person to my right, correctly takes his own bread plate. Now I'm left holding the roll."

When you sit down to a big banquet meal and all the glasses, plates and flatware seem to blend together, what is the first thing everyone says? Are those my glasses or yours? Is that my bread plate or yours? If you choose incorrectly, the entire round table will be thrown into chaos.

How do you tell what belongs to you? At Maria Everding's *Etiquette Institute,* I learned a quick trick. Put your thumb and index finger together on each hand, like you are giving the "okay" signal. Keep your other fingers straight. This makes a lowercase "b" and "d."

The "b" in your left hand stands for "bread plate on the left." The "d" in your right hand stands for "drinks on the right." Isn't that easy?

At one university, a professor came up after a dining tutorial and said, "That 'okay' signal is an obscene hand gesture in Brazil." Fair enough. Don't do "b" and "d" in Brazil.

What if, like my fundraising friend, you are left bread plate-less? Our guiding principle is to make people around us comfortable so don't say, "Hey! That's *MY* bread plate!" Set your bread on the upper left part of your dinner plate. In other words, roll with it.

Which Fork and When?

When you see all those forks, spoons and knives at your place setting, what initially comes to mind? (Besides, "Thank goodness I don't have to do the dishes.") Many ponder, "Which do I pick up first?"

There is an abundance of faulty etiquette advice out there. One of the most common is, "If you are not sure which fork to pick up, just watch what the people around you are doing."

What if they are WRONG? Many times, people are.

It's easier and less stressful to remember to start with the utensils on the outside and work your way in towards the plate with each course. The dessert fork and spoon are at the top of your place setting. If you don't see any fork or spoon at the top of the place setting, don't panic. Dessert utensils are often served on the dessert plate itself.

Sometimes I tell the college students, "I am going to ruin the dating pool for you, because some day you will be sitting across from a date, thinking, 'I can't believe this person just picked up the wrong fork.'"

The positions of utensils let you know the order of things. If the salad fork is on the outside, that means the salad will come before the main course. In a formal dinner, the salad fork might be on the inside, closest to the dinner plate or service plate. In that case, the salad will come after the main course (as shown in the graphic below).

Before You Begin

The first step in any meal is to wait for the host to tell you where to sit. Stand by your chair and sit down when the host sits.

Whether it's an interview or a meal at someone's home, follow the host's lead. When the host places the napkin in his or her lap, you follow suit. When the host begins eating, you may begin eating.

When to Begin at a Banquet

At a banquet for 200 people, it is not necessary to wait for all 200 people in the banquet hall to be served before you begin eating. If you had to wait for everyone, some people would be eating cold soup.

In a large banquet, the service is like a wave. The servers deliver one course and people begin eating, while the rest of the room is served. By the time they have finished serving, the next wave begins: the people served first will be finishing and the servers can start clearing. This saves time by allowing the caterer to be more efficient with fewer servers.

A university client said their previous etiquette instructor insisted everyone in a room of 150 people be served before anyone could eat and everyone be finished with each course, before plates could be removed. Their etiquette dinner, scheduled for two hours, lasted four hours.

If you are sitting at a table with eight or fewer people, begin eating when everyone at your table has been served. If there are nine or more at the table, wait until at least a few people have been served. The same rules of when to begin apply to each course.

With a buffet, you may begin eating as soon as you take your seat, but it is polite to wait until at least a few people have joined you. You never want to look like you are half-starved at a business meal.

The Napkin

Place your napkin in your lap when your host does. Otherwise, place your napkin in your lap as soon as you sit down. If there is a grace or an invocation being said, wait until after the grace or invocation to place your napkin in your lap.

A dinner napkin is large – fold it in half, making a rectangle in your lap. Even if it comes in a triangle-shape, fold it into a rectangle. This way, it covers more of your lap. A luncheon napkin is smaller – unfold it all the way, making a square in your lap.

You may not tie your napkin around your neck or stuff your napkin in your shirt collar or waistband. Gentlemen, do not flip your tie over your shoulder to save it from splatter. You must learn to eat neat.

There are two things you should never do with a napkin:

1. Never blow your nose on your napkin. Have tissues on hand for that.
2. Never spit anything into your napkin. (How to remove unwanted objects is covered in Chapter 4.2: *Awkward at the Table.*)

If you are dining at someone's home and leave a big wad of goo in a fine linen napkin – when they are cleaning up after, they will know you did this. (Unless you switch napkins with the person next to you.)

If you need to leave the table mid-meal, Maria Everding says there are two schools of thought about what to do with your napkin. She gives the rationale for both and lets people make up their own mind. I agree.

Traditional thinking: leave the napkin on your chair. If the napkin is soiled, you wouldn't want to put it on the table, while others are still eating, because it's an unappetizing sight.

Newer thinking: leave the napkin, slightly crumpled, on the table to the left of the place setting, with any blots turned in. Leaving it on the chair and then using it to wipe your mouth is unsanitary. (Who knows where that chair has been?) In some upscale restaurants, no matter where you leave the napkin, the wait staff is trained to pick it up and leave it folded over your chair handle for when you return.

At the end of the meal, when you leave, place the napkin, slightly crumpled, to the left of the place setting. Do not refold the napkin. (Even if you know how to turn it back into a fancy crane or rose.)

Breaking Bread

If you have a roll or slice of bread, break off a bite-size piece, butter it and eat it. Then repeat. Do not butter your whole roll or slice of bread, then bite into it. Do not make a "butter sandwich" by halving the roll and slathering butter in the middle.

When butter is passed around the table, use the serving knife with the butter to place butter on your bread plate. Use your butter knife to butter your bread. Place your knife horizontally across the top of the bread plate, with the blade facing in.

The bread plate is for bread and butter. It may also be used for items from a relish tray, such as radishes and olives. The bread plate may not be used for items from your dinner plate you don't like, such as icky mushrooms. What happens on the dinner plate stays on the dinner plate.

If you don't have a bread plate, place your roll on the upper left side of your dinner plate. Or skip the bread – at a big banquet meal, who needs another starch?

The next thing I must tell you will make some people very sad. You may not take your bread in hand and swab it through your gravy, salad dressing or spaghetti sauce. That's tragic, isn't it? But there is good news. You may take that bite-size piece of bread, spear it on the end of your fork, then soak up your gravy, salad dressing or spaghetti sauce.

Passing Fancy

When you are passing an item to be shared – a bread basket, salad dressing, a water pitcher – pass it counterclockwise. (That's from your left to your right, for those raised with a digital clock.) After items have gone around the table once, they may be passed by the shortest distance, to whoever is asking for them.

If there is a large platter of something, like eggplant, hold the platter for the person on your right, while that person uses the serving utensils to move the eggplant from the platter to his or her plate. Always turn the serving utensils toward the person who will be using them next.

Be a peach and don't reach. Say, "Please pass the..." and "Thank you" when it arrives.

Salt and Pepper

Salt and pepper are passed together, one in each hand. Even if someone asks for just the salt or just the pepper, you still pass them together. Some etiquette instructors say, "Salt and pepper are married." But it might just be a mutually beneficial, co-dependent relationship.

Don't grab the salt and pepper in hand by the tops. Do not try to balance them in one hand by the bottoms. Set both down on the table next to the person to whom you are passing. Do not deliver them directly into the person's hands.

When someone says, "Please pass the salt and pepper," you may not stop and use them for yourself first. That's pass interference. Speaking to a group of college athletes, I added, "That's a 10-yard penalty." A football player corrected me, "It's an automatic first down." I replied, "That's it – roughing the etiquette instructor, 15-yards."

Taste the food before you use the salt and pepper. And even then, use salt and pepper sparingly. When eating in someone's home, pouring on the salt is an insult to the cook, because you are suggesting the food was not adequately seasoned.

Can We Eat Already?

Now that we have the map of the place setting, we can get down to the business of eating. There are two different styles of eating: Continental (or European) Style and American Style. The good news is, they both have the same cutting position.

Cutting Your Food

There is a right way and a wrong way to cut items on your plate. Holding the knife or fork in your fist and pinning items with your fork straight up, pirate style (Arrrrrghhh!), is the wrong way.

The right way is to take the fork in your left hand and knife in your right hand. Put your index finger on the back of the fork at the base (where the handle ends and the fork begins) and the base of the knife (where the handle ends and the knife begins).

Pin items to be cut with your fork tines down, applying pressure with your index finger. Keep your wrists low and elbows in. (You too, lefties!) The fork should be between you and the knife as you are cutting.

When you have an entrée to cut, cut three bite-size pieces at a time. Some people will say only cut and eat one piece at a time. Either way is fine. The main idea is to avoid cutting up the entire main dish at once, like your mother used to do for you when you were little.

I often get the question, "If my entrée is not in the best position to cut, may I turn the plate?" The answer is, "Yes, you may turn your plate once." You may not continue to rotate your plate this way and that like you are driving a bus.

If something is tender enough to cut with a fork, like an omelette or fish, you need not use a knife.

American Style

Set your knife, blade in, horizontally across the top of your plate and switch your fork to your right hand (lefties, flip your fork over) and scoop. When eating American Style, you may not use your knife as a "pusher" to push items onto your fork. Your finger is not a pusher either.

Continental (or European) Style

Keep your knife in your right hand and your fork, tines down, in your left hand. Spear items that you cut and bring them to your mouth with the fork tines down. Some people say this is more efficient, because you don't have to keep setting your knife down and picking it up, like American Style.

But here is the tricky part: to eat your peas and carrots Continental Style, you must use your knife to push them onto the back of your fork and raise the fork to your mouth. Tricky, right? Rice, mashed potatoes, everything else... onto the back of the fork. If you are not used to doing that, it takes a little practice.

Can you use your bread to push items onto your fork? Some etiquette experts will say, "Yes." I think it looks a little too "hands-on" with your food and informal. In business dining, try not to distract others by your eating habits.

Which Style is Best?

When I ask college students at any university, how many eat Continental Style, at least a third of the audience will raise their hands. While American Style is still the most popular in the U.S., Continental Style seems to be how the rest of the world eats, with the exception of those who primarily use chopsticks or their hands.

The style which is more comfortable for you is the one you should use. If you are in Canada and everyone around you is eating Continental Style, if you are not adept at it, you will look sloppy. However, if you are in Canada (or any country where they eat Continental Style) for six months or more, you should learn how to eat Continental Style.

Stick with the same style throughout the meal. That means you may not spear pieces of your entree Continental Style and then scoop up your peas and carrots American Style.

The Scoop on Soup

When you are eating soup, move the spoon away from you through the soup, rather than toward you. This is to prevent splashing soup on yourself. All these rules have a purpose. They are not rules for the sake of rules. Sit up straight and bring the soup up to you, not your face down to the soup. Sip as noiselessly as possible from the side of the spoon.

Do not cool your soup by blowing on it or taking ice out of your beverage to put in the soup. Wait for the soup to cool – this shows patience. Same for a hot beverage – wait for it to cool.

Sometimes my university clients will order tricky French onion soup as part of their etiquette dinner to challenge their students.

French onion soup, with its stretchy strands of melted cheese is easily managed. Use your soup spoon to sever the cheese against the side of the soup cup, bowl or crock. (Better yet, order French onion soup when you are out with friends and family, not on business.)

To get that last drop, you may tip the bowl slightly, but tip it away, again, to prevent splashing soup on yourself. You may not lift the bowl or cup to your face and drink from it. (We know you do that with your cereal bowl in the privacy of your own home when nobody is looking. That can be our little secret.)

Exceptions to the ban on soup cup lifting: a bouillon cup, which is lifted by the handles, and some cultures that drink soup from the cup. Important reminder: always learn the meeting, greeting and eating customs of other cultures you will be dealing with, whether you visit their country or they visit yours.

When you are finished with your soup, if there is a service plate underneath your soup bowl or cup, leave the soup spoon on this plate, to the right of the soup bowl or cup. If there is no plate underneath, leave the soup spoon in the bowl or cup with the handle at about four o'clock (or lower right section).

Know Your Soup Spoons

A spoon is a spoon. Unless you are *The Exceptional Professional*, who recognizes the different types of spoons.

- Oval Soup Spoon: looks like a Table Spoon. (Try not to be scandalized, but many people just use Table Spoons.)
- Cream Soup Spoon: has a round bowl.
- Bouillon Spoon: looks like a Cream Soup Spoon, but smaller in size.
- Iced Tea Spoon: a long, skinny spoon with a small bowl. If there is no plate underneath the glass to place it on, this spoon stays in the glass while you sip. To do this, rap the spoon against the side of the glass with your index finger, while you wrap your other fingers around the glass.

- Demitasse Spoon: a more petite spoon used to stir coffee or espresso, served in the adorable, little demitasse cup. The Demitasse Spoon looks like it could be a prom date for the Seafood Fork. (Alas, the two shall never meet, as they reside at opposite ends of the meal.)
- The Tea Spoon is for... (drumroll)... hot tea.

There are many other spoons. "Why should I care?" you might ask. They talk about the Grapefruit Spoon on *Masterpiece Theater* – so it matters. There's a Chocolate Spoon, Ice Cream Spoon, After-Dinner Coffee Spoon, and Five O'clock Spoon (smaller than a Tea Spoon, larger than an After-Dinner Coffee Spoon) for high tea.

Salads and Food Fumbles

When I give a dining tutorial, a frequent question is, "What if something falls off my plate?" This is usually asked during a salad course.

Salads are tricky. They are made up of wacky shapes and textures that don't fit together like Legos®. Cherry tomatoes roll. Croutons bounce. Leaf lettuce flaps this way and that. Dressing just greases the skids. Of course, it's piled high onto a tiny plate. If a piece of lettuce lands on the table, leave it (no pun intended). When you are finished with your salad, put the leaf back on the plate before the plate is removed.

Traditionally, you were not supposed to use a knife to cut your salad. The reason: knives were made of nickel-plated steel, which would tarnish from the acid in the salad dressing. We don't have nickel-plated knives anymore, so if something is too big on your salad plate, by all means – cut it. You don't have to struggle with it.

BE EXCEPTIONAL: Conquering the Cherry Tomato

The cherry tomato: so little, round and cute atop your foothill of salad, yet so hazardous. There's the dilemma. Is it small enough to pop the whole tomato in my mouth? Or do I have to slice it in two? *The Exceptional Professional* never leaves a cherry tomato behind.

Have you ever tried to cut a cherry tomato only to have it explode like a geyser and splatter your outfit? Or in the attempt to cut the slippery orb in two, you launch it like a salad dressing-soaked cannon ball onto the floor or your neighbor's lap? (Murphy's Law says the more important the dinner, the more likely that tomato is headed for the lap.) Some fear the cherry tomato and let it sit there mocking them.

Trap the little monster against your knife and put one tine of your fork through the top, where the tomato was once connected to the vine. Push the fork in deeper – niiice and slow. With the fork in the tomato, use your knife to gently divide and conquer. Savor the victory.

Give It a Rest: Resting Position

If you are not finished with your meal, you may place the fork and knife in the "Resting Position." This is an efficient way of letting your wait staff or hosts know your plate should not be cleared. You are planning to nibble some more.

The Resting Position for the American Style of eating is different from Continental Style. But here is the easy part: just set the utensils down exactly as you were holding them.

With Continental Style, your fork is in your left hand and knife is in your right. Set them both down in an upside down "V" on your plate, fork on the left and knife on the right.

With American Style, your knife should already be resting horizontally across the top of your plate and your fork should be in your right hand.

Leave the knife right where it is and place the fork diagonally across the plate, with the tines pointing toward the upper left part of the plate and the handle at about four o'clock (or the lower right section of the plate.)

Finis Finesse: Finished Position

Just as there is a resting position, there a "Finished Position," which signals you are done with your meal.

Whether you are eating American or Continental Style, the Finished Position is the same. Place the fork and knife diagonally across your plate with the handles around four o'clock and the tines and blade around ten o'clock. The knife is to the right of the fork on the plate and always blade in, facing toward you.

Some people eating Continental Style will turn the fork tines down in the Finished Position. That's fine. I don't recommend another variation, that has the fork and knife overlapping in an

X-pattern in the middle of the plate. With the X-pattern, the utensils are more likely to slide off the plate and more likely to get scuffed up.

All these rules have a rationale. Resting and Finished Positions make it easier on your wait staff. Imagine a banquet hall with 300 guests. Instead of having to ask, "Are you done? Are you done?" to 300 people, the wait staff can look at the placement of your knife and fork and know.

At the End of the Meal

Do not stack your dishes or push them away. When you leave the table, place your napkin, slightly crumpled to the left side of your place setting.

Multi Course Meals

I gave a dining tutorial hosted by a very generous business owner, who was treating his fortunate staff to a seven-course meal – a feast, with etiquette training. The setting was a private club, with windows all around overlooking the city. The food was unbelievable.

It's not often we partake in a seven-course meal. But for *The Exceptional Professional*, it's good to recognize the courses, the order in which they are served and the utensils that go with each course.

Seven Course Meal

1st Course: Seafood
2nd Course: Soup
3rd Course: Fish
4th Course: Meat
5th Course: Salad and Cheese
6th Course: Dessert
7th Course: Coffee (or a Fruit Course)

A "palette cleanser," such as a sherbet or sorbet may be served between the Fish and Meat Courses.

We often think of coffee as a beverage served with dessert. However, in a formal meal, Coffee is a separate course after the dessert. This is when you may order espresso. Espresso is an after dinner drink. Do not order cappuccino after dinner. Cappuccino is a morning beverage.

Seven Courses Mapped Out

Here is the same place setting from earlier in this chapter, but this time, all the utensils and glasses are labeled. Remember how we start with the utensils on the outside and work our way in with each course? Those utensils are a map of what's to come in the meal.

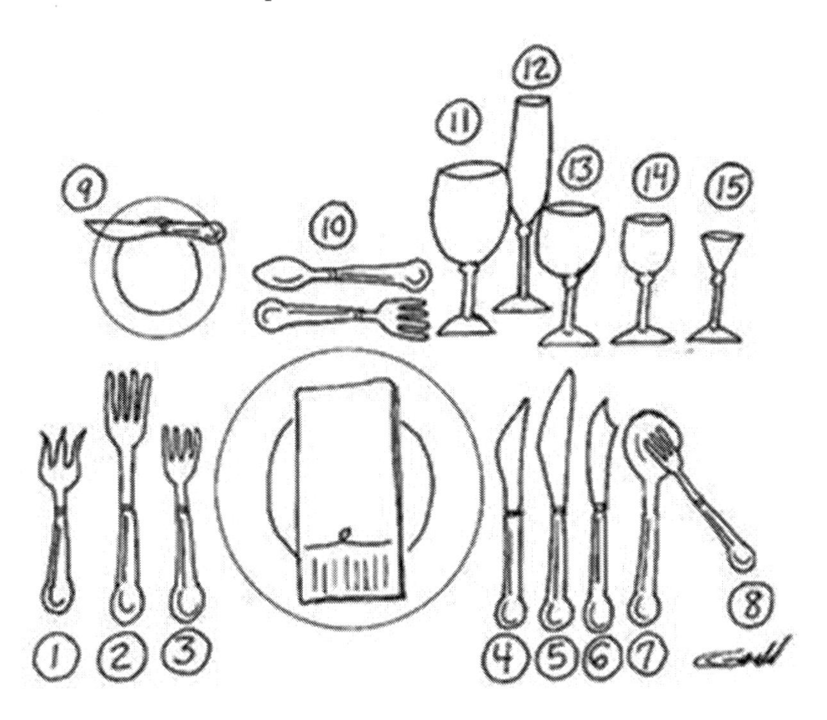

Utensils
1. Fish Fork
2. Entrée (or Main Course) Fork
3. Salad Fork *
4. Salad Knife
5. Entrée Knife
6. Fish Knife (curved)
7. Soup Spoon
8. Seafood Fork
9. Butter Knife **
10. Dessert Spoon/Fork

Beverages
11. Water Glass
12. Champagne (with Dessert)
13. Red Wine (with Entrée)
14. White Wine (with Fish Course)
15. Sherry (with Soup Course)

* The salad comes after the main course in a formal dinner, so the salad fork here is on the inside, closest to the service plate.

** There is a bread plate here, but traditionally, bread and butter are not served in a formal dinner.

The tiny fork resting in the bowl of the soup spoon, is a Seafood Fork (or Cocktail Fork). A Seafood Course might be shrimp cocktail, scallops, crab or something similar. Notice this fork has three prongs. A similar fork with two prongs is an Escargot Fork.

For fork snobs, there is also a Lobster Fork, Oyster Fork, Fruit Fork, Strawberry Fork, Pastry Fork and Ice Cream Fork (which resembles its hillbilly cousin, the "Spork.") Now that you're in the know, keep it under wraps from anyone about to go crazy with a bridal registry.

The funky, curvy shape of the Fish Fork and Knife are for deboning a fish. Sometimes the fish shows up on your plate with a face and tail still attached. (I know some find it disturbing when your third course is looking back at you, but it happens.) Make a cut across the fish near the top, and use the fork to gently pull the fish flesh away from the spine.

Often, both Dinner and Salad Forks will be the same size, so again, start with the fork on the outside.

There is Dessert, Isn't There?

The dessert fork is above the service plate. Don't despair if you go to a dinner and you don't see a dessert fork on your place setting. Sometimes the dessert fork arrives on the plate with the dessert. (Yay!)

When setting a table and placing a dessert fork above the plate, the handle goes to the right. But if there is a spoon and a fork with dessert (think fresh apple pie and ice cream), then the fork handle goes to the left and the spoon handle to the right.

Here's why: with just the fork, the fork is held in the right hand. The handle to the right makes it easier to grab. With a spoon and fork for dessert, the fork handle is to the left, because you are going to secure whatever you are eating with the fork in your left hand, then eat it with the spoon in your right hand.

The bigger picture? The utensils are placed for ease of use, not just because they look pretty that way.

Oh, but there's more. When you combine humans and food, there are so many things that can go wrong. Keep reading to our next chapter to learn how to avoid some of the dining pitfalls.

4.2 *Awkward at the Table*

"When may you place your elbows on the table?" I posed this question at a middle school. A young lady immediately raised her hand and said dreamily, "When you are gazing into each other's eyes."

Ei-yi-yi, junior high.

If you came up through the 4-H ranks, you might recite, "This is not a horse's stable, get your elbows off the table," or something similar. "Elbows off the table" is a favorite rule of grandmas everywhere.

When I ask during a dining tutorial, "When may you place your elbows on the table?" Several members of the audience will respond without hesitation, "Never."

Then I say, "Never say, 'Never.'" There is an exception to the "elbows off the table" rule. (Sorry, grandmas!) More about that in a bit. Just like the chapter on awkward things that happen while networking, we also need to navigate awkward things that happen while dining.

In this chapter, you will learn:

- What to do when you can't eat something
- How to get rid of things you can't spit into your napkin
- What to do when you have to sneeze
- When you can use your fingers

Elbows Off or On?

The exception to elbows off the table: you may place your elbows or forearms on the table between courses, when there is no food on the table. Usually, that happens in big banquet meals where there is a lot of background noise and you lean forward to converse with people across the table. It's not polite to use your elbows to prop up your sleepy head.

At all other times, you may rest your wrists on the edge of the table or in your lap. Keep your elbows in, to avoid bruising the ribs of your dining partners.

If There is Something You Can't Eat

Humorist Ogden Nash wrote, "I don't mind eels, except at meals." If we can't eat something, what are the reasons?

- Is it because we don't like it?
- Is it because we are allergic to it?
- Is it for religious, political or dietary reasons?

We all have certain things we just don't like. I don't like scallops. Or squid ink. I really don't like squid ink pasta with scallops. When dining in someone's home and you are served something you don't like, don't say anything. This might sound wasteful but cut it up (*whatever IT is*), push it around the plate and pretend to enjoy it, while keeping up the conversation. *(This is the most delicious sheep intestine I've ever had!)*

Eat what you can, leave what you can't. Telling people you don't like their food is like telling them their baby is ugly.

There are exceptions. If you have religious restrictions against certain foods, like pork or you are a vegan, you don't have to cut up a pork chop and move it around the plate. It's okay to let your hosts know you can't eat it, as long as you do it graciously and not with revulsion.

Allergies: Safety First

If you are allergic to certain foods, safety first. If you have to ask your host or the wait staff a few questions about ingredients, so be it.

If you are a vegan and need to find out whether a soup has a meat-based broth, go ahead and ask. Who knew tomato soup and broccoli cheese soup could be made with chicken broth?

If you know in advance the restaurant where your meeting will take place, go online and review the menu. If you need to ask questions about ingredients, call the restaurant ahead of your meeting and ask away.

Do Not Badger People for Their Food Choices

Dieters should not cast judgment on the non-dieters. *"I would have dessert, but I believe there is no worse poison for your body than sugar."*

Vegans should not scold meat-eaters. *"I used to eat meat, but I just couldn't stand the idea of killing a living, breathing creature for food."*

Similarly, carnivores should not harass the herbivores. *"How can you stand to give up steak? Are you sure you don't want to try a bite?"*

Whether a person is vegan or vegetarian for religious reasons, health reasons or political reasons, is none of your business. You may ask vegans or vegetarians about their favorite dishes or favorite restaurants.

The Bone of Contention: Removing Unwanted Objects

As you remove the fork from your mouth, you realize there is an unwanted object left behind. What is it? Fish bone? Olive stone? Icky mushroom? Or dare we speak its name – gristle? (Even the name sounds gross, doesn't it?) More importantly, how can you get rid of it? You cannot spit it into your napkin. But there are a few ways you can remove the offending object:

1. **Pinch it:** move the object to the front of your mouth, pinch it with your thumb and index finger and bring it down to your plate. Wipe your fingers on your napkin. This works well with a fish bone.
2. **Spit it out into your cupped fingers:** move your hand to your mouth and move the object into your cupped fingers. Bring it down to your plate. Wipe your fingers on your napkin. This is best for slippery items, like a melon seed.
3. **Take it out the way it went in:** bring your fork to your lips and push the object onto the fork. Move the fork down to your plate. This method takes finesse and it's a good way to deal with gristle.

The goal is to be discreet and attract as little attention as possible. If the unwanted object came from the dinner plate, it goes back to the dinner plate and gets pushed out of sight under a piece of parsley.

There's a Bug in My Soup

If you discover a bug or hair in your food or glass, don't shriek. Push it aside, don't make a scene. Ask a server for a new whatever it was.

Save the Knife

"Would you like to hold onto your knife?" asked the server. There you are, holding a knife dripping with salad dressing and you are not quite sure what to do with it. At a high-end restaurant, you usually get a knife with your salad and another knife with the main course. But not all restaurants have that. Here are your options:

- Give up the knife and ask for a new one.
- Place your knife, blade in, horizontally across the top of your bread plate. Or prop it up on a spoon, already on the table.
- If there are no other options, set the knife on the table itself.

Never lick the knife. And you know people who like to talk with their hands? Don't gesture with your fork and knife, set them down first.

When It Falls on the Floor

What happens when you drop your fork on the floor in a restaurant? I put this question to the audience at a Daddy-Daughter luncheon. One of the fathers immediately called out, "Five second rule."

If you drop your fork on the floor in a restaurant, let the wait staff pick it up. Discreetly ask the wait staff for a replacement.

If you are eating in someone's home and there is no serving staff, try to pick up the fork yourself, if you can do so without disrupting the diners on either side of you. If the floor could talk, it would tell you, "Do not even think about wiping that fork on your napkin and using it again." Discreetly ask your hosts for a replacement.

Dropping the Bread Crumbs

Do you ever feel self-conscious about bread crumbs left behind? It's probably because you are imagining everyone else at the table looking at your crumbs on the table cloth and thinking, "Did any of the bread make it into his or her mouth?"

Don't sweat the bread crumbs. Into all our lives a few crumbs must fall. In some fine dining venues, a wait person will come to your rescue by scooping up the crumbs with a magic wand called a crumber. Otherwise, leave them there.

What Happens if You Spill Something?

If you spill something on someone, offer to pay for the dry cleaning, be it an outfit or a linen tablecloth, If you break something, offer to replace it.

The Raw and The Cooked

If you heard people at a tasting describing what they experienced as sweet, fruity, crisp, subtle, salty, smoky, oak-y, you would think they were talking about fine wines. But they might be talking oysters.

Someone emailed me to ask about oysters: "Do I use a fork or raise the shell to my lips and slurp it?" I admit I had to research this topic, because the thought of eating oysters leaves me clammy.

I learned a great deal. I knew the raw and the cooked of it, but East Coast vs. West Coast? And that clams have necks? So here it is:

- In a formal dinner, oysters may be served as a "seafood course" at the beginning of the meal. Use the seafood fork to lift the oyster from the shell and to your mouth.
- In a more informal setting, and by that, I mean your waitress has more tattoos than Dennis Rodman, you may lift the shell and slurp.

In business, when dining with superiors, colleagues, clients or future clients, please use the fork. The same goes for clams and mussels served on a shell. Use the seafood fork or use a larger fork or spoon in the absence of the seafood fork. Fried clams may be eaten with your fingers, but it's better to use a fork in a business setting. At the end of the meal, no one wants to shake a clammy hand.

In the raging debate about West Coast Oysters vs. East Coast Oysters, East Coast oysters are a little more salty.

When I lived in Connecticut, I remember watching sea birds fly up in the air, drop oysters on the rocks to break them open, then swoop down to eat the meat. The animal kingdom is really gross.

Don't Multi-task with Your Mouth

Do not talk when you have food in your mouth. Do not drink when you have food in your mouth. Take small, bite sized pieces. If your face is distorted trying to chew all the food in your mouth, then you have taken too big of a bite (that happens with watermelon chunks).

BE EXCEPTIONAL: Be a Charming Conversationalist

The Exceptional Professional's job at a business meal or dinner party is not just to show up and eat the food. Your job is to be social and participate in the conversation. So no texting under the table.

Not sure what to say? The best conversationalists are listeners. Ask questions of others. If someone is not talking, invite him or her into the conversation. Change topics to make others feel included.

Topics to Avoid

Some say, "Avoid religion and politics." If you subscribe to that, you may miss out on some lively and interesting discussions. Be willing to discuss anything, as long as you keep it civil and treat people with differing opinions with respect.

Don't talk about your diet. *"I can't eat that – too many calories!"* No one cares if you had a pea and a tomato slice for lunch or how many carbs there are in a crouton. No one wants to hear about that or your rigorous workouts, when enjoying a feast.

Don't grouse about your health problems. "Oh my aching back!" People will think you are a real pain in the... well, you know.

Lemon Wedge vs. Slice

If there is a lemon wedge with your ice tea glass or on your plate, you may squeeze it. A lemon slice is a garnish – it's just there to look pretty.

Do not squeeze the lemon slice, nor grind nor pound it into the bottom of your glass with your iced tea spoon (no matter what kind of day you have had so far.) To keep lemon wedge from squirting:

- Pierce it with a fork before you squeeze it.
- Cup your left hand over it, while you squeeze it with your right.
- Squeeze it through the cheesecloth.

Sometimes when the lemon wedge comes wrapped in a piece of cheesecloth, it looks like little package and people are tempted to unwrap it. But don't – the cheesecloth keeps it from squirting all over the place.

Between the Teeth

You can feel it. An unidentified food object stuck in your teeth. What can it be? Parsley? Meat fragment? Couscous? While your colleagues continue to discuss business, you are wrestling with your own demon. You scold yourself, "I never should of agreed to fresh ground pepper on the salad!" You try to dislodge it with your tongue. Why aren't human tongues a little more pointed or sticky like a toad's?

If you try to remove it with your fingernail, a fork or the toothpick from your sandwich, your business associates will be appalled. (Even if you cup one hand over your mouth while mining with the other, they'll still know.) And while your attention to dental hygiene is appreciated, don't even think about using dental floss at the table. What can you do?

First, take a drink of water and swish it around your mouth to try and dislodge the object. (Swish, don't gargle.) If that does not work, excuse yourself to the restroom, where you may use a toothpick or floss.

Foiled by a Potato

Someone emailed me this question: "When you eat a baked potato during a business meal can you smush the sides with your fingers?"

For those of you not familiar with the term "smush," here's the definition: (Orig: from the Latin: smashibus, to smash + pushibus, to push) 1. *v.* to render an object more pliable by compressing it from the sides 2. *n.* an act or sound of something being smushed

The question behind the question was, "Is it impolite to touch the baked potato with my fingers?" Usually it's hands-off in a business meal. If the potato is served without a foil wrap, use a fork and knife. If the potato has a foil wrap, it's okay to briefly smush the sides with your fingers. Smushing allows the steam to escape and opens up the potato, making it easier to eat. Most baked potatoes are served pre-smushed with a slit in the top. If not, steady the spud with one hand, make an incision in the top with a knife or the side of your fork, then smush.

How to avoid all of this? When out on business, order the mashed potatoes or rice pilaf.

Settling the Spaghetti-Spoon Issue

There is nothing more controversial than the spaghetti-spoon issue. Once, I told a class I was teaching, that you should not use the spoon to twirl your spaghetti and a woman was so enraged, she stomped out.

Normally, you avoid spaghetti in a business meal and opt for something less messy – a smaller noodle like macaroni or penne. But sometimes, we are roped into spaghetti. That said, we are finally going to settle this spaghetti and spoon thing once and for all. The etiquette authorities are divided, so I will quote them directly:

No Spoon:

Letitia Baldrige: *Letitia Baldrige's New Manners for New Times*, 2003

> *"If you are a purist about eating spaghetti, linguine, or any other long, thin noodles, you will not use a spoon as a support. You will go it alone with the fork. The secret is in twining just a small number of strands*

around your fork (four or five.) Keep turning your fork around slowly until all the strands are rolled compactly around it and you're ready to put it into your mouth."[12]

Judith Martin: *Miss Manners' Guide to Excruciatingly Correct Behavior,* 2005

"A fork is the only utensil that may be used to eat spaghetti while anyone is looking. It must make do with whatever cooperation it may muster from the plate and the teeth. The fork is planted on the plate and the spaghetti is then twirled around the tines of the fork. If you can manage to use the grated cheese to add grit to the mixture for better control, so much the better. The twirled forkful is then presented to the mouth."[13]

Maria Everding, *Panache That Pays,* 2007

"Wind a few strands at a time, around a dinner fork, and lift to your mouth. Using a tablespoon and fork is archaic. Do not cut pasta."[14]

Pro-spoon:
Elizabeth Post, *Emily Post's Etiquette,* 1992

"The fork is used to spear a few strands of spaghetti, the tips are placed against the bowl of the spoon, which is held in the left hand and the fork is twirled, wrapping the spaghetti around itself as it turns. If no spoon is provided, the tips of the fork may be rested against the curve of the plate."[15]

Amy Vanderbilt, *Complete Book of Etiquette,* 1954

"The aficionado knows that the only graceful and satisfying way to eat real Italian spaghetti (which comes in full-length or perhaps half-length rounds) is to eat it with a large soup spoon and a fork."[16]

Pro-... Uh, Wait a Minute

Suzanne von Drachnenfels, *The Art of the Table,* 2008

> *"As a base to steady the fork while the noodles are wound, sometimes a spoon is held in one hand, a technique frowned upon in Italy."*[17]

Marjabelle Young (Stewart), *White Gloves and Party Manners,* 1967

> *"Spaghetti is quieter and less messy if you wind it around a dinner fork held against a large spoon. The Italian peasants do it this way."*[18]

Life is about choices. Next time you have spaghetti, you will have to take a side.

Can I Have Seconds?

At a dinner party, don't ask for seconds. Wait until they are offered. In a business dinner, avoid seconds. If there is one bun left in the bread basket, never say to your interviewer, "You gonna to eat that?" Leave it. If you eye your client's French fries and say, "Are you going to finish those?" you will be the one who will be finished.

Wait Till You Get Your Hands on It

Can I pick this up with my hands? Or should I use a fork and knife?

Here are some general rules:

- If it comes off a food truck, you may use your hands.
- In a formal dinner setting, use a fork and knife.
- If your host or hostess is using a fork and knife, you should too.

According to the late etiquette expert, Letitia Baldridge (who was always right), if you are eating "chicken, small birds, or lamb chops" outdoors, use your fingers. Indoors, use a fork and knife. (I haven't eaten any small birds lately, but I know a dog who finds them delicious.) Here are some guidelines for other tricky foods:

French Fries: if served with a sandwich that is eaten with the hands, you may eat the fries with your fingers. If served with steak (steak frites), an open-face sandwich or entree that is cut with a fork and knife, then eat the fries with a fork and knife.
Pizza: is usually eaten with the hands. Use a fork and knife if:

- It's too hot to handle
- It's deep-dish (Chicago-style)
- Dining with others who are eating entrees with a fork and knife

Asparagus: may be eaten with the fingers if the stalk is crisp and not flopping over like a wet noodle. In formal dining or if it is covered in sauce or dressing, it is best to use a fork and knife. Whether you pick it up or cut it up, asparagus is a good source of vitamins, protein and fiber. And it tastes way better than Brussels sprouts.
Chicken Fingers: Why are you ordering these? What are you, eight?
Bacon: if the bacon is crispy, you may eat it with your fingers; all other times use your fork and knife.

Finger Bowl

A finger bowl is a small, individual bowl of water placed in front of you on the table, usually before dessert. It may have a decorative flower or a slice of lemon floating in it. It may also have a doily underneath it.

The finger bowl is not for drinking. Although I have met a woman who said she was sitting next to a famous author at an event and she downed the finger bowl. "I didn't know what to do with it and I was very nervous," she said.

Dip your fingertips into the bowl, one hand at a time, then dry your fingers on your napkin. When finished, remove both doily and finger bowl to the upper left corner of your place setting.

No More on the Pour

"What if wine or coffee is being served and I don't want any?"

I get this question often. A simple, "No thank you," will do. Do not cover the top of the glass or cup with your hand (especially if you do not want hot coffee accidentally poured on your hand.) Do not turn your glass or your coffee cup upside down. If the coffee cup is already upside down on the table, leave it.

If you accept, leave your glass or coffee cup resting on the table while the beverage is poured. Don't try to hold it in the air while someone else pours.

Issues with Tissues

At certain times of the year (sniff), everyone is turning into a sneezing, wheezing (sniff), disgusting, dripping mess. If you are sniffing every five seconds, it's time to issue a tissue and dab or blow.

Once used, that tissue needs to go into a waste can, pocket, handbag or man-bag. Not balled up on the table or on your desk.

What To Do When You... *Ah-choo!*

If you are at a table with food and you have to sneeze or cough, try to get up and walk (or dive) away from the table.

Sometimes there is not time – the sneeze just sneaks up on you and wham! There it is. In that case, try to sneeze or cough down, away from the table, away from the food and into your tissue. Some will say, "Sneeze into your elbow," but if you are wedged in with people on either side, you might miss and hit your neighbor. (And if you have ever been on the receiving end of that, it's hard not to scream.)

In any case, excuse yourself from the table and go wash your hands. If the sneezing or coughing continues, you may have to excuse yourself from the meeting, party or event.

Don't take cold remedies in public. No one wants to sit next to people thrusting nose spray up their schnoz. Find a restroom or other discreet place. Ditto for popping pills, throat sprays or cough syrup. In any medical emergency, suspend the rules.

Not all who are sneezing, coughing or blowing their nose are viral. Some have food allergies or sensitivity to dusty or dry conditions.

Noises You Should Never Hear at the Table

Just before Thanksgiving, a man I met at a chamber of commerce event, said, "I dread Thanksgiving because it drives me crazy when my brother-in-law makes this smacking noise when he eats." There are certain noises you should not hear at the table:

- Lips smacking
- Knuckles cracking
- Teeth on fork scraping
- Ice crunching
- Fingers drumming
- Flatware jangling
- Glasses clinking
- "Ahhhh" after drinking
- Slurping
- Burping
- Open mouth chewing
- Backside tooting
- Under the table texting
- End of drink vacuuming
- Stuffy nose honking

What you should hear at the table:

- Please
- Thank you

Do I Hold My Pinkie Out?

There is only one time when you hold your pinkie out. That's when you are making a "pinkie swear," which as we all know from childhood, is the highest of all oaths.

"Pinkie out" was historically a European tradition. The first teacups, which came from China, had no handles. These cups were held by the brim between thumb and middle finger. The pinkie naturally went out for balance. Handles were added to teacups in the 18th century. Today, an extended pinkie just looks silly.

With a coffee or tea cup, do not loop your finger through the handle. Pinch the handle between your thumb and fingers. With a heavier mug, go ahead and loop your fingers through the handle for balance. Stir your hot beverage with a spoon by folding the liquid away from you. Try not to hit the sides of the cup.

What to Do with Butter and Sugar Wrappers

When finished with foil butter wrappers and paper sugar wrappers, tuck them under the rim of your bread plate to get them out of sight. If the butter came in plastic butter tubs, don't try to tuck those under the rim. Place them on or beside the bread plate.

You should not accumulate a large stack of these items, because in a business meal, you know to use butter and sugar in moderation.

Hint Worth a Mint

When people offer you a mint, do you ever wonder if they are doing it out of generosity or because your breath smells like an oyster bed at low tide and it's killing them? When your breath stinks, it's hard to do business. A few remedies to keep your breath fresh:

- Drink lemonade.
- Drink lots of water.
- Avoid coffee.
- Chew parsley. (And you thought it was only for hiding gristle!)
- Keep little mints on hand.
- Use peppermints offered by restaurants.
- Chew an antacid. Don't overdo, too many are not good for you.

- Carry a travel-size toothbrush and toothpaste, especially when traveling a distance for a meeting. Rinse with bottled water.

Do not chew gum. Unless you are the football coach, chewing gum is not professional.

If possible, avoid meals that are heavy in garlic. Even if you use a breath freshener, it will be emanating from your pores for the next 24 hours like a thick bank of foul fog. If you offer a mint to others, make sure you take one, too. They never have to know.

The End… Of the Meal

At the end of a meal, there should be no grooming at the table. Keep lipstick or lip balm in its holster at the dinner table. If you need to do any grooming, excuse yourself to the restroom.

The Delicate Question

When I am speaking at the universities, both undergrad and grad students will commonly ask the delicate question, "What if the person I am eating with is a total slob?"

The polite thing to do is not to notice. People often say things like, "I saw this man licking his fingers as he ate – you would have been horrified." The truth is, I would not have been horrified. One of the principles of professionalism is to make the people around us feel comfortable. That does not mean we join them in the bad behavior. It means we do not gasp and draw attention to it.

If we miss that professionalism is about being kind to others and making those around us more comfortable, then we are not behaving professionally at all.

If you drink alcohol, the next chapter is for you. If you have no interest in alcohol, you can skip it and go to the next chapter to learn about entertaining.

ALCOHOL

5.1 *Protocol and Excessive Celebration*

In college football, "excessive celebration," falls under "Unsportsmanlike Acts" – a 15-yard penalty. The NCAA defines it as: "Any delayed, excessive, prolonged or choreographed act by which a player (or players) attempts to focus attention upon himself (or themselves)."[19]

A university student told me about another excessive celebration. His fellow intern was the star intern for a multi-national firm. She was at the top of her university class and when it came to the end-of-internship presentations, hers was the best. She was going places. Everyone said so.

Then came the big party hosted by the executives to celebrate the end of the internships – part of the game plan to get the interns to think of the firm long term. The star of the intern class celebrated a little too much. She started with a Long Island Iced Tea. Then she had three more.

What's a Long Island Iced Tea? It has nothing to do with tea. It's a cocktail made up of a shot each of vodka, rum, gin, tequila, Triple Sec and a splash of cola. The highlight of the evening was the star intern loudly serenading the CEO with "Happy Birthday." And it wasn't even his birthday. This young woman was through. Everyone said so.

In this chapter, you will learn:

- How to hold different wine glasses
- What to order in a professional setting
- About use of alcohol and interviews
- How to avoid an alcohol incident

Whether you are in the mix or in the sticks, business and alcohol merges at business outings, conventions, chamber of commerce events, fundraisers, wine tastings, festivals and more. *The Exceptional Professional* knows how to handle alcohol with grace and taste and that sometimes, alcohol and business don't mix.

When you have an alcohol incident, no one will forget it. An alcohol incident doesn't have to involve four Long Island Iced Teas. It could be taking one sip too many and saying the wrong thing. First, we'll cover how to handle alcohol and finish with what not to do.

Alas! Which Glass?

At big banquet meals, sometimes there are two bottles of wine – a red and a white – and two glasses to choose from.

White wine goes into the glass with the smaller opening. White wine is usually served chilled, so hold it by the stem. That way, the warmth of your hand does not rob the wine of its chill too soon.

Red wine goes into the glass with the larger opening. Red wine is usually served at room temperature and held by the bowl of the glass (but not palm up like a brandy snifter). This is so the warmth of your hand can enhance the flavor. Some oenophiles insist red wine also be held by the stem. When holding a wine glass by the stem, you can't go wrong.

Stemless wine glasses, sometimes called "wine tumblers" are held with your hand wrapped around the sides. Never hold a glass by the rim.

Champagne, like white wine, is served chilled, so it is held by the stem. I can't tell you how many times I have seen New Year's Eve ads in magazines, featuring beautiful, elegant models in sophisticated holiday attire – millions of dollars spent on an advertising shoot – and they are all holding their champagne glasses wrong.

Champagne is served in two types of glasses: a tall, narrow champagne flute or the wide-open, shallow glass, which is the traditional champagne glass.

Wine Presentation

The sommelier brings the bottle to the table. (Diner thinks: "I have no idea what to do next.")

The sommelier presents the bottle with the label facing the customer. (Diner thinks: "I can't even remember what I ordered.") The sommelier opens the bottle and presents the cork. (Diner thinks: "Bonus! One more for my cork wreath.")

The sommelier pours a small amount into the customer's glass. (Diner thinks: "I've seen this before. I'm supposed to swirl it around then stick my nose in the glass.")

The sommelier does not let on that the diner need not aerate the white wine he has selected. That's what you do with red wines. (Diner thinks: "I've got them all fooled.")

Getting the nod, the sommelier fills the glasses of the others at the table, (Diner thinks: "Hey, where's he going?")

Lastly, the sommelier fills the glass of the host, the customer who ordered the wine. (Diner thinks: "Whew!")

A better way to handle the wine presentation:

- Look at the label to make sure the wine is what you ordered.
- Examine the cork: it should be moist, but not soggy, moldy or too dry and cracked. Set the cork down. Don't bite it or sniff it.
- With white wine, simply taste it.
- With red wine, swish it around to let it aerate. Then take a sip.
- If the wine tastes spoiled or vinegary, send it back.

The sommelier will serve others at the table before filling your glass.

BE EXCEPTIONAL: For Those Who Like the Details

Those are the basics, here are more tips for those who like the details:

- Check to see if the label on the cork matches the bottle's label.
- Hold up the glass to see that the color is clear and bright, not cloudy and to ensure that white wine is not brownish.
- Swish the wine around in your mouth to appreciate the full palette. The French call this, "Chewing the wine."

The Exceptional Professional knows and appreciates the details, but is not ostentatious about it. No one likes a wine snob.

Bon Aperitif: What is an Aperitif?

An aperitif (pronounced: ah-pear-ah-teef), often a fortified wine, is served before meals to stimulate the appetite. "Aperitif" comes from the Latin *aperire*: "to open" as in, to open the stomach or to open the meal.

Examples of aperitifs: sherry, vermouth, Campari and Dubonnet. Champagne or other sparkling wines may also be served as an aperitif. And for those who do not drink alcohol, there are non-alcohol aperitifs.

Aperitifs can be sweet or bitter. They are infused with spices, barks, fruits, flowers and other plants that give them their distinct flavors and colors. (The word "vermouth" has its root in the German word *Wermut*, meaning "wormwood.") If you have questions, don't be afraid to ask the restaurant's sommelier – they undergo extensive training to earn the title and are very knowledgeable.

A little alcohol will stimulate the appetite but too much will dull the palette. And spouting off about how much you know about wine to your dinner companions will dull your personality.

Cocktail and Mocktail Refresher

If you have a cocktail (or a mocktail) with a little straw in it, Maria Everding says, "Do not try to sip through that tiny hole. That straw is a stirrer, to stir your drink." Use it, then dispose of it.

You may eat olives or other fruit from your beverage off the toothpick. But do not go fishing for them with your fingers. If you cannot get it as you are drinking or it's stuck to the bottom of the glass, let it go.

Do not chew your ice. Like the cracking of knuckles or the scraping of teeth on a fork, it is a sound that sets some people's teeth on edge. Watch the ice – especially those crescent shaped ice cubes – that can create a log jam when you are taking a drink. When the dam bursts, your beverage pours out from both sides at once and misses your mouth.

What to Order in a Professional Setting

What do you order when you are out on business? First things first: if you don't drink, don't drink. In business, it is better not to have alcohol and keep a clear head. Never walk around with a glass of wine you don't plan to drink, just to fit in.

If you order alcohol, get a glass of red or white wine. "Merlot" is a common red wine to order. (I think it's common because it is easy to pronounce. *Mer-low like furlough.*)

Because I care, I will tell you not to order white zinfandel when out on business. It's a little tacky. That's why in many upscale restaurants, you won't find it on the wine list. If you want to keep the ball in the box of white zin in your fridge at home, fine. I promise not to tell anyone.

That said, never make bad comments on another's choice of wine. If someone is drinking white zinfandel, don't smirk or turn up your nose.

Avoid appletinis, tequila shots, or anything with a plastic alligator hanging off the side. Those are not professional drinks. Beer is reserved for more casual events, like a happy hour or an outing to the ball park.

In Someone's Home

When invited to a party in someone's home and that person asks, "What would you like to drink?" Your response should not be, *"I'd like a Bombay Sapphire® martini straight up with blue cheese stuffed olives and have the vermouth blow the martini a kiss."*

The right thing to say is, "What are you serving?" If your hosts do not have the Bombay Sapphire, blue cheese stuffed olives or do not know how to make a martini, you will embarrass them. What's our number one guideline? Make the people around us more comfortable.

If you are hosting a party, be able to recite a few of the beverages you have available, along with any specialty cocktails. Be sure to offer non-alcoholic beverages as well for non-drinkers and designated drivers. If you offer sodas/pop, make sure you have regular as well as diet.

A Gift of Wine

If you bring a bottle of wine or champagne as a hostess gift, it is the privilege of the host/hostess on whether to serve it. If your hosts carefully planned their wine selection, they may not want to serve your "Two Buck Chuck." If you bring something better than the hosts are serving, it makes the hosts look bad.

If they don't serve it, leave it. You may not open the bottle of wine and serve yourself. I remember someone bringing wine to one of my parties and when it wasn't served, the person reclaimed it on the way out.

Alcohol Alternatives

If you don't drink alcohol, there are plenty of beverages behind the bar that have no alcohol. Have a glass of club soda, cranberry juice, ginger ale or other sodas. If you want a beverage that resembles a cocktail, have a club soda with a twist of lime.

A beverage can be non-alcoholic and still inappropriate for business. Unless your business is on the *Good Ship Lollypop,* do not order a Shirley Temple. That's a combination of ginger-ale or lemon-lime soda and grenadine syrup. It's a child's pretend-cocktail.

I was presenting a dining tutorial for college students at a restaurant, where students had the option of ordering sodas/pop from the bar. A bunch of students ordered Shirley Temples, which probably drove the final bill for the school sky high, because Shirley Temples are often priced the same as more expensive mixed drinks.

Alcohol and Interviews

While waiting in a restaurant for your interviewer to arrive, do not order alcohol. If the interviewer arrives and sees you with alcohol or smells alcohol on your breath, it gives the impression you are either an alcoholic or need alcohol to settle your nerves.

If the interviewer asks you if you would like an alcohol beverage, ask first, "Are you having one?" (In an interview meal, the interviewee orders first and the interviewer orders second.)

If the interviewer is having alcohol, you may join him or her, or not.

If the interviewer is not having alcohol, you should not have alcohol.

If the interviewer is throwing back three and four alcohol beverages, do not join him or her in that practice. Stop after the first. An interviewer downing multiple cocktails is a red flag. Remember, you are interviewing the organization as much as they are interviewing you.

Group Interviews: When Someone Hands You the Wine List

A group interview for a large financial firm was held at a posh restaurant. One of the interviewers handed the wine list to a candidate and said, "Order for the table." This test has caused gastrointestinal turmoil for countless job candidates, but the guidelines to acing it are simple:

- Order a bottle of white wine and a bottle of red wine for the table.
- Select wine that is moderately priced, not the cheapest on the menu and not the most expensive.
- If you don't know a chardonnay from a cabernet, hold up the menu for the wine steward, discreetly point to a price point and say, "I'd like something from this area."

Most wine stewards recognize this as code for, "I don't have a clue about wine, so please pick out something from this price point to make me look good." No one else needs to know if you are talking about $35.99 or Chile.

If you do not drink, say, "I don't drink alcohol, so I must pass this on to someone else," then hand the wine list to the person next to you or back to the interviewer. No further explanation is required.

Why do interviewers put interview candidates through this? I met a woman who did group interviews for a law firm, who explained the wine list ritual. They are looking for three things:

1. Candidates who will not select the cheapest wine on the menu, because they want them to have good taste
2. Candidates who will not select the most expensive wine, because they don't want those who will run up the expense account
3. Candidates who spout off about their wine knowledge. That shows arrogance and those candidates get eliminated

You do not have to be interviewing to be put in this situation – there are a number of occasions in business dining where someone might hand you the wine list. Stick to these guidelines and you'll be fine.

Tipping the Wine Steward

If a wine steward assists you, tip him or her 20 percent of the cost of the wine (before tax). Designate that tip as a separate line item on the bill, after the tip for the food service. If you are waiting in the bar before you are seated in the dining room, tip a bartender at least $1 per drink.

Wine and Food Pairings

The right pairings of food and wine will enhance the flavors of the food. But what goes with what? In general, white wine goes with "white-flesh" (chicken or fish) and red wine goes with red flesh (steak). Order red wine with heavier "steak" fish like salmon, halibut, swordfish or tuna. A lighter red wine, like a pinot noir, goes well with fish.

White Wine

Order white wine with:

- White meats such as chicken or pork
- Seafood and shellfish and whitefish
- Vegetarian dishes
- Indian and Thai food

Red Wine

Order red wine with:

- Steak, veal, lamb or ham. I have heard it said that a great steak deserves a Bordeaux, which is a full-bodied, red wine.
- Comfort food like ribs, meatloaf, hamburgers
- Any kind of pasta (think "red sauce" and "red wine") – spaghetti, lasagna or ravioli
- Gamey foods, such as pheasant, duck, venison or rabbit

Be careful about drinking a lot of red wine, because it stains your teeth and makes them look darker.

BE EXCEPTIONAL: Take a Wine Tasting Course

The Exceptional Professional who enjoys wine and wants to learn more about it, takes a wine tasting course. Sommeliers teach classes through restaurants or wineries or even community education programs.

A friend of mine put together her own wine tasting class by gathering a group of friends and hiring a wine expert.

Wine tasting classes teach you how to evaluate the characteristics and flavors. "It has a hint of grapefruit or currents..." Classes also teach you how to appreciate wine and to speak with authority.

Unforgettable... In Every Way

If you do decide to drink, the most important point, is to know your limit.

Alcohol does different things to different people.

- Some people get plowed and then they get loud.
- It makes some people quiet, it makes some people riot.
- It makes some people flirty, it makes others talk dirty.
- It makes some explode in anger.
- It turns others into laughing hyenas.
- It causes people to say things they should have never said.

Alcohol might come after work – in happy hours, holiday parties and other special events. Such events are where careers are made and destroyed. When I worked in the music business, alcohol flowed like water over Yosemite Falls. During meetings at a local resort in the Chicago suburbs, one of my co-workers had too much to drink.

He went outside the resort, where he found a golf cart. He started driving drunk in the golf cart in the parking lot. Next, he drove the golf cart into the resort – the automatic sliding doors parted and he was in. The front desk was down the hallway, so they had no idea... yet.

Miraculously, he found our conference room. He drove the golf cart into the conference room, crashed into a buffet table, and knocked the food everywhere. Do you think he was able to keep his job?

Actually, he did – he was the son of one of the executives in New York. Anyone else would have been bounced... and billed for the damage. If you have "an alcohol incident," no one will forget it. You may have to change jobs. You may have to change cities.

I was making this point in room full of sales people and a bunch of them started laughing and saying, "Remember last year at this meeting when Jake (not his real name) got wasted? We found him curled up in the fetal position, crying like a baby." I am not sure what happened to Jake, but he is probably not on the promotion track.

The worst thing is to get so drunk, that you throw up in public. Those who witness it, never lose the image.

I remember when this kid with the flu in my third-grade Catechism class threw up all over himself and the main table in our classroom. For what seemed like an anxious eternity, the teacher made us sit there in the room with the sick kid and his vomit, while she tried to find a janitor.

Years later, I would see him around campus at the University of Iowa and we would exchange hellos. Friends with me would say, "Wow – he's so cute! Who is he?" And I would reply, "He's the kid who threw up in my third-grade Catechism class."

Moderate what you drink. Never drink so much that you are falling down drunk or have your head in the "oval office" with someone holding back your hair. If you throw up in public, no one will lose the image.

Peer Pressure and Alcohol

When alcohol is flowing freely and everyone around you is partaking, saying "no" is easier said than done,

In my first dinner out in the music business, people were chasing me around all night with a cart full of tequila shots saying, "You have to do a shot because *you're new – it's TRADITION*." I said, "I am not in college anymore." (I actually couldn't do a shot of anything in college.) Don't give in to peer pressure – especially if you are still in college. Never feel like you have to drink.

Dangers of a Drink Unattended

Never leave your beverage – alcohol or no-alcohol – unattended at any time. There are people out there who want to harm you, who can slip something into your drink if you are not looking. Known as "date rape drugs," several odorless substances can be dissolved into drinks and render victims unconscious or too weak to defend themselves. Never drink a beverage that has been out of your sight and never drink alone.

Drink Responsibly Or…

As mentioned before, it's better to keep a clear head in business. Leave childish college binge drinking behind. Celebrating birthdays, job offers or because it's the weekend, by getting drunk, is a road to nowhere. There may be hard choices ahead about leaving behind former drinking buddies. They're not looking for your friendship. They are looking for an enabler.

If you are reading this and thinking: "She just doesn't understand our profession – we have to drink to fit in." They used to say the same thing about smoking. If you are going to drink, drink responsibly, or don't drink at all.

ENTERTAINING

6.1 *Winner Dinners and Other Events*

My mother and I wanted to help out a first-time candidate who was running for a state congressional seat, so we threw a party at our home where we could introduce him to our friends and a few undecideds. We had a bountiful assortment of homemade appetizers, dips and desserts. The turnout was good and everything was going as planned.

Our candidate was about to say a few words to the group, when someone yelled, *"Hey! A big raccoon just came out of your house!"*

Everyone rushed to the bay window facing the back yard, to watch this 40-lb. resident of the workshop/garage in the back of the house, (aka, The Raccoon Ramada), slip from the roof to the top of a fence. Everyone was mesmerized while the raccoon delicately navigated the length of the fence. It was mortifying that now everyone knew we had a raccoon problem – including our future congressman.

The Exceptional Professional knows a healthy professional and social life means entertaining. In our busy professional lives, we are always grabbing food on the run. Sometimes you have to slow down and realize that entertaining is not just for holidays. But when you entertain, you have to be ready for anything.

In this chapter, you will learn:

- About dinner parties for beginners
- Who to invite and how
- Other parties in your home
- How to deal with crashers and other disasters

Dinner Parties for Beginners

Most business etiquette books with chapters on entertaining in your home begin with how to hire caterers, musicians and budget for 40+ people. I don't know about you, but that's not happening at my house anytime soon.

Start small. If your budget is limited, have 2-3 guests and a modest menu: salad, main course and dessert. You don't need a showcase home or a gourmet kitchen.

Can't cook? Grocery stores have prepared salads in bags, cut-up fruit and more. There are also markets, restaurants, bakeries and specialty shops for main dishes, desserts, etc.

Good cook? Let it rip. Showcase your talents, especially with a fabulous dessert. But make sure you have time to sit and enjoy your guests. A dinner party is no good if it becomes a chore. "Entertaining" does not mean you only feed your guests but also talk with them.

Have dinner ready on time, so you can serve it shortly after guests arrive. An invitation to dinner is not an invitation to watch you prepare the meal. Just as with meetings, if you hold the meal up for certain guests to arrive, you are wasting the time of everyone else.

How to Serve It

There are three different ways to serve food at a dinner party:

1. Butler Style: the food is portioned out for you and served on a prepared plate, often in a pretty presentation (butler not required).

2. Buffet Style: the food is set out on another table or set of tables and your guests serve themselves.
3. Banquet Style: shared platters or bowls of food are passed around the table and guests serve themselves.

One of the great ironies is when you go to a large banquet for business, it's usually served "Butler Style."

Whether a dinner is formal or informal also defines how the food is served and cleared (drinks, in either case, are served from the right):

- Formal: plates are served from the left and removed from the left.
- Informal: plates are served from the left and removed from the right.

How to Offer a Toast

It's time to raise a glass. At a wedding, the toast often comes before the meal. At a dinner party, the toast comes after the main course. It's the privilege of the host to offer the first toast. If the host does not offer a toast, any guest may ask the host's permission to offer a toast.

The guest of honor or recipient of the toast may offer a return toast *("Thank you for a wonderful evening and delicious food...")* The return toast may come after the host's toast or at dessert.

In an informal dinner, guests remain seated during the toast. For more formal occasions, all guests rise.

When delivering the toast, hold the glass at chest level. Then raise the glass to eye level and drink. Contrary to popular belief, you do not "clink" glasses with everyone around you. Some cultures clink glasses after a toast but in the United States, you should not clink.

What if someone next to you wants to clink your glass? You go ahead and clink. Why? Because your ultimate goal is to make the people around you comfortable. During one of my etiquette dinners, a college student from China said you clink glasses in China, but when clinking glasses with someone of a higher rank, you hold your glass lower.

Sip from the glass, don't drain it. If you are the one being honored by the toast, remain seated and do not drink to yourself. Drinking to yourself is like saying, "Hooray for me!"

There is an old myth that it is bad luck to toast with water – don't believe it. If you are not a drinker of alcohol, it is fine to toast with water or anything else.

What words do you use? Begin with:

"Please join me in a toast to..."
"It is my honor to offer a toast to..."
"I would like to offer a toast to..."

End with best wishes for the future:

"Here's to (name or names)"
"Here's to your health..."
"Here's to your happiness..."

Guests may respond with approval for the toaster, "Hear, hear," (not "Here, here,") which means, "Hear him or her."

A toast should last two minutes, not twenty. There's nothing worse than when a wedding toast turns into rambling, drunken rant that is like a verbal home movie. Nobody cares. Shut up and serve the wedding cake.

Hostess Gift is a Thank You

If someone brings you a hostess/host gift. That is like a "thank you" for hosting the party. You are not required to send a thank you note for a hostess gift, because it is like saying, "Thank you for the thank you."

BE EXCEPTIONAL: Finish Strong

The Exceptional Professional makes a meal memorable by finishing strong. End the meal with a really good signature, homemade dessert. Here are some of my favorites:

Chocolate molten cakes
Apple crisp with cinnamon ice cream
Bananas Foster
Key lime pie with raspberry sauce

My mother relies on an old Helen Corbitt cookbook for inspiration. She uses Corbitt's recipe for crepes, then wraps them around vanilla ice cream and serves them with fresh strawberries and a dusting of powdered sugar on top. Every person who entertains should have one Helen Corbitt cookbook in their collection.

Dinner Party Seating

Traditional seating at a dinner party: the host sits at one end of the table and the hostess at the other. A female guest of honor sits to the right of the host and a male guest of honor sits to the right of the hostess. Everyone else is male female, male female. Traditionally, spouses are not seated next to each other. You don't necessarily have to abide by these rules. But if you see people seated that way, you will know why.

Who To Invite?

When planning a dinner party, select guests from a variety of backgrounds and a mix of introverts and extroverts. If you have only introverts, nobody is talking. If you have only extroverts, nobody gets a word in edgewise.

Backyard Barbecue

If you are good at grilling, a backyard barbecue can be a great way to entertain. You can go elegant with steak, grilled swordfish or kebabs. Or go casual with hamburgers and brats. Where there is food to be eaten with the hands, provide lots of napkins.

Grilling can be tricky. Whatever you are serving, practice grilling it first. If you have never made barbecue ribs or pizza on the grill before, do a test run a week before, otherwise you may be sending out for pizza.

When serving an entree that needs to be cut with a fork and knife, provide tables. Make certain the utensils are suitable for the task. Don't make your guests saw through a chicken breast with a plastic knife.

If you are serving hamburgers and brats, it's fine to have people scattered on lawn chairs and benches, but provide small tables or trays in between, where guests can set down their drinks. Be sensitive to elderly or physically challenged guests, who may not be able to throw a leg over a picnic table bench or pull themselves out of a deep lounge chair. Find appropriate seating to make them comfortable.

Rein in the family pooch, who may be even less inhibited outdoors around guests with burgers on plates in their laps. Guests may not want to party with your dog as much as your dog wants to party with them.

You may not rope guests into cooking your meal or cleaning up. However, you may accept the kind offer of willing volunteers.

The biggest breach of barbecue etiquette is the BYOM Party. (Bring Your Own Meat). If you are going to throw a party, *throw a party*. Spring for food and drinks. Do not invite people to your house for dinner and tell them, "By the way... bring dinner."

If you are on a tight budget, limit the number of guests or plan a modest menu, like skirt steak fajitas. Not every backyard barbecue needs to be a block party. Start small, with two to four guests.

Are Potlucks Bad Etiquette?

If you ask guests to bring dishes, that's a potluck. Potlucks are not necessarily bad etiquette. They can be bad etiquette if:

1. The hosts do as little as possible and have guests provide the entire meal or the most expensive items, like the BYOM barbecue.
2. The hosts dictate to guests what to bring and how to prepare it.

When I lived in Connecticut, friends and I gathered once a month for "Comfort Food Sunday." Many of us were young, single and living far from home. This was like the substitute for the family dinner.

One month, the theme was "Food on a Stick." I provided cut-up meats, shrimp and vegetables and guests assembled their own kebabs. Guests cooked their kebabs on a small, portable gas grill on my porch.

Chad Himmel, a friend from Louisiana, wanted to stick to the food on a stick theme. He used giant pasta shells with his mother's macaroni and cheese recipe. He prepared the shells, skewered them on kebab sticks and poured the cheese sauce over them: cheeky but delicious.

The important thing was everyone was able to sit, laugh and enjoy each other's company, which is the point of entertaining.

What Not to Bring to a Potluck

The unwritten rule of a potluck is you must make an effort. People who show up with a bag of chips and a jar of processed salsa or dip or a grocery store-dessert encased in plastic, are not making an effort.

My sisters, Maureen and Catherine, were at a potluck for someone's birthday, when they saw what appeared to be a yummy-looking desert in a 13x9-inch pan with whipped cream and peanuts on top.

One of them took a spoon and started to dig to see what type of delicious cake or pudding was hidden underneath. There was nothing – it was just whipped cream and peanuts. Was there ice cream or something? No, only whipped cream and peanuts. This gave birth to much mirth.

> *"Sure that's good but did you try this whipped cream and peanuts?"*
> *"I want to be sure to save room for whipped cream and peanuts!"*
> *"Is this whipped cream and peanuts store-bought or homemade?"*
> *"I'd really like to get a recipe for this whipped cream and peanuts."*

Months later, Catherine sent Maureen an index-size recipe card for Whipped Cream and Peanuts. It listed two ingredients and the directions said, "Place whipped cream in a 13x9-inch pan. Fold in peanuts."

When there are leftovers from the potluck, let people take their leftovers if they want them. They have no right to demand your leftovers, but it's a nice idea to share leftovers and send people home with plates of extra food, if they want it.

Cocktail (or Mocktail) Party in Your Home

A "Cocktail Party" sounds so retro, but it's a perfectly good way to entertain. Instead of a dinner, provide appetizers – at different stations around the room, on a buffet or by circulating them on trays. Have a bar with both cocktails and mocktails for guests who don't drink alcohol.

When offering beverages, give a list of options. Supervise the beverages – make sure people are not getting the "Sahara treatment" (not being offered drinks) or drinking too much.

At any party, don't just feed and hydrate your guests and turn them loose. It's your responsibility to make sure everyone is engaged and having a good time. If someone is sitting alone in a corner, bring them back into the mix. Your policy should always be "No guest left behind."

Inviting Disaster

I had a friend who asked if he could bring an uninvited date to a dinner party in my home. I said, "Yes," because I needed his charming self to be there and assumed he would have a charming date who would get along well with everyone else.

I forgot the old adage that opposites attract.

The date was a miserable creature who wanted to draw everyone into a political battle. She made dismissive, cutting remarks to anyone who disagreed with her. I wanted to smash a dinner plate over her head. If I don't know the person who someone wants to bring, I am now more inclined to say, "No." As the host, it's your prerogative to decline requests for extra guests.

Count on people who don't respond to an invite to just show up. Have enough food and a little flexibility. That's easier than shutting off the lights and having all of your guests hit the deck and pretend like they are not there. In the future, leave non-responders off your invite list.

Party Crashers

My sister, Catherine, is a little more firm with the uninvited. She has a big party once every two years, where she rents tables and chairs and spends days preparing food. She allows people to bring their kids and even creates gift bags for the kids.

But the party is not come one, come all. She has a guest list. Frequently, people not invited, who she doesn't even know, call up and announce they will be attending, *plus-one.* Catherine is blunt and lets them know they were not invited and neither was their plus-one. The people who informed their friends this was okay, are left off future lists.

If you don't want party crashers, take preemptive measures and make it clear your invite is for the people listed on the invite only and say, "There will be no substitute guests or additional plus-ones."

Can you make exceptions? Of course. If someone calls and says, "My sister from out of town is staying with me, do you mind if I bring her to your party?" You might say, "Sure, bring her along."

A friend of mine getting married said, "I had someone who I haven't seen for 20+ years, reach out on *Facebook* because she heard I was getting married and ask if she could come to the wedding. I was as gracious as possible but it was really quite awful and uncomfortable."

Who Else Will Be There?

I don't care for digital or email invitations that reveal who has been invited and who is planning to attend or not attend. That accommodates rude people who want to know who else will be there before they decide to go. It's as if their attendance is contingent on the presence of people more important than the person who has so kindly invited them. (No one likes to feel like a tuna sandwich to a person who prefers grilled salmon.) If someone responds to your invitation by asking,

"Who else will be there?" you may respond, "I don't give out my guest lists."

The Things That Wouldn't Leave

Your party should have been over hours ago. All the other guests have gone home, but you have a couple of hangers-on that won't leave.

Saturday Night Live used to have a skit called, "The Thing That Wouldn't Leave." It was a fake preview for a horror movie. Jane Curtain and Bill Murray play a married couple sitting on their couch. In between them is, John Belushi, playing a guest who has overstayed his welcome, who they are trying to convince to leave. Curtain is screaming her lungs out in terror, while Belushi, smoking a cigar, says, "I'm thirsty, is there anything in the fridge?" The announcer comes on and says, "The Thing That Wouldn't Leave... *you may never have guests again!*"

Sometimes the last to go are people you enjoy hanging out with and you don't want the evening to end. But there are others who linger and won't stop talking. You just want them gone. You are doing everything you can to drop hints, like yawning, saying, "Well it's getting late..."

It would be great if you could just say, "Get out." What can you do? It's a five-step process and it involves "tough love."

Step One: Shut down the food and beverage service. Begin the clean-up process. Don't accept offers from the hangers-on to help clean up.
Step Two: Remain standing and move towards the door. If they are allowed to stay on the comfy couches, they will never leave.
Step Three: Offer verbal cues: "It's been so nice having you here but we really need to get up in the morning..." Yawn frequently.
Step Four: The direct approach: "It's been nice having you here but it is time for you to go now. Can I call you a taxi?"
Step Five: Expunge their names from future party lists.

The Peter Brady Party

In the music business, I learned that when you plan any event, you can count on about one-third of your invitees actually attending the event. When the turnout was less than that, it was called a "Peter Brady Party." The name came from an episode of the TV show, *The Brady Bunch,* where Peter Brady had a birthday party and no one showed up.

While I was interning in Washington D.C., I threw a party for my fellow-interns. I purchased all the food and beverages my meager intern's salary could afford. I spent two days preparing food – all kinds of sweet treats, plus appetizers and a variety of dips.

There were about 15 interns. Only two showed up. They said the others decided at the last minute to go try a new restaurant.

The next day, I was on the phone with my brother, Patrick, woefully describing my failed party. In college, Patrick roomed with his best friend from high school, nicknamed, "Angus." He said, "Callista, don't worry about it. Angus and I once threw a party and no one showed up."

Everyone has at least one Peter Brady Party. Don't let it deter you from trying again.

The best friends are the ones who reciprocate by inviting you to their parties. Read on to find out how to be on your best behavior when someone else is entertaining.

6.2 *You Have Arrived: Being Entertained*

My sister and her husband were at a Halloween costume party thrown by her supervisor at work. My brother-in-law heard the hostess's boyfriend was very shy and noticed him standing in a corner by himself. Being the kind person he is, my brother-in-law went over to make conversation.

The boyfriend was wearing overalls, so my brother-in-law asked, "What are you supposed to be? A farmer?"

The boyfriend said, "No."

"An old man?"

"No."

"A hobo?"

The boyfriend said, "I'm not wearing a costume."

My sister took her husband by the arm and said, "We have to go."

It's time to party. It's a chance to introduce yourself and be introduced. For *The Exceptional Professional*, this is not a room full of strangers. It's a room full of potential clients, vendors, advisors, colleagues and future friends.

In this chapter, you will learn:

- What R.S.V.P. means and how to respond
- How to behave when the party is part of work
- Your responsibilities as a guest at a dinner party
- The rules of eating out with friends

You Are Invited

Some think R.S.V.P. on an invite means, "Respond only if you are planning to attend." R.S.V.P. is short for the French "respondez s'il vous plait," or "Respond please." That's respond please, if you plan to attend or respond please, if you can't make it. It does not mean, "Regrets only."

Respond to an invitation within a week, not at the last minute or when all possibilities of a better offer have been exhausted. Say, "I am responding..." not "I am R.S.V.P.-ing." (Does not have a nice ring to it.)

- Respond to an email invite by email.
- Respond to a phone invite by phone.
- Respond to a formal invite through the postal mail by a written reply through the postal mail, using a fold-over note.

Guests Who Are Pests

Two guests are the bane of anyone who has ever hosted a party:

1. The No-shows, who respond affirmatively that they will be attending, then never show. Honor your commitments. If you say you are going to be there, be there. If an emergency arises, contact your hosts and let them know you will be unable to attend.
2. The Surprise-shows, who do not respond to an invite, then show up.

Surprise-shows think, "I'm one extra person. No big deal, every event has excess food."

Here's what your astonished host/hostess is too polite to tell you: *Are you out of your mind?! I have been working on this event for three months, you've had the invite for the last two months and now you show up without even bothering to respond? Do have any idea what goes into an event like this? Do you?*

Oh – you thought someone might not show and you could simply fill in? A lot of preparation went into this meal, but let me just snap my fingers and make more food appear. You brought a date? Maybe you didn't notice there was no 'plus one' on the invite? An event isn't enough of a mad scramble, but now you expect me to find room for two extra place settings? How did you get a date anyway? A three-dollar bottle of wine cannot buy me off.

Don't be a No-show or a Surprise-show in business and social events. An ideal guest responds to an invite as soon as possible and sticks to it. Doing so leads to more invites.

Workplace Parties and Other Events

During a dining tutorial, a college student asked, "Are office holiday parties for fun or are they work?" The answer: office holiday parties are work, in another venue. They are also an opportunity.

Never stick to only the people you know at a workplace party. Use the time to get to know people who work in other departments and expand your circle of influence. A workplace party is a chance to get to know to know the families of your colleagues, too.

Does Your Partner Help or Hurt at Work Events?

Do you have work events where you bring a spouse or a date? Can your partner mingle or does he or she cling to you like a barnacle on a boat and keep you from mingling? Does your partner help or hurt your career?

If you are attending a party or conference with your partner, you are there as your partner's champion:

- Speak well of your partner. It's not the time for teasing remarks.
- Know your partner's job and something about the organization.
- Don't be glued to your partner, jealous or controlling.
- Let your partner be the star. Don't outshine your partner or dominate the discussion.
- Put away your cell phone and be attentive to others.
- Don't flirt or make inappropriate remarks.
- Drink responsibly or don't drink at all.

Have a pre-party prep session with your partner. Discuss people your partner will meet, topics to talk about and topics that are taboo.

Workplace Party: Stag or Drag

At any event, consider the forgotten person: someone else's "plus-one," the person who is a spouse or date of the person who is supposed to be there. If you have ever been the plus-one, you know it can be awkward, especially at a workplace party. You're the hanger-on, the ball and chain. Nobody knows you or wants to make an effort to know you. You are not going to be in their workplace tomorrow.

When making the rounds at any work-related event, be attentive to any spouses or significant others. Here are some Dos and Don'ts:

- Do ask them about their interests, career, etc.
- Do introduce them to others in the room with similar interests.
- Do ask about other family members if you know the family, but don't get too personal.
- Do say you enjoy working with their spouse or significant other.
- Do dress appropriately, so people respect you, not inspect you.
- Don't dig for dirt on your boss or co-workers.
- Don't drink so much that you say something stupid.
- Don't try to sell them raffle tickets for your child's school fundraiser.
- Don't try to curry favor, if the plus-one is married to your boss.

(More about Workplace Parties in Chapter 10.3: *Sports, Holidays and Other Bonding*.)

The Dinner Party

Being invited to someone's home is the highest of compliments. It says, "We think enough of you that we want to show off our surroundings, but also we trust you enough to believe you won't steal the silverware."

Be on time. If you arrive late to a dinner party, you begin with the course everyone else is on. If you arrive at dessert, you get dessert. There are certain parties, such as an open house, where you may pop in, then leave. But you may not leap up in the middle of a dinner party and announce, "I have somewhere else I have to be!" (I'm so popular!)

Never overestimate your significance to the event. When you are the guest at a dinner party in someone else's home, your job is not just to show up and eat the food. Your job is to be a charming guest who takes part in the dinner conversation.

Sit Anywhere

Where should you sit in a dinner party? Wait for your hosts to tell you.

If your host says, "Sit anywhere," sit somewhere in the middle.

Follow your hosts' lead. Stand behind your chair and take your seat when your hosts do. Wait for your hosts to put their napkin in their lap. Wait for your hosts to begin eating.

Dinner Party Stew

When it's not your party, you don't get to dictate to the hosts what is served. If you are invited to someone's home, it's presumptuous to call your hosts and make special meal requests.

What if the hosts are making a special dish for the guest of honor and you can't eat it? Should the hosts deprive the guest of honor for your sake? Or should the hosts do extra work to give you an alternative meal?

Eat what you can. Leave what you can't.

Sometimes when I mention this in a dining tutorial, people will object. "I would want to know someone's dietary restrictions if I were the host, so I could accommodate them."

That's when I talk turkey. I call it "The Thanksgiving Exercise." I say, "You are planning a Thanksgiving dinner." I designate audience members as guests and invent their requests for the host.

- First guest calls: "I'm gluten free. Can you please stuff your turkey with gluten free bread? You should have gluten-free rolls, too."
- Second guest calls: "No salt for me. Please don't use any salt on the turkey, stuffing or anything else."

- Third guest calls: "I'm avoiding dairy. Can you make the mashed potatoes without butter or milk?"
- Fourth guest calls: "I'm dieting. It would be cruel to eat desserts in front of me. Can you skip the pies?"
- Fifth guest calls: "I don't like turkey. If it's okay, I'll just bring my own meal of halibut."
- Sixth guest calls: "The date I am bringing is against eating animals. You need to have a tofurkey instead of turkey, or she'll dump me."

If everyone called and made demands, it would be difficult to entertain. When hosting a dinner in your home, it's your prerogative to ask guests about special dietary needs. If it's not your party, it's not your place to dictate. To have it your way, throw your own party.

When being entertained, enjoy the company and don't grumble about the food. Thank your hosts for a lovely evening before you leave. There's always fast food on the way home.

Hostess Gift

When do you bring a hostess/host gift? The host/hostess gift is a small token to thank your hosts for inviting you to any occasion where someone has opened their home for entertaining, such as a dinner party, open house, sports watching party, graduation party, etc.

The hostess gift need not be expensive – somewhere in the range of $5-20 is fine. Ideal gifts include a small box of fine chocolates or mixed nuts, attractive note cards or anything you know your hosts have an interest in, such as a kitchen gadget or the latest business book. Specialty shops or museum gift shops are great places to find hostess gifts.

A student-athlete from the University of Minnesota could not make it home for Thanksgiving. When he was invited to Thanksgiving at a friend's home, he brought sports tickets to his sports-loving hosts. Score!

Here are some other ideas:

Miscellaneous

Gourmet coffee beans or a bean grinder for the coffee achiever
Box of notecards
Movie DVD or music CD
Black raspberry jam (not blackberry; harder to find, worth the effort)
Fresh fruit
Post-party pampering basket with bath salts, gel mask, etc.

Cooking enthusiasts

Fresh spices from a spice store or a spice grinder
Cookbook
Barbecue accessories
Hot pads, kitchen towels or a themed apron

Sports fans

Oddly colored or logoed tennis balls or golf balls
Latest sports biography
Accessories with a favorite team logo
Imported or locally manufactured specialty beverages

Families with kids

Special storybook or DVD
Interactive toy or puzzle
Supplies for a new baby
Coloring books and crayons or sticker books

Other hobbies

Gardening supplies
Scrapbooking supplies
Bird feeder or bird seed

Pet accessories
Addition to host's collectibles

Don't make the hostess gift giant or ostentatious. The idea is not to outdo or put to shame guests who came empty-handed.

Send Flowers Ahead

If you want to give flowers, send them ahead of the party. That way, your hosts are not scrambling to find a vase for them when you arrive. It also gives them time to find a place for it, so it does not conflict with a centerpiece they may already have.

Don't Force Feed Food Gifts

If you bring a dessert as a hostess gift, the intent is to bring an item that can be enjoyed by your hosts at a later time. Do not pick up an appetizer or dessert you intend to serve, as it disrupts the already planned menu.

I had a dinner party where someone brought a cake in a plastic container purchased from a grocery store. I left it in the kitchen, because I had a special, homemade dessert. The person who brought the grocery store cake retrieved it from the kitchen and put it in the middle of the table... plastic container and all.

And can we take a moment to talk about people who bring grocery-store-bought cookies on their own plate, trying to pass them off as something that came out of their own kitchen? Come on, these people cleaned their house to entertain you. Show a little effort.

Wear New Socks

I was invited to my boss's house for dinner. His wife had a rule of no shoes in the house. Unfortunately, I did not know that ahead of time.

When I took off my shoes, I had holes in my socks. (It's so hard to find good socks. Back then, I wore them until they were threadbare, then sewed them up.) It was embarrassing. But I think I got a raise after that.

Bored Games

How NOT to be the life of the party: show up with a board game. Nothing says, "The party's over" like a board game.

Clean Up

Offer to help with clean up, but if your offer is refused, stand down. Never force your help where it is not wanted. Don't start grabbing dishes and shoving them into the dishwasher.

Everyone has a particular way of packing their dishwasher and certain items they do not want in the dishwasher. When you mess with someone else's dishwasher, it's more work, because the owner ends up taking things out and reloading it.

Knowing When to Leave

In the last chapter, we talked about the *Saturday Night Live* skit where John Belushi plays, "The Thing That Wouldn't Leave." Don't be that person. Leave within half an hour of the party end time or within half an hour of the guest of honor leaving. Thank your hosts before you leave.

BE EXCEPTIONAL: Follow Up

The Exceptional Professional follows up with a handwritten thank you note to the hosts letting them know the event was enjoyable. A thank you email or text just won't do. If you brought a host or hostess gift, you still need to send the thank you note after the party. *"Thank you for inviting me, I had such a nice time. The crème brulee was delicious. I enjoyed meeting your friends ..."*

If someone invites you to their home for dinner, you should reciprocate. You don't need to go to the same lengths or expense. The best invite is an invite to your home. If you don't want to do that, you can always invite that person out for dinner and pay for their dinner.

Eating Out with a Group

An *Etiquette Tip of the Week* reader sent in this question: *"I was invited out for a birthday dinner at a restaurant. A few others ordered multiple cocktails, an appetizer, the most expensive entrees and dessert, while some, including myself, had no appetizer or dessert and a moderately-priced meal. When the check came, those who spent the most insisted the check be split evenly. How should I handle this situation?"*

Answer: Normally, the person who does the inviting, pays. There's nothing worse than when someone invites you to a large group dinner at an expensive restaurant for a birthday or another celebration, where you pay. That said, it is common for smaller groups of friends to get together for dinner and pay their own way. Establish payment rules before the dinner. Here are the options:

- Split the check evenly: each person pays the same amount, no matter what he or she ordered.
- The "honor system": pass the check around and everyone pays what they owe. (Most people will overpay in this situation to avoid the embarrassment of being called out to kick in more.)
- Separate checks: each person gets a check. However, if you have a table of 15, it is unkind to expect the wait staff to juggle 15 checks. (It's like asking the wait person to cover 15 tables. A typical wait staff person has 4-6 tables.) And some restaurants just won't do it.
- Group the checks: divide into several groups to negotiate payment with fewer people. Let the people with champagne tastes be a group.

Above all, know the difference between friends and those who want you to subsidize their lifestyle. I remember going out to dinner after an event with a small group of friends. But some invited others, who invited even more people. Suddenly, our group of 4-5, swelled to over 20.

Someone ordered a whole pie to celebrate a birthday of another person. The pie, which only a few enjoyed, cost $35. When reviewing the bill, I said, "Okay, who bought the pie?"

A young man said, "I did but I thought we could all split the cost."

I said, "Most of us didn't have your pie. You didn't ask if anyone wanted to split the cost. You ordered it. You are paying for it."

He said, "I don't have enough money."

I think he was expecting me to say, "Oh you don't have enough money? They we'll have everyone split it." Instead, I said, "Start collecting from your friends, we are not splitting the cost."

In the end, he was able to collect the money from others who ate the pie, who begrudgingly gave it up. Being invited out is a privilege and an opportunity. But you have to pay your way. You can't live large and expect others to foot the bill.

Next up, it's time to think about your look. Whether at a party or on the job, you want to look good.

PROFESSIONAL ATTIRE

7.1 *The Case For Dressing Better*

I was giving a talk to a group about professional attire. A woman sitting in the second row, was wearing a blouse with a neckline plunging so deep, it would make someone on *Dancing with the Stars* blush.

When I talk about professional dress, I tread gingerly, because I never want to call anyone out or hurt anyone's feelings. So, I am saying things like, "Modest is hottest" and "Dress so people respect you, *not inspect you,*" and I am trying not to look at her.

Then, an epiphany. "Has anyone seen the prom pictures in the newspaper and what young girls are wearing lately?" I said. "Low in front, nothing in back and more holes than a piece of swiss cheese."

The woman with the plunging neckline came to life. "Out-RAGEOUS!" she said. "I would NEVER let my kid out of the house dressed like THAT!"

Every head in the room turned to her like, "*Really?*" After that, she pulled her low cut neckline together. She became more conscious of it.

No matter what the dress code, *The Exceptional Professional* knows making wise wardrobe decisions gives us an advantage. It's as important to be role model with our image as much as our management style.

In this chapter, you will learn:

- The case for dressing better
- When high fashion gets low marks
- What to think before you get inked
- Bare vs. flair and dressing your age
- Clothing care and when not to use the dry cleaners

Workplace Attire is a Contentious Issue

Whenever I am asked to give a talk on professional attire, it is usually because a manager is at odds with his or her people. That manager is either tired of beating the drum for more dress code conformity or wants to avoid the uncomfortable conversation with the one or two employees who really need it.

Dress codes exist for a reason: because some make unfortunate choices in clothing and grooming. If you think it's mostly the youngest employees who make these unfortunate choices, you would be wrong.

The biggest violators of dress code policy? It's not the millennials. It's middle-aged women, age 50 and up. When I get called in, this is usually the group the employer is targeting.

Middle-aged women get comfortable in their positions and start dressing down. It starts with sweatshirt-like, knit blazers with t-shirts underneath. Then it devolves into sweat suits and capri pants (aka, cropped pants – those pants chopped off at half calf that flatter no one.)

I was speaking to a group of women who were assistants in various workplaces. A woman came up to me afterwards and said, "Young women in my office just don't know how to dress professionally. They wear tight skirts, hiked up to here… and blouses cut down to there…"

The woman telling me this, was wearing a homemade Halloween vest with pumpkins, ghosts and black cats on it.

We have a disconnect on what professional dress is. I don't want to completely absolve the millennials in the workplace. They also have problems with professional dress.

I was invited to a women's business group to hear a 20-something young lady, an assistant youth minister at her local church, give a talk on the millennials. As usual, I was dressed in one of my suits.

The young lady, wearing a loose baby doll top, with short, puffy, princess sleeves, fashionable at the time, talked about how millennials like experiences, rather than material things. They want to work from home whenever they want. And they prefer to dress casually in the workplace. Then she singled me out of the audience of about 40 women and said in a mocking tone, *"Sorry, Ms. Etiquette."*

I stood up and took off my earrings. Then I taught her a lesson about respecting her elders... *and her betters.*

I didn't really. I kept my mouth shut, which was the polite thing to do. But I wanted to say, "When you make it to the C-suite wearing that baby doll top, you can tweet me."

No superior wants to have the "Your attire is inappropriate" talk with his or her reports. It's second only to the "Your body odor is killing your co-workers" conversation. As a result, those that need the talk, don't always get the talk. They just get passed over for promotion.

Appropriate wear is a sensitive issue, because it's personal. People see their clothing choices as self-expression.

There's a Place For Us

There is a disconnect on what professional dress is, so let's define it:

> ***Professional dress*** *is attire that reflects your profession and represents your organization's brand, mission and culture well.*

The good news is, whatever your style, whatever you want to wear, there is a place for you. There are all kinds of options available:

- If you want to wear a suit and tie, there's a workplace for you.
- If you want to display tattoos that run the length of your arms, there is a workplace to welcome you with open arms.
- If you don't want to decide what to wear, there are workplaces that will issue you a standard uniform.

I know, because I have worked in all of these places. Sony Music was extreme casual – t-shirts and ripped jeans ruled. When I moved on to Amana Appliances, where the code was business dress, I spent piles of money to build a suit wardrobe. To my chagrin, Amana went business casual and I had to start over, purchasing business casual wear.

Working in the tech world for InterTech Media, the dress code was somewhat flexible between business casual and extreme casual. As an etiquette instructor, I'm a "suit" again.

In high school and college, I worked in restaurants where I wore a uniform every day. Don't knock the uniform. It saves money and cuts decision making time.

Sony Music had its Midwest branch in a 10-story granite, suburban, corporate complex. Each day, we rode the elevator with financial advisors in suits. One day, I was on the elevator with Vickie Strate, Sony Music's Midwest director of marketing. As the elevator reached our floor, an older gentleman in a suit looked at Vickie in her leather jacket and ripped jeans and said, "What exactly do you people DO in there?"

She said, "Smoke pot and listen to rock-n-roll music." Then we stepped out onto our floor and the elevator closed behind us. I said, "We don't smoke pot. Why did you say that?"

"Because that's what they think," she laughed.

There is a Dress Code… It's Just Not Written Down

Some workplaces flaunt their lack of a dress code. Internet companies make a lot of noise about this. Wear whatever you want – flip-flops, shorts, sweats. Suits are too stuffy. The workplace should be fun, they say, as they frolic among their bean bag chairs and ping pong tables.

> *"You can be serious without a suit,"* reads Number 9 of *Google's "Ten Things that we know to be true"* company philosophy. "... *Our atmosphere may be casual, but as new ideas emerge in a café line, at a team meeting or at the gym, they are traded, tested and put into practice with dizzying speed – and they may be the launch pad for a new project destined for worldwide use."*[20]

Written or not, every workplace has a dress code. If you don't believe me, try sending an attractive girl in a bikini into one of those open-minded, open floor-planned Silicon Valley organizations and see how fast it takes her yoga-gear-clad female colleagues to object.

There lies an important insight of professional dress: what we wear impacts how others respond to us. As the *Google* principle implies, we all want to be taken *seriously.* If you claim, "I don't want to be taken too seriously," you will find the world all too willing to accommodate you.

When I attended a Toastmasters meeting at a club at *Google* in Dublin, Ireland, most people there adopted a business casual look. On the elevator, my host introduced me to a woman who was wearing a tasteful, colorful dress. She stood out – in a positive way, because she was dressed a little better than those in more casual attire.

Even *Facebook*'s Mark Zuckerberg, known for his hoodies, dons a suit and tie when meeting with international leaders. He realizes other cultures can be more formal than the U.S. and suiting up is respectful.

O Pioneers! The Dual Wardrobe Professionals

At Iowa State University, I was talking about professional attire to young women studying agricultural and biosystems engineering. These pioneers in a growing industry will revolutionize our food production, balance industry and water quality, stem the scourge of hunger and conquer nutrition deficits. My topic seemed small in the greater scheme.

Today's professional dress is not "one size fits all." Like many pros, these agricultural and biosystems engineers will have two wardrobes:

1. **Casual:** functional wear for every day, hands-on work. They may be climbing on machinery, working with animals, researching in a lab or out in a lake testing water quality.
2. **Business:** suits for special events. In their pioneering industry, they may be presenting at conferences, lobbying and testifying before legislators or winning investors.

The dual-wardrobe extends to other industries, too. As public relations manager at Amana Appliances, even after the organization went business casual, I kept a navy blazer on the back of my office door, in case the media showed up unannounced. And I used it.

Executives to middle managers in business casual environments, wear jackets or blazers when they have important meetings. You should always have a suit ready, so you are prepared for anything.

The Case for Dressing Better

We have lost that sense of what it is to be dressed up for work. Growing up, I remember my grammar school teachers dressed up for school. Even the ones in polyester pant suits seemed to be making an effort. I am not sure teachers make an effort like that anymore.

Dressing better doesn't necessarily mean showing up to your casual workplace in a suit every day. Dressing better means taking the dress code you have been dealt and kicking it up a notch. But before we get to that, let's make a case for dressing better.

Dress better to distinguish work time from non-work time.

In *Forbes,* psychologist/author Jennifer Baumgartner talked about how casual dress environments have made it more difficult to distinguish between our "work selves" and "off-work selves." When we go home, we still feel like we are at work, because we're wearing the same thing.

Her advice? Make your casual work outfit slightly more dressy – with a nicer shirt or a blazer or sport coat. Then change when you get home to create that work/home boundary. Try it out. Dress for success, then go home and change to decompress.[21]

Dress better to stand out.

In Sony Music's extreme casual environment, Branch Manager Colin Willis wore a blazer and collared shirt with casual pants, if he had an important meeting. On other days he would wear a nice pair of jeans, with a tailored, collared shirt. Dressing a little better distinguished him as the one in charge of the branch. There are lots of ways to stand out. Dressing up rather than down creates a positive image.

Dress better to get hired or promoted.

A friend of mine was running a booth at a college career fair and he said all the college students were wearing black suits with dark shirts and dark ties. He said one student walked in wearing a navy suit, white shirt and red tie. *"Employers were knocking themselves out trying to get to this guy,"* said my friend. *"He looked professional and he stood out."* He was dressed slightly different and it set him apart.

A survey by OfficeTeam found 80 percent of executives interviewed said clothing choices affect an employee's chances of earning a promotion.[22]

Dress better to be more productive, self-confident.

When you are dressed better, you feel more confident. A new shirt or new accessory makes you feel good. Buy one stylish piece of clothing a year that you might not normally purchase, just to freshen your look.

Some get the same affect with a new hairstyle. My friend Tom Jenkot, a graphic designer I worked with at Sony Music, had hair down to his elbows. One day he shocked everyone when he came to work with his hair half an inch long. Some co-workers didn't recognize him at first. But he looked great. I don't think he ever went back to the long mane.

BE EXCEPTIONAL: Upgrading Business Casual

While business casual dress codes are supposed to make everyone more comfortable, they do a disservice to career-oriented people, especially women, because business casual attire makes people look ordinary. *The Exceptional Professional* takes business casual and upgrades it and turns an ordinary look to an extraordinary one.

I was interviewed by Susan Reimer, a columnist for *The Baltimore Sun*, who said people often talk about the "Don'ts" in professional attire. *Don't show too much skin. Don't have your boxer shorts or bra straps sticking out. Don't wear yoga or sweat pants.*

Ms. Reimer challenged me to come up with the "Dos." I like that. My goal has always been to have you see professionalism a little differently. When it comes to business casual, let's talk about the Dos. Here's how to upgrade your business casual wardrobe:

- Wear a pressed shirt, instead of a polo shirt.
- Try a collared shirt instead of a t-shirt.
- Wear a blazer or suit jacket with your open-collared shirt.
- Put on a tie without a blazer or suit jacket.
- Add color with a scarf. (Scarves are wardrobe extenders.)
- Enhance with a simple necklace – pearls, gold or silver chain, colorful stones.
- Improve a pair of casual pants with dressier shoes.
- Rock a pair of dress pants instead of dockers.
- Wear a professional-looking dress or skirt instead of slacks.

These are subtle changes that make a difference. The next chapter, will cover suiting up for business dress and even more formal occasions.

Should You Dress Fashionably?

An arrogant woman I worked with always dressed in the latest fashion. One day, she came to work wearing what looked like a sailor suit. It was a navy blue top and bell bottom pants with white stripes around the sleeves and the bottom of the pants. A square back flap on the top also had stripes. Only thing missing was one of those white sailor hats.

When she walked into the Engineering Department, the engineers saluted and yelled things like, "All hands on deck!" "Ahoy matey!" and "Man overboard!" She was the subject of much ridicule—and she was not the type of person who took it well.

I don't know if she paid a lot of money for that outfit, but we never saw it again. It didn't matter to the engineers. For weeks, they were still yelling, *"Thar she blows!"* whenever they saw her.

High fashion is valued in some industries, where it is important to look fashionable, current and hip. But always wearing the latest trendy things can also make you seem inconsistent or look like "a follower."

Two Perceptions of "Fashionable":

Positive: current, up-to-date, stylish, chic, fresh
Negative: inconsistent, "shift with the wind," follower, spendthrift

The fashion industry has a job to do – *sell clothes.* They change styles every season, so you have to buy more clothes to stay current. This is how they make money. This is how they pay their bills.

Dressing in the latest fashion is in the fashion industry's best interest, but not always in your best interest. In women's clothing alone, there are many silly looks sold as high fashion. Two words: *pilgrim shoes.* Remember those? They were huge black shoes with a big buckle on them that looked like something Benjamin Franklin would wear. (Making women dress like Ben Franklin was all about the "Benjamins.")

Women are not the only ones who fall victim to fashion. Men's suits with undersized jackets and skinny pants, or blazers and shirts with oversized lapels, have had their moment, too.

At one university, a young man who was a finance major asked me about shoes to go with his interview suit. On his cell phone, he showed me a pair of ankle boots that look like something William Shatner would have worn as Captain Kirk on the original *Star Trek.*

I said, "No boots."

He said, "What about this one?" showing a similar boot in a different color.

"No boots."

He let me borrow his phone and I pulled up a dark shoe with laces. "Really?" he said.

Back to our woman in the sailor suit. By their jokes, the engineers let her know she wasn't going to be taken seriously in that outfit. How many of her colleagues did not say anything, but thought the same thing? It's good to incorporate a little bit of fashion into your wardrobe, but don't go overboard.

Wearing Evening Wear as Workplace Wear

Fashion magazines really get it wrong on professional dress when they confuse evening wear with workplace wear. Hence, the perennial articles that say your cocktail dress can double as professional attire, if you throw a jacket over it. After work, toss the jacket and hit the town.

Having been a commuter in big cities like New York, Chicago and Washington D.C., that has a certain appeal. But no, your cocktail dress cannot double as business attire. Know the difference between workplace wear and evening wear. The following are evening wear:

- Sparkly jewels (worn after 6 p.m.)
- Sequins
- Satin anything
- Strappy sandals and spiked heels
- Cocktail dresses
- Tuxedo shirts

There may be occasions where you have an evening event for work that requires formal attire. We'll cover that in the next chapter.

What to Think Before You Get Inked

After a talk at a law school in Florida, a young woman has a question for me. She is gorgeous: a brown-eyed blonde, tall and slender and wearing a charcoal-gray suit with a crisp, white, collared shirt.

She said, "I have sleeve-tattoos running the length of both my arms. If I go to work in a law firm, should I keep them covered?"

This was not an isolated incident. Another time, it was a male student, with sleeve tattoos, who wanted to work at an accounting firm. One difference – his tattoos extended onto his wrists and peeked out from underneath his shirt cuffs.

The good news is, if you want visible tattoos, there are many workplaces to welcome you. I'm not just talking artsy jobs. I have tattooed friends who teach K-12.

But a lot of dress codes still say, "No visible tattoos." If you are considering a tattoo, consider this: visible tattoos, while welcome in some workplaces, can limit your opportunities. How many people have had a dramatic shift or re-evaluation of their career? How many are now in a position they never imagined in their youth? My sister, once a media buyer for a top global ad agency, is now a felony attorney for a public defender. (She doesn't have tattoos, but many of her clients do.)

About 23 percent of people regret their tattoos, according to a 2015 Harris poll.[23] What's to regret? U.K.-based Premier Laser Clinic identified the top removed tattoos as: name of ex-lover, dolphin and misspelled foreign quote.[24] If you are determined to get inked, get one that can be easily covered. Once you find your groove in your career, if you want another and another, go ahead. But if you get that dolphin tattoo, you'll probably regret it.

Tattoo Stories

People who have tattoos will tell you they are addictive. If you get one, you will want more. I like to ask people about their "tattoo story." Usually, the tattoo has some deeper meaning to the person and often there's an interesting story behind it.

The accounting student I mentioned earlier, told me his story. The tattoos that extended onto his wrists were bright bluebirds. A few years earlier, he had been in a serious car accident. He was airlifted to the hospital. The last thing he remembered was the emergency room, and a nurse – we'll call her Jamie – taking care of him.

After that, he was in a coma for a few weeks and when he emerged from the coma, he was in the hospital for another few weeks, recovering from all of his injuries.

When it came time to leave the hospital, he went around thanking the nurses, doctors and other medical personnel. He also went to the emergency room. He said to the staff, "There was also a nurse named Jamie who I wanted to thank."

The ER staff said, "There's no one here by that name."

He insisted, "She took care of me and I remember she had a bluebird pin on her uniform."

A few of them froze for a moment, then looked at each other. One finally said, "There was a nurse named Jamie. Three years ago, she left after her shift here and she was hit by a car and killed."

As I mentioned in the networking chapters, everyone has an interesting story. If we take an interest in people and ask questions, we will get those stories.

Multiple Piercings

Piercings, other than ear piercings, are like tattoos. Many workplaces don't care. But others have dress code policies that say the other piercings must be out of sight or removed during work hours. I also read one dress code policy that said, "and/or while representing (name of organization)." That was recognizing that many employees are often out in the field and dress codes extend beyond the workplace headquarters.

One woman I worked with, who was a graphic designer, had a pierced eyebrow and a pierced tongue. Whenever she was working with clients, however, she removed her eyebrow stud and put putty in the hole. She also removed the tongue stud. I don't think there was a dress code. She was just a thoughtful person who didn't want to make more traditional clients uncomfortable.

Tattoos can often be removed, but some piercings are permanent and beyond repair, like people who stretch their ear lobes with big, Inca-sized rings or medallions. Earlobes aren't easily stitched back together.

Bare vs. Flair

Only on TV do women wear tight, sexy outfits to work in the crime lab. The late comedian Joan Rivers had a feature on her hit TV show, *Fashion Police*, called, "Starlet or Streetwalker," where an image of a person in a sleazy outfit, with the face obscured, was presented and people were supposed to guess whether it was a famous person or a prostitute. Most of the time, you couldn't tell.

Hollywood used to be a place of glamour and style worth imitating. But now, when celebrities walk the red carpet in see-through outfits that are barely glued together, they just look trashy.

Unfortunately, women of all ages mimic celebrities with tops cut too low, skirts too short, heels that are too high and everything too tight. When I see a woman who dresses too sexy in a professional environment, I assume one of two things:

1. She doesn't have good mentors in professional dress.
2. She lacks attention.

There's a remedy for the former. For a woman who is willing to learn, there are good mentors in professional dress. For the latter, the person who lacks attention, that's a tougher nut to crack. Those who lack attention disrupt the workplace in other undesirable ways.

Develop a style worth emulating. That means not only dressing so others respect you, but also so you respect yourself:

- Let the skirt or dress hit your knee, not four or five inches above. Especially after age 40 – your knees just aren't that cute.
- Wear clothing with room to move, not skin tight. This allows you to glide down the hall, not waddle like a penguin.

- If you have to crouch down or bend, make sure there is not a big gap between your top and bottom.
- If people can see your underwear, you need something else to wear.

Dress Your Age, Not Your Shoe Size

Men go afoul of dress codes by dressing immaturely. A cartoon or superhero tie says, "I LOVE CARTOONS!! Cartoons are AWESOME!! What won't be heard is, "We need to go in a completely different direction with our sales strategy and here's why."

Don't wear sports logo ties, cartoon ties or other silly designs. And if your hair mimics the styles of teen boys in high school or younger, it's time to update your look.

Keep it simple. Some people think we have to dress outrageously to stand out. The biggest mistake is to wear clothing, so other people see the clothing but they don't see us. If I showed up to give a presentation in a day-glo orange suit or neon yellow suit, the audience would be distracted by that. They might not hear, all that I want them to hear.

Don't let your outfit or accessories be a distraction. Dress well, dress your age and let your personality shine through.

What to Wear to a Wake or Funeral

I went to the funeral for the wife of a colleague and saw young people wearing flip flops. That's too casual for the solemn occasion.

When attending wakes, funerals and memorial services for business associates or their family members, dress to blend in, so not to offend. Men should wear dark suits, dark ties and white shirts. (Do not wear a black shirt and silver tie, for this occasion – or ever.) Women should wear dark suits, dresses, skirts or dress pants. Avoid cocktail dresses, bare shoulders, spaghetti straps or mini-anything. Avoid bright accent colors in ties, scarves or other accessories. No sparkly jewelry – don't bring your bling.

Hats Off to Professionalism

While giving a talk to a Kiwanis group, a mostly male audience of about 80 people over 80 years-old, I was surprised to find their biggest etiquette pet peeve was not rude cell phone use. Their biggest pet peeve? Young men who enter restaurants without removing their baseball caps.

For those who want the bare bones hat etiquette: men remove their hats when entering a restaurant, church, office or a home. Women may keep their hats on under all these circumstances.

For those who crave details: men remove their hats when entering a restaurant, church (with the exception of an orthodox synagogue, where men might be required to cover their heads), office, home, apartment building, hotel lobby, elevator for a hotel or an apartment, store, theater or a courtroom.

Men may leave their hats on in a bank, an airport terminal, an office building, a public building like a post office, an elevator for a public building, office building or shopping mall. Men remove their hats when entering individual offices and individual stores.

A woman generally keeps her hat on, but a woman who is a military officer removes her hat in dining rooms and in the officers' clubs.

Clearing the Air in Business

When I was selling my house, I had a real estate professional, who wore perfume so overpowering, it had a life of its own. Half an hour after she left, my house smelled like she was still there. I had to open every window to clear the air, which is not advantageous in Iowa in February.

Scents in the professional world don't make sense. My olfactory system is not even that sensitive. Others have allergies or get sick to their stomach at the slightest whiff of something flowery or musky. You won't know who they are unless you notice them desperately trying to hold their breath or passing out.

Don't put on perfume or cologne for any business meetings, especially interviews. Your experience amounts to nothing, if you smell like a graduate of P.U. Avoid scents when you will be in close proximity to others – meetings, networking events, recreational sports. Even for evening events, when you are "putting on the dog," hold the fog.

Perfume or cologne does not mask body odor. It makes it worse, like it was mixed in a laboratory in some evil experiment to repel all opportunities and promotions. Other undesirable scents come from scented hand-creams, lotions, body splashes, aftershaves, smelly hair products, musky or fruity deodorants and "natural" alternatives like patchouli oil.

If you practice good hygiene, take showers or baths regularly, wear (unscented) deodorant and launder your clothing, there is no need for additional fragrance. Here are some hygiene basics:

- Shower daily
- Use deodorant, not just anti-perspirant
- Trim and clean your fingernails
- Clean and maintain your hair
- If you have facial hair, keep it trim
- Don't forget to clean out your ears
- Wash your hands before eating, after using the restroom and throughout the day
- Brush your teeth after meals, to freshen breath and prevent cavities (Remember what they told you in grammar school: ignore your teeth and they will go away!)

Launder What You Wear/Clothing Maintenance

If you shower every morning, put on deodorant and still give off an offensive odor, your clothes aren't adequately laundered. (People who never launder their leather jackets have this problem.) Do a smell check.

Some articles on clothing care will tell you dry cleaning is not good for suits, it wears them down. But not dry cleaning your suits is bad for your career – being stinky wears down your co-workers and clients.

Do not believe articles that say to only dry clean suits twice a year. Suits and other items should be laundered on an as-needed basis. Suits should go to the cleaners after you wear them 3-4 times. Some people are sweaty and need to launder more frequently. Air out suits after spending time in a restaurant with strong aromas – what smelled delicious in the air will not smell so pleasant on your suit later.

Shirts, blouses, undergarments and other items worn next to the skin should be laundered after each use.

Home Laundering

Dry cleaning shirts and blouses is convenient and gives them a more crisp look. But it can get pricey. And you have to watch out for sneaky dry cleaners that steal the extra buttons off your clothing.

Doing some of your own laundering saves money and can minimize damage on your clothing. Always read the user care instructions on an inside label for any garment first.

- Wash cotton shirts and blouses on cold in your washer's gentle or delicate cycle.
- Divide light colors and dark colors into separate loads.
- Don't put shirts through a complete dryer cycle. Dry them for 10 minutes, then hang them to dry. Often, the material will shrink, but the stitching will not, creating a buckling effect on the seams.

There is no such thing as completely wrinkle-free clothing. If you need to use an iron to press your clothes, do it. Some people like ironing, like some people like vacuuming. Both are a chore to me, but everyone should know how to do them. There may come a time when you arrive at your hotel for a conference or meetings and you don't have time to send your shirts or blouses out for a pressing. You may have to do it yourself.

Hand Washing Sweaters

I used to send cashmere sweaters to the dry cleaners, until I saw an article in the *Wall Street Journal* about Italian designer Brunello Cucinelli's instructions for hand washing them. Hand washing is easy, better for the sweaters and makes them much softer. Dry cleaning wears them out faster.[25] Here are the instructions, paraphrased:

- Gently hand wash the sweater in cold water. (He suggested using a gentle hand soap. I use *Woolite®*.)
- Don't wring it out. Place the wet sweater on a towel and roll it up. Press down on the towel roll to absorb more of the water.
- Lay out the sweater on another dry towel for half a day.
- When it is semi-dry, but no longer heavy with water, hang it over a line to let it air dry.
- Don't use any dryers, or irons.

These instructions are for sweaters. Send lined cashmere coats and blazers to the dry cleaners.

Much of what we covered in this chapter was about business casual. But there are certain times when we have to suit up. And that's where we are going next.

7.2 *Suiting Up and More Formal Codes*

One of my clients had a brother who was a university professor, who always wore a suit or blazer and tie to teach his class. His students gave him a hard time.

> *"You always look so formal."*
> *"You need to loosen up."*
> *"You should dress more casually."*

The following semester, he took their advice. He stopped wearing ties and any kind of a suit jacket or blazer. He taught the class the same as he had taught before. But at the end of the semester, his student evaluations, which were always very high, were noticeably lower than the previous semester. He went back to wearing the suits and blazers and ties. The evaluations went back up.

Despite the casual attire craze in workplaces, one thing still holds true: people treat us differently when we dress up. But suiting up, for both men and women, takes a little finesse. *The Exceptional Professional* knows it's not just enough to wear a suit, it's about knowing how to create the right combination of colors. Whether you don a suit regularly or once in a blue moon, this chapter is designed to help you make choices that will boost your image and your career.

In this chapter, you will learn:

- How what you wear impacts how others respond
- The best color combinations when you suit up
- How women in the C-suite dress differently
- The Professional Dress Challenge
- What to wear when the code is "formal"

People Treat You Differently

I was at *The Des Moines Register* having my photo taken by Art Fernandez, a former assistant photo editor. I noticed he was wearing a gray striped tie with a lighter gray shirt. I said, "That's a nice combination, but don't photographers usually dress more casually?"

"I want to bring credibility back to the photo department," he said. "News photographers are always into everything, so they often dress down. They are perceived as slobs."

"Sometimes I meet people who think they are photographers because they carry an expensive camera," he continued. "They are less likely to tell me what to do, when I am wearing a tie."

Art said his father-in-law retired and gave him a bunch of his ties and he was enjoying them. Art had it right. When you are dressed up, people treat you differently.

The Wardrobe According to Levitt and Molloy

My professional dress background started at age nine. My father, who used to wear three-piece suits to work every day, was an avid reader of John T. Molloy and Mortimer Levitt, the maharishis of menswear. At the breakfast table each morning, we would discuss color combinations – neutrals, bases and accents and other principles. You can wear a brown tie but never, ever wear a brown suit.

After a band concert at school, other dads were asking their kids, "Where would you like to go for pizza?" My dad was showing me how to identify the tweeds on the other dads. "That's a Harris tweed... this is a Herringbone tweed... Can you see the difference?"

My father also showed me how to tie a necktie. He told me how Mortimer Levitt, founder of *The Custom Shop* chain, said an expensive tie, not coordinated, can look like a cheap tie. And conversely, a cheap tie, coordinated and knotted well, can look like an expensive tie.[26]

Dress for Success Research and Controversy

In the 1970s, researcher John T. Molloy struck literary gold with his best-selling books *Dress for Success* and *Women's Dress for Success.*[27] But the books were not without their controversy. Even today, the fashion industry still howls over his pushing men's suits for women, with a floppy bow as the feminine version of the masculine necktie.

While the floppy bow may be long gone, Molloy's most important contribution, demonstrating how what we wear impacts how others respond to us, is timeless. Many of his principles of color combinations with traditional suits, are still followed by top managers and executives.

Molloy did exhaustive research from the 1970s through the 1990s on imaging. He dressed men and women in different business outfits, different colors and cuts and then gave them tasks to perform, such as:

- Interviewing for a job
- Walking into an office without an appointment and trying to get a meeting with someone
- Walking into popular restaurants to see if they could get a table without a reservation

He also had participants keep diaries of how people in their workplace responded to them on days when they were wearing certain color combinations or outfits. Here are some of Molloy's conclusions:

- Both men and women in management commanded more authority when they wore darker, more traditional colors.
- Both men and women wearing traditional suits, rather than fashionable attire, commanded higher salaries.
- When people were dressed more casually, especially women, their ideas were challenged more often in meetings.
- Women in suits or blazers had more authority. Women who wore dresses or sweater sets had their authority challenged more often.
- A woman wearing the most conservative, businesslike dress will be seen as a professional by only 40 percent of the business people she meets for the first time. If she wears a jacket over the dress, the number of business people who assume she has power, authority or potential will more than double.

Molloy also discovered differences in the colors people wore. When female managers wore pastel suits, their female colleagues would give compliments. But those same female colleagues, were more likely to challenge their authority. Men were more likely to challenge them, too.

If you have problems commanding respect or have people questioning your authority, Molloy suggested wearing darker colored suits. If you are perceived as too commanding or aggressive, he suggested wearing lighter colored suits in light taupe, medium gray, or medium blue-gray, to soften your image and be less intimidating.

These principles are still in play. Many times when large NFL or NBA players become TV sports commentators, they wear lighter colored suits, so they are not perceived as too intimidating.

In a business casual environment, you don't have to wear a suit. But if you are in the management ranks or aspire to management, you should wear a jacket. This goes for women as well as men. If a woman's cute sweater set or a man's sweater vest could talk, it would not say, "I am in charge." It would say, "What would you like from the deli?"

BE EXCEPTIONAL: A Different Take on Professional Dress

I mentioned how I grew up with the idea that if we wear a jacket or blazer, we command more respect. That's still true.

But a professor at Johns Hopkins gave me a different perspective. This woman was always wearing suits. I asked her, "Do you wear suits, so your students will respect you?"

She said, *"No. I dress this way out of respect for my students."*

That was a humbling moment. Here I was, an etiquette instructor, and my whole mantra was, "Be attentive to the people around you. Don't think of yourself, think of others..." Here is this professor showing me how it's really done.

Picture it: the students she is dressing up for are probably dressed like slobs – jeans hanging down, t-shirts and camisoles and sweat pants that say, "Juicy" on the backside. But they have also sacrificed to be there. They've worked hard, paid a lot of money – taken out loans or earned scholarships. Many have jobs on the side.

By dressing up, she is really saying something about Johns Hopkins – that it is an important place, it is aspirational. And she is recognizing her students as important.

That is something we don't always think about. How we dress, how we present ourselves: we are not just representing ourselves. We are also representing our organization and our profession. *The Exceptional Professional* dresses well out of respect for others.

Suiting Up: Finding the Right Color Combinations

The key to the professional suit is knowing how to mix and match colors of suits, shirts or blouses and accessories. We are going to start with the very basics and then we will branch out.

Begin with a traditional suit in one of the following colors:

- navy
- charcoal gray

These colors convey reliability and stability. Navy also conveys trust, which is why you will often see politicians wearing it. It is also a universal color that looks good on everyone.

There are also lighter-colored suit options, such as:

- medium gray
- taupe (brownish-gray color)
- lighter taupe
- medium gray-blue.

Sound pretty boring so far? "Positively institutional!" some might say. Let's brighten it up with a light-colored shirt for men or blouse for women in one of the following colors:

- white
- light blue
- French blue
- pale pink
- pale yellow

Okay, brighter, but still boring. What we need is a contrasting accent color. That is the part of the suit that announces, "Here I am!" without hitting people over the head. For men, the accent color can be a tie. Women can capture the same effect with a scarf or other accessories like a pin or necklace. Think basic crayon colors.

- red
- royal blue
- yellow
- green

Now for some variations on these crayon colors:

- maroon
- aqua blue
- light blue
- forest green
- gold
- pink
- magenta

Women can add more colorful options in blouses or shirts in the crayon colors, plus hot pink, shades of blue, green, etc. These colors might also work as blazers or jackets for women, in combination with darker pants or skirts. I would not recommend any of these colors for men's shirts. Men should also avoid dark shirts, such as dark gray, olive, black or brown, under a dark-colored suit.

Now we have some color options. Let's combine:
Start with a man in a navy suit

Add a white shirt.
Contrasting accent tie in: red, royal blue, yellow or green

Take the same navy suit
Change to a light blue shirt
Contrasting accent tie in red, yellow or green
Why not a royal blue tie here? Too much blue. Overkill.

Women's suits have a lot more variety in cuts and styles. There are skirt suits, pant suits, short jackets, long jackets, jewel necks, different shaped lapels or no lapels, buttons, snaps, zippers and other fasteners, etc. But right now, we're just thinking about colors.

Let's look at a woman in a charcoal gray suit
Add a white shirt or blouse
Contrasting scarf in red, royal blue, yellow or green

Take the same charcoal gray suit
Add a pale pink shirt
I would throw a set of pearls on with this. But other women might want a colorful piece of jewelry or brightly colored scarf.

People err with suits by not using the right color combinations. Eight percent of the male population is color-blind, which also leads to problems. Color blind people often have help organizing their color selections in their closet.

Knowing a few color basics can lead to unlimited combinations.

Minimize Jewelry

Besides a wedding ring, pick two of anything: earrings, necklace, bracelets, decorative pin, etc. Don't wear all four together. There is no need to look like you robbed King Tut's tomb.

Don't wear oversized jewelry. As sales guru Tom Hopkins says in *Selling for Dummies*, "You don't want to be remembered as 'that woman we talked with who had those humongous earrings.'"[28]

What About Suits in Basic Black?

For years, retailers were pushing black suits for women. Black suits are okay. They are more appropriate for funerals or evening wear than business. It's not a great color for an interview suit.

Black and red are supposed to go together, but a black suit with a red shirt underneath is a bad combination – for men or women. A maroon or other dark-colored shirt under a black suit is also a bad combination, because there is no contrast. I have seen women executives wearing black skirts, dresses or pants, with a more brightly colored jacket for contrast – that's a better way to go.

In the previous chapter, I mentioned the stand-out student at the college career fair, wearing a navy suit, white shirt and red tie. This set him apart from the sea of students in black suits and dark shirts.

Some Additional Guidelines

Do not mix too many stripes and patterns. If you have a pinstriped suit, do not wear a striped shirt and a striped tie. With a pinstriped suit, wear a solid shirt and a small-pattern tie or a solid tie. Pinstripes also make a large person look larger. Tweed jackets are for business casual, not professional dress. Same with seer-sucker jackets in warmer weather.

Wear Natural Fibers

Just like there is a glass ceiling, there is a fabric wall. Choose natural fibers over synthetics. Wool, cotton and silk allow the skin to breathe. They also last longer and are less likely to snag.

When I say, "wool," this is not about one of those thick, furry wool suits, that feels like you are wearing the sheep. This is about a lighter wool fabric that can be worn all year round, even in the summer.

Knit t-shirts are less professional. A lot of women wear them under suits but there are better options. Avoid 100 percent polyester, which is not as breathable and gets stinky faster.

Tying One On

If you are all thumbs when it comes to tying neckties, bowties or scarves, there are a lot of *YouTube* videos and other resources on the Internet.

Brooks Brothers has a section on their website with instructions of tying different knots for ties and scarves. I never knew there were so many ways to tie a man's tie: a Windsor, a Half-Windsor, a Four-in-Hand, a Prince Albert… For more info, visit: www.brooksbrothers.com

Shoes

The best shoes for men: laced-up shoes, in black or brown. Slip on loafers are business casual. The sock color should match the trousers. Avoid: Tan shoes with a dark suit, Bucks and Star Trek-like ankle boots.

For women: closed-toe and closed-heel shoes, either low-heeled pumps or flats. Avoid open-toed shoes, sandals and spiked heels. I never understood women walking around in New York City, or any big city, wearing open-toed shoes. Ick!

Should Women Wear Hosiery?

I get this question every so often when I am presenting. I sometimes pull back the sleeve of my jacket to reveal the underside of my arm, which, because of my Irish heritage, is as pale as a human being can get, this side of rigor mortis. (Cosmetics companies use more flattering terms like "alabaster" or "porcelain.")

"This is the color of my legs, if I were not wearing silk stockings," I say. "Without it, my legs would blind you." Put another way, no one would see me, they would just see my bright, white legs. For women who were blessed with more natural color in their legs, it's easier to get away with not wearing hosiery. But silk hosiery adds a nice, finishing touch. Orange, dollar store nylons, not so much.

Dressy Doesn't Always Mean Professional

Not every dress is professional. When I worked at Amana, some well-intentioned women would wear mother-of-the-bride dresses to work.

While those are dressy, they are not professional. Pale pink suits work for the mother-of-the-bride but not so well for the chair of the board. Ditto for shiny shantung or jackets with ruffles or big fabric flowers.

In one presentation on professional attire, I put up an image of a woman in a red jacket that had a big, frilly, ruffled collar and said, "This is not professional wear." One woman protested, "I would wear that for business." I could not convince her otherwise.

The ruffles fad comes and goes. I was looking at suits one time and I found this beautiful, traditional cut suit. I turned it around and to my great disappointment, it had a big ruffle on the back of the skirt. I thought, "What am I supposed to do in this? The cha-cha?"

Women on Top

In one of my presentations for women, I show multiple images of C-suite women executives, at the top of their game. I ask the audience to identify what elements they have in common. Here are traits they identify:

- Suits in mostly dark colors, but some variations – light gray and taupe, some bright colored jackets
- No wild patterns, big flowers, animal prints or busy designs
- Modest necklines and hemlines
- Light, natural makeup; no heavy mascara or dramatic eye shadow
- Nail colors in translucent or understated colors; no bright reds, hot pinks, blues, maroons or black
- Simple jewelry, not big and chunky, unobtrusive
- Simple hairstyles; hair not hanging in the face
- Latest fashion does not seem as important

Some of the female executives, even though they were multi-millionaires, were wearing the same jacket at different events. That suggests they are not "clothes horses" with overstuffed closets at home.

Another interesting feature I discovered after looking at hundreds of pictures of top women executives, is that most of them had one lipstick color. They did not match their lipstick to their outfit, they had one lipstick shade they wore with every outfit.

I do the same exercise for men, with multiple images of C-suite male executives. There is a little less variety in what they are wearing, but most have the traditional dark suit, light shirt and accent tie combination. They avoid distracting patterns.

Try The Professional Dress Challenge

John T. Molloy challenged people to test his theories for themselves, by taking his "Professional Dress Challenge." That meant dressing down for several weeks, then dressing up for several weeks and keeping a diary of how your colleagues, superiors and reports acted towards you.

I took the challenge, while working as manager of public relations at Amana Appliances. At the time, Amana was transitioning from business dress to business casual. For two weeks, I wore sweaters or a nice blouse and slacks. I even tried a short skirt, with a hemline at least four inches above my knees. For two weeks after that, I wore more traditional suits with jackets and skirts.

I sat in on a meeting with one of the vice presidents and a group of factory workers. I was wearing a suit. The vice president was wearing a shirt with his tie loosened but no jacket. The factory workers were in t-shirts and jeans.

I did not say anything during the meeting – I was there to observe. At the meeting's end, the factory workers bypassed the vice president and came to me with questions. They thought I was in charge.

When I wore the suits with jackets, both men and women treated me with more respect. In the sweaters, blouses and slacks, not so much. In the short skirt, people stared and I felt like a weird distraction. No one asked for my input on anything that day.

Try the John T. Molloy Professional Dress Challenge for a month. For two weeks, dress down. For the next two weeks, dress up. If you don't normally wear a suit or a jacket, wear one. Men, if you don't wear ties, wear ties. Women, if you wear t-shirts, change to blouses and collared shirts. If you usually wear low cut necklines, button up. Vary the colors you wear. Keep a diary and write down how people react to you in meetings and other business situations. You will notice a difference.

Are Casually Dressed People More Approachable?

"We deal with a lot of farmers and I feel like I am more approachable when I am dressed casually." That was an older woman, putting up the argument against her employer, a bank in a rural area, that was changing from a casual dress code to business dress. A few other women around the same age agreed. The manager felt like the casual dress had become too sloppy.

I countered, "You are suggesting the farmers are intimidated by suits. Does that mean you should wear overalls?" That touched a nerve. They became more vociferous in their objections to business attire.

But I pressed on. "Some people are intimidated by people who are attractive. Are you going to say to the most attractive employees, 'Can you ugly it down a little – you are frightening the customers away?'"

As we talked further, the real rationale for not liking suits surfaced.

"They're too uncomfortable,' said one. "I feel like I can't move in them," said another. (Ah, the truth comes out. This wasn't about customer service at all.)

A suit that doesn't fit can feel like a strait jacket. But suits come in all sizes. If your suit or shirts are uncomfortable, you might need a larger size or tailoring. If your weight fluctuates, have several sizes of suits. Don't try to squeeze into clothing that is too small. Clothes that are too big on you, make you look older. Clothes that are too tight make you look heavier.

I heard the "more approachable" argument from career counselors at a university, who preferred to wear t-shirts and big knit sweaters. "Suits are intimidating for students. I am afraid they won't open up to me."

But what kind of life after college were they preparing these students for? One where they would never have to speak to someone in a suit? What kind of example are they setting? Many college students these days are first generation college students – first in their family to go to college. They need good examples for professional dress.

At Amana Appliances, I learned that wearing suits never got in the way of fostering good relations with people who worked in the factory, who were dressed very casually. What was important to them was that I was attentive to them and I listened.

Money and Suiting Up

Any time you are dealing with people's money, their savings or retirement – whether you are in industries like financial services or law – people expect you to dress more formally. Because you give the impression you are more – here comes that word we heard in the previous chapter – *serious.*

In financial services, especially a bank, people are placing their savings, their home loans, their retirement, their livelihood in your hands. This is definitely a case where you would dress up out of respect for the customer. You don't want casual attire to give customers the impression you are casual with their life savings.

I worked with a financial services firm that trained their interns to shine their shoes and press their clothes, because many of their clients were seniors citizens. Seniors see sloppiness as a red flag: sloppy dress equals sloppy work. Never underestimate a senior's ability to notice the details.

Where to Shop for Suits

Buy the best suit you can afford. If you are serious about your career, get one or two good suits. Business suits come and go in the big box retailers. Sometimes they're everywhere, sometimes more scarce. Retail chains, online and offline, may have reasonably priced suits.

Take the looks from the more expensive retailers and copy them with pieces at less expensive retailers. Or take a less expensive suit and pair it with shirts or accessories from the more expensive retailers.

If you don't have money for a new suit, look through some resale/second-hand clothing stores for some good suit buys. If you get a second-hand suit or hand-me-down suit, get it tailored to fit you.

If you can't find a suit in the stores or online, seek out a good tailor and have one made. I knew an executive who would have suits made with one jacket and two pairs of pants, because he would often shuck the jacket in his office and wear out the pants faster.

My sister, an experienced felony attorney, finds inexpensive suits from Walmart for her defendants, who don't have anything to wear to court. Her outfit of choice for defendants is a charcoal gray or navy suit, white shirt and maroon tie. Whether you are trying to land the job of your dreams or trying not to land in prison, it helps to suit up.

Special Occasions and the Formal Dress Code

I was at a black tie benefit in Connecticut and it was like *Dress Barn®* and *Nordstrom's Rack®* collided in a train wreck. There were strap lines and tan lines going in different directions, fashion carnage everywhere.

There were women poured into tiny gowns that did not flatter them and men who were wearing silly-colored bow ties and cummerbunds that looked like souvenirs from a senior prom. There were more fake tans than a political party convention. One woman had the tag hanging out of her dress, because she obviously intended to return it. Oh, the humanity.

The first step to any formal event is to know the dress code. If the dress is "business attire" and you show up in a cocktail dress, you will stand out like a sore thumb. If you show up in business casual, you will be underdressed. Know the dress code.

Evening Wear and Formal Dress Codes

I learned the meaning of "evening attire" the hard way. At Sony Music in my mid-20s, we had a black-tie event for one of the artists. The dress I bought for the occasion was black velvet on top with a flouncy, shiny, tea-length skirt, the color of green beer on St. Patrick's Day. It looked like a bad bridesmaid dress.

When I entered the event, other women I worked with looked beautiful and chic in black floor-length gowns that were stylish and tasteful. I looked like I had lost my tacky wedding party. (Do you ever want to go home and start over?) It got worse. Another woman in my workplace asked what I was going to wear, then had a dress made to match what I described. All night, people said, "Hey, you're like twins!" To avoid my mistakes, here are some guidelines for evening wear:

Cocktail Attire

Men: jacket and tie
Women: cocktail (just above knee) or tea length (mid-calf) dress

Black Tie

Men: black tuxedo or dark suit with black tie (Navy blue won't do.)
Women: formal gown or dress, usually floor length
(Black tie "optional" is your host saying, "Just dress black tie, okay?")

White Tie

Men: black tailcoat and dress pants, white shirt, white vest with a white bow tie
Women: same as black tie attire

Other Tips for Women

- Stay simple. A little sparkly is fine. Dressing like a disco ball is bad.
- Wearing a dress that is tighter than a sausage casing, flatters no one.
- Don't wear a sawed-off bridesmaid dress you thought you could wear again. If it looks like a bridesmaid dress, just say, "I don't."
- A mermaid dress is a bad idea for any event.
- Avoid strapless. Have you ever seen a woman in a strapless dress who did not spend the entire evening pulling it up with her hands under her armpits, like she was doing the Chicken Dance?

- Carry a small clutch bag. Do not stuff your cell phone into your bra.
- Whatever you decide to wear, don't tell anybody.

Other Tips for Men

- No black shirts and silver ties
- Do not wear goofy-colored cummerbund and tie combinations. It's not that critical that you match your date's dress. If you could wear it to your high school prom, don't wear it to a grown-up event.
- Brown shoes do not go with black or white tuxedos.
- No top hats, canes, scarves or other accessories that look like they're from a Fred Astaire movie.

Whether you suit up regularly or once in a while, you should be confident and comfortable. There is no doubt, that when we are dressed up, people treat us differently.

When we dress up for a presentation, people pay attention. We are letting the audience know we have something important to say. That seems like a good segue into our next two chapters, on public speaking.

PUBLIC SPEAKING

8.1 *Capture Your Audience and Conquer Your Nerves*

My first paid presentation as a certified etiquette instructor was at a small college in Iowa. I was giving a dining tutorial to about 70 students and I planned a big opening joke guaranteed to get laughs: "I am going to ask you a serious question and I want you to be honest with me. Let me see a show of hands. How many of you... *were raised by wolves?*"

None of them raised their hand. Not one of them even cracked a smile. The silence was such, you could have heard a napkin hit the floor.

The presentation went downhill from there. Fortunately, I only had 1 hour, 59 minutes and 30 seconds to go, then a long drive home to think about it. At home, I called my etiquette mentor, Maria Everding, "Maria, I'm no good at this. Being an etiquette instructor was a big mistake."

She said, "Oh sweetie, everyone bombs their first time. Get back out there. You will be great."

Whether speaking to a packed auditorium or a smaller group meeting, *The Exceptional Professional* knows it's not enough just to impart information. We must be compelling. We must know our audience and be respectful of their time. And when we bomb, and we all will bomb at one time or another, we must get back out there.

In this chapter, you will learn:

- How to connect with the audience
- How to conquer your nerves
- How to grab the audience's attention from the start
- What to do when trouble comes

In addition to public speaking before a live audience, think of the digital possibilities. Can you speak into a camera and be entertaining, without seeing your audience, as in a web video? Can you be compelling on a webinar where the audience only hears your voice and sees your slides?

Connecting with Your Audience

I got back out there. The week after that first disastrous dining tutorial, I had another dining tutorial for 200, at a much larger university. I dropped the "raised by wolves" joke, which might have resonated with an older crowd, but fell flat with college students. That presentation went much better and that university became a repeat client.

Know Your Audience

To connect with your audience, you must know your audience.

I was speaking at an event for an association, whose the two biggest players were direct competitors. We'll call them Business A and B.

The speaker before me had a PowerPoint presentation, where all his examples were about how great Business A was and the big impact they made in the community. He was really piling it on. The problem? There was not one person from Business A in the room. The room was filled with managers from Business B, Business A's biggest rival.

It was like going to Auburn and telling them how great Alabama is.

I knew the room was filled with managers from Business B, because prior to the event, I asked the meeting planner for a list of the people who would be there and the organizations they represented.

If the meeting planner does not want to provide names, ask for a list of organizations that will be represented. At conventions, sometimes they publicize this on their website. In addition, ask your meeting planner about the audience demographics. You should know:

- Age range
- Male/Female ratio
- Education level
- Knowledge of your subject/Lack of knowledge of your subject
- Professions, interests
- Tech-savvy/Not tech-savvy
- Cultural differences

Cultural differences are especially important. At the University of Iowa, one of my professors for a fiction writing class was Justin Cronin, later a best-selling author of *The Passage* trilogy. He warned against using "American pop culture idioms" or popular expressions that might not translate well to other cultures.

Expressions like: "*Somebody let the cat out of the bag,*" or "*You can kill two birds with one stone,*" might have people from other cultures thinking, "Why are these barbarians bagging cats and killing birds with rocks?" Avoid slang and pop culture idioms that might be misconstrued.

What are the needs of your audience? What are their fears? What drives them? Determine what you want your audience to do as a result of your presentation. Do you want them to think or feel something? Do you want them to take action? The more you know about your audience, the easier it will be to connect and persuade them to your call of action.

—

BE EXCEPTIONAL: Connect Before Your Presentation

The Exceptional Professional knows if you show an interest in your audience, your audience will show an interest in you.

At the beginning of this chapter, I talked about the disastrous presentation at the small college and more successful presentation at the larger university. Besides dropping my opening joke, I also changed what I did *before the presentation*. At the small college, I stood off to the side before the event and reviewed my notes. At the larger university, I used the time before the presentation to mingle with the audience and ask the students, "Where are you from?" "What's your major?" I spent time getting to know them.

Instead of reviewing your notes or cooling your heels offstage, get out in the room and greet people who have arrived early. Mingling time with the audience is also "discovery" time. What you learn about audience members, you can refer to in your presentation.

Have a Conversation, Not a Lecture

My presentations were forever changed by a speaking coach named Dr. Morgan McArthur. I was competing in Toastmasters' International Speech Competition and I hired Dr. McArthur, a previous winner, whose legendary "Stuck to a Bucket" speech was about his decision to give up his career as a large animal veterinarian.

One of the first times I met with Dr. McArthur, we were sitting in chairs facing each other. He pulled up his chair so we were almost sitting knee to knee and said, "Tell me your speech."

I had memorized this seven-minute speech and I went, "Ahh... uhh... buhh..." I forgot my speech. I couldn't remember the opening line.

Then Dr. McArthur said, "I don't want you to *recite* your speech. I want you to *tell me* your speech like you and I are having a conversation and you are telling me the story. I sputtered ineptly through the speech and it took me awhile to get through it, but that exercise was invaluable.

Any presentation is a conversation with the audience. That's all it is. It's just like a one-on-one conversation we would have with a friend.

Think of a really powerful speaker you have heard before: a leader, a coach, a teacher, a preacher, a politician, an activist, a motivational speaker. Did it feel like that person was speaking directly to you? A good speaker makes you feel like he or she is speaking to you one-on-one.

Courage… Courage…

The problem with public speaking for many, is they fear they will fail, before they fail. They think of public speaking as a performance. Who wouldn't get nervous before performing? They become very self-conscious that everyone is looking at them and judging them negatively.

When people are nervous, it shows. Besides vocal tremors, there are many ways people manifest their nervousness in public speaking:

- Pacing
- Scratching their nose, touching their face or hair
- Clasping their hands in front of them
- Knuckle cracking
- Hands in their pockets
- Death grip on the lectern

Another learning point from Dr. McArthur: "Think of one of your best friends. Then picture the audience as a room full of that person." Audience members are not your enemies. They are your friends and they are pulling for you. If your video failed to launch or your laptop crashes, there is not one person in that audience who is not feeling bad for you.

Make eye contact with the audience. Don't look over their heads at the back wall. Some think you have to be constantly scanning the room like a lighthouse. Instead, if you want to make an important point, stop and focus on one person for a moment. Pause, then look to someone else.

Other ways to conquer nervousness:

- When you are introduced, take a deep breath and slowly exhale. This slows down your pounding heart rate.

- Transform nervousness into power in your delivery. Don't worry if you start a little shaky. Keep going.
- Keep your hands busy with gestures that emphasize your words.
- Stop pacing. Plant yourself in one spot for a while, then move to another spot.
- Practice your material over and over. The more you know your material, the less nervous you will be.

Nerves are natural. Even seasoned professional speakers admit they get nervous before each event. Once you get into your presentation, play to the audience. Feed off their energy. If someone is nodding in agreement with you, nod back to that person as you are speaking.

If you are preparing a presentation, try Dr. McArthur's method: sit across from a friend, a family member or one of your co-workers and talk it through, like it is a conversation.

Structure of a Speech

Before we deliver anything, we must structure our speech. If you are not organized, your speech might be scattered like a spilt jar of marbles. Every speech should have these three elements:

1. Introduction
2. Body
3. Conclusion

These are also known as:

1. *Tell them what you are going to tell them* (Introduction)
2. *Tell them* (Body)
3. *Tell them what you told them* (Conclusion)

Create a central theme and have all the points in your speech follow it. The structure is straightforward, so how can we make it interesting?

Grab Attention From The Start

The safe, but dull, predictable opening: *"It's nice to be here. Thanks for having me."* Or, *"I'd like to begin today with..."* Here are some more compelling ways to begin a speech, to grab the audience's attention:

Open with Humor

I have an opening that I call my "flight attendant routine." It goes like this: *"It's great to be a woman in business. Whenever I travel by air, and I'm wearing this suit, I always get mistaken for the flight attendant. I will be walking down the isle of the plane and someone will say, 'Can I get a pillow and blanket?' Or 'Can I get a cup of coffee?' And I tell them, 'You need to ask a flight attendant. There is one down there—'* (Then I do the flight attendant safety briefing point: two fingers or open hand point down the aisle.) *'And two behind me.'"* (Two hands pointing behind me.)

That really happens to me on airplanes. That's why it's funny – it's a comical observation on a true story. I watched flight attendants closely on many flights to perfect that routine. After a talk in Kansas City, a woman said, "I'm a former flight attendant, you did that very well."

Begin with a Question to the Audience

Raise your hand if you are tired of speakers at meetings and conferences asking you to raise your hand. Instead of saying, "Raise your hand, if..." or *"How many of you have...?"* Say, *"Have you ever...?"*

This was a concept I first heard in a workshop given by Patricia Fripp, a past president of the National Speakers Association.

What's the difference? When you say, *"How many of you..."* you are speaking to a set of people within the audience. When you say, *"Have you ever..."* you are speaking to everyone in the audience.

"Have you ever had your lunch stolen out of your workplace fridge?"

Your question to the audience could be hypothetical:

"What if there were a layoff at your organization and as a manager, you had to choose between a good friend and someone more qualified?"

When you ask a question, you are involving the audience. You are bringing them into your scene.

Start with a Story

The story at the beginning of this chapter about bombing with my first paid presentation, is what I sometimes use when speaking to audiences about public speaking. But when you start with a story, you don't have to begin at the beginning. You can begin at the height of the problem, in the middle or the end of the story and work your way back:

"When they gave me the bad news, I was sitting in the waiting room, my hands wrapped around a paper cup, my nose near the edge, breathing in the steam of the coffee. "It's over," he said. "We can't save her. She had a good, long life – you took such good care of her. I am sorry, there is nothing more we can do.... When my 13 year-old Toyota Corolla died on the New Jersey Turnpike, it was like part of me died too."

The last line is the surprise twist on that opening. Did you think I was talking about a car... or a person? Your opening story could be dramatic, outrageous, contentious, heartwarming, sad, happy or funny.

Use Your Own Stories

Many people underestimate the power of their own stories. The worst thing you can do is use fake stories off the Internet.

In the professional speaking industry, they joke about "The Starfish Story." The Starfish Story is about a little boy walking on the beach with thousands of starfish. He is flinging them one by one back into the ocean. Someone says to him, "There are miles of beach and thousands of starfish. You can't possibly make a difference." The boy flings another starfish and says, "It made a difference to that one." Aww!

The Starfish Story is overused and not real. If you find a story on the Internet or if it came from a forwarded junk email, your audience has heard it before. Respect your audience and use original content.

The key to using your own stories is to look for common emotions everyone can relate to: frustration, anger, happiness, joy, helplessness. Or look for common experiences. Everyone has:

- Made mistakes
- Felt ripped off
- Experienced love and loss
- Started a new job
- Worked with a toxic co-worker

Sometimes the ordinary stuff is magic, because it is relatable:

- What was it like for you growing up?
- What was your first job like?
- What was your education like?
- When did you feel challenged in your life?
- What were the lessons you learned along the way?

One warning: as in conversation, no one is as impressed by your kids as you are. If you are talking about parenthood, make it relatable or funny. It can't be about how your genius kids are wise beyond their years or how cute they are. As soon a speaker says, "Then my child said, 'Mommy' or 'Daddy... blah, blah, blah,'" I am looking for the exits.

Be Interactive

The more interactive your presentation, the more memorable it will be. The younger the audience, the more interactive you must be. Here's how:

- Give the audience an activity, challenge or exercise to practice
- Brainstorm: have audience members call out ideas

- Ask the audience to form groups of two or three to discuss a topic
- Create a social media challenge, where audience members post something immediately
- Provide access to a free download, which audience members can access on their phones
- Award prizes for participation

Don't play games or try to make your volunteers from the audience look foolish. When speakers say, "Repeat after me..." most people don't.

Question and Answer

If you have a question and answer session, compliment people on their questions. Change it up. Don't use the same compliment each time.

That's a very good question.
I'm glad you asked that.
Thank you for bringing that up.

Complimenting audience members on their questions:

- Makes the audience member feel smart
- Encourages more people to ask questions (Asking questions in front of a full room can be intimidating.)
- Gives you a moment to collect your thoughts for your answer

Sometimes an audience member wants to give their own speech, rather than ask a question. If someone goes on too long, interrupt. *"I am sorry to interrupt, but did you have a question?"*

Many presenters have a question and answer session at the end of their presentations. When I do presentations, I invite the audience to ask any question at any time throughout the presentation. It makes for a more lively, interactive experience. If you know your material well and you are comfortable with the audience, give this a try.

If you leave time for questions at the end of a presentation, don't let that be the end of your presentation. Have a strong closing planned after the questions, to leave your audience on a high note.

Presenting with Slides

When giving a presentation with slides, stand on the same side of the room as the screen. If you are in the back of the room and the screen is up front, the audience will feel like they are watching a tennis match, back and forth between you and the screen.

Never read your slides to the audience. An events planner for an association once commented to me, "When speakers read their slides to the audience, I want to say, 'Couldn't you just email those to me and I'll read them on my own time?'"

If slides aren't necessary to your presentation, don't use them.

Microphone Form

Somewhere, sometime, somebody will hand you a microphone. You might be in a large audience, asking a question of the speaker. You might be interviewed on stage or serving on a panel. You might be taking part in a video of spontaneous responses. Or you might lose all inhibition at a karaoke bar. In any case, you should know how to hold a hand mic.

I learned how to hold a microphone from Bill Stephens, a professional video producer, when I was participating in the Semifinals for Toastmasters International's World Championship of Public Speaking in Orlando, Florida. Bill produced recordings of Toastmasters' conventions for decades. He is an expert in making people look good.

Bill said not to hold the microphone tightly in your fist, as people do when they are nervous. Hold the middle of the mic lightly with your fingertips in the front and your thumb behind. Hold the microphone just beneath your chin, so anyone taking your photo will capture you and not the microphone.

Do not eat the microphone. Your mouth does not have to be on the mouthpiece for it to pick up your voice. Besides, you don't know where that mouthpiece has been, do you? When I see musicians resting the microphone on their chin or lip, I think, "Gross. Who has to use that microphone next? Who is going to wash that off?"

Other Microphone Options:

- Wireless lavalier that clips onto your lapel
- Wireless headset that fits over your head or over your ear
- Fixed microphone that is attached to a lectern or a mic stand

—

BE EXCEPTIONAL: Move the Mic Stand

The Exceptional Professional is smooth on stage. An interesting little move that I learned from comedian Gavin Jerome is when you take the stage and there is a mic stand, grab the microphone off the stand and with the other hand, move the mic stand out of your way. Set it down just behind you in a quick sweep. Then launch into your presentation.

That way, you are not tripping over the mic stand as you are moving around. I am very clumsy, so it took me a little while to perfect that move, but it really makes a difference.

—

Webinars and The Unseen Audience

I have listened to plenty of webinars, but the first time I presented one was a challenge. I use a lot of humor and stories when I speak, so audience interaction is important to me. But presenting in a webinar, I could not see my audience. I could not hear if they laughed at my jokes or get any feedback. I didn't know if I was killing it or getting killed.

Sometimes webinar participants might see you, but sometimes they won't. In the latter case, your voice is everything. Employ vocal variety – raise your voice, lower it, speed it up, slow it down. Practice your material, to do away with annoying speech tics – uh, um, ah, so... Keep hydrated by drinking little sips of water, because if your mouth is dry, you make smacking noises that a microphone will amplify. When you can't see the audience, you have to imagine them in front of you and speak with animation and enthusiasm.

Near the end of the webinar, a facilitator fielded questions, then read them to me. There were a lot of questions coming in, so that let me know people were engaged. Whew!

Don't multi-task on a webinar. My friend, Terry Harrington, who is a homebuilder, (married to Ben, mentioned in Chapter 2.2), said she could hear keyboard tapping on a webinar. Others noticed it, too. "Participants could read the questions and comments from others," she said. "Several people texted the presenter that the keyboard tapping was annoying. He was struggling with his presentation and equipment. I disconnected."

When Trouble Comes

I was giving a dining tutorial to a group of engineers at a country club and there was a lighted candle on my demo table. I was holding notes in one hand and I accidentally set them on fire. Then my flaming notes set the tablecloth on fire. In my panic, I started trying to pound out the fire with a dinner fork and finally extinguished it with a wet napkin.

It's hard to talk about poise and professionalism when your notes are on fire. When presenting, you have to be ready for anything.

Technical Difficulties

Into our presentations, a few technical difficulties must fall. In case of equipment failure, be able to give your presentation without any slides, video or other digital media. Be ready to work with a hand-held microphone if the lavalier or headset isn't working or work with no microphone if the sound system has gone awry.

To reduce the probability of technical difficulties, arrive at the venue early to test the equipment. Also, bring multiple copies of your slides: on your computer, on a zip drive, in the cloud, etc. Sometimes your presentation can be loaded onto another computer.

Presentation Time Squeeze

You were allotted 40 minutes to give a presentation. But the room was not set up correctly and it took longer than expected to herd all the participants into their seats. When the event did start, the windbag before you, who was supposed to take 10 minutes, took 30.

Some speakers dig in, thinking, "I have critical information to impart – I was prepared to speak for 40 minutes and I am going to take my 40 minutes." Then they speak for an hour. Every person in the room just wants that speaker dead, so they can go to lunch.

When things are not going according to schedule, your time may be cut short. Be prepared to give your 40 minute presentation in 20 minutes or even 10 minutes. If you have a slide show presentation, create a version with half the slides. Practice your presentation and time it. Those who are unprepared, tend to go over time. Be respectful of other people's time, even if your time is cut short.

The Stare Master

Every audience has one. That person who stares you down with either an angry look of contempt or abject boredom. When we see that person, we want to win them over, so we focus on them, to the detriment of the rest of our audience. Don't get distracted by the Stare Master. You can either:

1. Ignore them. Don't let them get to you.
2. Call them out. *"You look skeptical, do you have a question?"*

Sometimes people don't even realize they were making a face. I had a man glaring at me throughout a presentation. Afterwards, he came up to me with the same angry glare and said, "Thank you. I thoroughly enjoyed your presentation." He wasn't angry at all. That must be how he looked all the time. You never know what others are thinking.

The Heckler

The Heckler is like the Stare Master, only verbal. Hecklers interrupt to disagree, boast their own knowledge or make you the butt of their jokes. In any case, they crave attention and they want the floor. When you have a heckler, you have three choices:

1. Ignore them. Stay calm and don't get rattled.
2. Confront them. *"I have material I need to get through. I would be happy to discuss that more with you after the presentation."*
3. Incorporate them into your presentation. *"That was very funny, could you say that a little louder, so everyone can hear?"*

When Your Joke Bombs

When your joke falls flat, that's an opportunity for humor. Growing up, I remember watching Johnny Carson's opening monologue on *The Tonight Show.* Carson was funniest when he was bombing. If a joke failed, he turned it into a self-deprecating joke. Use your failed humor to connect with the audience.

> *"Wow, that one just went..."* (make a noise like airplane crashing)
> *"No one laughed at that... my mother thought it was hilarious."*

Don't be intimidated by larger audiences, because the bigger the audience, the more chances that someone is going to laugh at your jokes.

Audience Drifting Away

Everyone who has ever sat through a presentation by someone who was kill-yourself-boring, knows that it is more like a hostage situation. How do you know if you are boring? No one is going to tell you. (*Darling, I love you, but you're boring.*) Gage your audience's reaction. Here are the warning signs you have lost your audience:

- Glassy-eyed stares
- Emotion draining from the faces
- Nodding off
- Checking phone messages
- Shifting, crossing and uncrossing legs
- Having side conversations
- Folding arms
- Yawning

If you see these signs, stop what you are doing and change direction:

- Throw questions back to the audience to encourage participation.
- Become more animated and move around.
- Change the pace – move a little faster through your presentation.
- Ditch the slides and interact with the audience.

Some will say, "That audience was just rude." Don't make excuses. If you don't have their attention, that's on you. It may be an issue with content or delivery but either way, you need to be more compelling.

Don't be too quick to negatively judge people in the audience who are texting. They might be texting about your talk. Sometimes I'll check *Twitter* after an event and find out audience members were posting positive comments and photos during the event.

What If You Really Are a Bore?

When you talk, your co-workers' eyes glaze over. During your presentations, people nod off. One guy even snored. Before your meetings, attendees say, "Wait, I need some coffee." People only invite you over when they are having trouble getting their kids to sleep.

You have a boring problem. You may be intelligent, have a wealth of information to share and other fine qualities, but if you are boring, you won't get your message across. Avoid the hallmarks of a boring person:

- Boasting
- Talking over people's heads
- Big words, jargon
- Excessive detail
- Complaining

Some speakers go too long. Don't cram too much into your allotted time. Narrow your topic. Take a part of your speech and focus on that.

Sometimes it's not what you say but how you say it. If your voice is monotonous, vary the pitch, tone or inflection. Add emphasis and feeling to words in your sentences. We'll cover this in more detail in the next chapter. Boring doesn't have to be a terminal condition. Always look for ways to be more compelling.

The Toughest Audience: Kids

The toughest audiences are kids. They have a short attention span and some are looking for any opportunity for humor at your expense. When you have to speak to the K-12 range, consult the experts.

I was invited to talk to the home economics classes at a middle school. Before I did, I called a friend who was a substitute teacher at middle schools. She had this insight: "When you are a substitute or guest speaker, you are taking them out of their routine. Their routine is comfortable to them. Start by introducing yourself. Say, "I will give you 60-seconds to ask me any question you want about me. Go."

I have tried this. It's great. The students fire questions immediately, "Are you married? Do you have any kids? Do you have any pets?"

I answer their questions and it's a novel way to break the ice. This helps you make a connection, but after this, you still have work to do.

A Pro In Action

My friend Mark Brown, a Toastmasters World Champion of Public Speaking, is a master at speaking to kids. He gave talks on bullying to middle school and high school students throughout the U.S. I drove two hours to hear him speak at a high school in Denison, Iowa. He stood in the middle of the gym as the students filled the stands. When he began, some students were chattering away. By the time he finished, he had them so mesmerized, you could have heard a pin drop in that gym.

What did he do? He started out with slides with pictures of his family and showed him he had kids around their age. He used a lot of humor. Then, he just kept moving. Mark, a native of Jamaica, who came to the U.S. as a teenager, has this incredible voice and he uses it. He raised his voice, he lowered it, he sang, he laughed, he did imitations.

Next, he became very serious. He read letters from students who had written him about their bullying experiences. He paused dramatically. Some students wiped away tears. He brought them down, but then lifted them up with encouragement and a call for change, which is what great motivational speakers do.

What I learned from watching Mark is that younger people may have a short attention span, but if you keep moving, make it entertaining and make it relatable, you can do well with this audience. It helps to learn from experts like Mark Brown.

BE EXCEPTIONAL: Bring Treats

The Exceptional Professional never goes to school empty handed. I was speaking to a group of high school students in a business education class. Fortunately, I was at an event a few days before where I met a woman who was a business teacher for another high school. I said, "I don't talk to high school students very often. Do you have any advice for me?" She said two words, "Bring treats." She said all these corporate speakers who show up bring snacks or giveaways.

I brought chocolate chip cookies. This school was literally five minutes from my house. I had my coat on and car keys in hand when I pulled these cookies out of the oven, slid them onto a plate and put foil on top. When I handed them out, one of the students said, "These are still warm!" Those high students were like cookie dough in my hands.

Toastmasters: For More Confidence in Speaking

If you want to improve your public speaking skills, join Toastmasters. Toastmasters is a non-profit organization where people meet to practice public speaking. Toastmasters caters to all, from beginners to seasoned speakers. It's a safe, supportive environment and everyone goes at their own pace and chooses their own path.

I joined Toastmasters to improve my speaking skills and to network. It paid off on both accounts. Many fellow Toastmasters have referred me for paid speaking engagements.

Visit several clubs to find one with the right fit for you. Some clubs seem to have people who miss their high school theater days. I prefer the more business-oriented clubs. For more info: www.toastmasters.org.

Get Back Out There

Here is the thing about public speaking: some days you are going to bomb. Pick yourself up, dust yourself off and as Maria Everding says, "Get back out there."

Now that you know the basics of public speaking, next we will talk about how to add extra "oomph" to bring your presentations to life.

8.2 *Enhanced Delivery: Make it Memorable*

I gave a dining tutorial to engineering students at the University of Iowa. This is how I opened my presentation:

> *"My nephew is graduating in a few weeks from another university with a degree in electrical engineering. I asked him, "Jimmy, can you give me any insights into the life of an engineering student?*
> *"He said, 'Can you talk about coming home every night and crying in the shower?'"*

It got a lot of laughs – and a few nervous laughs. But it let the students know, "She's not an engineer but she gets us." I could have said, "My nephew said electrical engineering was very stressful." But his actual quote was more funny and something the students could relate to.

The other thing I did, was use dialogue – I gave the actually quotes from our conversation. Using dialogue, humor and storytelling techniques are just a few ways to enhance your delivery.

The Exceptional Professional knows that public speaking is not just what you say, but how you say it. The difference between an average speaker and one who knocks it out of the park, is found in simple techniques that anyone can put into practice.

In this chapter, you will learn:

- About adding your own humor to presentations
- Storytelling techniques to bring the audience with you
- How to create visual pictures for the audience
- Ways to use more vivid language
- How to stage your presentations

One thing about learning to be a better speaker, is that it made me a better writer. That is a benefit I hope you will get out of this chapter, too.

Using Humor in Speeches

Humor is great tool for business speaking with many benefits, including:

- Humor relaxes your audience.
- Humor helps you be more relatable.
- Humor makes your content memorable.

If your audience remembers the funny story, they will remember the point behind it. But use your own humor. Don't grab jokes from the Internet or steal other's material – it hurts your credibility. Give credit where credit is due.

Where Do We Get Humor?

Humor is all around us. We just have to open our eyes to it.

Here are some sources for humor and examples:

1. Your pain: mistakes, embarrassment, stress, awkward situations
   "There are no cars in sight, until you wander out into the middle of your driveway in your pajamas to retrieve a far-flung newspaper."
   "Nothing says, 'I'm single and I give up,' like getting a cat... my cat's name is Snowball."
2. Pet peeves: what drives you crazy drives others crazy too
   "We already have driverless cars. I was almost hit by a woman behind the wheel with a phone in one hand and a latte in the other."
   My friend Bill Telle says, *"I have this nightmare that I am going to wake up one day, looking like my driver's license."*
3. Ordinary events or disruptions to ordinary events
   My sister, Maureen, says: *"I'd love to homeschool my kids, if I could just drop them off at someone else's home."*
   "Women's tennis players let out a primal scream with every hit. Why must the audience be quiet, when the players are screaming?"

The most successful stand-up comedians have humor that is about every day, mundane things that happen to all of us. Comedian Bill Connolly, author of *Funny Business, Build Your Soft Skills Through Comedy*, says, "Don't try to be funny in your presentations, try to be human. Create real connections that are relatable to your audience, and inevitably, humor will result. Life is funny enough to draw upon, there is no need to overthink it. People appreciate when someone is clearly sincere in their presentation. It makes a big difference."

Put Awkward Situations in Your Presentations

Many people say, "I am not funny. I can't tell jokes." If that's what you think, you are the perfect candidate to do humor. If people don't expect it, you will be that much funnier.

After an etiquette presentation, an older woman said to me, "You are really funny. I saw you in that suit and thought you were going to be *a real stiff.*" There's truth in what she said. Some people see a suit and expect me to be boring. When I say something funny, it's funny because they didn't expect it. Humor is about incongruity: what's unexpected is funny. No insult is wasted if it can be used again. The woman calling me a "stiff in a suit" became fodder for future presentations.

Self-deprecating Humor is Best

Make fun of yourself, not others. Laugh at yourself and your mistakes.

> *"When I was a student at the University of Iowa, I was thrown out of Ballet II. On the first day, they showed us a routine, then the piano started up. The class went this way. I went that way. When I reached the hallway, the teacher shut the door behind me."*

At the time, it was not funny. Have you ever heard of the equation: Comedy = Tragedy + Time? (I have heard it attributed to many sources, but the earliest seems to be actor Steve Allen.)

How Do You Know It's Funny?

Test your humor in ordinary conversations. Don't preface it with, "Tell me if this is funny..." Just work the story into normal conversations. Did others laugh? If they didn't, the audience might not either.

Capture Humor

When you think of something funny, write it down. I have kept humor notebooks since college. When I think of something funny, hear a funny story or a funny line, I write it down. I don't worry about wordsmithing or making it perfect, I just capture it. When I need inspiration, I flip through those notebooks. Some of those stories ended up in this book.

Let the Audience Be Funny

Sometimes the audience is funnier than you. You have to let the audience be funny. It shows they are involved and having a good time.

At a middle school, I used my routine where I take out a big, colorful, toy "Elmo" (from *Sesame Street*) cell phone and carry on a fake conversation. After I finished, a young lady asked, *"I'd just like to know how long you've been seeing Elmo?"* It made the class laugh. It made me laugh. I said, "Good one!" Don't compete with your audience to prove you are funnier. Incorporate their humor into your presentation.

BE EXCEPTIONAL: Don't Step on the Laughter

My good friend Bill Telle, a talented speaker and songwriter, advised me, "Don't step on the laughter." That means if you have the audience laughing, don't interrupt them. *The Exceptional Professional* savors the moment and waits for the laughter to die down before continuing on to the next point.

That's different from stand-up comedy. I learned from comedian Gavin Jerome, that laughter comes in waves. After a joke, the laughter rises, peaks, then begins to fall. A skilled comedian launches into that next joke before the laughter dies down completely. The trick is to time it right, so you don't start the next joke while the audience laughter is at its peak. It's useful to master both of these techniques.

Storytelling: Take the Audience with You

Storytellers enhance a presentation by bringing the audience along for the ride. They put you in their scene by appealing to your senses and emotions, acting out and using both literary and vocal techniques.

Use Facial Expressions

Unless you are a sociopath, you have facial expressions. Use your expressions to emphasize what you are saying.

Every parent has a look that can stop their kids in their tracks. You don't even have to utter the words, "You are in so much trouble," because your look says it. Aunts, uncles and neighbors can give "the look," too. Stand before a mirror and practice that look.

Look surprised – someone catches you off guard. Do your eyes open wider? Do you step back? Does your mouth fall open? Say out loud, "I didn't know what to do!" What is your bewildered look?

You are dressed up for a client meeting and waiting to cross a street. A car comes flying through a curbside puddle and showers you with muddy water. What is your aggravated look? Do you roll your eyes? Do you exhale? Do you grimace? Let your expressions do the talking.

Gestures: Talk with Your Hands

Some people aren't sure what to do with their hands while they are speaking, so they put their hands in their pockets or they grip the lectern.

Just let go. We all know people who we would say, "Talk with their hands." While they are speaking, their hands move effortlessly. Let your hands flow naturally with what you are saying. If your gestures are too mechanical or robotic, they will be distracting.

Extend your arms to their length and use your full range of motion. Channel nervous energy into deliberate movements. Use gestures for emphasis on key points or no gestures when making a serious point.

Act It Out

When talking about networking, I ask my audience, *"What happens when you meet someone and they do this? 'Ah-choo!'"* (I pretend to sneeze into my hand, then hold out my hand for a handshake.)

People in the audience cringe. "Eiwwww!"

I could have said, "What if someone sneezes into their hand, then wants to shake your hand?" But the visual is more effective. Create visual pictures for your audience by acting things out as you speak. This is taking gestures to the next level. Try acting out these scenarios:

> *"I was driving to work."* (Show two hands on a pretend steering wheel.)
> *"I got my cup of coffee."* (Grasp an imaginary coffee cup, take a drink.)
> *"I ran through the airport to make my connection."* (Pump your arms.)
> *"I was waiting in a long line."* (Be impatient or look ahead in line.)

Always think of ways to make your presentation more visual. It need not be an Oscar-winning performance. You can act out emotions, too: "Ugh! I was so frustrated!" (Grit your teeth. Clench your fists.) Check back in with the audience: "Have you ever felt that way?"

BE EXCEPTIONAL: Stage Your Presentation

The Exceptional Professional moves with the story. The ultimate goal is to get out from behind the lectern. Sometimes we have no choice. The microphone is fixed to the lectern and that's where we stay.

But if it is possible to get a wireless lavalier (clip-on) mic or a head set, get out and move around. The lectern is a barrier between you and the audience. If you want to bond with your audience, get close to your audience.

Too many speakers will burn up a single line in the stage, pacing back and forth. Stage your talk. If there are different locations in your story, move to different parts of the speaking area to emphasize those changes. If there are different points you are trying to make, move to different parts of the speaking area to emphasize those points.

As part of *The Des Moines Register*'s "Storyteller Project," I told the story of two restaurants where I worked one summer during college. Each restaurant had a spot on the stage where I stood when I was talking about that restaurant.

If your format is problem and solution, your problem could be in one spot and your solution in another. Or you could start and end from the same spot. The key is to make your movements so fluid that the audience can't tell it's staged, but they feel the effects.

Appeal to the Senses

In the previous chapter, I mentioned my speaking coach, Dr. Morgan McArthur. The first time I heard him speak, he was giving a workshop on storytelling. He talked about the "creak" of a barn door and "crunch" of the snow underfoot. Those words bring you into his story by appealing to your senses. The five senses to which you can appeal are: sight, smell, sound, touch and taste.

Try this exercise: describe your favorite restaurant using all five senses. For example, let's think about an Italian restaurant:

- **Sight**: a family-owned restaurant, red and white checked tablecloths, red-glass candles on the tables and family pictures on the wall
- **Smell**: an aroma of spaghetti sauce, garlic and fresh baked bread
- **Sound**: noisy, you can hear people shouting to each other in the kitchen, the dining room is full of customers engaged in conversation
- **Touch**: the freshly baked rolls are almost too hot to handle and still steaming as you break off a piece, the vinyl tablecloths feel slippery

- **Taste**: the restaurant's signature sauce is meaty with just a hint of tomato, the house salad dressing is so heavy on the garlic that you'll still be breathing it, even after you brush your teeth

Think of other scenarios you might describe for the five senses. You don't need all the senses in every description, but try two or three.

Senses don't always have to be positive. A friend of mine grew up on a hog farm in northern Iowa. She and her siblings complained about the nasty, pervasive smell you couldn't get out of your nostrils. Her father, breathing deeply, would say, *"You know what that is? That's the smell of money."* (If you know anyone who raises hogs, they all say that.)

Create Visual Pictures with Literary Techniques

Another lesson I learned from Morgan McArthur is how to produce pictures for an audience using literary techniques.

In a 2017 commencement address at Iowa State University for the College of Veterinary Medicine, he talked about how he never learned anything from "the cozy cocoon of comfort." He mentioned how early in his career, he was "jelly-legged at the prospect of public speaking."

You might not have thought of the word "alliteration" when you read that, but you probably liked the way it sounded. You don't have to be an English major to incorporate these simple literary techniques to enhance your story. (I was an English major, *so I love this part.*)

Use Metaphors

Metaphors are a comparison of two dissimilar items, where you liken one to the other. Metaphors make your content more memorable.

I ordered the mega macchiato with the Matterhorn of whipped cream.
The professor could have left it with the letter grade. Instead, he threw a lifeline to a lost undergrad adrift in a sea of 30,000 students.

Vivid Language

Using more vivid language adds color to your content. Can you take an ordinary phrase and make it stronger with other words? Take the sentence: *The lights went out and we were in the dark.* And add more vivid language: *The lights went out and we were engulfed in darkness.*

Word choice makes a difference – vivid language produces more powerful images.

To Draw People Near, Please the Ear

Certain literary techniques are pleasing to the ears. People like the sound, but they often don't know why.

Rhyming

Do you remember having children's books read to you when you were little? Many of them had words with similar sounds. Rhyming works well for your presentations because it has a soothing sound.

> *Innovations in communications were supposed to bring us closer.*
> *With notes shaking and knees quaking, I pioneered through my frontier of fear.*

You don't need to be Dr. Seuss. Use rhyming words in small, subtle doses. A great resource for rhyming words: www.rhymer.com

Alliteration

Alliteration is the repetition of similar sounds of closely connected words. Instead of "We will cover table manners," I will say, "We will *tackle* table manners." (repeating the "t" sound) Here are other examples:

> *In fifth grade, I was skinnier than the science-class skeleton.* (s-sound)
> *We go throughout our day with so many digital distractions.* (d-sound)

Think about rhyming and alliteration when you are coming up with a clever title for a presentation or even a catchy email subject line.

Use Dialogue

Instead of saying, "He told me that..." Put a voice to the person, by using a quote. Dialogue gives your story a little more punch.

> Example: *She told me she did not want the dog in the house.*
> Better with Dialogue: *She said, "Get that dog out of the house!"*

Add Other Voices

Dialogue is even stronger if you can mimic someone else's voice. If you can do multiple voices and make each one unique, even better.

Some will say, *"I can't do voices."* Start with those you love and know best. Everyone can imitate their spouse, parents, kids or siblings.

I can think of my father's deep, sonorous voice. In high school, if you brought home a date to meet him, he would shout across the house to my mother, *"Ree, shall I ASK HIM if his intentions are HONORABLE?"*

Who else can you imitate? A celebrity? A teacher? A neighbor? It takes some practice, but it adds to your story if you can vary the voices.

Vocal Techniques to Enhance Your Storytelling

Nothing induces sleep faster than speakers who speak in a monotone, with no vocal variance. Don't be that speaker. Change it up.

Change the Volume

Raise or lower your voice for dramatic impact.

> (Loud): *I opened the door and stepped out onto the rooftop and felt the sun on my face. The view was incredible!* (Soft) *Then I realized the door had shut and locked behind me.*

Lowering your voice causes your audience to listen more intently. I have heard speakers lower their voices to almost a whisper, even though they are speaking in a huge auditorium.

Change the Tone

Tone is the character or mood of your voice. What emotions does your voice convey? Is your voice happy, solemn, excited, angry, shocked?

Let's look at a change in tone with the earlier example:

> (Excited, exhilarated): *I opened the door and stepped out onto the rooftop and felt the sun on my face. The view was incredible!* (uh-oh, disbelief) *Then I realized the door had shut and locked behind me.*

Change the Pace

Speed up the pace or slow it down. Here is an example of a change in pace I used to describe a car crash, where a large truck slid on the ice and hit my car, when I was at a stoplight:

> *(Fast talk, panicky) My car was HELPLESSLY, HOPELESSLY penned in! A car in front of me, a car behind me. (Normal rate) Have you ever seen a crash coming in (Slow down) slooowww moootion and had your life flash before your eyes?*

Pause and Effect

One of the greatest speech techniques anyone can master is the "pause." It's a moment or more of silence before you continue. A pause creates anticipation for what you are going to say next. Sometimes a pause gives your audience time to soak up what you said and reflect on it:

> *Have you ever had a bad boss?* (pause) This gives the audience time to think of their own experiences.

Pausing also helps you work out speech tics, like "Ah," "Um" or "So." Instead if using those filler words, try to pause instead.

Vocal Quality

If your voice is too shrill: practice reading something boring, like a textbook or encyclopedia. I've heard some people suggest Shakespeare but I like Shakespeare. I would suggest Ralph Waldo Emerson.

One of my cousins used to read *The Wall Street Journal* to his children in an animated voice, as if he were reading a children's book. *"And then, the Dow Jones Industrial Average rose 100 points, due to a surge in Consumer Staples..."*

Enunciate or pronounce each syllable. When you enunciate, you say, "lit-er-ature" instead of, "litter-chur." And when speaking about the weather, say, "temp-er-ature" instead of "temper-chur."

Pronounce the "ing." Instead of "*Doin', goin'...*" say, *"Doing, going..."*

Say, "You," not "ya." Instead of "*Do ya', can ya', will ya*?" Say, *"Do you, can you, will you?"*

As I mentioned earlier, learning to be a better speaker can make you a better writer. The next logical step in our professional journey is to look at writing in business. If you like writing, you will enjoy it. If writing intimidates you, well, just dip a little toe in the pool of the next chapter. It's easier than you think.

THE WRITE STUFF

9.1 *Better Business Writing*

My father once had a cardiac event at home and paramedics were called. As the paramedics moved him onto a stretcher, one said, "Lay down."

My father replied, "I think you mean lie."

"What did he say?" asked the paramedic.

"Never mind," said my sister the nurse, who was helping prepare him for the ambulance.

My father was a doctor, a scholar and a motorcycle hill climbing enthusiast. But foremost, he was a grammarian. If you said, "I am going to *lay* down," he would reply, "Then I expect there to be eggs when you get up."

Studying grammar was a lifelong practice for my father, because he knew, as *The Exceptional Professional* knows, that grammar determines one's station in life. The same goes for writing skills.

In this chapter, you will learn:

- How to write a memorable thank you note
- When to type or handwrite correspondence
- How to write, proofread and format a business letter
- The stationery you need as you advance
- A little bit about grammar

Writing can seem daunting, so we'll start with the simplest and most essential form of business correspondence: the thank you note.

It's Wise to Personalize

When I teach business writing, I read out loud two thank you notes. The first, from a client, who handed me the note before a presentation:

> *"Dear Callista, I would like to thank you for taking the time to speak at our conference. We appreciate your help in making our event a great success."*

The second, from a sixth grader, after a presentation at his school:

> *"Dear Ms. Gould, Thank you for telling me the proper way to use a napkin. My mom really appreciates it."*

Looking at those two, who wrote the more personal thank you note? The sixth grader was more personal, because he mentioned specific content from my presentation and that he discussed it with his mom.

The other note, written before my presentation, could have been for any speaker at the conference. I could have kicked over the lectern, set fire to the stage and had everyone screaming and running for the exits and still, I would have had a note saying I made the event a great success. If a sixth grader can write a better thank you note, you can too.

Writing a Thank You Note

Start with a fold-over note. If you fret over what to write in a thank you note, follow this easy formula. A basic thank you note is just three lines:

> Line 1: *Thank you for* ________
> Line 2: *It meant a great deal to me because* ________
> Line 3: *Thank you again!*

That's it. Don't overthink it. Knock it out and mail it. Some want to text it, tweet it or email it. But fold-over notes linger longer.

Keep a box of fold-over notes on hand in your workplace and at home. If you don't have them, any corner pharmacy store sells them.

Art museum shops have nice ones. If you are a manager or aspire to be one, you should have a box of note cards ready.

How Late is Too Late?

"I am about six months late in writing a thank you note. Is that too late? Should I just forget it?"

That was an excellent question from a college student in one of my dining tutorials. Many etiquette books say we have a year to write a thank you note. It's more advantageous to write that note as soon as possible. When you write a thank you within 24-hours, the sentiment is still fresh in your mind and you will write a better note.

Is it embarrassingly late? Write it anyway. Sometimes it will be a pleasant surprise to the person who has long given up on you. We all have those thank you notes we should have written. Make today your day. While it's in your head, get out a note card or some stationery and fire it off. One caveat: do not ask for favors in a thank you note.

Reasons for a Thank You Note

What do you write thank you notes for?

- Gifts received
- Help on projects
- Recommendations written
- Client referrals
- Informational interviews
- Acts of kindness or generosity
- Mentoring
- Classes well taught
- Dinner at someone's home
- Any meals or entertainment paid for by someone else
- Jobs well done
- To show appreciation

"Can't I email or text it and be done?" ask the digitally immersed. You could email or text a thank you, but your little effort means little. And generic, pre-printed, "Thank you for your thoughtful gift," cards are insulting. (Were you responding to a generic, pre-printed card that said, "Congratulations on your happy occasion?") The written note means more. It's not too late. Write that note.

Handwrite or Type?

When sending letters by mail (postal, not the celebrated e-kind), it's good to know when to type it or handwrite it. Here are some guidelines:

Type:

- Business correspondence
- Thank you notes for interviews or contracts
  (There's more about the post-interview thank you note in Chapter 12.1: *Interviewing: Misfires, Inspires and Attire.*)

Handwrite: (using dark blue or black ink)

- Thank you notes for gifts and other acts of kindness
- Replies to formal invitations
- Condolence letters
- Expressions of love (not in the workplace, please)

How to Write a Better Business Letter

First, we'll look at the content of a business letter and how to edit it. Then we'll cover how to format it.

As with everything in this book, we go back to the core principle of professionalism: make the people around you comfortable. Write the business letter you would want to read.

1. State your purpose early
2. Use plain language
3. Personalize it

4. **State your purpose early**

   What is your purpose for the communication?

Make a pitch	Collaborate
Set up a meeting	Send additional information
Follow up	Clarify
Check in on a client	Invite

   "I'm writing to follow up on our conversation yesterday."
   "Attached is the contract you requested."

5. **Use plain language**

   Keep it simple. Don't try to impress with more complicated words that people might trip over when they are reading. Some examples:

   "Use" instead of *"utilize."*
   I was watching a major sports network cover a college basketball game and one of the color commentators used the word "utilize" repeatedly, even saying, *"If he utilized a little more patience..."*

   "Agree" instead of *"concur"*
   Some people stumble over "concur." It means "to agree." But the "con" makes people think it means the opposite, like "contrary." (Contrary is from the Latin "contra" which means "against." Concur is from the Latin "concurrere" which means "to run together.")

   "Irregardless" is not a word. The word is *"regardless."*
   I worked for a manager who would frequently say, *"Irregardless of the circumstances..."* It caused a lot of eye rolling around the conference table.

6. **Personalize it**

   People crave connection. Make people feel like you are talking to them and not just anyone.

   Generic: *"As a follow up to our meeting, here is additional information on the plan."*

   Personalized: *"Attached is the schedule and distribution channels we talked about. Thank you for taking time to meet with me."*

   "I will follow up with you when you are back in the office on the week of June 8th. Enjoy your vacation."

   Personalize with other details you remember from the conversation:

   "I enjoyed your story about your first job in manufacturing."

   When you personalize it, that says to the person, "I was listening."

BE EXCEPTIONAL: Reduce "I"s and Make it About Them

It's not about you. Well, sometimes it is. As *The Exceptional Professional,* you just don't let everyone else know it's about you.

When you review emails, business letters or speeches, reduce the number of sentences or paragraphs that start with "I." Review your letter and think, "How can I rephrase some of these?"

"I" focused: *"I would like to tell you about our new product..."*
Change to "you" focused: *"There is a new product we offer..."*

"I" focused: *"I wanted to congratulate you on your promotion..."*
Change to "you" focused: *"Congratulations on your promotion..."*

You don't have to eliminate all the "I"s, but reduce the number.

Don't Forget the Magic Words

Remember to write, "Please," and "Thank you."

> *"Thank you for seeing me on such short notice."*
> *"Please let me know if you have any questions."*

Writer's Block

What happens when you feel stuck and can't think of what to write? Ann Humbert, my predecessor at Amana Appliances, advised, "Pretend like you are explaining it to your mother." I always found that helpful.

Think out loud what you would say if you were talking to someone, then write it down. Don't edit as you go. Get your thoughts on the page – *splat!* Then edit.

Editing Your Correspondence

We have a draft. Now it's time to edit.

To Proofread Any Document, Read it Twice

Proofread, so it's easy to read. A little extra time can save you from a bad impression that lasts a lifetime. Read over documents twice. Read first for grammar, then second, to see if the words make sense.

First: Read for Grammar

I work with a lot of career services professionals at universities and they say the number one complaint from employers is that students contact them with sloppy emails full of texting jargon, misspelled words and grammatical errors. Proofread your email first for grammar:

- Are you using correct punctuation: periods, commas, question marks and even an occasional exclamation point?
- Did you correctly use words like, there/their, to/too/two, our/ are,
- where/wear/ware, its/it's? (It's "it's" if you can break it into "it is.")
- Did you eliminate duplicate or excess words from prior edits?
- Did you split run-on sentences into smaller sentences? (A run-on sentence has too many thoughts crammed into one sentence.)

Grammar and spell check features are helpful. But never rely on these completely. They often get it wrong and miss errors.

Second: Read to Ensure It Makes Sense

Recite each word slowly and deliberately, so you hear each word and how they connect. Mistakes are overlooked when you hear your "composing" voice and what you meant to say, instead of reading the actual words.

Eliminate Excess Words

In Chapter 2.2: *How to Prevail on Email,* I introduced the idea of writing so our correspondence could be read quickly to respect the reader's time. The best way is to eliminate excess words. *Draft it, then half it.*

Exercise: In the following sample paragraph, strike through as many excess words as you can find, without moving words around or adding additional words. Try not to peek at the solution below.

> *When you hand someone a business card, you should hand it between your thumb and your index finger, with the words on the card facing towards the person you are handing it to. When you are in China, you should hand someone a business card with two hands and then when someone hands you a business card, you should receive the business card with two hands.* (66 words)

How did you do? You should be able to pare it down to 35 words. Below is the solution and how the paragraph reads without the excess words.

Edited Solution:

> ~~**When you**~~ *Hand someone a business card*~~**, you should hand it**~~ *between your thumb and* ~~**your**~~ *index finger, with the words* ~~**on the card**~~ *facing* ~~**towards**~~ *the person* ~~**you are handing it to**~~. ~~**When you are**~~ *In China,* ~~**you should**~~ *hand someone a business card with two hands and* ~~**then when someone hands you a business card, you should**~~ *receive a business card with two hands.*

After Eliminating Excess Words:

> *Hand someone a business card between your thumb and index finger, with the words facing the person. In China, hand someone a business card with two hands and receive a business card with two hands.*
> (35 words)

Other Excess Words to Eliminate

The easiest excess words to eliminate are "I think" and "in my opinion".

If you are writing it, of course it's your opinion. There may be instances to use, "I think," but most of the time it comes off as wishy-washy.

One of the first words I eliminate, is "that." Find excess "thats," by reading sentences without "that." *I told him ~~that~~ networking is more effective than online applications.*

Here are other excess words:

> "In order to" *In order to start the engine...* Edited: *To start the engine...*
> "Absolutely" *That is absolutely true.* Edited: *That is true.*
> "Really" *It's really not necessary.* Really?

There's also the redundant phrases:

> "Added bonus" – if it's a bonus, it is added
> "Past experience" – if it's experience, it's usually in the past
> "End result" – the result is something that comes at the end

Reduce Syllables or Characters

Simplify words to make your letter faster to read:

- *"insignificant"* (5 syllables) change to: *"minor"* (2 syllables) or *"trivial"* (3 syllables)
- *"considerable"* (5 syllables) change to *"large"* (1 syllable) or *"substantial"* (3 syllables)
- *"meticulous"* (4 syllables) change to *"careful"* or *"detailed"* (2 syllables)

Best place to practice eliminating excess words? *Twitter* with its 280 character limit.

Formatting a Business Letter: Full Block Style

The most popular business letter format is called *Full Block Style.* It's easy to remember because everything is lined up against the left margin. (See Example Format on the next page.)

Use Full Block Style for cover letters to thank you letters and any other business correspondence. *Modified Block Style* has the date and closing lined up closer to the right side of the page. Another variation is to indent the beginning of each paragraph five spaces.

Full Block Style

Date (month, day year – spelled out)
(space two lines)

Name of person you are addressing
Title
Organization
Address
City, State Zip (two spaces between State and Zip)
(space two lines)

Dear __________: (This is the Salutation.)
(space two lines)
(This is the Body or text of the letter – lines single spaced, one extra line space between paragraphs.)
(space two lines)
Sincerely, (This is the Closing.)
(space three lines - place written signature here after printing out the letter)

Name of person writing letter
Title of person writing letter
(Include your address and phone number if it is not on the letterhead. You might include your email, too.)

Salutations

A business letter begins with the "salutation" or greeting. Should a colon or comma be used in a salutation? Use a colon with a formal business letter or email, especially when contacting someone you don't know well. *Dear Mr. Spire:*

Use a colon or a comma with people who are more familiar to you.

Dear Ms. Tower: or Dear Belle:
Dear Ms. Tower, or Dear Belle,

Punctuation for an even less formal salutation might be:

Hi, Max, or *Max*—

With people who are completely unfamiliar:

To The Consumer Affairs Department:

Always try to find the name of the person you are trying to reach. If you are unable to discover a name, use the title, section or division. Avoid, *"To whom it may concern."* It may not concern anyone.

Honorifics

Use honorifics (Mr., Ms., Dr., etc.) until the person gives permission to use their first name. In general, if someone seems old enough to be your parent, use the honorific.

Closings

Ever get to the end of a letter and ask yourself, "How do I end this?" There are many ways to close a business letter:

Best closing for a business letter:
Sincerely, Sincerely yours, Very sincerely,

Also appropriate for business and slightly more personal:
Yours truly, or Very truly yours,

Acceptable, but a little on the chilly side:
Cordially or Cordially yours,

To someone you know well, but not are not that close with:
Regards, Warm regards, Kindest regards, Best wishes, All the best, As always, As ever,

For a family member or close friend:
Love, With much love, Fondly, AffectionatΩely, Affectionately yours,

Addressing clergy or members of high political office:
Respectfully, or Respectfully yours, Faithfully, Faithfully yours,

Thanking someone:
Gratefully, Gratefully yours

The Flap on Envelopes

When mailing a business letter through postal mail, the return address should be on the front of the envelope in the upper left corner. When sending a personal letter by mail, the return address should be on the back flap of the envelope. A typical address on the envelope has:

(Mr., Ms., Dr....) and person's name
The person's title
Name of the organization
Address of the organization
City, ST Zip Code

An honorific is not used, if a professional title follows the name:

Right: *Dr. Charlie Horse* or *Charlie Horse, M.D.*
Wrong: *Dr. Charlie Horse, M.D.*

If a letter is typed, the envelope should be typed. If the letter is handwritten, the envelope should be handwritten. But I'll let you in on a little secret: I handwrite all my envelopes, because handwritten envelopes usually get opened first.

How to Stuff It

You print out your business letter and proofread it – it's perfect! It's the most stunning business letter ever (and it only took five printings.) You fold it and it goes terribly wrong. It won't fit in the envelope.

A business letter is folded in thirds. Take the bottom edge of the stationery and place it two-thirds of the way up the page (or one-third from the top) and press down to make the fold. Then take the top edge of the stationery and fold it over. Another way, is to place the stationery next to the envelope as you are bringing up the bottom edge for the first fold. Then fold the top of the letter over.

Place the letter in the envelope, with the open side facing the back of the envelope, so when the recipient slides it out, it opens toward them. Place a fold-over notecard in an envelope fold side down, so the opening is at the top of the envelope. The front of the notecard should face the back of the envelope.

Forms of Address

How someone is addressed in a salutation sometimes differs from how that person is addressed on an envelope or in person. People who are out of office, still retain their title. Example: a former governor is still addressed as "Governor (last name)." Here are examples of how different people are addressed in letters vs. in person:

Title	Envelope Address	Letter Salutation	Addressing in Person
Any person, no title	Mr. or Ms. Client	Dear Mr. Client: or Ms. Client:	Mr. or Ms. Client
Medical doctor	Dr. Carson Noyed or Carson Noyed, M.D. or D.O.	Dear Dr. Noyed:	Dr. Noyed
Professor – PhD	Dr. Paige Turner or Paige Turner, PhD	Dear Dr. Turner:	Dr. Turner
Professor – non-PhD	Prof. August Lecture or Mr. August Lecture	Dear. Professor Lecture:	Professor Lecture
Dean, Associate Dean or Assistant Dean	Mack Ademia, Dean (or Associate or Assistant Dean)	Dear Dean Ademia:	Dean Ademia
Attorney	Ms. Dee Facto or Dee Facto, Esq.	Dear Ms. Facto:	Ms. Facto
Judge	The Honorable Judge Justin Case	Dear Judge Case:	Judge Case
Justice	Justice Gilda Cage	Dear Justice Cage:	Justice Cage or Madam Justice
Chief Justice	The Chief Justice of the Supreme Court	Dear Mr. or Madam Chief Justice:	Mr./Madam Chief Justice
U.S. Senator	The Honorable Marc Thyme	Dear Senator Thyme:	Senator Thyme or Senator
U.S. Representative	The Honorable Carmel Korn	Dear Ms. Korn:	Ms. Korn
Governor	The Honorable Rich Fields	Dear Governor Fields: or Dear Governor:	Governor Fields or Governor
State Senator	The Honorable Ginger Root	Dear Senator Root:	Senator Root
State Representative	The Honorable Otto Maddock	Dear Mr. Maddock:	Mr. Maddock
Mayor	The Honorable Ann Oversight Mayor of Nicetown	Dear Mayor Oversight: or Dear Madam	Mayor Oversight
Ambassador	The Honorable Cary Water	Dear Mr. Ambassador:	Mr. Ambassador

Honorable Mention

"The Honorable" is a title given to those elected or appointed to high office at the federal, state or city levels. This includes cabinet members, heads of federal agencies (but not heads of divisions or bureaus of a department), ambassadors, senators, representatives, governors, mayors and judges. When sending correspondence to these, "The Honorable" appears on the first line and the person's name on the second line:

The Honorable
Harold P. Goodwill
House of Representatives
(address)

Exceptions: correspondence to the president and vice president of the United States and the chief justice and associate justices of the Supreme Court are addressed with their titles. With the first three of these, the person's name is not necessary.

The President (or The Vice President)
The White House

The Chief Justice
The Supreme Court

Example for Associate Justice:
Justice Harold P. Lawful
The Supreme Court

BE EXCEPTIONAL: Stationery You Need as You Move Up

Letterhead and fold-over notes are staples for any person in business. *The Exceptional Professional* also looks to the future and additional stationery, like Monarch Stationery for executives.

Letterhead (8 ½ x 11 inches)
This is the standard business stationery that everyone uses. Letterhead usually has an organization's logo, as well as the address and contact.

Fold-over Notes (usually 6 x 4 inches, but it varies)
Fold-over notes are for handwritten thank yous and can be used for other types of notes. Some people in business have personalized fold-over notes with their name or initials printed or engraved on them.

Correspondence Cards (6 ½ x 4 ½ inches)
Correspondence cards are around the same size as a fold-over note, without the fold-over. They are a little less formal and can be used for thank you notes, invitations or brief notes.

Monarch Stationery (7 ½ x 10 ½ inches)
Monarch stationery is slightly smaller than letterhead. It's used by executives, who usually have their name printed on it.

You may use your organization's official stationery for personal notes related to business. Do not use it without permission for personal correspondence that might be misconstrued as coming from your organization, such as a letter to the editor, a political endorsement or letter of complaint, lawsuit, etc.

Grammar Helpers

This chapter began with the story of my father correcting the paramedic who said, "Lay down," instead of "Lie down."

Thanks to the knowledge and professionalism of the paramedics, my father didn't leave us that day. When he did pass away, several years later, one of the legacies he left us was that our grammar education didn't end in the sixth grade. It's a life-long practice.

My father peppered us with grammar questions. Coming home from college, before you dropped your bag, he would say, "Tell me the difference between *lie* (to recline) and *lay* (to put something down)."

Today, I lie down. (present tense)
Yesterday, I lay down. (past)
In the past, I have lain down. (past participle)
Today, I lay the book down. (present)
Yesterday, I laid the book down. (past)
In the past, I have laid the book down. (past participle)

Grammar is about credibility. Would you invest with a financial planner who says, "Me and him have a financial plan if yours ain't producing real good returns?" Employers regularly pigeonhole resumes and cover letters full of grammatical errors. What kind of errors would these people make if hired?

Instead of tackling all grammar, I'll cover one that made my *Etiquette Tip of the Week* readers howl, when I asked about bothersome buzzwords. It's the confusion over pronouns used as subjects and objects. Then I will give some good sources for grammar.

Is it I? Or Is it Me?

He/she and I? Or he/she and me? Without going into too much detail:

"I" is a subject, which creates the action.
"Me" is an object, which receives the action.

Rudolph and I excel at reindeer games. ("I" am the subject.)
Rudolph and me excel at reindeer games. (Incorrect)

The other reindeer were nasty to Rudolph and me. ("Me" is the object.)
The other reindeer were nasty to Rudolph and I. (Incorrect)

Another way: separate it into two sentences.
Rudolph excels at reindeer games. I excel at reindeer games.
(You wouldn't say, *"Me excel at reindeer games."*)

Where it gets tricky:

> *Rudolph is better at reindeer games than I.* (Correct)
> *Rudolph is better at reindeer games than me.* (Incorrect*)

Complete the sentence in your head:

> *Rudolph is better at reindeer games than I am at reindeer games.*
> (*Here's where grammarians split hairs. If "than" is used as a conjunction, it's "than I." If "than" is a preposition, it's "than me.")

Instead of Rudolph, try a pronoun:

> "He" is the subject.
> "Him" is the object.

> *He and I excel at reindeer games.* (*He excels at reindeer games. I excel at reindeer games.*)
> Not: *Him and I excel at reindeer games.* Certainly not: *"Me and him…"*

Painless, right? You and I are going places.

A Few Good Grammar References

To improve your grammar, do so by increments. Grammar books are not to be read like novels. Pick one topic or one chapter a week and study it.

> *The Elements of Style* by William Strunk, Jr. and E.B. White
> *Booher's Rules of Business Grammar* by Dianna Booher
> *Associated Press Style Book* or *Chicago Style Book*

Online sources:

Purdue University Online Writing Lab (OWL): owl.english.purdue.edu
Grammar for Dummies online: www.dummies.com/education/language-arts/grammar/

Grammar is part of professionalism, because out of respect for others, we speak and write to the best of our abilities, without pretension. A lot of business writing takes place in our workspaces and that is what is coming up in the next chapter.

WORKSPACES

10.1 *Embrace Your Space*

I went into work early one morning at Sony Music, because I needed extra time to work on a big project. I thought I was alone.

My desk was surrounded by a half-wall, about four feet high, which a colleague dubbed, "the veal fattening pen." Suddenly, 20 feet away, the office door of my boss, Marketing Manager Dave Fisher, opened. "Fish" stuck his head out, looked at me, quickly pulled back and shut the door.

Not even a, "Good morning?" What's going on? I walked over to the door. No sound. I knocked. No response. I knocked again. I put my hand on the door handle and slowly opened it a crack. The office was the size of a large SUV parking space and Fish was nowhere.

I opened the door a little wider and leaned in. Out of the corner of my eye, I saw him. He was hiding behind the door, his back pressed up against the wall. I rolled my eyes, backed out and slammed the door shut.

There are all kinds of workspaces and different organizational cultures. *The Exceptional Professional* knows that every workspace is what we make of it. What's most important is that we interact with our colleagues and other stakeholders in a satisfying way that results in productive and profitable results.

In this chapter, you will learn:

- What's great about an office environment
- Different types of workspaces

- How to make your workplace inviting
- Respecting each other's workspace
- Your best friends in the workplace

Don't Shun the Office

A lot of college students tell me, "I don't want to work in an office." They are influenced by stereotypes from Hollywood, where offices are portrayed as a dull drumbeat of daily incarceration. Such stereotypes are likely created by people who never worked in an office.

I come not to bury the office, but to defend it. With offices come great camaraderie, creative collaboration and support. I tell students when I worked for a music label, it was crazy fun and in an office.

Sony Music's Midwest branch was in the Chicago suburbs. The layout was a long hallway with offices all the way down. But what made Sony Music so enjoyable was the unique group of creative and funny people. Whatever your workspace, the people make the difference.

A Workspace for Everyone

Back in the day, many workspaces were organized with manager offices on the perimeters and desks in the middle for everyone else. Then came cubicles, which exploded in the 1980s, and allowed employers to pack more employees into tighter spaces and provide some semblance of privacy and personal space.

With the tech boom, came the advent of "open workspaces" with everyone at open tables, regardless of rank. Open workspaces allow you to see and hear what's going on at all times. The idea is to inspire more collaboration and creativity. Most open workspaces still have conference rooms for meetings that don't require the collaboration of the entire staff.

Some organizations are now going to hybrid workspaces, with open tables, but also private workspaces or "pods" (like library study carrels), for those who want fewer distractions.

The Cube Dwellers

My first job out of college was at Johns Hopkins Hospital in the Public Relations Department. My cubicle was pretty spectacular, with a window and a partial view of Baltimore's Inner Harbor. This was not your average burlap-walled and metal trimmed box.

Cubicles provide some protection from outside distractions, but fail to keep out microwave popcorn smells, loud conversations and the constant drone of the cubicle neighbor listening to techno music with headphones. For a private call, you must find a conference room.

Cubicles do provide some sense of your own space. You may decorate the walls. There is a bit of privacy, to focus on projects.

In an office, your chair behind your desk usually faces the door. In a cubicle, your back is often to your doorless doorway. If you don't like people sneaking up behind you and looking over your shoulder, position your computer screen so it faces away from the doorway.

Respect Cubicle Boundaries

A cubicle should be treated like an office. Even without a door, there should be boundaries. If someone is on the phone, don't enter the cubicle. It's annoying when you are on the phone and people park themselves in your cubicle doorway, waiting for you to finish.

If someone chooses to eat at their desk, respect the lunch. Do not interrupt them and try to do business. Do not loom and ask them, "What's for lunch?" Let them eat lunch. If someone interrupts you at lunch, you are under no obligation to feed them.

An Office of Your Own

At Amana Appliances, I had a corner office. And by "corner office," I mean my office was on a corner that jutted out into a hallway. Instead of a window to the outside, I had two walls with large windows that faced the hallway. It was a nice office, but a bit like working in a fishbowl.

Still, having an office has its perks. If you have an important phone call or conference call, shutting the door affords privacy. Whenever I had writing to do, that closed door blocked out a lot of noise.

When you have an office, you can decorate. That may sound silly, but it's a perk. You can put artwork on the wall. It's hard to hang framed artwork in a cubicle. At Sony Music in my veal fattening pen, I just had a framed corkboard on the wall, where I posted a few cartoons and photos.

It's also nice to be able to lock your door when you go home each night and not worry about anyone having access.

The Open Floor Plan

The first time I worked in an open floor plan was at InterTech Media in New York. InterTech was on Madison Avenue on the fifth floor of an older building. Big windows let in the light and you could stick your head out the window and look up Madison Avenue. From the north windows, you could see the Empire State Building, just around the corner and up a block. It was exciting to be in the swim of it all.

In an open floor plan, everyone sits together at tables with no special treatment for rank or seniority. Our CEO would come in and pull up a chair anywhere. Although the idea is that no one has a regular spot where they sit, people do settle into regular spots.

There's no doubt an open floor plan fosters creative collaboration. Another benefit is you are constantly in tune with everything that is going on in the organization. With a tech start-up, new ideas and innovations are exciting and everyone feels like a part of the progress.

A by-product of sitting around together all the time, is that it yields some incredible conversations. One of our directors of content was a former producer for a major news network in New York. I asked him, "What's the craziest story you have ever covered?"

He said, "An elevator in an old building was stalled between two floors. A man tried to hold the elevator open and the elevator moved suddenly and beheaded him." But that was not all. "His head fell into the elevator, where there was a pregnant woman. At that moment, she went into labor." He always had riveting stories. That was the most shocking.

With an open floor plan, there are distractions. It was like eating at the former *Grill Room* at *The Four Seasons* in New York. When a new person walked in, everyone's head whipped around to see who it was.

Working in an open floor plan takes self-discipline, because sometimes you need to focus and tune out all the moving parts. The only one in that workspace who had an office was the office manager, because she had to do payroll. No one wanted her to be distracted.

Your Space

No matter whether you had an office, cubicle or part of a table, Jeanine Longeway, the office manager at Sony Music, taught me if you cleared off your desk at the end of the day and put everything away somewhere, you would have a fresh start the next day. It helps your frame of mind.

Ann Humbert at Amana Appliances, said, "It's okay to leave some work on your desk each night. That's why we come back the next day." I usually aimed for something in between.

Try to keep your workspace as neat as possible. If you were buying insurance and the insurance salesperson invited you into a workspace where there were papers piled high, garbage on the floor, soda cans on the desk, would you buy insurance from that person?

Your workspace should be neat but also look worked-in. When a workspace is too clean, it looks like there is no business going on and that doesn't look good either.

The photos you choose to display say a lot about you. I was at a bank speaking to a young woman who had photos taped to her file cabinet behind her desk. In the photos, she was in a strapless evening gown, grinning from ear to ear with friends, looking a little schnockered. It wasn't flattering. Nor, did it raise my confidence in the bank.

Think about what kind of statement any personal photos say about you. It's okay to have family photos, but unless you are

Michael Phelps, there should not be a photo of you in a swimsuit in your workspace.

Shared Spaces

At Amana Appliances, someone posted a printed sign in the supply closet that said, "Clean up after yourself – your mother doesn't work here." Another person came and wrote on it in ballpoint pen, "I wish she did, because then I could go back to having my lunch served."

Every workplace has its shared spaces – conference rooms, supply closets, break rooms, kitchens. With shared spaces comes responsibility. Right away, you find out who grew up with a mother who waited on them hand and foot.

Better Breakroom Behavior

Whose food is that? It's so old and rotting, it's knocking on the refrigerator door and asking to be let out.

Our Sony Music branch instituted a policy that if a container in the workplace refrigerator had an old, moldy product inside, the item was tossed out, container and all. There was no attempt to identify the owner or clean it out and leave the spotless Tupperware® or glass Pyrex® dish for the owner to claim. Here are tips for better break room behavior:

The Fridge: Keep the refrigerator clean. Take home storage containers and uneaten food. Discard old styrofoam containers. Do not eat what is not yours. Just because that Lean Cuisine® in the workplace freezer doesn't have a name scrawled on it, doesn't mean it's up for grabs.

The Coffee Maker: If you drink coffee, share in the coffee making. *"I don't know how,"* won't work forever. How on earth did you learn to do your job? If you finish (or nearly finish) the pot of coffee, make another. If it's approaching the end of the day, turn it off and rinse out the pot.

When I worked in the Washington D.C. area, a man in my workplace, who never talked to me, showed me how to make a fresh pot of coffee. I thought he was being nice. When he finished he said, "Good. Now you can make the coffee all the time." I stopped drinking coffee. After that, he still had to make his own. (It was long before I was an etiquette instructor. Actually, I would probably still do the same thing.)

The Microwave: Place a paper towel over dishes in the microwave to keep the food from splattering. If your lunch explodes in the microwave, wipe down the inside. Otherwise it will become a dried, caked-on mess. Not to mention the undesirable seasoning it adds to others' food.

Avoid foods that emit strong aromas, good or bad. (The good smells make everyone hungry and envious. The bad smells annoy.) That includes food heavy in garlic or spices that will waft through the workplace. Ditto for popcorn – enjoy popcorn at the movies or at home.

The Watercooler: Do not place a water bottle or cup you have been drinking from against the water cooler tap or against any beverage dispenser. Use clean, unused cups only. The watercooler is a great place to socialize, but be conscious of others working nearby.

The Sink or Dishwasher: Don't leave dirty dishes or food debris in the sink or on the counter. Clean up after yourself. Wash and put away any coffee mugs, dishes or flatware or place them in a dishwasher.

Workplace Restroom

At Sony Music, the marketing coordinator was looking for a manager.

"Is he in?" he asked me.

"I think I saw him headed towards the restroom."

"Then I will just wait for him."

"He was carrying a magazine."

"Oh," he said, "I'll come back."

Fortunately, Sony Music had men's and women's restrooms. There is nothing worse than a restroom shared by all, because as everyone knows, men pollute the restroom much more than women. In a small workplace, everyone knows who was last to render the restroom unusable. There are solutions, so we can all get along:

- No magazine rack or pile. Don't let anyone get too comfortable.
- Flush the toilet as soon as possible, to minimize a lingering odor.
- You could use air sanitizers or fresheners, but know that some people are sensitive to floral scents.
- Don't use a burning candle as an air freshener. I had a coworker whose candle in a glass on her desk broke and started a fire, while she was away at lunch.
- Nurse's trick: put a few drops of mouthwash in the toilet to diffuse the odor.

And remember these words of wisdom: *"If you sprinkle when you tinkle, be a sweetie and wipe the seatie."* That was scrawled on a stall inside a restroom at the University of Iowa when I was an undergrad. I have never been able to get it out of my mind.

Can't We Just All Get Along?

Sometimes when we work in close quarters, we get in each other's way. Here are a few common conflicts to avoid.

Pregnant Pause with Pregnant Coworker

It's common to see pregnant women in the workplace these days. But before you open your mouth to comment, have a pregnant pause. The following is a list of inappropriate things to ask or say that I have compiled from pregnant women:

"*Are you expecting?*" (Hard to walk this back if you are wrong. Ask me how I know.)
"*Was this an accident?*"
"*Did you get pregnant by in vitro or the old fashioned way?*"
"*Do you know what it is?*" (Answer: "*The doctor tells me it's a baby.*")
"*Is this it or do you plan on having more?*"
"*Are you going to try again for a boy/girl next time?*"
"*Who's the father?*"
"*Are you planning to breastfeed?*"
"*Are you going to have a C-section?*"
"*You are really getting huge!*"
"*When are you going to have that thing?*"
"*Are you having twins?*" (Again, hard to walk back.)
"*You look like you could go any day now!*"

Don't ask about names unless you are ready to act supportive and enthusiastic for whatever comes out of the mother's mouth. ("*You're naming her Saturn? Terrific!*") Don't offer unsolicited advice, no matter what you've read or your own experience with pregnancy. And most importantly, hands off. Never put a hand on a woman's pregnant belly, unless invited to do so. Don't ask to do that, either. It's awkward.

Treat your pregnant colleague with the same professionalism you would before the pregnancy. What can you say? "Congratulations," after the new arrival has been announced.

The Music Next Door

We're surrounded by music – and that's a beautiful thing. Unless, it is the unwanted buzz escaping the "noise cancelling" headphones of the guy in the next cubicle next to you. What do you do?

First, lay the groundwork for good relations before there is a problem. Be a good cubicle or open workplace table neighbor. Offer a friendly greeting each day. It's much easier to take, "I hate to bother you, but could you please turn down your music?" from a person who is kind to you than from a cold fish who ignores you.

Looting the Workspaces of Those Who Left

Whether someone has been fired or resigned, unless someone seals off their area like a crime scene, others swarm in like vultures and steal office supplies, equipment and sometimes a good chair.

Before Amana Appliances hired me for the public relations manager position, my colleague Dan Sandersfeld, caught someone carting off a large computer screen from the public relations office. He said, "Hey, where are you going? That's not yours." The person said, "The new CEO wants it for his office." Dan said, "Oh...well, I guess he can have it."

A Real Steal at the Workplace

Only a thief would pocket a candy bar or energy bar from a store without paying for it. But what about those who pilfer pens or post-it pads from their employers? Employee theft adds up:

- Taking office supplies for personal use
- Using printers or copiers to print personal documents
- Pilfering printed postage for personal mail
- Snatching coffee supplies or snacks provided for workplace use

There is also theft of time. There must be reasonable time for lunch, breaks and room for emergencies. Sometimes, we take more. Who hasn't been guilty of intending to spend 10 minutes surfing the web, only to find 45 minutes have passed?

A woman I worked with spent most of her work time on the phone planning her next vacation. Back from vacation, she spent her work time sharing hundreds of vacation photos with co-workers. Was it fair to the employer paying for her time? Theft of time includes:

- Personal phone calls, texts or email during work hours
- Non-work Internet surfing
- Chronic lateness, early departures
- Long lunches
- Extended coffee or smoke breaks

Many try to justify these little thefts:

"*The organization has an excess.*"
"*No one will miss it.*"
"*This makes up for the lack of salary that I get.*"
"*I am entitled to it, because of the long hours I put in here.*"

It is wrong to steal from a store and wrong to steal from your employer. Be honest. Honesty leads to a better relationship with your employer and more self-respect for yourself.

Selling to Your Co-workers

Have you ever had a moment in life when you felt your career hit rock bottom? I remember my moment. It was the day I had to throw a Mary Kay® party for a boss's wife. She was trying to start a Mary Kay business and my boss put me in charge of throwing her first party.

The boss was a nice man but this was an overreach. His wife wanted me to invite my friends. I was working 60 hours a week, going to grad school and living off Ramen noodles, to afford my rent and text books. Most nights I fell asleep on my couch with a textbook across my face. Outside work, *I didn't have any friends.*

I went down the hallway inviting other women in my workplace. No one wanted to come. Except for one – Martha Nelson, a field marketing rep. Martha was the only one who stayed after hours in the conference room, while my boss's wife put robin-egg blue eye shadow on us and told us how great it looked.

The boss's wife did not sell a thing that night. A week later, I was demoted. A few weeks after that, I was re-promoted, under a different boss, who wasn't married.

Multi-level marketing sales, whether makeup, baskets, candles, organic cleaning products or kitchen tools, should have no place in the workplace. It's uncomfortable to have people putting catalogs under your nose and pressuring you to buy products from them at work.

But It's For the Children

Then there are child fundraisers: Girl Scout cookies, Boy Scout caramel corn, bricks of cheese and candy bars to help fund the school band trip. Some bring their wide-eyed kids into the workplace to stare you down.

Is there a difference between this and multi-level marketing? Yes. No one likes overpriced candles and baskets. Almost everyone likes overpriced chocolate bars. But you should never feel coerced to buy.

At Sony Music, Mike Scheid, a radio promotion manager, took a no-pressure approach. He brought in a case of boxes of Peanut M&Ms® his daughter was selling for a school fundraiser. He put the case in the kitchen, with a jar for contributions. Then he opened one box, poured out the M&Ms onto a paper plate and labeled it, "Free samples." By the end of the day, he, (I mean, his daughter) sold all the boxes.

Workplace Romance

In full disclosure, if not for a workplace romance, I wouldn't be here. My parents met while working at a hospital in Chicago. Workplace romances may end in wedded bliss or end badly. Here are some guidelines:

- Never date anyone you directly supervise or who reports to you.
- Avoid dating people with whom you work in close proximity. If the romance fails, it's awkward not just for you, but also for co-workers.
- Before dating a person you work with, visualize how you would feel if the person broke up with you and started dating another co-worker.
- All dating-related activities must take place outside the workplace (not in the parking lot).
- Avoid public displays of affection: no holding hands in the hallway, no footsie or texting under the conference room table.
- Do not send romantic messages through workplace email. Workplace email is not private.
- Absolutely no sneaking off to the supply closet for hanky panky.
- Do not display romantic gifts from co-workers, including flowers, balloons or boxes of chocolate.
- Break up immediately with the person who gives you one of those stuffed animal monkeys with a heart that says, "I Wuv You."

These same guidelines apply to your clients and vendors, too. Doug Sullivan, a professional speaker who gave seminars on *How to Have a Successful Marriage*, said, "The first rule to a successful marriage is: *don't date other people.*" Keep it professional and don't act on impulses that compromise your marriage or the marriage of others.

The Fungal Jungle

I saw a woman sneeze without covering her mouth. That happens. Sometimes the sneeze sneaks up on us and we don't have time to cover our mouth. This person unfortunately sprayed the ATM machine in front of her. She was also in a hospital lobby, wearing scrubs...but I digress.

It's a fungal jungle out there. Hand sanitizer and packages of antibacterial wipes are not just for people with children. They are for everyone. Avoid sneezing on ATMs, vending machines, shared workplace coffee pots, doorknobs or any other public dispensers. If you do, wipe them off with an antibacterial wipe or some hand sanitizer on a paper towel. Take care of others while you are taking care of yourself.

Who Gets to Tell the Sick Person to Go Home?

Some people relish this task. *"You're going to make us all sick! Go home!"* Show a little mercy. Don't badger suffering fellow employees to leave. Colds can last a month or more. Calling in sick for a month isn't realistic. Just take your vitamins and give them wide berth.

To Health and Back

When a co-worker returns to the workplace after a medical leave, most want to ease back into work without too many people fussing or asking probing questions. Here are some things to think about:

- Never say, "I know what you're going through." Each case is unique.
- Avoid prying questions about the person's condition or treatment. If the person wants you to know, he or she will tell you.
- Don't corner the person with your own treatment or health advice.
- If you are not sure what to say, smile and say, "We're glad you are back. Anything I can do to help?"
- Don't bombard the person with your own, a relative's or friend's health story. Each diagnosis is different and talking about another person's health issues may only frighten the person.
- Be there for them if they want to talk, but don't force it.

A Death in the Work Family

When a co-worker loses a member of his or her family, go to the wake and funeral and express your sympathies. Bring a condolence card and write a check for the chosen charity or memorial fund.

What to say: *"I am very sorry for your loss."*

What not to say: *"I know how you feel."* (Again, every situation is unique.) Or *"At least they are no longer in pain."* (Though well-intentioned, no one needs a reminder their loved one was in pain.)

When a co-worker loses someone suddenly, he or she may be in shock or may be grieving a long time. Make sure you let them know you are there for them, but also give them time and space to grieve.

If your co-worker passes away, reach out to that person's family, whether you knew the family well or not. I was organizing a reunion of Sony Music colleagues when I stumbled on an obituary for Shelley Mori, a former radio promotion manager for Epic Records. Everyone loved Shelley and we all grieved – it was like losing a member of our family, even though we were no longer working together.

Everyone shared stories over email of what Shelley meant to them. I gathered the stories and sent them to the funeral home, hoping they would forward them to her family. I received a response from one of Shelley's sisters, who wrote that words could not express how touched the family was that her friends and former co-workers took the time to put their thoughts, memories and love on paper.

There is a reoccurring theme in this book: *write that note.* If you knew the deceased and have positive things to say, let the family know.

Your Best Friends in the Workplace

You should always be nice to everyone in your workplace. But there are two groups of people who should be your best friends in the workplace: administrative professionals and IT professionals.

Administrative Professionals

Behind every successful manager, there is the ultimate multi-tasking, negotiating, organizing, master scheduling, event planning, crisis managing, psychological counseling administrative professional.

They go by different titles: executive assistants, secretaries, receptionists. Sometimes they serve one person. Sometimes they serve many. Certain administrative professionals direct legions of other administrative professionals. They are the ones in the organization who make the rest of us look good by covering all the details that we don't have the time or – let's be honest – the competence to do.

Administrative professionals know how to get things done. Often, we know not how and it's better not to ask. A good one is hard to find. Even those who are not your direct assistants, can pave the way for you to meet with others or direct opportunities your way.

With administrative professionals, don't condescend, it's better to befriend. They are a manager's most trusted allies and their opinion carries weight. Whatever is going on in an organization, the administrative professionals are always in the know.

Administrative Professional's Day falls in late April. On that day – take them to lunch, buy flowers, a gift or gift certificate or let them go home early. But don't make it a single day. Celebrate them all year long.

IT (Information Technology) Professionals

On Valentine's Day, my *Etiquette Tip of the Week* is always a tribute to those we hold dearest. The ones who deal with us at our worst and bring out our best. The ones who lift us up when technology lets us down. Of course, I am speaking of the IT Department.

Unless you are a technical genius, there is no more helpless feeling than when your computer goes "poof." The men and women of IT are our port of last resort, when we have lost the PowerPoint presentation we have been working on the last five hours, and with it, the will to live.

Where would we be without this team of dedicated professionals to fix our computers and other digital devices? Down the hall crying in the restroom, that's where. Or tossing our malfunctioning electronics into the "fake lake" on the corporate campus. (Who uses that lake besides disgusting Canadian geese, anyway?)

Here's how many communicate with the IT professionals in their organization: "Just fix it." Don't do that. Be kind and attentive to your IT professionals. All of them have a name. Use it.

Do not project your anger or pass along your stress. They didn't break your computer, but they may be the only ones who can fix it. Treat them with kindness, patience and appreciation. Follow up with a handwritten thank you note. If you are really a star, you will write a note of high praise to their supervisor.

It never hurts to send some treats down to the IT Department. And would it kill you to say, "Hello" when you pass them in the hallway? Be kind to your IT people all year round – not just when you are in a fix.

Manufacturing: Factory vs. Office

One of the great advantages of a large organization, is the opportunity to meet new people every day. As manager of public relations at Amana Appliances, I loved to grab my safety glasses and go out into the factory and talk to people on the refrigerator line. It was loud, there were a lot of moving parts, hazards like forklifts flying around corners – here was the lifeblood of the organization.

My favorite machine shaped the interior liners for the refrigerators. A thick sheet of plastic would enter the machine at one end, heat up in seconds, then inflate like a giant piece of bubble gum. Then a rectangular mold would punch the bubble from beneath and the melted plastic would immediately fall into shape around the mold. It would cool for a few minutes, before ejecting from the machine.

Some people farmed during the day and worked in the factory at night. The second shift employees were usually a little younger and more boisterous. If an argument broke out, it was usually on second shift.

Two of my favorite people in the factory were Margie and Jeff, who worked on the refrigerator line. Both were young and would talk about their families and take out pictures of their kids to show me. They would ask how it was going in the offices and I would tell them about our advertising campaign or magazines featuring our product. They would tell me how it was going on the line.

Jeff always talked about a woman, who worked in the factory on another shift. He said, "She looks like you, but she's not *like you.*"

I said, "What do you mean?"

He said, "She's like, Harley Biker Chick." To demonstrate, he lifted up his t-shirt and said, "Whoooooooo!"

I said, "How do you know I'm not Harley Biker Chick on weekends?"

He said, "You just don't seem like the type."

"You're right, I'm not." I conceded.

In manufacturing companies, there can be a gulf between office and factory and an "us and them" mentality. There doesn't have to be. Every work environment is what you make of it. If you choose to hide in your office or cubicle and lunch at your desk, you are limiting yourself.

Working with a manufacturer was also a big learning curve for me. To celebrate the launch of a new advertising campaign, we had Amana t-shirts made for everyone. This was a no-brainer for me, having ordered t-shirts many times in the music business. I had a guy in Kansas City – his t-shirts were beautiful, soft, 100 percent cotton.

The people in the factory took one look at the shirts and were furious – the label did not say, "Made in the USA." I discovered that was a sensitive issue, especially in a unionized organization.

BE EXCEPTIONAL: Leading Means Listening

The Exceptional Professional is a problem solver. To solve problems, sometimes you need to listen to the people who know the most about them, even if it means putting yourself on the spot.

Whenever one organization takes over another, there is a cultural shift and a lot of unease. This was the case, when Goodman Manufacturing purchased Amana Appliances from Raytheon. Frank Murray, the Goodman CEO, would hold employee meetings of 200 people at a time, give a ten minute "State of the Company" report, then say, "Ask any question you want."

The office people were very reserved, but the factory people would jump up, rant and gesture wildly about issues on the line. Once, a man asking a question let slip the F-word. Everyone gasped. (I had become desensitized to the word in the music business, so it flew right by me.)

Frank Murray listened, did not react to the F-bomb, but answered the factory worker's question and eased his frustration. He assigned someone to take care of it. Problems were solved. I admired that about him. That took courage to get in front of 200 people and invite complaints. People working in the factory worked hard and took pride in the product. They appreciated that he listened to their input.

Emergency Exits

Do you know the way out if there is a fire? Do you know what to do if there is a tornado or an earthquake? Or, in a scenario none of us likes to imagine, do you know what to do if someone starts shooting?

Know your organization's emergency procedures. Consider the worst situations. Think about the different escape routes if you had to get out of the building. Think about hiding places if you had to get out of sight. If your organization does not have emergency drills, encourage your leadership to put them into practice.

Now that we've covered workplaces, it's time to look at special instructions for when you are new to a workplace.

10.2 *What to Do When You are New*

My first job out of college was publications assistant in public relations at Johns Hopkins Hospital in Baltimore. It was in the middle of Hopkins' Sesquicentennial Celebration, so everyone was very busy.

I was asked to copy a few documents in a room down the hall. The copy machine filled the room. I lifted the lid, put a document on top, but couldn't find the button to start the machine. I looked over and around, I was feeling under the edges for some hidden button. A big, unlabeled button on a nearby machine, appeared to be connected, so I pressed that.

It turned out to be the main server. That flick of a button shut down every computer in the office of about 50 people. Did I mention this was before "Auto save?" Some people lost five or six hours of work, because they hadn't saved their work. I thought they were going to tie me up, light me on fire and throw me into the Baltimore Harbor. I had to eat lunch by myself for at least two weeks.

While your first job out of college may not be the perfect fit, *The Exceptional Professional* finds there is great value in learning how to land on your feet in each new situation in your career.

In this chapter, you will learn:

- How to get to know people in a new workplace
- Strategies for new people and interns
- Boss loyalty and protocol
- The lost art of phone etiquette

Getting to Know You

When you pass people in the hallway, do you:

1. Look off in another direction?
2. Look down at your cell phone, glued to your hand at all times?
3. Make eye contact, smile and say, "Hello" or "Good morning"?

Ding, ding, ding...the correct answer is 3. Be convivial. In your workplace, greet people, even those you don't know – a simple, "Good morning," or "Hello" will do. Maybe they say, "Hello" back. Maybe they haven't had their coffee and grunt, "'Lo." (That's okay – it's contact.)

What if they say nothing? Maybe they are conceited. But try not to assume the worst of others. They might be painfully shy, preoccupied, just focused on getting from point A to point B, have earbuds on under their hair or not used to anyone acknowledging them or saying, "Hello."

A simple act of making eye contact and greeting another in passing is validating that person. Validate early and often. At Amana Appliances, I walked through the factory to get from the parking lot to my office. On my way in, I would wave to the first shift people working on the refrigerator line and on my way out, wave to the second shift. Waving led to shouted greetings back and forth, then small talk, then work talk. As I mentioned in the last chapter, sometimes there is a gulf between office and factory in a manufacturing environment. Simple greetings led to trust and communication that was helpful in my job.

Make friends with the administrative professionals. If you see people on your way into the workplace each day, you should know them by name and greet them when you pass by.

Know your security guards by name. They are there to protect you.

When I was at Chestnut Hill College in Philadelphia, it was still a women's college. Some students would jokingly question the ability of the security guards, who seemed older and carrying a little extra weight. Then one night, we saw one of them take down a large, unruly boyfriend, who had been asked to leave. No one doubted them again.

BE EXCEPTIONAL: Don't Wait for an Introduction

Being the new person can feel a bit like being plunged into the deep end of the pool. *The Exceptional Professional* knows if we start moving and treading on our own, we'll get along swimmingly.

Sometimes in a new job, we get introduced to a few people, then deposited into an office, cubicle or highly-collaborative, ergonomic, open floor plan workplace. Then it's sink or swim.

When I was first hired at Amana Appliances, Ann Humbert, my boss in public relations, did a smart thing. She introduced me to a few people, then sent me out to the department heads to introduce myself.

Instead of a fleeting introduction, I had the opportunity to sit down with each vice president and listen to their different perspectives and plans for the organization. The great thing about these leaders – they had an open door policy and were generous with their time. I could talk to them any time and ask any question. Less than a year later, when Ann left the organization, those relationships fostered early, allowed me to step into her position.

Introducing yourself shows initiative. Start first with the people in your area, then gradually widen your circle. Whenever you encounter someone you do not know, introduce yourself.

Do More Listening than Talking

I met a wise young woman who was an event planner at a luxury hotel in Chicago. She had only been in the job a few months, but she spoke with enthusiasm about how much she had learned from the servers on the banquet staff, many who had been with the hotel for years.

From her interaction, it was clear that she had a good rapport with the staff and they liked her very much. The reason is, she took the time to listen and get to know them.

A frequent complaint I hear from employers is that many young, new hires want to be boss right out of the chute. When you start a new job, spend some time listening and learning before putting forth your brilliant, turn-the-earth-on-its axis ideas. Don't be condescending to those without college degrees. Anyone who has been at an organization longer than you has more experience and can be your teacher.

Learn the culture – get to know your colleagues and how they do things. Listen and learn from those with more experience. If you do this, your ideas will have a better chance of being well-received than if you started spouting ideas like a fountain the day you walked in the door.

Not My Job

Do everything to be helpful. Not in your job description? Do it anyway. If you don't, there are plenty of candidates for your job (especially if it's entry-level) who will. Come early and stay late, without complaint. Don't be a clock-watcher. If work begins at 9 a.m., get your coffee before 9 a.m. If work ends at 5 p.m., do not start packing up at 4:45 p.m.

Don't Eat Lunch at Your Desk

When you are trying to make a good impression by working hard, it is easy to get holed up in your workspace during lunch, doing work or surfing the web. Don't eat lunch at your desk. Eat in the cafeteria, breakroom or wherever people gather. Have lunch at different times each day and eat with new groups of people. If someone is sitting by himself or herself, ask, "May I join you?"

Lunching with co-workers is a great way to learn the workplace culture. At Amana Appliances, I lunched with people in customer service, engineering, sales, finance and other departments. The customer service people always had funny stories about their contacts with consumers. Learning from them about questions and issues consumers were raising helped me know what was going on with our products. That was valuable for me as the public relations manager, because some consumers complained to the media, who in turn, contacted me.

Engineers, who were constantly taking apart our competitors' products, would tell me about weaknesses in competitive products vs. strengths in our products. Sales people let me know what products were in demand and the promotions and events our competitors had at retail.

Getting out to lunch can be a good way to bond. Up the road from Amana Appliances, was a restaurant called The Garden of

Eatin'. My colleagues and I always joked about trying it. We finally did have pizza at the Garden of Eatin'. It's no longer there but I still think of it fondly.

Be Friendly, But Wary

When starting a job in a new workplace, the first person who makes friendly overtures to you is hard to resist. But be cautious. The first person who befriends you is not always your friend. Beware of the workplace gossip who takes a personal interest in you, to mine for information to later use against you. Make no mistake, anything you say to the workplace gossip can and will be used against you.

In one of my jobs, a young woman cozied up to me my first few days and started talking down my supervisor. She acted like she was doing me a big favor by bringing me into her inner circle and educating me on how things were. She tried to get me to give negative impressions of my supervisor. I didn't bite. I said, "(The supervisor) has been very nice to me and I feel like I am learning a lot." Eventually, this woman spent less time with me, because she wasn't getting what she wanted.

Conversely, people who, at first impression, may seem to be against you, might end up as your greatest allies. My mother wisely said, "Be nice to everyone, because those who seem like enemies at first, may end up being your closet friends." I have found that to be true. Take time to get to know people, before committing to friends and allies.

Be Loyal to Your Boss

Your job is not only to advance your own career, but also to make your superior look good. Here are ways to make the boss look good:

- Speak well of your boss to others. Whatever you say about another person will get back to that person, so say something positive.
- Support your boss's initiatives. Work with, not against him or her.

- Defend your boss, when he or she is not present. You are on your boss's team – make sure you have your boss's back.

You owe some allegiance and respect to your boss, unless that boss is behaving in a less than respectable way. Never do anything illegal or unethical for your supervisor, because you will be held accountable.

Seek out supervisors and mentors who are ethical, that you will be proud to support. Look for the good mentors in life and learn all you can from them. Most bosses will support you in return. Some won't.

Superior Protocol

Every new person should know that in most organizations, there is a protocol to follow. If there are people, such as your supervisor, who outrank you in an organization, do not invite them to lunch. Wait for an invitation from them.

Buying holiday or birthday gifts for your superior is not appropriate. Others may think you are currying favor with the boss. Also, it puts your superior in an awkward position of whether or not to reciprocate.

Ask Questions

Question authority. Not in a rebellious sense. I mean, if you really don't know what you are doing, ask someone. New hires, especially those just out of college, often worry others will be judging them and thinking, "Don't you know anything?" You don't. So ask. The server disaster I mentioned at the beginning of this chapter could have been avoided, if only I had asked one person, "How do I work this copy machine?"

BE EXCEPTIONAL: Accepting Constructive Criticism

One of the hardest things to take, especially when we first enter the professional world, is how to accept "constructive criticism." *The Exceptional Professional* accepts constructive criticism graciously, because how we advance in our professional lives depends on our ability to accept and incorporate feedback. As the old saw goes, "We need to take guff in order to give guff."

It's not easy. None of us likes to be reminded by others we are not perfect. Even when you call it "constructive," the word "criticism" still sticks. (Calling it "feedback" doesn't neutralize this.) The worst part? When it comes from people we don't like. Or at least we don't like them after their feedback. Here are some things to consider:

- Don't take it personally or begrudge the person who gave it.
- Hear the person out; no interrupting with excuses or self-defense.
- Work on your flaws. Aim higher by breaking bad habits and raising your standards.
- If the criticism is warranted and you did work to overcome it, thank the person who brought it to your attention.

If you are serious about advancement, ask for feedback:

"How was my presentation received?"
"Do you have suggestions for improving my content or delivery?"
"I am interested in a management position. What things do I need to work on to get there?"

What you know will help you grow.

Learn from Your Mistakes

A wise CEO once told me that an employee who makes mistakes and learns from them is far more valuable (and more cost efficient) than a replacement employee. Admit mistakes and apologize. (*"I am sorry you were offended,"* is not an apology.)

Eat a big piece of humble pie. Learn from your mistakes and move on. Even the trials in our lives are a learning experience.

Interns and Internships

I worked with an intern, who I'll call Dylan (not his real name). His father was friends with the owner of the organization, which is how he got the internship.

I assigned him tasks that were interesting and designed to help him learn about our industry and our competition. These projects were nothing I wasn't willing to do myself and had not done before. But he did not want to do any of them.

I was spending all this time having conversations with him and trying to come up with projects. With each project, he would slack off or not do anything. When I asked for his progress, he was flippant. He didn't behave that way with men in the workplace. I began to suspect one of his issues was he didn't like taking direction from a woman.

One day Dylan said, "I don't think you realize, my father is a *good friend of your boss.*" As if I were going to lose my job if I did not cooperate with his slacking off. I looked at him and said, "Okay." He smiled, thinking victory was his. I smiled back.

My solution was to stop knocking myself out, wasting my time coming up with projects for him. Dylan's father's friend would say, "Do you have anything for Dylan?" And I would say, "Nope. Not a thing."

Pretty soon, Dylan was onto the game. He was begging me for projects. I said, "Sorry, I don't have anything for you to do." Eventually, he was let go because we had nothing for him to do.

Internships should be a learning experience for the interns. They should be exposed to different aspects of the organization and not just used for grunt work that no one else wants to do. But in order for internships to be a learning experience, interns must be willing to learn.

When you are in an internship, you are a low person on the totem pole and you have to prove yourself. Everyone deserves your respect. Interns do not outrank others, no matter who their parents know.

Here are more guidelines for interns, or anyone new to an organization:

- Show up. Internships are not like college, where you can sleep in, then borrow someone else's notes.
- Work with gusto. Don't grouse about assignments. When you are in charge, you can assign them to others. Earn it until you learn it.
- *"Please, may I have some more?"* Ask for more assignments, not more time off.
- Graduate to a working wardrobe. If you can wear it to the beach, don't wear it to your workplace (unless you work at the beach.)
- Get to know people and processes, before offering your opinions.
- Holster that cell phone. No texting under the table during meetings.
- Leave the earbuds at home. No person is an island, but every person is a piece of the continent (with apologies to John Donne.) Be attentive to your co-workers.

Someone told me about an intern with a wandering eye and wandering feet. He kept wandering from his department into the next department to hit on a female assistant. His attentions were unwanted by the assistant. As a result, his continued employment was unwanted by the organization. What the wandering intern didn't get: "No" still means, "No." The rebuff says, "Enough!" Focus on being professional in your internship and your career will take off.

When to Pick Up the Phone

One complaint I hear from managers working with new college grads, is that they are so digitally focused, they are hesitant to use the phone.

A manager in Kansas City said she will ask a new employee, "Did you call the client?" The response, *"No, but I emailed him three times."*

Or the manager says, "Did you talk to your co-worker?"

New employee: *"No, but I texted her and she did not respond."*
Manager: "She works two cubicles away – go talk to her."

Tech-savvy is good, but in today's workplace, you have to be skilled in multiple forms of communication. Be willing to make a phone call or have a face-to-face meeting, when necessary.

Answering the Call: Phone Etiquette

Earlier in my career when I worked for Sony Music, I started on the front phones. You can imagine the people that call into a music label.

"I am a very close friend of Mariah Carey, but I lost her phone number. Could you give it to me?"
Me: "Sure, it's right here in my rolodex." (Click)

Radio people would call to prank the radio promotion managers by pretending to be someone else. One day, a man called in saying he was Eddie Money. I said, "Right." I put him on hold and said to the woman at the next desk, "Get this, this guy says he's Eddie Money."

She said, "Did he ask for Mike?"
I said with some hesitation, "...Yes."
She said, "That *IS EDDIE MONEY.*"
I grabbed the phone and said, "Mr. Money, he'll be right with you."

Before there were cell phones and laptops, there were telephones. (If you were born after 1980, you probably don't remember.) It's good to review the fundamental niceties of telephone etiquette, because they extend to current digital devices.

Professionally Speaking

Especially in this era of start-ups and sprouting industries, everyone grabs the phone at some time. Your title doesn't matter. When you answer the phone, you are the voice of the organization to potential investors, clients, job seekers and other stakeholders. Make sure your first impression is a good one.

What do they always tell you about phone etiquette? Answer the phone with a smile in your voice and a song in your heart. In other words, sound pleasant. Never sound like someone who is jarred out of sleep by a 2:00 a.m. phone call that turns out to be a wrong number. Sit up straight to maximize your vocal tone. Speak distinctly and enunciate.

Try not to let the phone ring more than twice. Business phones that ring more give the impression the workplace or person is disorganized.

Say, "Hello." That's two syllables. Some try and squeeze it into one: 'Lo' (The one on the other end is thinking, *"Did he just say Yo?"*)

Give the organization or department name, then your own name. This creates a personal connection and puts the other person at ease. (If you are worried about security, exclude your last name.)

"Hello, Sensation Investigations, this is Polly Graff."
"Hello, Kenny Ketcham's office, this is Willie speaking."

When the person provides his or her name, use it. If you have trouble remembering names, make a note of the caller's name on a piece of scratch paper so you can repeat it back to him or her.

"Mr. Steele, how may I help you?"

If the person does not give his or her name, ask for it.

"May I tell Ms. Graff who is calling?"

If it is customer service-related, repeat the person's issue back, so the person knows he or she has been heard.

"I don't know why your road has not been plowed for four days so you feel as if you've been forgotten and left for dead... but I'll find out."

Give the Caller Your Full Attention

Have you ever been on the phone with someone and you could hear them softly tapping away at their computer keyboard? Tapping on a computer keyboard, clicking a mouse or texting, can be heard over the phone. When someone is web surfing, checking messages or watching TV, you can feel the distraction in how that person responds.

Put down your sandwich and spit out your gum. If you must cough, cough away from the receiver. Be interested in the person who is calling.

Know When to Hold 'em

Try not to put anyone on hold for more than 10 seconds. Years ago, I called United Airlines, expecting to be on hold for a long time. When the agent picked up after five seconds, I was taken off guard. I said, "I'm sorry, I wasn't ready, I thought there was going to be more hold music." The agent said, "I can hum a few bars of the 'Lion King' if you like."

It's good to talk to a live voice. If you know Mr. Ketcham is not available, let the person know before you ask for a name. No one wants: *"Can I tell him who is calling?... Please hold... I'm sorry, he's busy."*

Instead, say: *"Mr. Ketcham is out of the office, but he should be back this afternoon. Would you like to leave a message on his voicemail?"*

Once in a while, a grumpy person will say, *"I don't want to leave a message on voicemail. I want YOU to WRITE DOWN my message."* Don't argue, write it down. It will cost you 30 seconds and satisfy the grumpy person. Then you can put the message on voicemail.

If your organization has music hold, you should know what it sounds like. On hold with another department at Amana Appliances, I heard an elevator music version of "Light My Fire" by The Doors. I couldn't help picturing a lonely musician, whose dreams of being famous had long been crushed, sitting in a studio somewhere in front of a keyboard tapping out this perky, Easy Listening version of Light My Fire.

Transferring a Call

There is nothing more frustrating than being bounced around like a hot potato from department to department and having to start over with each person and explain the reason for your call.

When transferring a call, do not hit transfer and hang up. Wait until the person picks up, let that person know who's calling and why. It keeps the caller from having to repeat their story and prepares the person taking the call. *"Mr. Bass is on the line. He has a question about his account."*

If the person does not pick up or you get voicemail, retrieve the caller, let them know the person is not available and ask if he or she would like to leave a message on the person's voicemail.

Digital Menu Rescue

I once went through a 20-minute process to get to a live person for technical assistance on my computer. My cell phone cut out for a second and the person hung up. I thought my next call would be to a drywall person to patch the wall I was about to hurl the computer through.

If your organization has a digital voice menu that callers must navigate before they get a live voice, be sensitive to what they have been through. Few things are worse than the hell of a digital voice menu.

> *"If you would like to continue in English...press 1..."*
> *"Please enter your ten digit phone number, followed by the pound sign."*
> *"Please enter your account number, followed by the pound sign."*
> *"Please enter the last four digits of your social security number, followed by the pound sign."*
> *"Please enter your PIN number, followed by the pound sign."*
> *"Please enter how many pounds you weigh, followed by the pound sign."*

When digital menus give the option of using voice instead of pushing buttons, it really pushes people's buttons. It never fails that you hear someone on their cell phone in the airport dealing with this. *"Two....*

TWOOO!... Service Department... SERRVICCE DEPARRT-MMENNT!!" Be especially kind and patient to the person who has been through the digital voice menu, even if they seem cranky.

Making a Call

Always be nice to the person who answers the phone – he or she is the gatekeeper – the person who puts your call through *or not.* When calling a business, announce yourself to the person answering the phone:

> *"Hello, this is (first and last name), May I please speak to Lou Ming?"*

Add your organization name or department if calling for business:

> *"Hello, this is (first and last name), I am calling from X Incorporated."*
> *"Hello, this is (first and last name), in the IT Department."*

Don't make it awkward by saying, "Don't you recognize my voice yet?" That your voice is not memorable is not that person's fault.

If you leave a message with a live body, be gracious and thank the person for taking the message. I can't say this enough – be kind to the gatekeepers who answer the phone. They may recommend you or condemn you. End the call with "Goodbye." (not BUH-bye)

Leaving a Voicemail Message

Ever get a voicemail message where you couldn't quite make out what the caller was saying? The person may have been mumbling or yelling like their house was on fire. Perhaps they were calling from out where the elephants go to die and cell service was a little spotty.

When leaving a voicemail, speak clearly. State your name, organization and phone number at the beginning of the message and repeat your name and phone number at the end of the message.

Say the phone number slowly each time, as if you are standing in front of the person who is writing it down. That way, the person listening does not have to keep replaying the message to take down your info. Or if the number was hard to understand at the beginning of the message, the repeat number will confirm it. Return a call within 24 hours.

Your Voicemail Message

Make sure your answering message on voicemail represents yourself and your organization well. Your voicemail should:

- Project a professional impression
- Have a warm and welcoming tone
- Be clear and concise
- Avoid cutesy, joking or lengthy messages

Years ago, I had a message on my home answering machine where I said, as fast as I could, "Not here. Leave a message at the beep." It went so fast, callers were taken off guard and all the messages started with, "Uh...um...uh...." It was funny. Then one "Uh...um...uh..." message was from my supervisor at work. I changed the message after that.

Embrace Your New Workplace

When you are new, be enthusiastic about your workplace. Don't regale your co-workers with stories about everything that was great about your previous job. How does that old Crosby, Stills and Nash song go? "Love the One You're With." (The Luther Vandross remake is also awesome.)

Always look forward. College was fun, but look for the fun in your future. Learn all you can about your organization's products, services and competition. Get to know people. In the next chapter, we'll find some of that fun when we cover how to be more involved in your organization's extracurricular activities.

10.3 *Sports, Holidays and Other Bonding*

I was invited by some co-workers to join their volleyball league. A friend was dating a man on our team, who seemed like a great catch: handsome, physically fit, charming and nice... until we played volleyball with him.

He turned out to be one of those people who took recreational volleyball very seriously. He went ballistic on the court, screaming and cursing at people on his own team when they missed a shot. He made some of the women cry. He made some of the men cry, too. Everyone dropped out of volleyball that summer.

There are many activities, inside and outside your organization, where you can bond with your co-workers. *The Exceptional Professional* seizes opportunities to expand social circles, get some exercise and fresh air and even do something good for the community.

The Exceptional Professional also knows to eschew activities that work against his or her reputation and career goals and not to give in to pressure by people who don't have his or her best interests at heart.

In this chapter, you will learn:

- How to use sports to bond with colleagues
- What's so great about golf
- The case against costumes and Secret Santas
- About lottery pools and other forms of gambling

The Sporting Side of Employee Bonding

At Amana Appliances, I was invited to join the employees' volleyball league one summer. They probably figured, "She's tall, so she must be good at the net." Next summer I was not invited back. That's okay, because volleyball hurts my delicate, little, hothouse flower wrists.

Amana's bowling league only wanted me for one season, too. It's not as if I have no athletic ability. I just have no hand-eye coordination for any sport that involves a ball. In a foot race, I know I could have taken any of those bowlers and volleyball players.

Here's the great thing about recreational sports: you don't have to be an Olympic athlete. Can you watch sports? Can you work a cooler full of beverages? Go for the social side.

Of course, if you are an Olympic athlete, that helps. My brother was part of a water polo team and had a teammate, a big bear of a man, who actually competed in the Olympics in swimming. Someone from the other team joked, "I'll cover the big boy," thinking he would be slow in the water. He had no idea of his Olympic experience but soon learned.

There are many different sports leagues for adults – softball, basketball, kickball, volleyball, soccer, rugby, flag football, bowling and more. Whether you are playing or not, it's fun to hang out and watch. There is often a lot of joking, good-natured trash talking and taunting. But there is also cheering, coaching and encouragement. And there is certainly the benefit of learning to work together as a team.

You get to know people you might have known only in passing. You see a different side of them when playing sports. Sometimes it's not pretty. Other times, leadership qualities emerge.

Sportsmanship: From the Field to the Workplace

Here are some guidelines for being a good sport:

- Win or lose, thank the other team for the game and let them know you enjoyed playing against them.
- Congratulate the winners. Compliment them on a good game.
- Be gracious to the losers. Tell them they were worthy opponents, compliment them on what they did well.
- Be humble. Don't boast of your higher athletic ability. Tell opponents that they made the game challenging and fun.
- If the winner is gloating, smile and nod and don't say anything. To have the upper hand, you need to take the higher road.

BE EXCEPTIONAL: Apply Sportsmanship to the Workplace

The same sportsmanship guidelines can be applied back in the workplace. *The Exceptional Professional* is a gracious winner, when he or she gets the promotion others didn't. There's no victory lap around the workspace.

Similarly, when competing against another person for a promotion and the other person gets the promotion, congratulate that person. Don't be a poor loser. You'll never be a success if you waste time hating other people for their success.

—

Individual Sports

Then there are individual sports where a team isn't required, although sometimes you team up.

The Golf Outing

My brother Michael says, "Here's the mystique behind golf: it's one of the best uninterrupted places to talk business." While there is much ado about how business deals are made on golf courses, it's more about building relationships – getting to know your clients, investors, vendors, your boss or other stakeholders. And sometimes it's a relaxing respite with friends.

Golf is a game of rules and manners but also of rituals. And there is much you can learn about people from how they play golf:

- Do they get frustrated when they make a bad shot or take it in stride?
- Do they really blow their stack and throw clubs?
- Do they have a sense of humor or none at all?
- Are they patient or intolerant with hackers (bad golfers)?
- Will they let you use your "foot iron" or "foot wedge" to move the ball from behind a tree?
- Will they give you a Mulligan?
- Do they remember their own strokes correctly?

- Do they talk too much or talk at inappropriate times?
- Did they turn off their cell phone?

While there is a lot of talk that goes on in golf, there are times when you need to keep your yap shut:

- When someone is teeing up
- In the middle of someone's backswing
- When someone is putting

It's also important not to walk in front of someone when that person is putting or not walk around when someone is teeing up.

Then comes the ethical dilemma – should you let your boss win? That's a judgment call. If you have never played golf, but want to learn, sign up for lessons through community education or a local golf course.

Raising a Racket

Racket sports like tennis, racquetball and squash are great for one-on-one or two-on-two play, but bring your athleticism and endurance. Those with bad knees need not apply.

I love tennis, but I am sloppy tennis player. Amana Appliances had community tennis courts not far from headquarters, so a few of us would play after work. Once, I ran back to the baseline to return a shot, slipped in a puddle of mud and went down sideways. I was covered in mud.

Brett Vladika, one of Amana's design engineers, was an excellent tennis player and was teaching me how to improve. He was shouting directions across the court, while his boss's wife was playing on the next court. The next day, his boss told him his wife said, "I saw Brett on the tennis court with a girl. He was sure bossing her around!"

Like golf, you can learn something about people when you play racket sports. Do they get frustrated easily? Are they patient? Are they aggressive or laid back? Are they a good sport?

BE EXCEPTIONAL: The Birth of Bad Tennis

If there is not an extracurricular sport that fits your talents, make one. *The Exceptional Professional* always looks for ways to be as inclusive as possible with events.

In Connecticut, I organized events for a group of young professionals and a few people expressed an interest in tennis. However, when I organized a tennis event, only one or two people out of a group with over 300 members showed up. I went back to people who said they liked tennis and said, "What gives?" They all said the same thing: "I like to play tennis, but I'm *not that good at tennis.*"

I remedied the situation by calling the event "Bad Tennis." The description on our website and in the promotional email started with, "Do you stink at tennis? Then we have an event for you."

With Bad Tennis, everybody showed up. We ended up commandeering 2-3 courts and everyone with a racket got on the court and started swinging wildly. (They weren't kidding. Some were truly awful.) The better players went off to another court to play each other. A good time was had by all.

People who are not good at sports often feel intimidated and stay away. But if you are not looking for perfection, advertise it as such.

Unconventional Sports

There are also unconventional sports like frisbee golf, pickleball or paintball. Paintball is often sold as a team-building exercise for organizations. Not everyone is into donning coveralls and masks and shooting each other with paint pellets in order to work well together.

Some larger companies have yoga or other exercise classes available in house or discounted memberships to nearby health clubs. Running or walking groups are another good way to bond with colleagues or friends. My brother Michael runs five miles at lunch with a group of men and women from different professions who work nearby.

Working out together can be a good bonding experience with colleagues. As long as you are aware that some prefer to work out alone or use that as cerebral think time. Don't badger your boss by always selecting the machine near him or her. Allow people their space.

Spectator Sports

Sometimes organizations have outings to spectator sporting events. Inexpensive tickets and group packages can be had for minor league "farm team" baseball. Even if you don't like baseball, go for the social aspect, because there are so many activities to keep your attention besides the game, like mascot races, contests that involve audience members and even a hotdog cannon. Who doesn't love a device that shoots food into the air? Bring your catcher's mitt.

Chambers of commerce often sponsor "Chamber Night" at the ballpark, which are a great networking opportunity to get to know people from other businesses.

Company Seats

When I worked at Sony Music, we had season tickets to the Chicago Bears football and Chicago Bulls basketball games.

I was still new to Sony Music when I won a pair of tickets in a workplace lottery to see the Bulls in the playoffs against the Cleveland Cavaliers. Seeing Michael Jordan and Scottie Pippen in action from the 10th row, center court seats was unforgettable.

With great seats, comes accountability. Season tickets often take years to secure. I have heard of organizations losing their seats, because the people they treated behaved badly, by becoming drunk or argumentative and obnoxious to the people around them. Always treat good seats that aren't your own as if they were your own.

Volunteer for Organization Sponsored Events

When your organization is a major sponsor of a community or charitable event, like a marathon, 5K run, golf tournament, Special Olympics®, or other event, don't just attend, volunteer. Help check people in, run a water station, be a gopher who runs errands, help set up or tear down.

Volunteer work can be fun. It gets you out of the workplace and it feels good to do something for your community. And one of the best benefits is you meet nice people, because nice people volunteer.

Holidays and Other Celebrations in the Workplace

There are certain times where you want the staff to cut loose and have fun. But trust me, precious few want to play games or wear costumes.

We covered the Workplace Party in Chapter 6.2: *You Have Arrived: Being Entertained.* Now to cover the other occasions where there is pressure to participate, that may not be in your best career interests.

Halloween In the Workplace is Scary

"Are you a fun hater?" said an angry woman on the phone. This was my first call of the day when I had an article in the newspaper about how wearing a Halloween costume to work is not great career move, especially when there's no costume party.

"Sometimes we just need to let our hair down," protested the woman. "Is it so wrong to have a little fun?"

While I am no hater of fun, I know the higher you aspire, the more you must guard your image. Once, I made the mistake of making an appointment at an eye clinic on Halloween. The woman who checked me in was dressed like Tippi Hedren from Alfred Hitchcock's *The Birds.* She had on a white shirt with fake blood and fake black crows attached to her shirt and to her blonde hair.

What's the most graphic scene in *The Birds*? It has to do with eyes and birds. Enough said. Why would anyone think that was a good idea to remind people of that at an eye clinic?

I don't get Halloween. I don't get it.

I don't get adults who come to work in a Halloween costume.

I don't get the woman who brings her kids to my door and reaches over their heads into my basket of treats and says, "You don't mind if we (moms) have some too, right?" If I were your kid, I'd wear a mask, too.

I really don't get people that hand out *Raisinets*®. You can't even trade those for anything.

At the eye doctor's office, other members of the staff were in costume, but the doctor was not.

"Why aren't you in costume?" I asked.

"I need to be taken seriously," said the doctor.

Did that mean others at the practice were not to be taken seriously?

A friend of mine described a similar situation, with a doctor, who took the opposite view. My friend was diagnosed with breast cancer and her doctor referred her to a cancer specialist. Her appointment was on Halloween and everyone at the doctor's office was in costume. The receptionist was dressed like the Devil. She had horns on her head and a dog collar around her neck, tied with a string holding up a tail at the other end. One nurse was dressed as a vampire. The doctor was dressed as a clown.

She said it was awful. None of the women in the waiting room were laughing. They were sitting there shell shocked – feeling anxious and nervous, dealing with their mortality. She could not believe the insensitivity of the medical staff.

Some want to inject a little fun into the workplace, release their inner child. So what's the harm? Some think it creates a fun and festive mood. But it can really cause anxiety and discomfort and erode the trust factor. While staff is on board, clients may not be.

I went to a bank on Halloween where my teller was dressed as a vampire, with fake blood streaming from his mouth. It was gross and disturbing. This is the person I am supposed to trust with my savings?

Dressing in a Halloween costume gets especially weird if your organization doesn't have any costume events or party. In several places I've worked, a few people just showed up in costume.

Many managers I have talked to frown on Halloween costumes at work, as distracting and unprofessional. Talk about a career killer.

Nobody loses that image. Months later, when several are vying for the same promotion, it may not go to Elvis or Frankenstein's Bride.

Still, there are those in the workplace who insist on foisting a workplace Halloween costume party on everyone else. Is it because if they held the party at home, few people would show? A workplace costume party is a celebration with a captive audience.

Whatever you do, don't harangue the people who bring in their leftover Halloween candy. Even if you're on a diet. It's not about you. It's about people who like leftover candy.

Lose the Secret Santa

When it comes to the workplace holiday party, forget the Secret Santa. Secret Santas are where people pull a name of a co-worker from a hat and then buy (or re-gift) that person a secret "gag" gift. Don't do it. We all have enough to do outside the workplace this month. Most men don't buy their own Secret Santa gift anyway, their wives or assistants do it.

I have sat through too many uncomfortable exchanges where someone who purchased a nice gift got a discount store gag gift in exchange. I remember comforting my assistant crying in the restroom after a thoughtless jerk gave her an insulting book that hurt her feelings.

Like the workplace costume party, the Secret Santa is a holiday hostage situation, usually proposed by someone who is not looking to advance in their career. It's okay to opt out.

There are better ways to celebrate at the office. At Amana Appliances, the Consumer Affairs Department had incredible potlucks. Everyone would bring in homemade appetizers, salads and desserts. It was always a huge spread and people would gnosh on that all day.

The most important takeaway here is not everyone likes to put on costumes and have a Secret Santa. But everyone likes food. Workplace potlucks are easy to execute. Non-cooks can contribute plates, utensils and beverages. Moochers who don't contribute anything kick in $10 to go to a local soup kitchen or go towards the next office party. If you want a workplace party, don't play games, just have food.

The Group Gift Shake Down

Also banned, should be the workplace elf who says, "I'm collecting money so we can get the boss a gift." Usually this ends up with the boss getting a $100 decorative candle or a snow globe.

Someone told me about a gift collector in a workplace that was using "the boss's gift" as a self-enrichment program. About half the money collected was actually spent on the boss's gift and the collector pocketed the rest. If someone is buying a group gift, ask to see receipts.

One person told me about a group gift to a superior that came with a card that said, "THESE PEOPLE WHO SIGNED THE CARD are the ONLY ONES WHO CONTRIBUTED." That was certainly not in the spirit of the season.

Collective gifts should be used sparingly – there should not be a collections agent in the workplace shaking co-workers down for every birthday, engagement, wedding, new baby, etc. If you do have a collective gift, contributions should be optional and not under duress.

Birthday Celebrations

At one place I worked, I used to get invited to birthday lunches, while my supervisor, who was not well-liked, and a few others I worked with, were not invited. I still went. I was young and the birthday lunch people were fun. But it was always awkward when I got back to the office.

When you celebrate birthdays, anniversaries or other occasions in your workplace or department, celebrate each person's birthday, not a select few. Or have a monthly cake to celebrate the birthdays of that month. If a group of people go out for lunch to celebrate someone's birthday, everyone should be invited or the group should keep it quiet.

It's My Party

Don't hand out in the workplace, invitations to private, non-work related celebrations, unless everyone is invited. Don't use your work email to invite people to a private party.

Workplace Lottery Pools

My sister was in a workplace lottery pool where a group of 23 employees won more than $40 million. But there were many people in her workplace who played regularly who did not play that week.

Rumors started flying that the lottery winners were going to split the winnings with everyone, even those who didn't play. The winners were not about to do that, because they had assumed the risk in the first place. The lottery win created a lot of hard feelings.

Workplace lottery pools erupt when one person purchases tickets for the group, then claims a winning ticket was a separate purchase with the person's own money. Some plaintiffs in these cases have sued successfully to have the winnings divided. Others, who had no contracts or documentation, were out of luck.

In my sister's workplace, everyone who participated each week put in a dollar and signed their name to a sheet of paper. One person would make the ticket purchase, then make copies of all the tickets available to each participant before the drawing. That way, all the participants had access to the group's numbers.

NCAA Brackets

It's a given that the die-hard sports fan who follows basketball religiously never wins the workplace pool for the NCAA Basketball Tournament, aka "March Madness." The winner will be someone who knows nothing about basketball, who picked the teams because he or she had been to the team towns or liked the color of their uniforms.

March Madness pools are fun, but you must ensure they don't take over the workplace, so that work is not getting done. No watching games on your smartphone while you are on a conference call.

Stick to the rules. All filled out brackets must be in before the first tip-off. Like the office lottery pool, document participants' picks.

So whether you got game or are really lame, add sports and other activities to your bonding with co-workers. When the activity is not in your best career interest, opt out.

In this chapter, we've opened the door a crack on little annoyances in the workplace. Now it's time to address the big annoyances. The name of the chapter says it all. It's time to talk about working with knuckleheads.

10.4 *Knuckleheads*

Have you ever had a bad boss? One who really made your blood boil? Early in my career, I was an assistant to an awful human being. Every day, it felt like he wanted to squash me like a bug.

> *"You're not very smart, are you?"*
> *"You'll never be as good as my LAST assistant."*

One day, he was reviewing a research article I had worked on for two weeks. It was one where I had to call up people who did not want to talk to me and coax information out of them. He glanced at the article and exhaled loudly. I braced myself for what was coming. *"Are you kidding me? Can't you do anything? I'll have to re-write this!"*

Then he switched two sentences around and put his name at the top of *my article.* He put my name underneath, as the secondary author.

My resentment was volcanic. I felt the lava bubbling and rising inside me. My face was getting hot and I started to shake. I was seething with anger as I faced my boss and I… turned and went down the hallway to the bathroom and cried. (Did I mention it was early in my career?)

Call them "toxic," "people with issues" or "difficult people." They fall under one category: knuckleheads. Being an *Exceptional Professional* isn't just about how to act, *but how to react* to people who behave in a not-so-professional manner.

In this chapter, you will learn:

- How to deal with, deflect or dodge knuckleheads
- What do to before you escalate
- How to work things out
- How to deal with a bully boss
- When to move on

Who are the knuckleheads? The people who hinder productivity:

The ones who can't live without drama
The ones who are ruled by their insecurities

The ones who start the gossip
The ones who are socially challenged
The ones who are miserable and want others to be miserable, too
The ones who lack attention and will do anything to get it
The ones who need to be right, at all costs
The ones who are just plain mean

Sound like anyone you have worked with? We live in a world of flawed individuals. Some lacked good mentors or examples in life. Others have inner struggles. A few have what John Cusack's character in the movie *Grosse Pointe Blank* called, "a certain moral flexibility."

At the beginning of my career, I thought anyone who worked hard, helped others and was nice to everyone, would be valued. But we run into bad circumstances and difficult people. Our ability to work with others and navigate challenging circumstances determines our success.

Tough Love

Let's begin with some "tough love." This is difficult for me to say, but I only say this because I care. *Not everybody is going to like you.*

Hard to believe, isn't it? Because you are a nice person, right? It's very sad! No matter how nice you are, how hard you work or how much you contribute, some people will find something not to like about you.

What is WRONG with them? (sniff...sigh) Step number one on the road to recovery is realizing *they have a problem.*

While it's always healthy to self-reflect, it's also important to realize people who don't like you may have other challenges going on. Maybe you look like someone who treated them badly. Maybe you remind them of a relative to whom they no longer speak. Maybe you are better looking than them or smarter. Maybe it is some insecurity on their part. Who knows? Whatever it is, it's out of your control.

Don't Let Them Make Their Problems, *Your Problems*

You can't control other people's rude behavior but you can control how you react to it. On the inside, you decide. As a wise CEO once told me, "Try not to let them make their problems, your problems."

When people treat us badly, it's usually *not ABOUT us.* Dr. P.M. Forni of the Johns Hopkins Civility Initiative, and author of *The Civility Solution: What to Do When People are Rude,* said rudeness originates "from a bad state of mind" in the person who is behaving rudely. It might be stress, unhappiness or lack of time. While rudeness often feels personal, it isn't. Dr. Forni says, "When we realize that the rudeness others send our way stems from their own problems, it is much easier not to become deeply upset. We just leave the package of rudeness unopened, since it doesn't belong to us."[29]

Practice Restraint

When dealing with knuckleheads or toxic employees, one of the best practices is to keep a cool head.

Not Every Wisecrack Needs a Comeback

Practicing restraint means not every remark or slight needs a response. We're so conditioned to think, "I have to have a clever comeback." Ever beat yourself up later because you thought of a great comeback *too late? "I should have said THIS... Rats!"*

Have you ever allowed a co-worker to rattle your confidence or make you feel inadequate? Have you ever worried about what a workplace gossip was saying behind your back? When we let rude people get to us or let others make us feel bad, we hand over control of our lives to them.

Earlier in my career, I spent a lot of time talking when I should have been listening. I never liked to lose an argument. I grew up in a large family where we were always challenging and debating each other. When it came to the art of verbal self-defense, I was skilled. But a strong person uses restraint. Dr. P.M. Forni, said in his first civility book, *Choosing Civility*, "Restraint is the art of feeling good later."[30]

At Amana Appliances, I said to one of the engineers, "The people in Marketing are going at each other today – so many strong personalities and personality conflicts." The engineer said, "We don't have that problem in Engineering, because engineers don't have any personality."

Don't Take the Bait

Using restraint also means deflecting people who want to draw you into conflict. An organization I worked for had a policy against discussing your salary with your co-workers. A woman came to me one day and said, "I heard a rumor that (So and so) makes more money than you." My response was, "If I am happy with what I make, what does it matter what other people make?"

She stood looking at me for a minute, then went, "Huh," and moved on. She wanted a reaction from me – jealousy, indignation or rage. She was trying to start a fire so she could stand on the sidelines and watch it combust. I chose to give her nothing.

Gossips spread harmful rumors and hearsay to damage others' reputations. Gossips use people. Gossiping is addictive – gossips crave it like a narcotic and want more and more. Managers sometimes listen to gossips, but almost never promote them. Whatever you say about others will get back to them. So why not say something positive? There are several ways to deflect gossips:

- Counteract: say admirable things about the objects of their gossip
- Object: *"I don't think that's any of our business."*
- Walk away: refuse to participate
- Guilt trip: *"I wonder what you say about me when I'm not around."*

Gossips may try to alienate you if you don't play their game. That will be offset by the trust you will gain from others by not participating.

It Doesn't Pay to Be Jealous

We all encounter co-workers who brag about money, cars, homes, vacations and all things material. A friend of mine in Washington D.C. had a great way of dispatching notorious braggarts. She would smile and say, (the emphasis is important) *"How nice FOR you."* Her inflection was so subtle and her smile so sweet, sometimes they did not realize they were being neutralized and brought down to size.

This is different from saying, "How nice for YOU," which implies a tinge of jealously on your part.

No need to be envious of people boasting of material wealth, because many live beyond their means. It's what Thomas J. Stanley and William D. Danko, authors of *The Millionaire Next Door*, called the "Big Hat, No Cattle" theory.[31] It's all for show when your yearnings get ahead of your earnings. When people are not smart with their own money, why should anyone trust theme to be smart with the organization's money?

Before You Escalate

Before making a formal complaint against a person, consider the options.

Weigh Pros and Cons of Doing Nothing

Sometimes a person's behavior is so egregious, someone needs to tell them off. Everyone in your workplace says so. You decide to step up and tell that person off publicly, so everyone can witness it and be satisfied a hot plate of comeuppance was served. You'll do it, because you're a doer. You could be the superhero of your workplace. Everyone will be cheering for you. Right? Step back, take a breath. Then think:

- Could the situation be handled better with a side-conversation, not a public flogging? It is not professional to correct the behavior of others in public, unless they call you, "Mom" or "Dad."

- Should the message come from someone else, like a supervisor?
- Is it best to let it go?

Don't even think about an anonymous note. What was awful in grammar school is worse in the professional world. If you can't say it in person, don't say it.

Keep in mind, if you lodge a complaint against your co-worker, Barb, it might still reflect poorly on you. Management may not interpret that as, "Barb is a problem," but rather, "You and Barb don't get along." If you are perceived to be one who can't get along with others, you will never advance or get good assignments.

Acting as a referee for petty complaints costs a manager time and money. Before you escalate, take time to let it percolate.

Don't Argue

These following words of wisdom for the road pop up in various forms from Dale Carnegie to Louis Untermeyer's *Golden Treasury of Poetry*:

Here lies the body of Michael Shay,
who died maintaining his right of way.
His case was clear and his will was strong,
But he's just as dead as if he'd been wrong.

Dale Carnegie, in *How to Win Friends and Influence People,* pointed out when you win arguments, you really lose. It "will be an empty victory because you will never get your opponent's good will."[32]

I worked in a workplace with a man who would barge into conversations and ask inappropriate, prying questions. Also in the workplace was a woman from New Jersey who had a singular way of dealing with him. "Shut up, you jerk!" she would say.

While a surprisingly effective deterrent, it's not one I would recommend. With someone like this butt-in-ski, you don't need to be hostile, but you do need to set boundaries. *"Hold that thought - we're in mid-conversation." Or "If you need me, I'll be with you shortly."*

Have Lunch, Not War

Before running your complaint up the chain of command, try to resolve differences on your own. Problem solvers are evolvers. Problem solvers get promoted. Complainers get to complain about working for them. Invite the person you are having a dispute with out to coffee or lunch.

I had a jealous co-worker who was always talking behind my back and making power grabs for my job. The problem peaked when my supervisor came to me with copies of my press releases, all marked up. My supervisor said my jealous co-worker found many mistakes and suggested I run press releases by the co-worker before sending them out. My supervisor was not confident in her own proofreading or grammar skills, so this was unsettling for her.

I glanced at the corrections and said, "I'm an English major. I can cite the rules that show why these corrections are not correct." I assured the supervisor she had nothing to worry about, that I would have a conversation with my co-worker. I went to my co-worker and said, "Why don't we go to lunch in the cafeteria?"

"I don't eat in the cafeteria," she huffed. I said, "Fine. How about if we leave the building and eat at this place down the street?" We did. Over lunch, I just let her talk. It turns out, she had a difficult life and her family had failed her. Growing up, she shouldered responsibilities no young person should. I gained respect for her perseverance in adversity.

When we returned to the workplace, nothing changed. She still talked behind my back and made power grabs for my job. But at least I knew where she was coming from *and that helped me.*

We should strive for peace in the workplace and try to get along, no matter what our differences. Always make an effort towards that end. Sometimes you will be pleasantly surprised. Admit your differences and make a case for working together:

"We both have our differences, but if we could agree to work on them, we could be a great team."
"I don't want to be at odds. I want us to work together. We have been fighting each other. Our competition is who we should be fighting."

Taking It to the Next Level

Always try to resolve conflict on your own first. If you are not able to resolve the issue, then it's time to consider the next steps.

It's Not Personal, It's Financial

Knuckleheads in the workplace are no longer a personal issue. They are a financial issue. Not many people care if your feelings are hurt. But top management cares when the bottom line is hurt.

Christine Pearson and Christine Porath, authors of *The Cost of Bad Behavior*, assert that businesses try to cut costs, but miss a significant expense caused by bad behavior, estimated to cost American businesses billions annually.[33] When filing a formal complaint, don't make it about a personality conflict, make it about the money.

I had a co-worker who went into a shared server and deleted a large number of edits I made on shared content. My mistake was not keeping a back-up copy. That sabotage cost me over two weeks of work.

A saboteur costs an organization money and time. Human resources doesn't always care about money like upper management, so bypass human resources on a case like this. That's what I did and the person was let go.

Steps to Filing a Formal Complaint

The formal complaint should always be your port of last resort. But if you must file a formal complaint, here are the steps:

Step 1: Document, Document, Document

Write down any discussions or confrontations in detail:

- Date, time and place
- What was said
- The circumstances

- How you felt
- Capture details. If the person swore at you, write down the words. If the person slammed their hand down on the desk, write that down.

Keep your notes locked up and keep an additional copy at home. Print out emails and put them in your documentation folder. Get legal counsel if you feel you need it.

Sexual Harassment

Sexual harassment is an instance where you need to document every detail. According to the U.S. Equal Employment Opportunity Commission, "...Harassment can include 'sexual harassment' or unwelcome sexual advances, requests for sexual favors, and other verbal or physical harassment of a sexual nature. Harassment does not have to be of a sexual nature, however, and can include offensive remarks about a person's sex. For example, it is illegal to harass a woman by making offensive comments about women in general..."[34]

Be clear in your communication. Use the words, "Stop," "No" and "Unwelcome." If the harassing behavior persists or you feel threatened, consult an attorney, then make a formal complaint. In the case of a physical attack, contact the police immediately.

Hollywood often portrays sexual harassers as men 30 years older than their victims. What surprised me, is the worst sexual harassers I faced in my 20s were close to my age or just a few years older. Shouldn't men raised in an era of sexual harassment awareness know better?

One supervisor said the most awful, disgusting things to me, often publicly in meetings in front of others. It made me appreciate all the men I worked with later in my career who behaved like gentlemen.

Step 2: Talk to Someone You Trust

If your efforts to solve the problem on your own fail, the next step is to talk to someone you trust. It could be a supervisor, mentor or anyone else above you in the chain of command with whom you have a good working relationship. Review the issue or conflict with that person and get his or her feedback on your next steps. Decide if the issue is serious enough to consult an attorney or other experts.

Step 3: Filing the Formal Complaint

Follow your organization's instructions for filing a formal complaint. If you fill out any paperwork, do not leave without a copy for yourself. Your other option is to write a formal business letter. (See "How to Format a Business Letter" in Chapter 9.1: *Better Business Writing*.) Depending on the nature or gravity of your complaint, it may go to:

- Your supervisor
- Department head
- Human resources
- CEO or chairman of the board
- An outside regulating association

Follow the protocol in your organization. Every complaint doesn't need to go straight to the CEO. Start with your supervisor. If you are not satisfied with the response, take it to the next level and so on.

The Bully Boss

If you have ever had a bully boss, you know "Monday dread." That is when, on Sunday night, you hate the thought of getting up the next morning and having to face another work week with a despot. When a bully boss rouses a reign of terror, some employees band together and hunker down in survival mode. Others flee for their professional lives.

Types of Bully Bosses

Screamers: explosive, temper tantrum throwers that go off at a moment's notice. They rule by intimidating and keeping people on edge.

Verbal Abusers: constantly criticize, use put-downs, resort to name-calling and try to humiliate employees in front of others.

Control Freaks: are micromanagers who want to control minute details. They are often terrified of making mistakes and worried about losing their job. Some block employees from networking with others.

Slave Drivers: are punishing superiors that pile on work and make employees feel they will lose their job if they don't get it done. Some slave drivers are workaholics themselves, but not always.

Characteristics of the Bully Boss:

- Insecure: driven by fear, envy or self-doubt
- Indecisive: frequently changes direction
- Good at "kissing up" to his or her own superiors
- Isolationist: will often attack their targets where they can't be heard or observed

Who is Their Target?

- Independent
- Self-starting
- More technically skilled than their bullies
- Team player
- Better liked
- Honest and ethical
- Non-confrontive[35]

If you are the target of an abusive boss, take it as a compliment. I had a boss who said, "You wouldn't understand any of this – *it's a 'numbers' thing*." I responded, "I have an MBA with a concentration in accounting, so actually, I do understand the numbers."

Immediately, I saw his face change and I knew, despite his slight, this was a case of talking when I should have been listening. After that, he made my life miserable. He gave me demeaning tasks, he started demanding PowerPoint decks describing my responsibilities, he wanted to move me out of my office into a cubicle.

He was an inherited boss – not the one who hired me. So he never saw my resume and didn't realize I out-degreed him. It wasn't something I broadcasted. But this is a case where I would have been better off had I used some restraint and not relished having the last word.

Dealing with The Bully Boss

Many stay in place and put up with a bully boss, thinking they can wait it out. There is another option besides "put up and shut up."

Confront the Bully Boss

Talk to the bully boss and be direct.

> *"There is a better way to deal with this than calling me names. Let me know how I can address the situation."*

> *"While I appreciate that you care about my work, I feel like you are too involved in the details. I would like to discuss with you ways I can gain your trust."*

Some have told me how they stood up to their bully boss and ended up earning that person's respect. But this could also make the boss even more crazy and he or she could make your life worse.

Show No Emotion

If people are screaming at you, they have already lost control and they want you to lose control too, by crying or screaming back.

Don't do it. Show no emotion, be Stoic. Speak in a calm, soft tone. If you want people to know you mean business, speak slower and lower your volume. The same bully boss who said, "You wouldn't understand ... it's a 'numbers' thing," came completely unglued once and was yelling at me in his office. "Why don't YOU JUST QUIT?!" he raged.

I think he expected a woman to burst into tears and fold. But bully bosses early in my career made me tough. Instead of crumbling, I leaned forward and said slowly and calmly, "If you want to fire me, *then fire me.* I will not quit, because I am doing a good job." He was completely taken aback.

Finally, at his boiling point, he screamed, "You know what I can't stand about you? I CAN'T READ YOU!" And that's how it works. He was baffled and frustrated. But in a powerless situation, I felt powerful.

Don't show anger, surprise, shock, fear. Give them nothing. Do not be afraid to say, *"Let's take a step back and discuss this later."* Or, *"That discussion was a little heated, can we try again?"*

Don't Cry at Work

Try not to let people see you cry at work. If you feel the impulse to bawl, remove yourself from the situation. Head for the restroom, head out the door. Get some air. Walk around, stretch. Change your mindset from the hopelessness of the current situation to a positive outlook for the future.

If you are the supervisor dealing with an emotional person who burst into tears, give them some space. *"I can see how this is affecting you, let's take a few moments and reconvene."*

Going Over the Bully's Head

It bears repeating: try to resolve any conflict on your own first, before taking it to the next level. Then follow the Steps for Filing a Formal Complaint, outlined earlier in this chapter.

Warning: Before you file the formal complaint against a bad boss, have a Plan B – somewhere else to go. In most bad boss situations, the bad boss stays in place. The bad boss who told me to quit, did end up firing me. He fired me on a Friday and by Monday, I had a new job.

Action might be swifter if instead of a personnel issue, bully bosses were weighed financially. Does the department despot raise enough revenue to offset the costs of employee turnover? These costs include recruitment, time of others involved in the interview process and training and learning curve productivity loss. As with other knuckleheads, don't make your case a personality conflict, make it about financial costs.

Unseat those who mistreat. Organizations should be encouraged to weed out bullies and toxic employees. Recognize warning signs like increased absenteeism or turnover. Pay attention to exit interviews. Keep lines of communication open and reward good behavior.

When to Move On

If a resolution cannot be reached, leave the organization, especially if your health is affected. Most people who leave a bad boss situation end up in happier circumstances. Before you quit:

- Can you make a lateral move to another department?
- How much time before you are vested?
- Look at other options in marketplace. Are other organizations hiring?
- In order to move to another job, would you need additional training?

Have your resume ready to go if it doesn't work out. Whether you quit, get fired or laid off, leaving a toxic environment is a golden opportunity to try new things. My brother-in-law, who volunteered to do readings in church, had a deep, sonorous voice. People said to him, "You have a great voice – you should do voice-over work."

When he was laid off from his tech job, he took voice-over and acting classes. Soon enough, he became the voice of different products from Butterball Turkey® to Mercedes Benz®. Organizations also hired him for training videos and other presentations. Today, he still works full time in the tech industry, but also does voice-over work on the side.

Make Your Workplace a Better Place

We've spent a lot of space talking about how to battle or deflect the knuckleheads in the workplace. How do we keep the peace? How can we make our workplace a better place?

The Opposite of Conflict is Connection

People crave connection – that authentic person to person "heartspark" contact that lends meaning, security and value to our lives. What are some ways to connect with people in your workplace?

- Greet people you pass in the hallway or on your way in and out of the building.
- Take an interest in people and get to know them.
- Be a good team player who shares credit and builds other up.
- Reach out to people who are new and introduce them to others.

Validate Others

Give people your attention. *Choosing Civility* author, Dr. P.M. Forni said, "Listening is the most fundamental form of validation." Validate early and often. Give unexpected compliments and encouragement to others. Be sincere. Don't flatter with false words.

> *"You did an excellent job on that presentation."*
> *"Thank you for your help with that project."*

Sometimes you can turn around a knucklehead co-worker who feels neglected and under-appreciated. Keep your guard up but never write off anyone. Keep responding with kindness. There are enough people in this world to make people feel bad about themselves. Why not make people feel good about themselves?

Have Confidence in Yourself

It comes back to the tough love: not everybody is going to like you. It doesn't matter. Do you like you? Know your gifts and your limitations, but don't be ruled by your limitations. Knuckleheads prey on others' insecurities. When you are more confident and resilient, it's difficult for knuckleheads to get to you. See the good in yourself and in others.

Let Peace Begin with You

Work on workplace relationships. Begin with that annoying knucklehead co-worker you want to kick to the moon. Start with a clean slate. Try to be accepting or forgiving of quirks and character flaws.

Don't plot revenge. People that focus on revenge hurt themselves. They stress themselves out and their hate eats them from the inside out. Plotting revenge:

- Wastes your organization's time and makes you less productive
- Sucks the energy out of you and wears you out
- Is unhealthy – it creates tension and stress as anger builds

Never demand an apology. That's a hollow power play. Who cares if the person never apologizes? You may not be able to fix people that were damaged long before you started working together. But you always have control over how you react to them. Let peace begin with you.

Getting Past The Grudge

Insults and incidents roll off some people like water off a duck. Why is it that some people can forget an insult by lunchtime, while others will carry it with them all week...and possibly to the grave?

When we hold in anger, the hate does not dissipate, it turns into real estate. That is what a grudge is – allowing the person who has wounded us to rent real estate in our head and our heart. When we hold a grudge, it only hurts one person. My anger held me back for years, because the space in my head that could have been used for more productive, creative thinking, was occupied by people from the past who had hurt me. Then I found a secret weapon against words that wound, more powerful than a punch in the nose.

Use the F-Word

The secret weapon, is to use the F-word. Most people don't like to use the F-word, but trust me, it's liberating.

The F-word is... *Forgive.* Words can wound or they can heal. Forgiveness is a healing word. It's not always easy to use. The root is "give," because it requires us to give of ourselves, sometimes to people who don't seem to deserve it. Mother Teresa said, "Forgive endlessly." What a call to action! People think Mother Teresa was this sweet, little nun who helped poor people, but she was tough as nails. She would not have accomplished everything she did if she had not been tough.

Forgive...*endlessly.* She said we need to start with the people in our own families. Obviously, Mother Teresa never met *my family.* Growing up, we fought like barbarians. Still do. Whether you have one sibling, or eight siblings as I did, you never lose anything. If you can't find it, it's because somebody took it.

Forgiveness was easier when we were kids, wasn't it? We could fight like wild animals and the next day, be back in the sandbox, like nothing ever happened. Why as adults do we hang on to our anger? Do you have family members who don't speak to each other? One will say, "I can NEVER forgive him or her." We all have the power to forgive.

Maybe, it's time to get back to the sandbox. Start talking to those you have refused to talk to in the past. Mend fences. Forgiving others is sometimes difficult, but you need to forgive in order to move forward. The solution is *resolution.*

The good news is, no workplace conflict is wasted time. It's a character building experience and a learning opportunity. When I was still green out of college, I worked for a few powder-keg bosses with explosive tempers who made me tear up. If I were to meet them now, I would say this: "Thank you. You made me tough."

All this talk about knuckleheads in the workplace makes you realize, it's good to get out of the workplace once in a while. Next up, we'll talk about hitting the road.

TRAVEL

11.1 *Get Packing for Air Travel*

It was the Sanitation Department's pick-up day for bulky trash. You know, where people put out all sorts of furniture and other large items that would not fit in the regular trash? One of my brother-in-law's friends was driving to work and he spotted a set of luggage in good condition.

While he was not normally the type to pick up someone else's trash, he said to himself, "I can't believe what people throw out." He pulled over and tossed the luggage in his trunk. The luggage felt like it had a little weight to it, but he shrugged it off because he was late for work.

At home that evening, he opened the luggage. It was packed with dress shirts, ties and a shaving kit – for a business trip. The owner was not discarding it after all. He must have been waiting for a taxi or limo and left his luggage on the curb, while he went back into his house. The unwitting luggage thief, left the luggage stealthily on the porch of the house where he found it, along with an anonymous apology note.

In business travel, when things go wrong, you must be strong. *The Exceptional Professional* is prepared for anything and is as at ease on the road as much as at home. In this chapter, we'll cover business travel by air. The next chapter covers transportation by car and hotels.

In this chapter, you will learn:

- How to select the right bag for business travel
- How to pack for a business trip without checking a bag

- The best way to get through airport security
- In-flight insights for a smooth trip

A Bag That is Easy to Identify

Have you ever lost your luggage and had to describe your bag to the airline customer service agents? "It's black and rectangular." The agent turns around and faces a sea of 100-plus bags, all black and rectangular.

Some people tie a ribbon around the handle to make it easier to identify. At one point, I thought about getting one of those Hello Kitty® bags. That way, when I lose my luggage, I can tell the airline agent, "It's pink and it has a big white cat face on it... two eyes, a nose, no mouth." The agent will say, "Oh yes, I remember it well. It's right here."

When selecting the right piece of luggage, find a bag that is easy to distinguish, so you can pick it out of the line-up of suitcases on the jet bridge, find it easily on a baggage claim turnaround or recognize it sitting on the tarmac in the rain as your plane is pulling away.

You don't want it to be too distinctive. If someone were stealing luggage, wouldn't they go for the most expensive looking ones? Or if you are traveling with your boss, you might not want a bag with designer logos all over it – especially if you are trying for a salary increase.

Learn to Live Without Checked Luggage

I traveled with a team of executives from Iowa to New York to interview advertising agencies for Amana Appliances' brand revitalization campaign. We landed at New York's LaGuardia Airport and with our carry-on luggage, started heading for the taxi stand.

But one of the team had checked a bag. The rest of us had to wait 45 minutes for his bag to appear on the baggage turnaround. When it did appear, it was enormous, like he was packing for a family of four. We were only going to be away for three days. Usually, men have an easier time packing light than women. He was embarrassed but he learned from it. I never saw him with a checked bag again.

In business, learn to live without checked luggage. It's more efficient – you can grab your bag and be on your way. And with airlines requiring extra fees for checked bags, it's more economical.

At smaller airports, the wait at the baggage carousel might be 15 minutes or so. At larger airports, it could be 30 minutes or more. Think of how far you could have been away from the airport in that 30 minutes.

Most airlines limit carry-ons to a combined length, plus width, plus height of 45 inches. That's usually a bag with wheels, around 22 inches tall, that will fit into most overhead bins. A duffel on wheels can be squished to go where framed luggage cannot.

How to Pack for a Business Trip

Packing a carry-on is a skill and requires practice. There's no need to bring shoes to match every outfit.

What to Pack for a Four-Day Conference

This is the plan for packing a 22 inch carry-on for air travel. If you are driving on business, you can pack more and bring extra bags.

For Women:

dress shoes and walking shoes
2 skirt or pant suits (or 1 suit with an extra jacket or extra skirt or pants)
4 shirts/blouses
extra pair of pants
1 sweater (I bring a light cashmere that's warm, but not bulky)
2 pairs of silk stockings, plus 2-3 pairs of dress socks
5 pairs of underwear (always carry a spare)
pashmina scarf (as an accessory or warm wrap in a chilly conference)
sleepwear
makeup kit

For Men:
dress shoes and walking shoes
2 suits (or 1 suit with an extra jacket or extra pants)
4 shirts
extra pair of pants
1 sweater
2 neckties
4 pairs of dress socks
5 pairs of underwear (again, the spare)
sleepwear
shaving-kit

Bring clothing with colors that mix and match. For instance, a navy suit, an extra pair of pants in gray and shirts or blouses that can be worn with either. When traveling for business, there are two things to consider when selecting what sleepwear to pack:

1. Comfort
2. What you would not mind your supervisor, co-workers or the TV cameras seeing you in outside on the curb if the hotel must be evacuated during the night, because of a fire or other emergency. You don't want to be caught in your ripped Metallica t-shirt and boxers, that nightie that makes you feel sexy or... well, you know.

The Packing Order

You will wear one outfit and one pair of shoes in transit, so you won't have to pack that. I wear the sweater, too, because I am usually freezing on airplanes. It's wise to dress in layers, in case you are on a sauna flight.

- The other pair of shoes goes up against one side of the carry-on.
- Roll or fold the outfit you plan to wear last and put it in the bottom of the suitcase.

- Fit the pajamas into the front of the suitcase (near the top handle) with makeup or shaving kit on top.
- Layer other shirts and pants in the order you plan to wear them.
- Fill in socks and other items around any gaps.
- Fold suit jackets on top.

BE EXCEPTIONAL: Carol Moy's Packing Tips for Women

My long-time friend Carol Moy, who I first met at Sony Music, knows how to be professional and chic, while packing light, so I asked for her packing tips for women for a four-day conference:

1. Black or white are the most versatile colors for tops and bottoms, either as a solid color or coordinates. These colors instantly look sleek mix and matched.
2. Jersey material is comfortable to wear, packs well and generally does not wrinkle.
3. If it is truly dressy event, then a sleek top with a skirt, either pencil or A-line is great. Dresses are fine, but if the material wrinkles easily, you will look like an unmade bed.
4. Pants must be appropriate for the occasion. They should be dress pants or pants with easy movement, as that is sometimes dressy.
5. For shoes, black pumps or silver strappy sandals with off-black or flesh-colored hosiery.
6. The clothes and shoes above can be mixed and matched with jackets, pants, etc. to create other outfits during the 4-day conference, reducing the amount of clothing you need to pack.
7. Accessories distinguish the outfit: earrings, necklaces in gold or silver, bold costume jewelry, scarves (double as shawls, cover-ups, etc.) They are small to pack and make a huge impact.
8. Bring a small clutch bag with a hidden strap for versatility.

Carol says, "If there will be more than one dressy event, pack more dressy blouses. I prefer lightweight polyester/rayon in a feminine print, as it does not wrinkle. If it does, the design makes it less visible. You can also hang it in the shower and the steam will help the wrinkles fall out."

The Bag of Liquids

Take any liquids (makeup, toothpaste, shaving gel, hair gel, etc.) and put it in a plastic baggie in an outer pocket of the carry-on, so you can take it out going through airport security. I never like putting all these liquids in a see-through bag – it feels like all my beauty secrets, laid bare to the world. Most women's makeup is a hodge podge of different brands purchased from a variety of locations. If your plastic baggie gets lost or left behind, that makeup cannot be replaced overnight.

If you forget something, most hotels have complimentary razors, toothbrushes, toothpaste, deodorant and other hygiene products at the front desk. I usually bring my own shampoo, because I don't always like the smell of the complimentary hotel shampoo. I do like the hotel hand lotions with the lemon and sage scents. But aren't those both things people put on turkeys before they cook them?

Never overpack. The more disorganized your bag is, the more likely it will be opened at the airport security checkpoint. You don't want your carry-on to be like one of those jack-in-the-boxes as the security agents are unzipping it. *Da-dat-da-dat-da-da-da-dat...* KA-BOOM!! Shirts, socks, underwear... everywhere.

For Frequent Travelers

I know a man in sales who travels so frequently for business, he keeps a second carry-on packed at home. When he arrives home late one night from a trip and has to take off early the next day, he picks up the second, already packed bag.

Handbag or Man Bag

Along with your carry-on, airlines allow one "personal item" (handbag, man bag, attaché, computer bag or backpack). The personal item can be sizeable, as long as it fits under the seat in front of you.

I usually bring a computer bag. I lighten my load by carrying a tablet with a keyboard cover, instead of a 5-6 lb. laptop. If I need extra room, I bring a backpack for my carry-on. I don't want to bring a backpack to meetings, so I have a purse I can flatten into my carry-on. Before meetings, I transfer the tablet, any important documents, business cards and other items into the purse.

If you use reading glasses, pack a spare pair. I nearly went out of my mind at a convention at a resort when I lost my one pair of glasses. The resort shops did not have any reading glasses and there were no stores in walking distance. I thought I would not be able to read my plane tickets to get home. Fortunately, someone turned in my glasses.

Workout Clothes

It's even possible to fit a t-shirt, workout pants and shoes if you plan to use the exercise room at your hotel. I have running shoes that are light weight with a soft-knit shell, designed to flatten into a suitcase. They slide easily into a carry-on or computer bag. Some hotels offer workout clothes they can give you as "loaners." I prefer to bring my own.

Take Advantage of Hotel Amenities

I attended a four-day conference with two evening events. I needed a pair of evening shoes because my normal dress shoes with my suit were a little too "Marian the Librarian" for evening wear. (It's a shame you can't rent dress shoes the way you rent bowling shoes. "I'd like a pair of black slingbacks. I don't care how many people have worn them.")

I packed four pairs of shoes for that trip: dress shoes to go with my suit, dressy but comfortable shoes to go with pants, running shoes and a pair of evening-wear shoes. How was this possible? I was able to pack fewer clothes by using the hotel's laundry services.

Most hotels and resorts have guest laundry rooms, as well as dry cleaning and laundering services. You can send out your cleaning in the morning and have it back by the evening. If you take advantage of this, you can bring fewer clothes and still be like new. I have had mostly good luck with this, except once, when I was traveling abroad and the hotel's dry cleaner put a hole in a new Brooks Brothers® blouse.

Bring wrinkle-resistant clothing you can hang up when you get to your hotel. Most hotels have an iron and ironing board in the rooms to press clothing, because as we all know, there is wrinkle-resistant clothing, but no such thing as wrinkle-free.

Before you turn on the iron, give it a smell check, in case the person before you used it to iron a sweaty, stinky shirt. I was halfway through ironing a shirt when I said, "What is that smell?... *Oh no.*" Somebody else's sweaty, stinky smell was now on my shirt.

Air Wear

A young executive was traveling to a conference at a resort in Arizona. He decided to dress down for the plane trip, in a t-shirt, shorts and flip flops. He was seated in the front row of the coach section. Unfortunately, he was spotted by his CEO, who was seated in the last row of first class – dressed in a business suit and tie.

When traveling on business, always project a professional image. You never know who you might run into on the airplane or if the person sitting next to you will be your next big client, investor or employer. Dress for the business meeting to which you are traveling. Do not dress like you are on vacation. (I don't get people who wear shorts, flip flops and tank tops on the airplane, then ask for a blanket. Wouldn't it be easier to wear clothes?)

If you dressed down and your flight is delayed and your luggage lost, you may have to step off the plane and go straight to your meeting. Stick with professional attire for the trip out and the trip home.

The Airport

Traveling for work has taken me through every major airport in this country. I have seen it all. I've been stuck in the security line at JFK in

New York behind a woman in thigh-high boots screaming at the security agents why she should not have to remove them. I have had a gate door shut on my nose at Dallas-Fort Worth, because of a connection that was too short.

At LaGuardia in New York, I saw a huge rat under the seats along the wall in the terminal. He was dragging a tiny Samsonite carry-on with wheels behind him. I'm kidding, it was a Gucci backpack. In Pittsburgh, I discovered my gate-checked carry-on was carried off in Milwaukee.

Airport Security

Once, I was going through security in the Des Moines Airport in Iowa and the baggage screener said, "You have a knife in your bag."

"A knife?" I said, "I don't have a knife in my bag."

"Yes, you do." he insisted.

One of the other agents started rifling through my computer bag and produced a large cake knife. We had a party at my workplace in Connecticut and I made a cake. The cake knife, which belonged to the office manager, came home with me on the plate with the leftover cake. I washed the knife and put it in my bag, to drop off back at work. Then I forgot about it. A few days later, I flew home for a visit to Iowa.

The scary thing? The cake knife made it through security at a New York airport, when I flew home to Iowa. The Des Moines Airport security confiscated it. At least it was a cake knife and not a steak knife. Otherwise, they would have kept me too.

Be nice to the airport security people, because airport security is thankless job. Everybody coming through is cranky and complaining. Many of them are taking off their shoes. Feet do not smell nice. The security agents are there to keep us safe. They deserve our respect.

I was chatting with a TSA agent and mentioned the woman in thigh-high boots at LaGuardia. He said, "The airport is no place to be fashionable." Have shoes you can slip on and off going through security – this makes things go faster for you and everyone in line behind you.

Going through airport security in Sydney, Australia, I went through my routine of shedding everything – shoes, jacket, passport pouch. I walked through the scanning arch with my hands in the air, as if I were already under arrest. The security agent looked down at my socks and said, "Nice shoes." No one was taking off their shoes or anything else.

Put a luggage lock on your carry-on when you get past security, so if you have to check the bag at the gate, it's secure. And if you sleep on the plane, no one can reach into your carry-on in the overhead bin.

TSA Pre-check

If you travel by air a great deal, it's worthwhile to get TSA Pre-check.

TSA Pre-check is a designation on your airline ticket that allows you to go through an expedited security line. You can keep your shoes on and you are less likely to get the full-body scan. Some airports have a wall between the Pre-check line and everyone else. That way, the Pre-check people don't have to feel guilty gazing upon the hundreds of people who have been in this long, snaking line since before they got out of bed.

You can apply online through the TSA (Transportation Security Administration, a division of the U.S. Department of Homeland Security). The website will send you to a local agency that will take your fingerprints as part of the background check process.

There is a fee. (As of the publication of this book, it was $85 for five years.) When you pass the background check, the TSA issues a number. Register your Pre-check number when you buy airplane tickets, so the designation appears on your tickets.

Making a Pass

There is a passing lane and not just on the street. There is a passing lane on sidewalks, on bike paths, in corridors and at the airport. The most important place to keep the passing lane open is at the airport. Because sometimes, through a series of unfortunate events, a responsible, law-abiding citizen with careful planning, can be late for her plane.

I was struggling to get to my flight out of JFK Airport and it took me longer than anticipated to find a parking space for my car. As I was running pell-mell through the airport, the zipper on my computer bag gave way, sending my laptop and all sorts of papers flying. I scrambled to pick up everything and sprinted for the escalator.

The plane was a few minutes late and the door was still open. When I reached my seat on the plane, I was still trying to catch my breath. A few minutes later, I realized why I was able to make the plane. They were holding it for Senator Chuck Schumer. I wonder where he parked?

If there are two escalators moving in the same direction and you want to plant yourself on one step, take the escalator on the right and let the people who come flying like bats out of hell with arms, legs and bags akimbo, pass by on the escalator to the left.

If there is one escalator, stay to the right side and let them squeeze by you on the left. (There should be escalator signs like those road signs in Canada that say: "Squeeze Right.") This means also moving your carry-on bags to the right, too – on the stair above or below you.

If you need to get by some escalator squatters blocking the way, say "Please excuse me." Have patience with parents traveling with small children, who are slower to get out of the way.

The Gate Wait

A lot of people are traveling with their dogs these days. In Chicago O'Hare Airport, I sat opposite a man who took his dog from its carrier and put it on the seat next to him. I wondered if people would think twice about sitting on an airport terminal seat if they knew a dog's rear end had been there. I wondered if the airport terminal seat I was sitting on had a dog's rear end on it before me.

At airport gates, the waiting area before you board the plane seems to be getting smaller and more crowded. The seats are all welded together. Just because you are sitting in a welded seat, facing the opposite direction of others, yapping loudly on your cell phone, does not mean you are not bothering them.

I always look for a quiet area so I can work. Once, a woman sat in the next seat and start playing Solitaire on her laptop… with the sound turned up. It made a *zzoooop!* sound, like a casino, every time she moved a card. I didn't even know Solitaire had a sound. I packed up and moved. Solitaire is such a waste of time and battery power. Not to mention, if you are spotted playing Solitaire by a colleague or a client, you will look thick as a brick. Feed your brain. Read a book or news online.

Gate Hogs

In a busy airport gate area with few empty seats, a tiny woman set down her laptop on one seat with her bag in front of it and left an empty seat next to it where she planned to sit. Then she went to another set of seats, to sit and chat with two co-workers. An elderly gentleman toting his luggage, comes along and makes for the empty seat. She stops him and says, "Oh no, *that's mine*." The man looks at her for a minute, then shuffles on. This thoughtless woman was hogging three seats at the crowded gate and preventing others from taking their rest.

There's no such thing as "this seat is saved" when the seating area is filled or the train or bus is filled or the seminar is filled. If your friend is not there, that is not the problem of the person who is there and looking for a place to sit down. In adulthood, there is no such thing as "I called it!" Be aware of the people around you and make room. Take your bags and stack them up in front of you or put them in your lap.

BE EXCEPTIONAL: Offer It Up

The Exceptional Professional does not hesitate to give up a seat, when others need it more.

If there is an elderly person standing in the gate area, or a mother with a small child and you are able-bodied, offer your seat. You might be thinking, "That's not exceptional behavior – it's what you should do." In this day and age, sometimes doing the right thing is exceptional.

To Air is Human

On airplanes, you are in a confined space, breathing re-cycled air and forced to sit elbow to elbow with some of the most unhygienic people on the planet. I take lots of vitamins when I travel, because I am usually seated in front of Typhoid Mary and next to Patient Zero.

Not to mention the kid that is kicking your seat from behind for the entire flight. Jeannie Gaffigan, wife of comedian Jim Gaffigan, said on *Twitter*: "Airlines should just seat all kids one behind the other so they can kick each other's chair backs."[36] The worst flight is anywhere to Orlando, Florida. Orlando, home to Disney World, is consistently ranked in the top five conference and meeting destinations in the U.S.

Any plane to Orlando is always mobbed with kids melting down and parents who overpacked. On a full flight to Orlando, I was next to a small child who was sprawled out in the middle seat, kicking me the entire flight. By flight's end, I wanted to give her mother a big kick.

(Parents, please, if your kid is two or three years-old, he or she is not going to remember the Disney experience. For the sake of all the other passengers, just stay home and give it another four years.)

That said, be patient with traveling families. It is never fun to be in the seat in front of the screaming child. It is even less fun to be the person holding the screaming child. My nephew described a cross-country flight where his two year-old screamed non-stop. He said to me with wide eyes, "On the plane, we were *THAT family*." Please don't give parents angry looks or make snide remarks. They get enough of that already.

Changing Seats

You see the enormous man coming down the center aisle and he is sweating profusely. You are thinking to yourself, "Please, please do not be in the seat next to me." Of course, he is. The first thing he wants is to raise the armrest between you, so he can be more comfortable. And he smells like he hasn't had a bath in a month.

Before you flip open the Exit door and jump, ask a flight attendant if you can be reseated. If there are open seats on the plane, they will usually accommodate you. However, some seats may cost extra. Don't balk – they might just be worth the investment.

Other In-flight Etiquette Practices

People are sensitive to strong odors, so avoid heavy perfumes, colognes or smelly food. Keep your shoes on. Air hot feet in the privacy of a hotel room, not in public. In a small, confined place on an airplane, do not do personal grooming in your seat, like clipping or painting your nails.

Keep your seat upright if possible. There is so little room between rows, that putting your seat back can pin the tall person behind you in his or her seat. Someone told me about sitting behind a young woman who tipped her seat back all the way. The person in the seat behind was so penned in, she could not use her laptop. She politely asked the young woman if she could put her seat back up. The young woman scoffed at her and kept her seat tipped back.

At that point, the person in the seat behind turned on the air vent above full bore and pointed it in the direction of the young woman's head. Soon enough, she protested, "Can you turn that off?" To which the passenger behind her said, "I am sorry, I need the air, because I am feeling a little claustrophobic with your seat tipped back all the way." The young woman put her seat upright. The air came off.

If you want to avoid tipped back seats, book a seat in the front row of your section. On larger planes, there are usually three classes of seats: first class, business class and economy class. First class has a lot of perks but it will cost you. Business class provides a bit more wiggle room than economy and is worth the $20-30 upgrade for a flight six hours or more.

Be proactive. Greet the people sitting next to and around you when you first board, so you start out in a positive light. That way, any requests you make of them after that, have more chance for success.

Before take-off and after landing, respect people around you by avoiding non-emergency cell phone conversations. Hold that crucial, "We're on the ground," conversation until you are off the plane. Be careful of phone conversations in close quarters. I have overheard conversations from people talking about strategic decisions to gossiping about co-workers. Make sure you are not giving competitive or reputation-damaging info to prying ears.

Long Flights

On some international flights, you might be on the plane for 20 hours or more. Get up and walk around several times during the flight. Stretch your arms and legs. This is important to keep your circulation going and to prevent blood clots. Accept water every time it is offered, because you need to stay hydrated on a long flight. They feed you a lot, but not always well, on international flights, so bring packaged snacks.

Bring an eye mask in case you need to sleep while the people around use their overhead lights, digital devices or seatback movie screens. Bring a neck pillow to support your head while you sleep.

Try to be cognizant of people sleeping around you. When the plane is dark and it is still bright outside, leave your window shade down, so it won't keep people awake. (Okay, maybe just a quick peek when you are flying over the Arctic Circle.) Also, minimize digital device use when the people around you are sleeping. Or read from your tablet in "night" or "dark" mode, so the glow will not disturb others.

Listen to the Safety Instructions

The people who are working hard to make you as safe and comfortable as possible are flight attendants – not stewardesses (and definitely not "honey" or "toots"). Be kind and respectful to the flight attendants because they have the power to throw you off the plane.

> Them: *"How is the Salisbury steak?,"*
> You: *"Ugh! It's awf— I mean, DELICIOUS!"*

Even if you have been on an airplane a million times, listen to flight attendants going over the safety features. Talking during the safety instructions may distract others around you. Do you want to be the reason someone drowns because they didn't hear how to use their seat cushion as a life vest? I didn't think so. Be good example to any young people sitting around you. If you need to exit the plane in the dark, do you know how many rows the nearest exit is in front of you or behind you? Thank the flight crew and attendants as you leave the plane.

Air Food

I was sitting with my mother on an airplane bound for Nashville and next to us was a young, beautiful, skinny girl in a shabby chic top and distressed jeans. She ordered Baileys with her coffee, then went to use the restroom. I said to my mother, "I bet she is a musician."

My mother said, "How do you know?" I said, "Because she is headed to Nashville, she is young, beautiful and she is already drinking." (She was an accountant. The economy at the time explained the drinking.) Avoid alcohol on an airplane – drinking at high altitudes makes you more inebriated. One drink on an airplane counts for two drinks on the ground. If you deplane on one of those mobile staircases and you fall down it and take out a senior citizen in the process, that won't look good for you or your organization.

I bring a sandwich with me on domestic flights. I also bring healthy snacks like almonds and granola bars. These will sustain you through unexpected travel delays. (If I have time before a trip, I make my own granola bars. Friends are like, "What are you, Martha Stewart?")

You can buy snacks on the plane, but they are expensive and leave a lot to be desired. Airport terminal food can also be pricy. And you should never count on having enough time between connecting flights to get something to eat. If you get fast food or any other strong-smelling food, try to eat it before boarding.

Crisis

The Denver Airport is my Bermuda Triangle. I always get stuck there. Once, I had a talk in Santa Barbara. My flight was late getting out of Des Moines, so I missed my connection in Denver. The customer service line lasted an hour. When I got to the end of it, the agent said, "We can get you to Santa Barbara by 1:00 p.m. tomorrow." My talk was at 10:00 a.m.

I began looking for other options that would get me closer to Santa Barbara. They said, "We have a flight across the terminal leaving for Los Angeles-LAX in moments. Decide now." It was the last seat on the plane and they sandwiched me between two men, the size of linebackers. I didn't have any armrest. I was squeezed in so tight, my arms were out in front of me and my elbows were together. I was thinking, "This can't get any worse," until the man in front of me tipped his seat back.

When I reached LAX, I was just about to leave the terminal in search for ground transportation, when I noticed a Departures board. There was a flight to Santa Barbara. I went back to the nearest gate. Two gate agents worked to get me onto that flight. And it was complicated, because with my change to LAX, they had my trip ending at LAX.

If your flight is delayed or cancelled, be patient and kind to gate agents, who are trying to find a way to get you to your destination. Do not transfer your stress to them. They didn't break the airplane or cause the bad weather. Sometimes they will do amazing things for you.

I once had a cancelled flight where the airline paid for a four-hour taxi ride, so I could get to another airport and make an international flight. If not for that, I would have had to wait for a flight the next day.

Instead of whining and complaining, help them help you. Maybe you can't reach your destination, but can they get you to an airport closer to your destination? I was in Baltimore trying to get home to Des Moines. The airline agent suggested a flight from Baltimore to Las Vegas and then connect to a flight from Las Vegas to Des Moines. I nixed that idea, but asked, "Can you get me to Chicago?" I have a sister in Chicago, so I stayed overnight with her and flew home the next day.

BE EXCEPTIONAL: Thank You for All You Do

The Exceptional Professional is attentive to all the people around him or her, not for ulterior motives, but because it's the right thing to do.

My friend Mark Brown is a professional speaker based down in Georgia. Whenever he travels by air, he approaches the gate agents and says, "I just want to thank you for serving my fellow travelers and me. I appreciate you!"

On board the plane, he says to the flight attendants, "Thank you for all you do for us as passengers." At hotels, he says to the people at the front desk, "I just want to apologize for any guests who have treated you rudely today."

And what do you think happens when he does this? He gets upgraded to first class. Free drinks. Free snacks. Extra bags of pretzels. Gift baskets left in his hotel room.

Here's the thing about Mark: it's not an act. He doesn't do it to get things. He is a genuinely kind, thoughtful and attentive person. One time he overheard a flight attendant telling a fellow attendant, "That man in 3A thanked me as he boarded the plane and it kind of threw me. I've been doing this for over 20 years, and I've NEVER been greeted like THAT before!"

It didn't cost him a thing to say those kind words. When you treat people well, good things come back to you. Don't just treat people well so you get stuff. Mark Brown says it best, "I taught my children to be engaging, friendly and courteous to anyone who serves them, not for the rewards or the benefits, but because it's the right thing to do."

Traveling by air can be stressful, because there are so many uncertainties. But if you know how to pack, bring snacks to get you through any delays and treat your security people and flight crew with kindness and patience, you will reach your final destination more easily.

There's more to business travel than airplanes. Read on to learn more about rental cars and other modes of transportation, as well as hotel accommodations.

11.2 *Transportation and Accommodations*

As I deplaned after midnight at LAX airport in Los Angeles, the pull handle on my wheeled carry-on jammed and was stuck inside the case. Now I'm going through the country's third largest airport and it's like I am lugging a sleeping calf.

It's half an hour before the rental car shuttle comes. I am first in line at the counter but I get the slowest agent. Anyone behind me is ahead of me outside in the lot. The word in the lot: "We have no more cars."

Not true. They had cars. But not many, so whatever came out Door #2 is what you drove away, no matter what your reservation. Everybody was complaining loudly, stamping their feet and making audible exhaling noises. I turned to a weary looking agent in the lot and said, "It's been a rough night, hasn't it?" She said, "You don't know the half of it!"

A Toyota Corolla comes out. I said, "I think that's mine, because I ordered a smaller car." But this angry woman with her husband and two teenage sons, who had been behind me in line inside, hissed, "We're taking that one!" The four folded uncomfortably into the Toyota. The agent said to me, "Would you like that one?" She pointed to a shiny, full-sized car nearby, which the angry woman had asked for, but didn't get.

Is it so wrong for an etiquette instructor to smile at the woman still sitting in the exit line unhappily crammed with three tall men into the Corolla she just pinched from the etiquette instructor?

In this chapter, you will learn:

- How to navigate car rentals
- The variety of rides for hire
- Making tracks on trains and subways
- Selecting hotels and other accommodations

The message behind the opening car rental story is, in any sticky situation when people are angry and complaining, pour some sugar on it. Remember, the purpose of etiquette is to make the people around you feel comfortable. Sometimes the people who are there to serve you need to be made comfortable. Be kind, empathetic and patient to people helping you on your way.

Rental Cars and the Gender Gap

When traveling for business, I use a lot of rental cars. Usually, I am picking a car up at an airport, but sometimes on long trips, I rent a car to save wear and tear on my own car. One thing I have found is that women are treated differently when it comes to renting cars.

Men often know more about cars than women. As a result, I feel like some agents try to sweet talk me into an uncomfortable car, when more comfortable cars are available. If you find yourself being steered towards one vehicle, ask what other cars are available in that class.

Sometimes car rental places want to give women the silly car. One time I ordered a standard-size car for a 10-hour trip and when I arrived at the car rental office, the agents showed me a powder blue Volkswagen Bug. I said, "No way."

The agent said, "Really? Most women are thrilled to have this car." I said, "As a woman in business, I need to be taken seriously. I can't show up to meet with clients in that."

Agent: "I'm sorry, it's the last standard-size we have. If you want something else, you will have to pay for the upgrade."

I know there are free upgrades in certain circumstances. Because I have been standing next to men at the rental counter when the free upgrades are offered to them. With the powder blue Volkswagen Bug, I shelled out the money for the upgrade. But I wasn't happy. When I returned the car and was asked about my experience, I told the manager about the powder blue Bug and said, "If I were a man, that car would not have been offered to me. I would have had a free upgrade."

He apologized and gave me a free upgrade on my next rental. That's important. In some cases, the agents may not be helpful. But you can get compensation or a concession from customer service or management later. Don't write companies off. Give them a chance to make it right.

Another time, in Montana, my plane arrived late and the rental car agent was kind to stay and wait for me. He handed me the keys to a Kia Soul, a boxy-looking car, but a comfortable ride. I thanked him and headed out to the lot. It was dark and I had to follow the fence to the far end of the lot where I found the car… *in Kermit-the-frog green.*

No one else in Montana was driving a Kermit-the-frog green car, so I attracted a lot of stares. Sometimes an oddly-hued rental car might come in handy. I lost my white rental car in the parking lot at a convention resort in Phoenix. The parking lot was the size of Phoenix itself. I was clicking away at the keychain in every direction, with no response. Did I mention it was July and it was 114 degrees?

Imagine trying to explain the dilemma to resort personnel. "It's a white car… and I left it parked between two white cars." The sun was so intense, I felt like an ant under a magnifying glass. I thought the sun would burn me into a pile of ashes before I found the car. (*"All we found was a pile of ashes… and a tasteful handbag."*)

I did find the car, but the lesson burned into me that day was to take careful notes and maybe snap a picture of your car's location. I had a Nestle's Crunch® bar in my bag. When I reached airport security at the Phoenix Airport, it had to be confiscated as a liquid.

Checking Out the Car

Before you drive that rental car off the lot, go all the way around the car with the rental agent to make sure there are no scratches, dents or cracks in the windshield. Lift the trunk to see if the opening is scraped from people trying to get luggage in and out. Check the seats to make sure there are no tears or stains in the upholstery. Sometimes an agent will try and rush you through this. Better to be thorough now than sorry later.

Should you buy the extra insurance coverage? Check with your car insurance carrier. Some plans will cover rental cars. If I know the weather is going to be bad or if I am driving through moose territory, I buy the additional coverage as a precaution.

The roadside assistance is good to have. I once locked my key in my rental car in Florida. I had to pay someone $75 to come out and unlock it. If I had purchased the roadside assistance for $15, my additional cost would have been zero.

Clean out your rental car. My sister saw a family drop off their rented minivan and proceed to leave. But an agent took one look inside the car and called them back, saying, "If you leave that minivan in that condition, we will have to charge you $100 to clean the inside." The family went back to the minivan and began hauling out fast food bags, disposable cups, bottles, spilled snacks and other miscellaneous trash.

Factor into your schedule, time for rental car check out or return time. At some airports, you can walk right out of the airport onto the rental car lot. In others, you have to wait for a shuttle to take you to an off-site location. When the shuttle drops off multiple customers at once, you may have to wait in line.

Compare prices. Vehicles rented at the airport can sometimes be significantly higher than off-site rental locations, not far from the airport. Sometimes you can save money by using your hotel's shuttle to and from the airport and renting your vehicle at a location near your hotel.

Your Own Vehicle

We live in such a beautiful country, I like to drive when traveling for business. When there is time, I stop and take pictures along the way. (Sometimes I don't stop while taking pictures, which usually causes any passengers in my car to let out an occasional blood-curdling scream.)

If something is four or five hours away, driving is sometimes easier and faster than air travel and you can pack more. When you use your car for business travel, be good to it. Get the oil changed every 3,000 miles, rotate the tires and keep up the regular maintenance.

Business Colleagues in Your Car

A friend was on an interview, where the interviewer was to pick him up and drive him on a multiple site tour. The interviewer arrived, but then his car died. "Do you mind driving us to our corporate office?" he asked.

Fortunately, my friend had cleaned his car. "Can you imagine how embarrassed I would have been if I hadn't removed the dust, soda cans and smelly gym bag from my auto the night before?" he said.

How's the inside of your ride? Is it fit to transport an interviewer, supervisor or client? I once had to pick up eight executives at Chicago O'Hare Airport and drive them to a meeting downtown. The plan: drive my car from Iowa to Chicago, stay with my sister, Maureen and rent a van to pick them up. At 10 p.m. the night before the meeting, I couldn't find my driver's license. I couldn't rent a van without it.

Maureen said, "You could use our minivan."

For a moment I considered the smell of spilt milk, juice and diaper wipes, cup-holders caked in mud (How did that happen?) and oat cereal pieces everywhere. "Absolutely not." I said.

Half an hour later, I was scrubbing down that minivan with PineSol®, vacuuming and drying it with a hair dryer. I called it a night at 2 a.m., leaving scented dryer sheets on the seats to kill the stench that seemed entrenched. The next morning, I drove to the airport with windows rolled down – in freezing temperatures. The executives were delivered to and from the airport. No one passed out. I kept my job.

My friend's call to action: "When getting ready for an interview or important meeting, put "clean car" on your to-do checklist!" Clean your car inside and out. I would add to that, never pan a proffered minivan.

For the Driven: Taxis, Limos and Ride-Hailing

If you would rather leave the driving to someone else, there are many options: taxicabs, ride-hailing services, limos, shuttles and public transportation like trains, subways and buses. Factors like your location, budget and time constraints determine which of these are viable.

Hailing a Taxi

In large cities, flagging down a taxi is easy. If the light on top of the taxi is on, that taxi is available. If it's off, it's not. Stand near the edge of the curb, raise your hand and try to make eye contact with the driver. The driver should pull over and pick you up.

How to Get a Taxi to the Airport During Shift Change

With the convenience of ride-hailing services, this may be a moot point. But if you are still relying on taxis, there are certain times when it is harder to catch a taxi. When it's raining, there is a greater demand and a shorter supply of taxis. The other time is when there is a shift change. Taxi drivers usually change shifts around 4 or 5 p.m. in the evening.

If you are standing on the curb with your luggage at around 3 p.m. or later in Midtown Manhattan, most taxi drivers will pass you by, because they don't want to haul you all the way out to LaGuardia, JFK or Newark Airport, when they are so close to their shift end. Legally, taxi drivers in New York cannot refuse to pick someone up based on race, disability or destination in New York City. The exception to this rule is when the trip would result in the driver operating the vehicle for more than 12 hours.

A friend who is a native New Yorker, showed me how to hide my carry-on luggage between two parked cars when hailing the taxi near the shift change. When drivers spot your luggage, sometimes they get mad. But once they have pulled over, they are not supposed to drive off. Make sure you tip them well.

Tip the driver 20 percent of the fare. More, if you like. If a bell person at your hotel hailed the taxi, tip that person $3-5.

The Best Seat in the Taxi

The best seat in the taxi is behind the front passenger seat. Offer this seat to a client or the senior-most executive. A junior staff member hails the taxi for those of higher rank. A host hails the taxi for clients.

Uber/Lyft or other Ride-hailing Services

Ride-hailing services like Uber or Lyft, make it easy to dial up a driver on an app on your cell phone. You pay in advance, the driver shows up and takes you to your destination. Since the drivers for these services use their own vehicles, you never know what you are going to be riding in. But it can be very convenient and many swear by it.

When you order an UberTAXI, available in certain cities, you get a licensed yellow cab who you are contracting with through Uber.

No Need to Tip?

Ride-hailing service Uber boasts a "cashless experience." You summon the driver on your phone app and at the ride's conclusion, you pay electronically. According to Uber's website, "As a rider, you are not obligated to offer your driver a gratuity in cash."[37]

But should you tip? In the United States, the answer is, "Yes." The reason we tip, for any service, is not to rate the service, though many tip extra for outstanding service. We tip because the service was personal. Give your Uber driver a cash tip, because the driver picked you up and delivered you, not wherever the driver felt like it, but to your chosen destination. That's personal. (The drawback of cash tips is the driver could be robbed, because people might expect the driver to have cash.)

Lyft and UberTAXI allow you to add a tip electronically. But one of Lyft's tipping choices is $1. A $1 tip means your ride was $5. Your tip should be 20 percent the cost of the ride.

At the end of your Lyft ride, you get a payment screen on your app, where you can add a tip and rate the driver. Tips are itemized for the Lyft driver on a weekly statement. If you skip Lyft's payment screen, your credit card is automatically charged 16 hours later, without a tip. Lyft allows you to locate the record of your ride in the app and add a tip up to 72 hours after the ride.

Ridesharing

Ridesharing services also allow you to order your ride through an app on your cell phone. The only difference is you may have multiple passengers that ride with you and split the fee. Ridesharing is economical, but it requires you to be a little more flexible with your time.

Limousines

Limousines or limos are more upscale than a taxi and can be scheduled and paid for in advance. People hear the word limo and think "stretch limo" that people use for weddings and parties. But a limo might be a full-size vehicle like a Lincoln Town Car® or Ford Crown Victoria®.

They are good for entertaining clients, because they are usually nicer and more comfortable than taxis. You can schedule a limo to take your client to and from the airport.

Limo drivers can be hired for the day. I was staying in Krakow, Poland and I wanted to see Czestochowa, which was about two hours away. The tour bus that went there, didn't go the day I wanted to go. When the hotel concierge suggested hiring a driver for the day, I thought it might be out of my price range, but it was surprisingly affordable.

Shuttles

Shuttles, usually small buses or vans that pick up multiple passengers and transport them to and from hotels or other locations, can offer significant savings. Hotels often have dedicated shuttles to and from major airports that are free or have a minimal fee. You can also book independent shuttle services but the bummer is the shuttle often makes multiple stops, which can eat up a lot of time.

Compare prices between shuttles, because prices vary. A person at an airport information booth clued me into this. The first shuttle service outside the airport had agents practically grabbing my carry-on bag to get me onto their shuttle. But when I checked the shuttle next to them, the fare was $20 lower.

While free sounds good, it's not always the best deal. When I was stranded at the Denver Airport in a snow storm, an airline gave me a hotel voucher. I waited with a group of people more than an hour for a shuttle bus that was supposed to take us to our hotel. Finally, we decided to split the fare for a taxi that took us to the hotel. It pays to network! Don't forget to tip your shuttle driver, even with a free hotel shuttle.

Commuting by Train

When you work or do business in large cities, commuter trains are the way to go. Early in my career, I used to commute from Columbia, Maryland to Alexandria, Virginia. That meant taking a commuter train from Laurel, Maryland to Union Station in Washington, D.C. and transferring to the Metro® train Red Line to Gallery Place. From there, I transferred to the Yellow Line, to go to King Street in Alexandria. From there, I walked 11 blocks.

That sounds like a sizable nuisance. But if I drove my car, it would have taken the exact same time, with the traffic on Washington's beltway. Monthly parking fees were greater than the train fare. The 11 block walk was good exercise, but a zero on the fun scale when it rained.

The bigger advantage to commuting by train, is you have time to work, read or just relax, while someone else drives. There's camaraderie on the train. After seeing people every day on the same train, you strike up friendships. Now and then, groups form on the commuter trains and on Fridays, they bring beer or share pizzas on the train for the ride home.

Disadvantages of Commuting by Train

One disadvantage is a loss of privacy and dealing with obnoxious behavior, like noisy conversations and cell phone calls. In New York, I sat across the aisle from a man loudly complaining on the phone about his girlfriend. He imitated her high-pitched voice demanding to be taken out to breakfast, ordering blueberry pancakes, then saying, *"I'm not gonna eat it! It's nasty!"* Tell it to Dr. Phil.

The other disadvantage of commuting by train is exposure to everyone else's plague. When I commuted, I caught colds much more frequently, because I was in overheated, enclosed train cars, with people coughing in all directions. Not to mention the germs on the grab handles and seats. A regular vitamin regimen and using hand sanitizer helps.

Amtrak

On the East Coast, if you have ever sat in stop and go traffic for eight hours on I-95, in a drive that should take half that time, you will appreciate the wonder that is Amtrak®. An hour and 20 minutes from Philadelphia to New York – some people make that commute every day. Amtrak is a government-subsidized, passenger train service that provides medium and long-distance options throughout the U.S.

In the Midwest, Amtrak means something different. It's more about leisure travel – a novel way to see the country with lots of beautiful scenery. People in Iowa jump on the Amtrak at Osceola and take it to Chicago to shop or out to Colorado. Amtrak seats are a little more comfortable than airline seats. You can get specific reserved seats or more economical general seating.

Disadvantages of Amtrak

I don't care for Amtrak. I feel like it is sitting in the back seat of America's station wagon. There are people falling asleep next to you with their head dropping onto your shoulder. There are people behind you sticking their bare feet on your armrest, in between the seats. The stations have fast food, so people bring their smelly meals on board. And then, there are the loud cell phone calls.

For the experience, Amtrak can seem a little pricy. If you are booking for holiday travel on the East Coast, like Thanksgiving, you better book far in advance, because they sell out. As with any mass transit, there are occasional weather snafus and delays. A friend of mine talked about waiting at the Amtrak station in Osceola, Iowa for a train two hours behind schedule. Delays on cross-country Amtrak trains can be much longer, because many of the tracks are owned by railroad freight companies and Amtrak must share the tracks with freight trains.

Amtrak's high speed Acela trains travel up to 125 or 150 miles per hour. But there are faster high speed trains in the world. The Shinkansen trains in Japan, which get up to around 200 miles per hour, are a smoother ride and more comfortable than Amtrak. The world's fastest train is China's Shanghai Maglev, which travels at 267 mph.

Buses

I am not a bus person. When I was in middle school, I used to walk two miles to and from school (uphill and in the snow) to avoid riding the school bus, because the school bus made me feel a little motion sick.

I have taken many city buses in my professional life. The schedules look intimidating at first and there's that nagging fear you will jump on the wrong bus in unfamiliar territory and end up miles from where you need to be with no idea how to get back.

But it's not rocket science. Look for the location at the end of the line in the direction you are going. That should be posted on the marquee on the front of the bus. When you near your destination, pull the cord above any of the windows to ring the bell for the driver to stop.

Taking the High Road: Professionalism on Public Transportation

There are certain practices that are the right thing to do when riding any public transportation:

- Offer your seat to people who are elderly, physically challenged or women who are pregnant or traveling with small children.
- Stay out of the seats designated for disabled travelers.
- On a crowded train or bus, there are no "saved seats."
- If your bag, purse, umbrella or other items did not buy a seat, then take them off the seat next to you.
- Small bags go on your lap. Luggage goes on the luggage rack above.
- Avoid loud conversations and keep cell phone calls to a minimum.
- Board and depart in an orderly fashion.

Where to Stay When Traveling on Business

I grew up in a large family. You've heard it takes a village? We *were a village.* My friends' parents splurged on vacations to Disney World.

We could never afford that. Our "Magic Kingdom" was The Holiday Inn®... where kids stay for free. (wink, wink)

Now Marriott®, Holiday Inn and a host of other companies have hotels that cater to business travelers. To me, the ideal is a mid-priced hotel ($100-150/per night), with a free breakfast and a work-out room.

Just like the car rental, as a woman, you may have to assert yourself. I figured this out after at different hotels, I was repeatedly placed in the room next to the elevator shaft. Have you ever had that room? All night, you can hear rrrrrrr... shhhhhh... rrrrrrr... Anytime anyone is going up or down, you know it.

Finally, at one hotel, I asked for a room away from the elevator. I was given the room up against the stairwell. In that room, you could hear every single person tromping up and down the stairs.

I forgot something down in my car. As I was coming in through the lobby, I noticed a man checking in after me was offered a special treat – a bag of chips and a granola bar – because it was Customer Appreciation Week. I stopped and looked at the man behind the desk without saying anything. He said, "Oh, I forgot... you can have a treat, too."

Maybe it was Male Customer Appreciation Night? Maybe it was an oversight. In any case, if you don't want the room up against the elevator shaft or stairwell, or if you want to be off the first floor, speak up.

Budget Hotels

Budget hotels and motels can offer substantial savings. The rooms usually aren't as nice, with dimmer lighting and an automatic bathroom fan that turns on with the light and sounds like a cargo plane taking off.

If the hotel is in a high-crime area, it's not worth it. Before booking, look at the online reviews. You can also view online crime maps of cities that identify the type of crimes committed near any location.

Higher End Hotels

Many conferences are held at higher end or resort hotels. There are several reasons to stay at the conference hotel and not a more economical hotel down the street:

- You have more time for networking.
- It's more convenient if you have to change for evening events.
- If you are feeling tired, you can go upstairs and cat nap to recharge.

Usually, the conference will offer a discounted rate for their block of rooms. Book early for conferences, because blocks of rooms sell out. Higher end hotels offer more amenities. Want your shirts starched and pressed? Need a fitness class? Salon touch up? More handouts for your meeting printed up? And there is usually a variety of restaurants on site, depending on whether you want a cup of coffee or a steak dinner. You pay for the extras. *"Internet access costs WHAT per day?"*

Reservations

Making reservations online is easy and allows you to review all the options. Double with two queen beds? Two or three bedroom suite?

There are discounts available for seniors, active military, government workers, AAA members. Check the availability twice – once with and without the discount code. More than once, I have put in a discount code, to find no rooms available. When I took away the discount code and searched again, available rooms appeared.

Always sign up for the frequent guest/points programs. My brother Michael, a seasoned business traveler, says hotels that are booked can sometimes make a room magically appear for priority guests.

In the Doghouse

One feature I try to avoid when making a reservation: "Pet friendly." I like dogs, I like cats. But people with animals have a different standard of clean than I do. When I walk into someone's home and they have cats walking across the kitchen counter or put plates used by the humans in the house on the floor for the dog to lick clean, it makes me a little crazy.

I remember staying overnight at one pet friendly hotel that smelled like a kennel, from the lobby on up. Another hotel had a couch in the room that had a pillow with a cutout of a dog on it. Thanks for the reminder that there have been multiple dogs on this couch, and the upholstery is not likely to have been cleaned between guests. If you are not pet friendly, watch for that designation in hotels.

The Free Breakfast

One time, I remember thinking, "I wonder why the Internet seems so slow in this hotel?" When I went down to the free breakfast, it looked like a tech convention. Everywhere in the breakfast nook there were young men and women completely absorbed in open laptops, tablets and cell phones. Whenever that free breakfast nook opens, is the time to get there. The more you sleep in, the more crowded it will be.

It's tempting to go for the eggs and sausage or the waffle maker. But there are healthier options: cereal, fruit, yogurt and if you are lucky, hot oatmeal. Oatmeal packets where you add hot water are not as good.

The free breakfast means self-serve and also that you self-bus your own table. There are trash receptacles for this purpose. I remember seeing how some chaperones traveling with a young gymnastics team, walked away from the breakfast area at a hotel, after allowing the youngsters to trash the eating area, leaving used plates, cups, napkins and food debris all over the tables, chairs and floor. It was really thoughtless.

If you have an early flight to catch before the breakfast area is open, you can usually ask the front desk the night before if you can grab a yogurt or box of cereal and a carton of milk. If there is no refrigerator in your room, put the items on ice overnight in your ice bucket. If you have access to a grocery store, it's also possible to stock your room with individual cereal containers, milk, fruit, juice or bottled water.

BE EXCEPTIONAL: Be Convivial and Conversational

Out on the road, *The Exceptional Professional* is kind and convivial to people whose job is to serve us along the way.

The hotel had a breakfast bar with a menu of breakfast items for sale. When I placed my order, I was friendly and conversational with the woman behind the counter. She put a spotty banana on the counter. "This has a few spots and we were going to throw it out anyway."

A free banana—I was ecstatic. And effusive in my thanks.

I sat down to eat and a few minutes later, the woman brought out a small rectangular plate with a bowl of hot oatmeal and all the trimmings: cream, brown sugar, Craisins®, nuts and all. "We were going to throw out this, too," she said. If I had stayed longer, this woman might have given me a free Thanksgiving dinner.

Would I have received a free banana and oatmeal if I had approached the counter while texting on my phone, barely making eye contact? There was a residual effect of that spotty banana, besides potassium. It made me happy to get something free and infused me with positive energy for the rest of the day.

When you are kind and attentive to others, good things will come back to you. What is a little thing you can do for someone else? Start with please and thank you.

Wake-up Call

Whether you use your phone or the digital alarm clock in the room, call the front desk or guest services and ask for a wake-up call as a back-up. It's a free service and gives you peace of mind. In this age, most hotels should have wake-up calls that are digitally programmed. Occasionally, I have had wake-up call come 10-15 minutes late or not at all. Don't rely on the wake-up call alone.

The 13th Floor

Have you ever been in a high rise hotel elevator and noticed there is no button for the 13th floor? Some people don't like to be booked on the 13th floor, because of the superstition that 13 is unlucky. So some hotels do not have a 13th floor. Actually, they do. It's just called the "14th floor."

Emergency Exits

When traveling for business and staying in a hotel, know your escape routes. The most travelled person in our family is my sister, Marie Therese, who, as the associate dean of the School of Nursing at Johns Hopkins, speaks all over the world. She says, "As soon as you are settled in your hotel room, step outside the door to your room and locate your closest emergency exit. Next, count the steps it would take to get to that exit." That way, if emergency lights are not working or are somehow obscured, you can still find your way to the exit.

This is especially important when traveling abroad to countries that may have varying emergency exit standards. You might want to follow the route all the way out of the building just once. I remember being in one hotel where the emergency stairs ended in a maze of tunnels behind the banquet halls.

The Thoughtful Guest

In any hotel, be courteous to your neighbors. Keep your voice down on phone or video chatting. Make sure the TV volume is not too loud. Don't carry on loud conversations near the elevators.

If there are ever problems with noisy neighbors keeping you awake, call hotel security. Do not bang on the walls, the floors or the ceilings or confront the noisy guests on your own.

Even though the hotels have housekeepers that will clean the room, tidy up after yourself. Put trash in the trash receptacles, place all the used towels in a pile and remove any hair out of the tub.

Hotel Tipping

Leave a $3-5 or more tip for the hotel housekeeper each day. Tip more if you made a big mess of the hotel room. Some people suggest only tip the housekeeper at the end of a multiple-day stay. But it's better to tip daily, in case different housekeepers are working on your room each day.

The more upscale the hotel, the more people there are to tip. Here are some other instances where you tip at a hotel:

- Bell person: $2-5-plus per bag for carrying bags; $4-5 for hailing taxi
- Room service: 20 percent the cost of the meal
- Laundry service: 20 percent the cost of the laundry service
- Concierge: $5-10 or more for securing tickets, reservations, directions, etc., depending on the service
- Engineer: $4-5 for fixing the TV or anything else going haywire
- Valet: $4-5 for retrieving your car

BE EXCEPTIONAL: Professional Panache

Each November, Marine Corps Balls are held throughout the world in celebration of the Marine Corps birthday. At one of the Marine Corps Balls at a hotel in Washington D.C., there was a colonel standing in the hotel lobby in his dress uniform, with a chest full of medals.

An elderly lady came into the lobby, and mistaking the colonel for a bellman, said, "Son, will you carry my bags to the front desk?"

He could have said, "You are mistaken, I am not a bellman for the hotel." He could have directed her to a bellman or flagged one down for her. Instead, he said, "Yes, Ma'am," and picked up her bags and carried them to the front desk.

Rather than correct her or declare, "That's not my job," he humbled himself and picked up the bags. That is professionalism. And panache. *The Exceptional Professional* knows professionalism is not about memorizing rules or correcting others. It's about being attentive to the people around us, no matter what our rank.

Avoid The Wrong Impression

I was traveling on business with a male colleague, who was an older gentleman. When we checked into our hotel, the person at the front desk said, "Would you like adjoining rooms?" I was stunned someone would even ask that. My colleague said, "Opposite sides of the hotel."

Don't let anyone get even a whiff of anything that might give the wrong impression. Never invite a client into your hotel room. If a client or colleague surprises you with a knock on your hotel room door, refusing to open the door is perfectly acceptable. Never over imbibe with clients or colleagues in the hotel bar. Never drink alone in the hotel bar.

Other Accommodations

If you are a little more adventurous and a standard hotel seems too boring, there are services like Airbnb, which offer an online marketplace of apartments, houses, rooms or other properties to rent. There are photos and reviews on Airbnb's website to help you make your selection.

When you are doing business in smaller towns, and you really want to get to know the community, sometimes a bed and breakfast is the way to go. A bed and breakfast is usually a home that has been divided into rooms for guests. The owners provide guests with a hearty breakfast in the morning. Most bed and breakfast owners like to talk to their guests and can tell you about the history of the area or fill you in on the local gossip.

Pick the Options that are Right for You

There are so many options when it comes to hotels and travel for business. Select the lodging and transportation that is the most attractive, efficient and cost-effective for you, while considering safety and reliability. Remember to assert yourself when necessary but prioritize consideration when you want to reach your destination.

Our next destination is all about interviews and interviewing.

INTERVIEWING

12.1 *Misfires, Inspires and Attire*

The interview was not going well. I was a sneezing, dripping mess. I left all my Kleenix in the car and I had one, tiny tissue to mop up the Niagara Falls pouring from my nose. The three women interviewing me sat across the table, leaning back in their chairs to avoid my cloud of contagion. My head was so stuffed up, I couldn't think.

The interviewers repeatedly asked, "How are you at dealing with difficult people?" I finally asked why they kept asking that. They said, "Because the engineers who work here don't respect us." Red flag.

Then something happened that has only happened to me once before in my life. I lost my voice. When I tried to answer, nothing came out. I thought I was going to have to complete the interview by hand gestures and charades. *"She's moving her hands around wildly... she's MESSY... no, no... she likes to STAY BUSY... First word...sounds like..."*

Interviewing can be both exhilarating and terrifying, because it is such a process to get the interview. *The Exceptional Professional* is aware that the interview begins long before we meet the interviewer and continues long after we leave the building. How we present ourselves and how we follow up can mean the difference between getting the job and getting a "Your skills were not a good fit at this time..." letter. In this chapter, we'll start with the interview itself.

In this chapter, you will learn:

- How to make the best impression when arriving
- What to wear for an interview
- Ways to follow up after the interview
- About asking for a higher salary

The great thing about interviewing is, it's the one time you get to tell people how great you are and they are actually willing to listen. Throughout my career, there are two interviews I remember with great clarity. The first one was the worst interview I've ever had, which I mentioned at the beginning of this chapter. The second, was my best interview. Funny thing: they were only a few days apart.

Four months before my worst interview, I was laid off from Amana Appliances. It was nothing personal – an organization-wide cut back after Goodman Holding Company purchased Amana from Raytheon.

It was January in Iowa and the temperatures were dipping below zero. I was sick as a dog with a head cold and I drove two hours to the interview. Besides the "difficult people" questions, there were other red flags. I was almost 10 years out of college and in the organizational chart they showed me, my box was hanging like fringe off the bottom. It would have been like erasing my previous experience and starting over.

It didn't matter. I drove home two hours in the dark feeling completely dejected. That interview was horrible. I was never going to find a job. Who would hire a disgusting, dripping, sick mess like me?

As I was driving, I listened to one of those radio programs where people call in and talk about their troubles and the host selects a terrible, overplayed pop song to make them feel better. This eight-year-old girl called in and talked about living with her grandparents, because her parents abandoned her. She wondered why her parents didn't love her.

Now I am unemployed, miles from home, driving in the dark and bawling my eyes out for this little girl on the radio. I reached home and went to bed. The next day, I got a phone call. They offered me the job.

I turned it down. I thought if they would hire me in that condition, they were too desperate. I would not have hired me. Not to mention those red flags. My father was frustrated. "Take the job," he said. "You have been out of work for four months. You can't afford to turn it down."

But I had another interview. It was back at Amana, the organization that laid me off. Two weeks after the layoff, my supervisor had quit Amana. That left her position open: manager of public relations. It was a key position covering Amana's five factory locations and the new owners were being careful about their selection. I had to go back to Amana five times and interview with at least 12 different people, mostly vice presidents. I had only been at Amana for nine months before the layoffs, so I was a long shot.

This was my fifth interview, it was with Goodman's new CEO, Frank Murray, whom I had not met before. What I knew: native New Yorker, young, Harvard MBA, Wall Street success story. And he had an uncanny resemblance to Christopher Reeves playing "Clark Kent" in the Superman movies. Whenever he was at headquarters, word in the factory was: "Superman's in the building."

I was still sick with the cold. Mr. Murray was having a busy day, I sat in the waiting room for 45 minutes before the interview. His executive secretary showed me into his office. Her name is Marion. She plays an important role in this – we'll come back to her later.

Mr. Murray can tell I'm sick. He has a cold, too. He offers a lozenge, then takes one for himself. I said, "I know I came in with a cold, but I wanted to show you than I don't call in sick. Unless I am throwing up or in the hospital, I will always be here."

He went through my resume line by line. I was an English major in college, so he said, "What do you like to read?" We talked about literature. We talked about art. I always carry a sketchbook, so I showed him my work. I said, "It's just a hobby but it helps me think creatively."

There is one quirky thing on my resume: a minor in Medieval Studies. The Medieval period, also called the Middle Ages, roughly covers the years 500-1500. Professionals and friends who reviewed my resume, said, "Lose the Medieval Studies. People will think you are one of those weird Renaissance fair people, running around a park in big, musty, period costumes, drinking out of bowls, telling bawdy jokes and having jousting contests."

But I kept it, because you can earn an English major by coasting on easy classes. I wanted people to know I took the hard classes. Few can read Chaucer from the Middle English. Anyone can read Virginia Woolf and write an essay saying, "It spoke to my inner turmoil..." (That's not completely true. I got a "B" in "Woolf and Lessing.")

It turns out Frank Murray was a collector of Medieval Maps. At the time of the interview, his maps were showing at the Smithsonian Museum in Washington D.C. We talked about that in the interview.

A few days later, I was offered the job. I asked for a bump in the salary. After five different trips to the manufacturer and interviews with 12 different people, I felt like I earned it. Again, my father freaked. "What? Are you crazy? You asked for more money? You have been out of work for four months. You should have taken their generous offer!"

Amana countered and I accepted. It was a great career move and a very challenging and enjoyable job. When Frank Murray left Amana a few years later to form his own innovative tech company, he invited me to come work for him again. He was a great mentor, best boss ever.

When I took the job as manager of public relations at Amana, a few of my co-workers said, "I heard you interviewed with Superman. What did you two talk about?" I replied, "The Middle Ages."

The Moral of the Story

The moral of the story is, when you have an interview, just get there. I am going to say something a little controversial here. Unless you have the flu or a flesh eating bacteria, get to the interview. On both those interviews where I was sick as a dog, I was offered a job. It sends the message that you are reliable and will show up no matter what.

If you have accepted an appointment for an interview – whether it be in an office, restaurant or at a career fair, be there. Can't make the appointment? Call your contact to let them know.

Be 10-15 minutes early for appointments. Never under any circumstances be a no-show. If you can't make your interview or have accepted another offer, call and cancel the interview.

Marion the Secretary

I want to go back to Marion the executive secretary at Amana. Marion had been with the manufacturer for years, working for several CEOs. She was regal, very formal and businesslike. Her desk was right next to a main thoroughfare at Amana. I would pass her desk several times a day, smile and say, "Hello Marion!"

When I came in for that final interview, Marion smiled and said, "Good luck!" I later found out there were other candidates vying for my job who had more public relations experience than I did. There were also long-time Amana employees who wanted the job. I later asked Frank, "What tipped the balance in my favor?" He said, "Marion spoke very highly of you." Marion and I are still friends today.

The Second Moral of the Story

The second moral is your interview does not begin when you meet the interviewer. Your interview begins at the front door with the security guards, the receptionists or any administrative professionals. They are the gatekeepers and sometimes the deciding factor as to who gets the job. Be kind and respectful to them, because they are part of your process. Make eye contact, smile and greet them.

Overlook or be aloof to the gatekeepers at your own peril. A hiring manager will often ask the receptionist or assistants for their impressions of an interview candidate. It's like the Colosseum in the movie, *Gladiator*. The assistant extends a hand in judgment, followed by a big *thumbs up* or *thumbs down*. Thumbs down means the candidate is toast.

Dressing for an Interview

Casual workplaces have created a dilemma for interview candidates.

> *Should I dress up in a suit because that's what you wear to an interview?*
> *Or should I dress casual, so I look like I belong?*

I have a friend who told me his brother-in-law refused to wear a tie for interviews, because he was a computer programmer and programming is a casual attire industry. He believed he must dress casually to fit in. "How's that working out for him?" I asked.

"He has been out of work for three years," he said. It's better to err on the side of formality. Suit up, even for an interview at a casual workplace. Dressing up shows respect for the interviewers.

When I worked for Sony Music in Chicago, some interview candidates would come for interviews in ripped jeans and t-shirts, because that is how they thought people in the music business dressed.

Let me let you in on a little secret. *That is* how people in the music business dress. But that is not the way interviewees were expected to dress. We expected people to dress up a little more.

For my interview with Sony Music, I wore a conventional skirt suit – navy blue with gold buttons, with a crisp, collared white blouse. I found out later, one of the reasons I was hired was that my two predecessors called in sick after a big concert. Our branch was in Chicago and one called in sick from St. Louis and the other called in sick from Kansas City. Each one had backstage passes through Sony Music and ended up on a tour bus with a band that came through town.

Management took one look at me in my suit and said, "We think it's a safe bet she won't get on the bus with a band." They were right.

If you feel uneasy about how you should dress for the interview, you can always call the organization's human resources department and ask about the dress code for interview candidates. You might even do an Internet search for images of the organization's leaders to see how they dress day-to-day and for special events.

The Overdressed Need Not Apply

Even companies that boast no code, have a code. A college student in Florida told me how a well-known tech company flew him out to California for an interview. He wore his interview suit and tie.

The first interviewer said, "Before you speak to me, you need to take off your tie." He took off his tie. The next interviewer said, "Take off your jacket." He shucked the jacket.

The third person in the interview process said, "I am not going to talk to you unless you come back in a pair of jeans." The student didn't have any jeans with him. So he left to go shopping, purchased a pair of jeans and returned to the organization. (Easy enough for a man. If I had to shop for jeans, I'd say, "See you in three days... if I'm feeling lucky.") The third interviewer talked to him and he completed the interview.

This would be a sad story if the student from Florida bought the jeans and didn't get the job, right? They offered him the job. He turned it down. A future boss who had the arrogance to make a poor college student buy a pair of jeans in one of the most expensive retail markets, just to speak to him, was not a good fit.

The main point of this story is, it's easier to take things off if you are over-dressed, than to put things on if you are under-dressed. This student showed up in a suit and still had a job offer at the end of the interview. I hear from employers more often that candidates were underdressed and being underdressed caused them to get rejected.

Modest is Hottest

I had a 20-something woman show up for an interview with me in New York wearing a halter top. It looked like it was macramé – like something from the 1970s that plants should be hanging in rather than the human form. There was no back to it and very little in front.

The job she was applying for? Public relations. I wanted to tell her, "In order to be the face for our organization, you need to have a back to your shirt." Dress better. Suit up. Press your clothes. Brush off the pet hair. And dress so people respect you, *not inspect you.*

Automated Video Screening

What could possibly go wrong? Employers are using automated online processes to screen candidates with pre-recorded video. Candidates get questions, hit "record" and answer into their computer's video camera. The video answers disappear into the pipeline for employers to review.

It should be a win-win. Candidates can show more personality and earnestness with facial expressions and gestures that wouldn't come through in a phone interview. Employers save time, because if the interview isn't going well, they can just click to the next candidate. That's a lot easier than saying early in an interview, "You're not going to work out," and pushing a sobbing, pleading mess out the door. But one employer told me what gets recorded, is sometimes sordid:

- Candidates in pajamas with uncombed hair
- Candidates sitting in their bedrooms on unmade beds and clothes strewn about, an open closet-door in the background
- Candidates lounging around on a big couch
- One candidate was whispering into the camera from a cubicle at his current job.

Now that you know what your competition is up to, you can do better. Treat a video interview like a meeting with a live person.

- Dress the part. Wear a suit or upgraded business casual you would for an interview.
- Sit up, lean forward in your chair, speak clearly and enunciate.
- Have the camera at eye level. If you are looking down at the camera, there will be additional chins and more visible lines under your eyes.
- Check your background. Are there open closets? Stuffed animals? Mirrors or glass covered pictures reflecting anywhere else? If you don't have a suitable background, find a library with a study room.

Record a few practice questions on your computer, then critique them. Smile, be confident and hit "record."

Waiting Room

Now you are in the waiting room. You have a few minutes, you'll just take out your phone and check your messages. Right? Wrong.

In Chapter 2.1: *Attached at the Phone and Other Devices*, I mentioned the Oklahoma receptionist, who told me the hiring manager asked her to watch the interview candidates in the waiting room and make note of ones who are texting or checking messages.

The big fear organizations have is they will hire someone, and instead of working, he or she will be texting and checking personal messages all day or be otherwise distracted. A university career services professional told me about an intern who was fired after he was caught watching movies on a digital device he was holding under his desk.

It's better to sit quietly before an interview and review your notes (for surely you have done your research on this organization – their leadership, mission statement, sales figures, etc.) Go over the answers to tricky questions in your head. Leave the impression you are focused on the business at hand and not distracted by other things.

Anyone who sees you looking at your phone does not know whether you are reading your notes on the organization or doing something else. I walked by a young woman waiting for an interview in a reception area, playing a video game on her phone. Why risk the wrong impression?

Turn off your cell phone before interviews. Don't put it on buzz, stun or vibrate. A phone on vibrate still makes an imposing noise. If it goes off in an interview, you will seem unfocused and easily distracted.

When can you use your cell phone? When you are alone. A woman told me how she was interviewing a college student and the student's phone went off. The student answered it, talked for a minute, then turned to the interviewer and said, *"How much longer is this going to take?"*

The interviewer said, *"We're done now."*

Meeting the Interviewer

Give a firm handshake. The handshake is the most important part of the interview and the one most people mess up, according to professionals I have talked to in human resources. Your handshake should say, *"I'm confident, I am enthusiastic, and I am darn glad to meet you."*

Prepare for the handshake. Warm up a cold hand. I remember having a meeting at the top of a skyscraper on a very cold day. I was alone in the elevator for most of the ride to the top, so I was furiously rubbing my hands together to warm them up.

When you shake hands with the interviewer, say, "How do you do, Mr./Ms. (last name)?" Don't call anyone by their first name until that person says, "Call me John" or "Call me Judy." Smile. Smiling shows you are open to communication and it helps you feel more relaxed.

If the interviewer says, "How are you doing today?" be positive. Say, "I am happy to be here." Or "I am looking forward to speaking to you." Don't say, "I don't know, it depends how this interview goes."

Bring extra copies of your resume in case the interviewer misplaced his or her copy.

Seating When Meeting

Wait for the interviewer to tell you where to sit. Remain standing in front of your chair, until the interviewer moves to take his or her seat. Lower yourself into your seat at the same time as the interviewer.

Sit up straight on the edge of your chair with your legs together. Lean forward to let the interviewer know you are listening intently. If other people walk into the room and the interviewer introduces you, stand up to greet them.

Conclusion of the Interview

At the end of the interview, give a firm handshake to your interviewer(s). Say, "Goodbye" to the gatekeepers and anyone you met on the way in.

Employers are Watching

A friend of mine who owned a packaging and mailing business, said interview candidates would ask, "Is it okay if I bring my boyfriend?"

"No," she said, "Not okay." Show up alone. Do not bring your significant other, or in the case of career fairs, *your significant mother.*

Even before you enter the building, your interviewers might be watching out the windows. A woman who works for a trucking firm told me she watches interview candidates all the way to the parking lot. "I want to see what their cars look like," she said. "If we are going to trust them with a $120,000 vehicle, we want to see if they take care of their own car. Is it clean? Does it have scrapes or dents? Bumper stickers?"

Another employer said she saw an interview candidate park in the handicapped parking, without a handicapped badge hanging from the rear-view mirror or handicapped license plate. That person was not hired.

Here are more comments given to me by watchful employers:

- *"He was on his cell phone as soon as he walked out the door. I assume he was calling his mom to tell her how his interview went."*
- *"I spotted our candidate touching up her makeup and putting on lipstick, using her car window as a mirror."*
- *"Before getting into his car he took off his jacket and his tie... then his shirt... and then his t-shirt. I covered my eyes after that."*
- *"She got into a screaming match with someone over a taxi outside our building."*
- *"From the window, we could see inside his car. He was not as organized as his resume said."*

The interview is not over with the final handshake or when the front door closes behind you. Make sure your behavior outside the business is professional and do not hang around.

Follow Up After an Interview

The most important thing you can do is follow through. After an interview, you should send two thank you notes:

- An email thank you, in case the decision is being made immediately
- A typed letter by postal mail, to leave a more lasting impression

Enclose a copy of your resume, so it is fresh in the interviewer's mind and he or she does not have to search around for it.

The Second Thank You Note

Hiring managers say over and over that candidates who send the thank you letter by postal mail, stand out. This typed letter does three things:

1. Proves you are willing to make an extra effort
2. Showcases your writing skills (lack of writing skills is a huge issue in hiring these days)
3. Indicates how you will communicate with co-workers, clients and other stakeholders, if hired

Employers know if you are thoughtful enough to send a thank you letter through postal mail, you will be thoughtful to the organization's clients and stakeholders.

Think about all the work that goes into the interview process: preparing your resume, sending a cover letter or filling out an online application, researching the organization, practicing interview questions with family or friends and then the actual interview. If typing and sending a letter through the mail would make all the difference in whether you get the job, why wouldn't you go that extra step?

It's Wise to Personalize

A post-interview thank you note should thank the interviewer for his or her time, briefly express your continued interest in the organization and why you would be a good fit. More importantly, it should be personal and include details of what you talked about in the interview.

Do not send a cookie-cutter, generic thank you that looks like it could have been re-used for any job title or organization:

> *"Thank you for speaking to me about the position at your organization. I feel like my skills would make me a valuable member of your team."*

Make people feel like you are talking to them, not just anyone:

> *"I was inspired by your story of how you started out in manufacturing..."*
> *"You are interested in a greater online presence for your athletic clothing line and I have proven experience in growing several student organizations through social media."*
> *"I enjoyed meeting you and Manny Products, your vice president of consumer research."*

The most valuable part of personalizing a business letter? It says to the person, "I was listening."

BE EXCEPTIONAL: Many Thanks

If you are interviewed by a group, should you write one thank you note to the most senior person and cc or email the rest? Or should you send an individual thank you note to each interviewer?

How badly do you want the job? *The Exceptional Professional* writes individual notes to each interviewer in a group interview and varies what each one says, in case the recipients send copies around to each other. It helps establish a connection with each person. That's a valuable jump start if you do get the job.

In my interview process with Amana, mentioned previously in this chapter, I went back five times and interviewed with 12 different people. Every person along the way received a typed thank you note from me.

The Follow Up Call

A lot of interview candidates sit back and wait for the phone to ring. Make things happen with a follow up call to inquire about the status of the position. It shows enthusiasm and persistence. It says, "If you hire me, I won't disappear." Phone calling can be an uncomfortable task, so excuses are legion:

"I don't want to bug the person."
"The online application said not to call."

Unless you are applying for a position where you are expected to sit around waiting for the phone to ring, you should make the call. It bears repeating, how we behave in the interview process is an indication of how we will behave in the job. Make the call. Show them you are a self-starter with initiative, not someone they will have to light a fire under.

Is the person you are calling not available? Gently coax information: "Is there a better time to reach him/her?" Again, be kind to the gatekeepers. They can make sure your call gets through *or not.* You don't have to make the extra effort but know there's a good chance you will lose the job to someone who did. If you want the job, go after it.

Job Offer: Let the Negotiation Begin

The interview was a success. You have an offer with a salary. Now is the time for negotiation. Some people want to take the first offer and be done with it. But salary negotiation is a normal and expected part of the interview process. If you ask for more money, you must make a case why you deserve it.

Don't overshoot. I interviewed a young person, green out of college, who asked for over $100,000 for an entry-level public relations position. It wasn't realistic. Benefits are also part of your negotiation. Now is the time to ask those questions.

- Do you have a 401(k) program and do you match contributions?
- Do you have health insurance plan options?
- Do you offer tuition reimbursement?
- How much vacation time is offered? Do unused vacation days expire or carry over to the next year?

In the end, the organization will either make a counter-offer or not. And you may choose to accept or not.

Follow Through With the I Do

Do you accept this job, for rich benefits or poor ones, in sick days and in health, till layoffs do you part?

If you are offered a job and you accept, follow up a verbal agreement with a letter of acceptance, thanking them for the opportunity and expressing your enthusiasm for the job. Send out the note before your first day on the job. *"Thank you for your confidence in me for the director of operations position. I am very enthusiastic to meet the entire team and I am looking forward to getting started..."*

If you decide not to take an offer, send a letter of regret (by postal mail, not email). *"Thank you for your kind offer. While you have an impressive organization and I believe you would be a wonderful person to work for, I feel like the manager position is not a good fit with my skills at this time..."*

BE EXCEPTIONAL: Thank You for Not Hiring Me

So you didn't get the job. The interview went well, but they are moving forward with someone else. You feel disappointed and discouraged. What should you do? Say, "Thank you."

That's right. Thank the people who did not hire you. Type out a letter, send it through the postal mail. Send an email, too, if you like. Why? Because *The Exceptional Professional* knows that sometimes, being the runner-up is good.

Twice in my career, I have been the runner-up. Both times, I followed up with thank you notes. In one case, the person hired instead of me, turned out to be a disaster and was let go after only a month. Rather than start the interview process over, the organization called me. I gladly accepted. (Had I known then what I know now, I would have asked for more money.)

In the second case, I didn't get the job I originally applied for, but the organization had another opening. A savvy human resources person contacted me and said, "We have another opening and your experience would be a great fit. Are you interested?" Again, the result was an enjoyable job and a career boost.

What should your letter say?

Thank you for the opportunity to interview for the (name it) position. I was glad to hear you found the person you were seeking. You have an impressive organization and I enjoyed speaking with you. If there is another opportunity to work for your organization, I would be very enthusiastic to continue our conversation.
Thank you again for the opportunity.
Best Wishes,

The hiring process is costly and time consuming for employers. Most will jump at viable candidates they have already vetted, rather than start the process over. Don't be miserable, be memorable. Sometimes being number two works out for you.

The interview process, while it is work on your part, is also a lot of work on the employer's part. If you are turning down a job, be complimentary, even if you would rather be buried in a box of snakes than work there. You never know if you might cross paths with people from that organization down the road.

Don't Burn Bridges

Early in this chapter, I mentioned my interview with Amana Appliances. I want to finish the chapter with a "prequel" to that story.

It was the dreaded day of the big layoff at Amana. The manufacturer had just been sold by Raytheon of Waltham, Massachusetts to Goodman Holding Company of Houston, Texas. One by one we were called into the office of one of Goodman's vice presidents, to be let go by a man we did not know. I had heard a few people before me had lashed out at him with angry words, some had burst into tears.

When it came to my turn, this vice president looked like he had been through it. Instead of issuing a parting shot, I smiled and said to him, "I was only here nine months, but I enjoyed my time here and I learned a great deal. I am grateful for the experience and I thank you for that." He was pleasantly surprised. We chatted for a minute, he smiled, shook my hand and I went on my way.

When I returned a few months later to interview for the public relations manager position, one of the people I had to interview with was this same vice president. When I walked into his office, he smiled and said, “I remember you.” It was another factor that helped me get that job.

Every face-to-face contact you make, even in the worst of circumstances, is an opportunity to make a good impression. Build bridges, don’t burn them. Be nice to everyone, because the most unlikely characters may become the greatest asset to your career.

For more information about the meat of the interview: questions and answers to interview questions, read on.

12.2 *What Employers Want or Weed Out*

My sister had a friend in law school who listed on her resume that one of her hobbies was "bulldog breeding." Only she misspelled breeding. Her resume said that her hobby was "bulldog breading."

One law firm that received her resume responded, "Thank you for your interest. We do not have any openings at this time. Oh, by the way, we are very curious about your recipe for 'bulldog breading.'"

Two-thirds of the job search is surviving the weeding-out process. *The Exceptional Professional* knows what employers want and how to get their attention with a compelling resume and thoughtful answers to interview questions. *The Exceptional Professional* also knows if you want to make some bread, always have someone else look at your resume before a potential employer does.

In this chapter, you will learn:

- What employers are looking for in job candidates
- Common interview questions and how to answer them
- About action words for your resume that show initiative
- What to include and what to leave off your resume

What Employers are Looking for in an Employee

On an airplane between Baltimore and Chicago, I sat next to a man in commercial real estate. He told me that he hires a number of candidates right out of college. I asked what he looked for in the candidates.

"The main thing I want to know," he said, "is can they carry on a conversation?" This is important he explained, because they must be able to communicate with clients. He looks for eye contact, whether they researched his organization and if they show an interest in his organization by asking questions. And he wants to see if they can do all this, without checking or answering their phone.

What else are employers looking for in a candidate of any age? If you were running a business, what type of employee would you want? Before we cover interview questions, let's take a closer look at this.

The Employer's Hierarchy of Needs

Maslow's Hierarchy of Needs is a pyramid that begins at the base with the most vital needs: Physiological Needs, such as food, water and rest. The next higher level: Safety Needs, includes safety and security. Once you have met those needs, the next two layers are Social Needs and Esteem, a sense of belonging and feeling of accomplishment. Topping off the pyramid is Self-Actualization, or achieving one's full potential. [38]

If there were an Employer Hierarchy of Needs, here's what it might look like:

Shows Up / Punctual / Full Day

At its base, would be an employee who shows up. That's a low bar everyone must clear, but what's amazing is the number of people who don't clear it. Also at the most basic, an employee who is on time and doesn't cut out early.

Gets Along / No Drama

The next level would be an employee who gets along with others and does not cause any drama. That means no gossiping, back-biting or jealous backlash. So much work today involves teams. Employers want a person who is mature, respectful, attentive and works well with others.

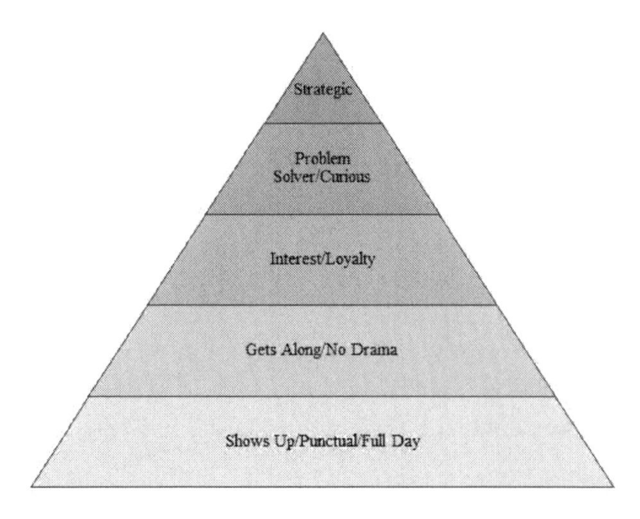

Interest / Loyalty

Next up on the Employee Hierarchy of Needs – an employee who is loyal and takes an interest in the organization. This person cares about the quality of the products or services. When the going gets tough, this person will stick by the organization. It also means the employee understands his or her job is not just to self-promote, but to also promote his or her boss or supervisor.

Problem Solver / Curious

One more level up, is an employee who is a problem solver and intellectually curious. When you ask this employee a question, he or she does not shrug and say, "I dunno," or "That's not in my job description." But instead says, "I don't know but I will find out and get back to you today." This person is motivated and thinking about advancement.

Strategic

At the top of the hierarchy, is an employee is who is a strategic thinker who sees all the moving parts of the organization and its stakeholders. This person always asks, "How can we do this better?" and looks ahead to future opportunities, as well as shifts in the market. This person is management material.

Another Perspective

Another way to think of this is how we evaluate our friendships. There are certain measures we look for in a friend.

> *Can I count on you?*
> *Will you be kind? Will you be honest with me?*
> *Will you be interested in what I have to say? Will you put aside your cell phone and not text or check messages when you spend time with me?*
> *Will you be loyal? Will you be there for me in good times and in bad?*
> *Will you care about my well-being?*

These are qualities employers are looking for in an employee or an intern. Be a friend to your employer or potential employer. In interviews, your preparation, research, clothing choices and attitude, should all say, "You can count on me."

What Interviewers Don't Care About

It's time again for a little tough love. And the last thing I want is for you to take this the wrong way. *Interviewers don't care what they can do for you.* There it is. The skunk is on the table.

They don't care that the job might be a great stepping stone in your career or that you would have a tremendous sense of accomplishment if you worked for them. I know! That is so selfish, isn't it? Who knew they could be this uncaring and unfeeling? It's all about them… so typical. Employers want to know what you can do for them. When answering interview questions, avoid, "I feel like this job would be a great opportunity *for me.*" Make it about them:

> *"My legal expertise and writing skills would be an asset to your firm."*
> *"I am confident my social media experience could expand your reach."*

Ultimately, it really is about you, but that can be our little secret. With what an employer is looking for (and not looking for) in mind, let's look at some of the common interview questions.

Interview Questions

Do not interrupt the interviewer. Let the interviewer finish the question before you start answering.

Where do you see yourself in five years?

I hate this question. I've never seen myself in five years. My first few jobs after college were a disaster. It took me awhile to find my groove. Employers tell me college students have replied to this question,

"Doing your job." One employer responded, "It took me 20 years to get here, but good luck with that."

Focus on the job at hand. When you are interviewing for an entry level job in advertising or accounting, don't tell them your goal in five years is to "go to law school." A better answer lets the interviewer know you are consistent and won't be hopping to another job, but also that you are ambitious and would like to earn a promotion.

> *"In five years, I would like to still be making a difference for this organization. I would like the opportunity to advance and I am willing to work towards that, as an individual or part of a team."*

Tell me about yourself.

Sometimes the toughest questions are the open-ended ones. The real question being asked here: *"Who are you and why should I care?"* The answer, is the "elevator speech" (covered in Chapter 1.2).

Your answer has three parts:

4. Where I have been (experience)
5. Where I am going (goals)
6. What I can do for you and your organization (qualifications)

> *"I majored in mathematics and finance in college and made some extra money on the side, tutoring students who had trouble in math. I enjoyed tutoring so much, that I went on to get a teaching certificate and do my student teaching at Central High. I know my subject and I have a lot of patience with young people. I know I could be an asset to your school. I hear you are also looking for an assistant track coach and I could fill that role as well."*

What is your greatest strength?

When preparing for an interview, think in stories. What are the stories of your life that demonstrate your strengths or other good qualities?

Answer these type of questions with stories. *"I am a good negotiator. I was able to reduce our costs in raw materials by $20,000 by taking bids from multiple vendors and then convincing them to give us discounts because of the volume of our business."*

Be brief. If you give too many details or talk too long, you will lose your interviewer. Think about other stories that demonstrate when you:

- Overcame a challenge
- Solved a problem
- Accomplished something you are proud of
- Learned a vital lesson
- Had to deal with a difficult customer

What is your greatest weakness?

Some try to con the interviewer with "a strength in cunning disguise."

"I work way too hard."
"I'm a perfectionist."
"I'm too detail-oriented."

Don't pull a muscle patting yourself on the back. Interviewers are on to you. Not being able to admit any weakness is a weakness. Admitting weakness can be a strength. Tell the story about a weakness you conquered and how. *"I see weaknesses as challenges to overcome. I used to be so disorganized. A great supervisor early in my career advised me to make a list every day and prioritize it. I made that a regular practice and now I am very organized."*

Why do you want to work here?

When I worked at Sony Music, interviewees were asked, "Why do you want to work here?" Most would say, *"Because I love music."* Which would cause the interviewer to say, "Who doesn't?" What seems like the most obvious answer isn't always the best. Consider other answers. *"I like that there are constant promotions and events going on, which will require creative ideas. I will work hard and I don't mind putting in the long hours this job demands."*

Other Common Interview Questions

Again, think about your stories that help you answer these questions:

Why did you leave your last job?
What motivates you?
What do you like to read?
What are your hobbies?
What characteristics do you look for in a supervisor?
Are you good at working with a team?
Have you ever had a conflict with a supervisor?
Tell me about your educational background?
Why should I hire you over other candidates?
What can you tell me about this organization?

(Hopefully, you did your research. More on that in Chapter 12.4: *The Great Job Hunt.*)

Sell Me This Pencil

Sometimes an interviewer will take a random object, hand it to the interview candidate and say, "Sell me this."

Larry Daniels, a long-time family friend, and a skilled sales professional, explained how a woman he interviewed aced this test, before the sale: *"I recently interviewed three candidates for a national account sales position. At some point during the interview, I reach into my desk and grab a toy (I keep them around for co-workers' kids who visit). I hand it to them and ask them to sell it to me.*

"The two men were flustered. The woman composed herself for a few seconds, stuck out her hand to shake my hand, and said, "I'm (Jane Doe) and I work for (Acme Products)." I did not have to hear the rest of it, though I let her go on for a minute or two. Natural abilities are revealed in the most subtle ways."

The Interviewer Throws a Curve Ball

My friend Tamara said her interviewer stopped in the middle of an interview and asked, "How do you think you're doing so far?" Tamara, soft spoken and intellectual, froze. Then she turned on the swagger, "I think I'm holding my own." The interviewer smiled, "I think you are too." She got the job. I told that story to another person who knew the interviewer and that person said, "He is the kind of guy where, had she waivered on that question, she might not have been hired."

When You Don't Know the Answer to a Question

This is a lot like when you can't remember someone's name. Don't try to finesse, just confess.

> *"I don't know the answer to that, but I am willing to learn."*
> *"I don't have the answer, but I will find out for you."* If you do promise further information, follow through. Don't let "I don't know" be the end of the show. Use it to highlight your problem-solving skills.

Inappropriate Questions

The Wall Street Journal had a great feature about the "Worst Interview Questions," that included "bizarre, inappropriate or just plain illegal questions." Here are some of the zingers:

> *"Are you currently looking for a husband?"*
> *"Do you believe there is life in outer space?"*
> *"Are you black?"*
> *"Do you believe in ghosts?"*
> *"Can you set up your own VCR?"*
> *"Can you count to 50?"*
> *"A math question about how many fleas a dog had"*
> *"Just entertain me for five minutes, I'm not going to talk."*
> *"Are you a Muslim?"*

—

BE EXCEPTIONAL: How to Answer The Illegal Question

What if you get, "The Illegal Question" in an interview? The Illegal Question is usually directed at women: "Are you married? Do you or will you have kids?" The question behind the question: "Will you be coming late and bolting early for school programs, teacher conferences, medical issues and sports?" *The Exceptional Professional* knows there are different options.

There is an abundance of advice online on how to dodge or rebuff this question. But Natalie McCandies, attorney at law, has another suggestion: answer it. I contacted Natalie, because I was impressed by her answer, which I first heard when we were both speaking at Valparaiso University Law School.

"I am a mother, I have a son. We are planning on having more. But that won't have any effect on how I do my job. I try to keep my professional and family life separate. But my family is very important to me and I am a mother first."

Natalie had the question when interviewing for a position with a public defender. Obviously, they would know asking about family or kids is illegal. So why ask it? "They are looking for your response," explains Natalie. "In the legal field, you deal with all kinds of people and people will test you. Will you fly off the handle or be defensive?"

Natalie got the job. "They liked my honesty," she said. She even brought her son into the workplace while working long hours as second chair with another attorney on a murder trial.

Natalie now works as a prosecutor. But she said people in that public defender's office appreciated her hard work and still provide excellent references for her. The askers of The Illegal Question, were nice people and good mentors after all.

I had an interviewer ask, "I noticed you are not wearing a wedding band. Do you have any plans to get married or have a family?" I made a motion like I was pulling back an invisible bow and arrow and I said, "Do you mean, am I on the hunt?" I laughed – I was really making fun of the question. The interviewer laughed too.

My answer after that, like Natalie's, was honest and direct. Like Natalie, I too, was offered the job. The interviewer turned out to be a kind person and strong advocate for women in management positions.

How you answer is really up to you. The main point is, if you get a similar question, you have options:

1. Dodge it
2. Object to it
3. Answer it

Answering it with honesty and candor is a good option.

Questions You Should Ask the Interviewer

There is nothing more disappointing to an interviewer than to have the question, "Do you have any questions for me?" met with stony silence. Asking questions, shows you are interested in the organization and in the interviewer, personally. Here are some questions you might ask:

What made you choose this career?
What led you to work for this organization?
What do you like best about working here?
If you could change anything about this organization, what would it be?
How would you describe your management style?
What do you see as the biggest challenge for you or your team here?
What are the next steps in this interview process?

You may also have technical questions about products, services, innovation or research, based on your skills and area of expertise.

Heed the Red Flags in an Interview

If you ask people about the worst job in their career, many will admit, "I saw red flags in the interview." Early in my career, an interviewer asked me to submit a photo with my resume. I thought it was strange – I was applying for an assistant editor job, not a modeling job. But I needed a job, so I sent a photo. After that, he told me,

"Another candidate, competing against you for this job, had 10 letters of reference." I had three. I rounded up more reference letters, but not 10.

I got the job. I lasted nine months. Never have I been so badly treated by a supervisor. It was the same bully boss I described at the beginning of Chapter 10.4: *Knuckleheads*. Had I heeded the red flags in the interview process, I would have never take the job.

You are interviewing the interviewer as much as they are interviewing you. Look for a job and organization that is a good fit. Look for good mentors. How else can you elude a bad employment situation?

1. Ask about your predecessor. Why did he or she leave? How long had that person been with the organization? Quick turnover is a bad sign.
2. Ask to see an organizational chart. How many layers of management are there? Is what you thought was a middle-management position hanging like fringe off the bottom of the chart?
3. Google "(organization name)" and "sucks." (Otherwise, don't use the word "sucks." As my high school literature teacher, Mr. Mitchell, would say, "Cultured people don't use that language.")
4. Review the social media of your interviewer and your predecessor.
5. If the interviewer is walking you in or out, observe how others in the workplace react to the interviewer. Are they genuinely friendly?
   Or more guarded? How does the interviewer behave towards them?

The End of the Interview

When the interview comes to a close, give a firm handshake to your interviewer and express your appreciation for the interviewer's time.

BE EXCEPTIONAL: Have a Closing Statement

Just as you would conclude a speech, *The Exceptional Professional* knows you should have a concluding statement for your interview, expressing your enthusiasm and interest for the job.

> *"Your organization is very impressive, especially the upcoming product innovations. I am still enthusiastic about the position. I know I could be an asset to your organization with my technical skills and consumer products background. I look forward to working with you."*

Resumes That Rise to the Top

Have you ever made this mistake? A child shows you original artwork and you say, "That's a really nice hippopotamus."

The child says, "It's a butterfly."

You say, "Oh yes, I see it now. That's the best butterfly ever."

As my nieces and nephews have grown, I've been promoted from art appraiser to resume coach. I am better at the latter. My record of them landing jobs after my resume re-dos was so good, I ended up assisting their friends too. What is the secret? It's all in the bullet points. Highlighting skills with bullet points makes your resume easier to skim. Here are some pointers on bullet points:

- Begin bullet points with an action verb: *Directed, Fostered, Negotiated, Developed, Designed, Produced...* Action verbs say, "I seized the bull by the horns. I had initiative."
- Lose "did the minimum" verbs such as: *Maintained, Implemented, Distributed.* Those verbs say, "I did what I was told."
- Change action verbs from present to past tense: *Led,* not *Leading.* Current experience is considered "past."
- Quantify results where possible. Did sales, clients, subscribers, attendees or audience reach increase under you? If numbers can show how you made things run more efficiently,

that is important too. Was there money saved or earned? Put a dollar quantity to it.

- Avoid repeating the same verbs. Find synonyms – instead of using *Created* twice, replace one *Created* with *Initiated.*
- As you gain experience, reduce the bullet points from previous jobs. The most recent experience should have the most bullet points. Everything after should have fewer.
- Drop some things from your resume as you get further into your career. If you have been in accounting the last 10 years, your job as a teenager scooping ice cream becomes less relevant.

When you update your resume, you can view it proudly and say, "That's the best resume ever," and really mean it.

Action Words that Show Teamwork

In a me-focused world, employers want to know if you will get along with others or be a human tornado of bickering, fighting, gossiping, whining and blaming. Nobody wants that in their workplace. There's a better way to show you get along with others and that's to say it on your resume by starting some bullet points with, "I-work-well-with-others action words:"

Collaborated with
Teamed with
Involved with team
Negotiated
Joined
Joined forces with
Assembled group of
Worked together with
Supported
Cooperated
Co-authored
Resolved
Contributed

Mix these words with bullet points of individual initiative and leadership action words and you have a winning resume:

Managed
Specialized in
Supervised
Motivated
Directed
Drove

Initiated	*Created*
Delivered	*Trained*
Designed	*Coached*
Selected	*Counseled*
Researched	*Enhanced*
Edited	*Fostered*
Produced	

All of these action words work well in your cover letters and the interview, too. If you are new to the job market, don't worry about the lack of *Managed* or *Directed* on your resume. Entry level experience is more likely to have verbs like: *Coordinated, Assisted, Researched.*

Other Resume Design Tips

Here are some quick design guidelines for drafting your resume:

Don't Use Too Many Fonts

I remember helping one person with a resume that had 4-5 fonts. The constantly changing fonts were a distraction. Stick with one or two fonts and keep them simple. Scripted fonts are harder to read. Not everyone's computer programs have the same fonts, so save your resume as a PDF to make sure employers see what you see.

Be Brief

Unless you are a college professor with an extensive CV (Curriculum Vitae), your resume should be 1-2 pages. A woman asked me to look at her daughter's resume. Her daughter was a new college graduate and had a four-page resume. Few employers will look past the first page.

Include a "Summary" Instead of an "Objective" at the Top

A Summary statement is a synopsis of your top skills. An Objective statement, about where you want to be, seems redundant. If the employer knows you are after a certain position, why waste space restating that?

Example of a Summary statement:

Public relations and media specialist with proven writing and speaking skills and the ability to perform on deadline. Experience in a variety of industries, including dealing directly with consumers in retail.

Have Someone Else Review Your Resume

A fellow chamber of commerce member told me the resumes his firm gets are terrible. He said, "They are written in paragraphs instead of bullet points, full of grammatical errors and not organized."

When you have been working on your resume for so long, you are too close to it and you will not see the grammatical errors and other flaws. Have a professional or a trusted friend review your resume.

Don't Sell Yourself Short

When I interviewed people whose resumes I was re-doing, I found many of them were leaving off great experience or underplaying it. College students, in particular, will leave fast food or retail experience off their resume, thinking it doesn't sound important enough. Humility is laudable, but when marketing yourself to employers, don't sell yourself short. Employers value skills from fast food and retail experience:

- Customer Service: you ask questions, listen to customers' needs, make suggestions and ensure they have an enjoyable experience.
- Teamwork: you work well with others.
- Multi-tasking: you can juggle assignments and work under pressure.
- Dealing with Difficult People: you keep calm, when others are blowing their stack.

One college student, who worked at a big box retail store, told me about a customer who became completely unhinged and started knocking over shopping carts. Security had to be called. If that's not experience in dealing with difficult people, I don't know what is.

Let's look at a fast food job description on a resume:

> Ordinary: *"Waited on customers who came into the restaurant."*
> Extraordinary: *"Learned to increase revenues and customer satisfaction by offering customers additional options."*

Which one would you hire?

Other Things That Go on Your Resume

- Special research projects you worked on
- Awards
- Volunteer work
- Engineers, IT people or other technical professions may include college class work or GPAs on their resumes. Communications majors, not so much – nobody thinks you flunked Communications.
- Have a professional email. If your email is "partygirl@_" or "kegboy@_," get a more professional email for your resume.

What to Leave Off Your Resume

- A photo of yourself (no matter how camera-friendly you are)
- Your age, birth date
- Height, weight or any other measurements
- *"References available upon request."* It's assumed there is someone who will speak to your good character. It's like saying, "Available for interviews." Of course, you are.

A Toss Up

Should you have information about your college fraternity or sorority? It can be a big plus if you know the person doing the hiring came from that same fraternity or sorority. Otherwise, people who did not participate in the Greek system may not see it as a positive but more of a negative.

A co-ed business, law or other professional fraternity might be okay, but add the words "business fraternity" after the Greek letters, for the uninitiated.

Your Skill Set

If the job description specifies knowledge of specific software or coding language, list those in a "Skills" section. Never put anything on a resume you can't defend in an interview. Never list computer skills you don't have. If an employer gives you a skills test on the spot, the ruse is up.

You don't need to list knowledge of *Microsoft Office* suite. Most employers are going to assume you already know that.

Honesty is the Best Policy

Do not lie about anything on your resume. That includes degrees, advanced degrees, awards or titles. I knew someone who boasted about having an MBA from an Ivy League university. It turns out, he attended a workshop at the university once, but in no way earned a degree. Anytime you lie, you are digging yourself into a hole.

Quirky Things on Your Resume

In the last chapter, I told the story about how everyone told me to drop the "Minor in Medieval Studies" from my resume, because people would think I was one of those weird Renaissance Fair types. But then I found out one of my interviewers had a medieval map collection.

Oscar Wilde said, "Be yourself, everyone else is taken." If there is something a little different or quirky on your resume that distinguishes you, leave it on there.

After telling that to a group of college students, one young woman who was a finance major, interested in working for a large financial firm, wanted to know if she should add her hobby to her resume: tattoo artist.

"Maybe not," I said.

If the quirky thing runs contrary to the industry you are aiming for, you might leave it off. Although I liked how this young woman was personable and ambitious. I imagine that, at whatever financial firm she landed, they are all covered in tattoos by now.

The Best Times For a Follow Up Call

In a competitive job market, it is important after sending a resume to follow up – not just with an email, but also by phone. When is the best time to call? Here are a few tricks I learned in my cold calling days. (Actually, I am still in my cold calling days.)

The normal work day used to be 9 a.m. to 5 p.m., but for many, it has shifted from 8:30 a.m. to 4:30 p.m. Here are the worst times to call:

- 10 to 11:30 a.m. is prime meeting time
- 11:30 a.m. to 2 p.m. is when people are lunching
- 2 to 4 p.m. is prime meeting time again

Try to reach people early in their work day from 8:30 to 9:30 a.m., before they get into meetings. If you want to reach an executive, try calling at 7:45 a.m. or earlier. Many are already in their workplace by then and a surprising number will pick up their own phone before their executive assistant arrives. If you don't reach your person in the morning, try again in late afternoon: 4 to 4:30 p.m. or 5 p.m.

And of course, you can always ask an assistant, "When is the best time to reach him/her?"

Now we've covered interviewing and resumes. What happens when the interview takes place over lunch? We'll tackle that set of challenges next.

12.3 *What Interview Meals Reveal*

At an upscale restaurant, an executive recruiter was interviewing a woman for a C-suite position. It was going smoothly, until a wait person set down a water glass to the left of the interview candidate. The candidate noticed the error. It should have been placed on the right.

Have you ever heard those stories about employers who have the wait staff purposely make errors to see how the interview candidates react? This was not one of those occasions.

The candidate lifted the glass in the air, noisily placed it on her right and loudly chided the wait person, "It goes on the right!" And for extra emphasis, *"I guess they are hiring anyone as waitresses these days!"*

Why do employers have interview meals? Because sometimes, it's like cracking open a can of crazy. Character flaws that would not appear in a regular interview, suddenly surface. Relating the story, the executive recruiter said, "I've never been so appalled and embarrassed in my life."

Many a career and client are lost over the breaking of bread. *The Exceptional Professional* knows how you behave at the restaurant reflects what kind of manager or employee you will be in the workplace.

In this chapter, you will learn:

- What interviewers are looking for in an interview meal
- What you should order in an interview meal
- Random interview meal rules and what they mean
- The dynamics of group interview meals
- How to ask for an informational interview

Another employer told me about interviewing a man over lunch. The interview was going well, until a wait person brought the interview candidate the wrong order. He exploded like an egg in a microwave. "How hard is it to get a (expletive) order right?!" he screamed at the wait person. This wasn't a test either.

In interview meals, most interviewers are not trying to trick you. They want to know how you will be viewed when dining with clients, potential clients and other stakeholders. What employers are looking for is someone to represent their organization well.

A friend of mine said her daughter-in-law interviews candidates for an insurance organization. She takes the candidates out for lunch and dinner and she is looking for three things:

1. Reasonable table manners: someone who knows which fork to use and doesn't have sloppy habits.
2. Social skills: can they carry on a conversation?
3. Alcohol use: do they drink too much?

Very few employers will say, "I hired or promoted her because of her beautiful table manners." But they will say, "I didn't hire or promote him because he ate like a pig." People tell me about colleagues passed up for promotion because their table manners were problematic. It was sloppy stuff: holding the fork in a fist; talking and chewing and spraying food in the process; shoveling food; licking fingers; licking the knife; reaching over other plates instead of saying, "Please pass." One person said the spouse was the eating disaster who prevented the promotion.

Some college students think, "I'll never have an interview meal. Interview meals are for finance majors and law students." But interview meals are not the only time our table manners are on display. Here is a list of instances in my own career where food was mixed with business:

- Dining out with clients and vendors
- Lunching at work with co-workers or friends in business
- Lunching out with colleagues
- Lunch ordered in for meetings gone long
- Dinner ordered in for work after hours
- Breakfast meetings with coffee, Danishes and fruit ordered in
- Someone treating the staff to donuts, bagels or muffins
- Boss treating employees to a meal
- Employee picnics
- Employee potlucks at work
- Meetings over coffee
- Workplace holiday parties
- After work happy hours with co-workers

- Chamber of commerce breakfasts, lunches and dinners
- Networking events
- Charitable breakfasts, lunches and dinners
- Conferences: dining with new people you meet
- Traveling with co-workers: meeting in the "free breakfast" area or hotel restaurant; lunch and dinner out; airport layover dining
- Anniversary and retirement dinners

No matter what business you're in, you're always eating with others.

Should I Eat Before?

"Should I eat before I go to an interview meal?" This question pops up during my dining tutorials at universities. There's a little confusion here. Eat before a networking event, not before an interview meal.

Eat before a networking event so you will focus on the greeting and not the eating. Some see appetizers and think, "Dinner!" That's bad.

Before an interview meal, don't fill up. If you are too full to eat, that raises questions in the mind of the interviewer. Is this person a picky eater? Does this person not like anything from our chosen restaurant? Is this person too nervous? Eat during the interview meal, to demonstrate that you are at ease in dining situations.

Beginning of the Interview Meal

If you are meeting at a restaurant, arrive at least 10 minutes early. The interviewer is considered the "host." Follow the host's lead. When the maître d' shows you to your table, wait for your interviewer to tell you where to sit. If you have a choice and you are sitting at a four-top table, it is better to sit next to the interviewer, rather than opposite him or her, because you are more in a position to negotiate. (More about seating in Chapter 3.1: *Making Meetings More Effective.*)

During a dining tutorial at a university, one young lady asked, "What if we are sitting in a booth? Should I sit next to the interviewer?"

I said, "No. In a booth, sit opposite the interviewer. If you sit next to the interviewer in a booth, some interviewer might say, 'Hired!' But that is not the person you want to work for."

What to Order

Place your napkin in your lap when your host does. As the guest, you will order first. So what should you order?

1. Order Something Inexpensive

If there is a choice of sandwiches or more substantial entrees on the menu, get a moderately-priced sandwich. If you order something pricey, the interviewer will see you as someone who will run up the expense account and cost the organization a lot of money.

If you were running a business, would you want employees to eat extravagant meals at the most expensive restaurants, then charge it back to the business? Don't assume you can order high-priced items on the menu because you think your host is flush with cash.

A candidate in a group interview told me how a few college students found this out the hard way. Knowing the interviewer was footing the bill at this high-end restaurant, several students ordered lobster. Not a lobster bisque or a mac and cheese with lobster pieces but a claws, tail and all, green gunk in the trunk, full-size, live lobster.

The interviewer was angry that so many ordered the most expensive entree. At the meal's end, he told them why that was wrong and said, "By the way, we're all getting separate checks tonight." When someone else is buying, order something moderately priced.

2. Order Something Neat

Avoid big, messy items, like a French Dip sandwich or barbecue sandwich with coleslaw on top or anything dripping with dressing. At an Italian restaurant, don't order a long, stringy pasta like spaghetti, linguini or angel hair. Look for a small noodle, like a penne pasta or macaroni.

Avoid finger foods like fried chicken or ribs. The interviewer won't want to shake a greasy hand at the end of the meal. Don't order chicken fingers. Those are for small children whose parents can't get them to eat anything else. Would you like a sippy cup with that?

3. Order Something You Have Tried Before

Try new things, but not on an interview. If you've never had turtle soup, your interview meal is not the time. After you get the job, go back on your own time and own dime and order up all the turtle soup you want.

An executive treated the employees on her team to dinner at an exclusive restaurant. The menu was limited and a la carte. An intern was talked into ordering foie gras. He had never tried foie gras and was a little hesitant because he didn't know what it was (a fatty duck liver pate, that came in a gelatinous form). But two others ordering it urged him, "You simply must try it! You will absolutely love it!" So he did.

After the first bite, I could see the uneasy, queasy look on his face. And he still had a piece the size of Normandy left. He took a few more small bites, swallowing fast and hard, his face distorting to suppress a grimace, while the others exclaimed, "Isn't this delicious? It's so rich!" Finding out what he was eating only made it worse.

Ordering something and not eating it, was a waste of money. In any business dining situation, especially interviews (and interns are still interviewing), if you haven't tried it, don't order it. The response to, "You simply must try it!" is to smile and say, "No thank you."

Random Rules of the Interview Meal

There are a variety of other practices that often define whether you go forward in the interview process.

Taste Before Seasoning

Taste your food before seasoning it. Seasoning first, makes you look impulsive, like you don't think before you leap.

Let It Cool

Don't try to cool hot soup or hot coffee with ice from your water glass. Don't blow on them, either. Waiting for things to cool shows patience.

Don't Do Anything Quirky

Try not to do anything quirky, like mixing the food on your plate into a pile of hash. That makes you seem messy and unorganized. On the other hand, don't be the person who must finish one thing at a time – first the corn, then the mashed potatoes, then the entrée.

In a long meeting where sandwiches were ordered in, I grabbed a sandwich, opened a bag of potato chips and started layering them on my sandwich. I was about to take a bite, when I noticed everyone at the table staring at me. Someone started cracking jokes about the potato chips on my sandwich. What was I thinking? You want to be remembered for your ideas, not how you played with your food.

All Things in Moderation

There is no such thing as "all you can eat" in a business meal.

- Do not reach for a second roll out of the bread basket.
- Do not order your steak "rare." What is delicious to you, might be an unappetizing, bloody sight to others. Try "medium rare" or "medium."
- Go easy on the salt and pepper. Season once, not between every bite.

- Do not smother your food with ketchup or steak sauce. That shows you do not have good judgment...or taste.
- Do not over-imbibe. Better yet, avoid alcohol to keep a clear head.

Don't Order Items on the Side

Don't order items like condiments, salad dressings or sauces on the side. It makes you look high maintenance. Your diet resumes after the interview.

Try Not to Send Items Back

If the wait staff brings you the wrong dish, don't say, "I ordered this flounder *broiled* and *not fried*!" This looks like you don't adjust well and can't go with the flow. Never send anything back during an interview unless it's so dangerously undercooked, it's crawling off your plate.

In dining tutorials, some will argue, "If I don't send it back, the interviewer may think I overlook mistakes or that I am not a take charge person." When you reach a stage where the position warrants an interview meal, no one is looking for you to take charge of the wait staff. Nitpicking and making demands of the wait staff is more concerning.

Keep Pace with the Interviewer

During a business meal, try to keep pace with the people with whom you are eating. Finishing too far ahead, will make them feel rushed. Finishing too far behind, will keep them waiting.

This is not always easy to do. I worked with a CEO who was a native New Yorker and whenever I ate with him, I felt like I was in one of those New York hotdog eating contests. I did learn to speed it up. Though when I went home to Iowa for a visit, my mother would say, "Goodness! Why are you inhaling your food?"

No Sampling Others' Food

You should ask your interviewer questions during the interview. But one of those questions should not be, "Are you going to eat the rest of those fries?" Or "Can I have a bite of that?" When you are out with family and friends, it is fine to sample each other's food. But not on an interview.

What if the interviewer wants to sample your food? That depends. How badly do you want the job?

Kill the Wait Staff with Kindness

How you treat the wait staff is a reflection of how you will treat others in the workplace. Berating the wait staff is the most cowardly act, because they can't fight back, without endangering their job. Make eye contact with the wait person when you are ordering and say, "Please." "I would like the grilled salmon, please." Say, "Thank you" when it arrives.

No Doggie Bags

Don't order a doggie bag or to-go box in business, no matter how much food is left. Your dog never has to know.

Since you will be answering questions, you may only make it through half your meal. A student told me she didn't have a chance to eat while being interviewed by three people over lunch. The three interviewers finished eating, then one piped up, "It looks like we didn't give you a chance to eat – go ahead and eat now." She said, "With three people staring at me eating, I couldn't eat another bite."

If others finish before you and you must leave food on the plate, leave it. You are there to do business first, and eat, second.

In a different situation, my friend took her client out for a meal. The client ordered a doggie bag and said, "I'm going to bring the rest home for my husband." My friend said, "I felt like I was paying for two."

Answering Questions

Take small bites, so you can answer questions or discuss business. We've all had someone ask us a question, just as we put food in our mouth. When that happens, use the universal symbol for "I have food in my mouth" – put up your index finger, which says, "Just a moment," and point to your mouth, which says, "I have food in my mouth."

How to Flunk an Interview Meal

Talking with food in your mouth is an obvious way to flunk an interview meal. Here are other, more subtle ways to botch an interview meal:

- Chewing your ice
- Dragging your teeth on a fork or spoon
- Using a finger to push food onto your fork
- Saying "Aaaaahhhh" after every sip of your drink
- Licking your knife
- Talking about your diet
- Trying to dislodge food from your teeth with your fingernail
- Leaving your cell phone on the table or glancing at your phone
- Applying lipstick or lip balm at the table

If you are wondering why "Making yummy noises" didn't make the list, it's because that's one rule I always break.

Should You Say Something?

In dining tutorials, I pose the question, "If your interviewer has spinach on his or her teeth, should you say something?" At one university, a young lady raised her hand instantly and said, "I would say something."

"Why would you say something?" I asked.

"Because it's grossing me out," she said.

Not quite the answer I was looking for. I look for more responses. The audience is usually divided 50/50. I want to hear both sides.

"I wouldn't say anything because I don't want to embarrass the person."
"I would tell the person, because I wouldn't want him/her to look bad."

The answer: it's a judgment call. The spinach in the teeth question came from my mentor and friend, Maria Everding. If you think that pointing out the spinach in the teeth would make the person embarrassed or self-conscious, you might not say anything. However, if that person is about to walk into a room full of people, you might mention the spinach to save that person from further embarrassment. I want audience members to reason out their decision. In either instance, your first thought is for the comfort of the other person.

College students like to throw curve balls: "If someone tells you there is something in your teeth, can you say, 'Is it gone now?'" If you feel like there is something still in your teeth, no need to badger your fellow diners. Excuse yourself to the restroom to take care of it.

Allergies: When All Etiquette Bets are Off

A college student with a severe seafood allergy told me about an interview where she was eating soup, that unbeknownst to her, had a seafood base. Suddenly, she felt overheated and her face and neck were flush. She began to swell up and could feel her throat starting to close.

Her interviewer called 911. The interviewer rode in the ambulance with her to the hospital. Upon hearing this, college students will interrupt with the vital question foremost on their mind: "Did she get the job?"

Yes, she did get the job. Once, I was telling that story at a law school. When I said, "She got the job," a law student called out, "And more importantly... *she lived.*"

In a dangerous situation, all etiquette bets are off. Do whatever you have to do. If you knock over tables to give someone the Heimlich maneuver, so be it. If you have to ask the wait staff a few questions about ingredients for your safety, so be it.

BE EXCEPTIONAL: Preview The Menu

If you know in advance the restaurant where your interview or meeting will take place, *The Exceptional Professional* looks at the menu before going to the restaurant. Go online, review the menu and select a few moderately-priced options that you might order.

If you have allergies or food restrictions and need to ask questions about ingredients, call the restaurant ahead of your meeting and ask away. Then you won't have to do it during your interview.

Interview Check

A frequent question from college students is: "If I have an interview meal, should I offer to pay the bill or at least pay for myself?" I understand the thinking behind that:

"I want the interviewer to see I am a nice person."
"I would buy the interviewer a Thanksgiving dinner to get this job."
"I'm highly competitive and I've never lost a fight over a check."

No, you should not offer to pay. The interviewer has invited you, so the interviewer, as the host, should pay. If you invite someone out for a meal or coffee for an informational interview, you should pay the bill.

A man told me about a lunch interview, where his interviewer paid the bill, but refused to leave a tip for the wait staff. He asked the interviewer, "Would you like me to leave the tip?" The interviewer said, "Nah! They make enough money."

The interviewee was horribly embarrassed but didn't dare correct the interviewer. He was offered the job, but turned it down. A person who would stiff the wait staff wasn't someone he wanted to work for.

Group Interview

Some companies, rather than interview one candidate over lunch or dinner, will interview a group of candidates.

Beware the group interview. While you may be tempted to distinguish yourself from those "complete losers," by wowing the interviewers with your superior wit, intellect, and experience – don't do it. One thing interviewers look for in a group interview is how well you get along with others. So attempts to play "I can top that story" or crush your fellow candidates like a bug, may be frowned upon.

What is a person of your superior wit, intellect, and experience to do?

- Greet and shake hands with the interviewers and other candidates.
- Be convivial – chat with the other candidates before the interview.
- Listen intently when others are speaking.
- Direct answers to interview questions to the interviewer, but also make eye contact with everyone else.
- If there is a shy candidate, invite that person into the discussion.
- Don't get drawn into arguments. Maintain your composure.

Don't join others who are behaving badly. If several candidates are ordering the most expensive items on the menu, over-imbibing, making fun of others or texting under the table, don't join them. Also skip the side-whispers, eye rolls and other evil alliances. Focus on the interview.

(In some group interviews, the interviewer will hand one person the wine list and say, "Order for the table." That is covered in Chapter 5.1: *Alcohol Protocol and Excessive Celebration.*)

Informational Interviews Over Coffee

An executive recruiter in a major metropolitan area was granting an informational interview to a college student as a favor to a friend. The recruiter received a phone call from the student, who lived across town from the recruiter's office.

"I live in (this neighborhood)," said the college student.
"I don't," said the recruiter.

When you invite someone out for an informational interview over coffee, he or she is doing you a favor. Make it convenient for that person:

- Scout out coffee locations near the person's workplace.
- Give them the choice of two coffee places.
- Provide a time limit: "Could we meet for 20-30 minutes? I want to be respectful of your time."
- Confirm the meeting either the night before or the day of by email.

Prepare for the meeting by researching the person's background and organization. "Informational interview" means you are there to listen. Make sure you listen more than you talk.

The rule of "all things in moderation" mentioned earlier, applies here. Don't distract from your meeting by dumping a lot of cream and sugar in your coffee. It's coffee, not "hot ice cream."

Coffee Meetings Without the Coffee

"What if I have a meeting over coffee and I don't like coffee?" This is a common question I get from many people in business, but especially college students fretting that first interview over coffee.

If you don't like coffee, keep it simple: order water, hot tea or an iced tea. Ordering nothing puts the interviewer in the uncomfortable position of enjoying coffee while you watch. What not to order:

- Big, pastel-colored or green smoothie
- Cold or hot coffee drink topped with whipped cream
- Specialty tea beverage, like bubble tea

The reasons not to order one of these "fun" drinks:

- Specialty drinks take longer to make. Your interviewer is left waiting while you keep glancing back at the counter, listening for your name.

- These drinks cost your interviewer more. One who is careless with an organization's budget on the little things is certain to be careless with the bigger expenses – dinners out, first class flights and hotels.
- It looks immature. The smoothie might seem healthy but it looks like a child's drink. Ditto for whipped cream-topped anything.
- It's a distraction. You want the interviewer thinking, "How fast can I hire this talented person?" Not, "What did this crazy person order?"

When out with family and friends, get that mega macchiato with the mound of whipped cream. Go wild. But not on business. Also, don't order a bagel, doughnut or Danish, if your interviewer is not having one.

The Other Person Wants to Pay

Whoever does the inviting, pays. Even if you invite the world's wealthiest person out to coffee for an informational interview, you buy the coffee... and maybe a pecan roll, too.

If you order at a cash register, allow your guest to order first, then say to the person behind the register, "These are together," and whip out your cash or credit card. Don't be slow on the draw.

The question often comes up, "What if the other person insists on paying?" Protest once. Maybe twice. "Please let me pay, I am grateful for your time." If the person still insists, let him or her pay. What is the alternative – a knock-down, drag-out fight over the check? Sometimes it's better to let nice people do a nice thing and graciously accept.

(For more info on eating while meeting, don't forget to check out Chapters 4.1: *Table Manners: Eating in Front of Others* and 6.2: *You Have Arrived: Being Entertained.*)

Now it's time to look at how to land that interview in the first place. If you are tired of filling out online applications and not hearing back, read on.

12.4 *The Great Job Hunt*

There was an opening with the Public Defender's office in Dallas, Texas. A recent law school graduate set her sights on that job. She made several phone calls but was unable to get through to the public defender. So she went to the Public Defender's office early one morning and parked herself in the waiting room. Finally, he came out of his office and said, "Okay – I will give you five minutes."

She told him how she had worked for a global advertising agency as a media buyer for some major brands. But she felt unfulfilled. She went to law school because she wanted to help people.

The public defender listened, then turned his chair and grabbed a stack of papers about a foot high off the credenza behind him. He set the stack on his desk before her and said, "These are the resumes for this one job opening. What I'm looking for is someone like you." There was one opening and she got it.

The Exceptional Professional knows you should never limit yourself to filling out online applications. If you want a job – go get it.

In this chapter, you will learn:

- Why face-to-face is the best way to market yourself
- Ideal places to network for a job
- Who wants you to get a job
- About temp agencies, career fairs and other opportunities

Bypassing the Online Applicants

"I filled out over a hundred online applications and did not get one response." This is a familiar complaint I hear from job seekers. If your application is first screened by a software program, it may be discarded before a human being ever sees it. Even if your application makes it past the software screen, your personality doesn't always come through. Filling out online applications and waiting for your phone to ring is at worst, a fruitless effort and at best, a strategy for mediocrity. Nothing can sell you like you, in person. When you meet people face-to-face, you have a chance to make a stronger connection.

I don't want to discourage you from filling out any online applications, but instead, refocus some of your efforts into more productive job hunting. When people get to meet you and see how great you are, why wouldn't they hire you?

I have never been able to get my hands on the study behind the oft quoted statistic from the U.S. Bureau of Labor Statistics that says, "70 percent of jobs come from networking." But when I look back on my career, only one of my jobs came from an advertised position. All the rest came from networking. Nothing can sell you like you, in person.

The Hierarchy of No

If you are still thinking, *"I can better my odds if I fill out 100 more online applications..." or "If I just re-write my solicitation email again..."* It just isn't so, because there is a "Hierarchy of No."

Bottom Level: Email When the request comes by email or text, it is easiest to say, "No." (Just hit "delete.")

Mid-Level: Phone Call When you hear someone's voice, it's a little harder to say, "No." Because now you can hear their tone and it's a little more personal.

Top Level: Face-to-Face When you are looking someone in the eye, it's the hardest to say, "No." Now you can see the facial expression, body language and how they react.

If you want a job, persuasion is best face-to-face. Look for opportunities to connect in person.

BE EXCEPTIONAL: How You Sell You

The Exceptional Professional knows when you are networking for a job or career leads, you are really in sales. And the product you are selling is you. There are two key principles to be successful in sales:

1. **You have to like the product you are selling**
   You have to like yourself. Believe you are a good product that any organization would be lucky to have. Be confident, but not cocky. You are asset, not God's gift, to an organization.

2. **Realize selling is about problem solving**
   Selling is not about pushing a product on people who don't need it. Selling is about discovering the goals of businesses and their owners. It's also about finding their pain. What are their challenges? What can you do to solve their business issues or enhance their bottom line?

Keep these two principles in mind as you are on your job hunt.

Five Great Places to Network for Job Contacts

Now it's time to get out there and meet people. If you are feeling a little rusty, go back and review Chapter 1.1: *Networking: The Basics.*

1. **Toastmasters**
   Had I known all the benefits of Toastmasters, I would have joined in college. Toastmasters is a place to practice public speaking in a friendly, supportive environment.
   A young man joined our club after his college graduation. A long time member, who was a vice president at one of the top employers in our area, was so impressed with his abilities and his enthusiasm, he hired him. When someone in our Toastmasters club has been out of work, other members offered help and referrals. To find a Toastmasters club near you, visit: www.toastmasters.org
2. **Alumni Events**
   When I moved to the New York City area for work, I didn't know many people in the area. I went to the website of my alma mater, the University of Iowa, and found they had an alumni club in Manhattan.

There were so many events: mixers with other Big Ten schools; walking tours; special backstage tours at some of New York's most famous venues. But my favorite events were the football watches at a bar in Manhattan on Saturdays. I met a lot of friends there and met alum from whatever Big Ten school we were playing each week.

The Iowa-Iowa State game was the best, because you would have over 100 people from the two schools filling the bar. There was a lot of good-natured bombast, as each side was convinced it was their year. I even went hiking on Bear Mountain in New York with fellow alum. (Important: never get caught three miles from your car, with the sun going down, at a place with "Bear" in the name.)

Alumni organizations can connect you with professional mentors who want to help fellow alumni. I meet many of these mentors when they take part in university etiquette dinners, where I present. The larger the university, the more clubs it will have across the globe. Visit your university's alumni website and look for a club near you.

3. **Trade Associations**

Whatever your occupation or field of interest, there is a trade group for it and chapters nationwide. Actuaries? Corporate attorneys? Truck drivers? Meeting planners? Electrical engineers? Administrative professionals? They all have associations or societies.

Most associations have local or state chapters and a national umbrella organization. Local and state chapters offer monthly meetings and events with educational programs and speakers, where you can learn a great deal. There is also time for networking.

Even if you are not a member, most associations allow visitors to attend events by paying a non-member fee. There are student discounts for college students and some associations even have collegiate chapters.

Networking within a professional association gives you the inside track to job opportunities and mentors.

4. **Volunteer Events**

   Business leaders and community movers and shakers often chair volunteer events and projects, so volunteering is a good way to meet them – and show off your skills.

   The younger you are, the more excited the charity's planning committee is to see you walk through their door. Younger, tech savvy volunteers can take over the social media promotion for a charity and also attract other younger volunteers.

   When I lived in Connecticut, I volunteered for the Multiple Myeloma Ball at the Hyatt Regency in Greenwich. One year, comedian Joan Rivers paid my friend, Kim, a nice compliment on her dress. Kim was thrilled to pieces, since Rivers was the fashion authority known for searing celebrities on the red carpet for their style missteps.

   Kim had funny run-ins with celebrities. When her future husband proposed to her on a golf course in Stamford, Connecticut, actor Gene Wilder was playing with a group on the hole behind. Wilder congratulated the happy couple and posed for photos with them. Kim, bawling from the proposal, cried, "Oh Mr. Wilder – I love your movies!"

   Besides putting you in the path of business leaders who have the power to create positions or refer you to other high-powered friends, volunteering can also be a great boost to your social life. It's the best way to meet nice people, because nice people volunteer.

5. **Chambers of Commerce**

   Your local chamber of commerce offers access to events and networking opportunities with business and community leaders. These events show you what's going on in the community, such as economic initiatives and new or expanding organizations.

   Chambers help organizations grow their business and growing organizations are always hiring. Chamber events are a great place to connect with professionals and ask them questions.

I belong to my local chamber and my favorite events are the "Ribbon Cuttings," where chamber leaders show up with a ribbon and a giant scissors to businesses that have just opened, joined the chamber or having a special anniversary or milestone.

I used to think, "Why would I go to a Ribbon Cutting, if I don't know the business owners?" But now I know you go to offer your congratulations for their success. I have made a lot of friends in the business community through chamber events.

Many chambers have "YP" (Young Professionals) groups for those in their 20s and 30s. Like regular chamber events, YPs have access to great speakers and community leaders to help grow their skills and find new opportunities. YP groups offer a chance to assume leadership roles early in your career.

Other civic organizations include convention and visitors bureaus, Rotary Clubs and breakfast clubs. (For more networking places, see Chapter 1.4: *Networking Strategy: Turn Your Contacts Into Advocates.*)

When you get out and meet people, you learn about opportunities and openings before they come open. And you may have a chance to secure an interview, bypassing the software screening process.

People Who Want You to Get a Job

Have you ever hit a rough patch in life where nothing seems to go right? Years ago, on the day after Christmas, I was at a local pharmacy chain, near my parents' home, buying a leftover Christmas tree. A young woman from my high school class sauntered over and said, "How are you?! I just came from my workout at 'the club' (as if I am supposed to know which "club.") What are you up to?"

I replied, "I just lost my job, our Great Dane died Christmas Eve and now I am buying a Christmas tree." She said, "Oh. Well, I need to look at some candles over there," and she took off.

When you tell people you are out of work, some will flee. Others will offer assistance or leads. The latter are why you need to get out there. Don't avoid holiday parties, networking events, kids' concerts and other gatherings. When you are unemployed, these are exactly the places you should be. The more you get out, the more you have a chance of meeting someone who can help you. Networking skills honed in holiday season are valuable assets when you do find a job.

Don't feel embarrassed to ask for help when looking for a job. There are people who want to help. How do you tell people, "I am unemployed?" Keep it positive:

> *"I was recently laid off, but am actively looking for a new position."*
> *"I am in between jobs, but looking for something in the (area of expertise) field."*
> *"My employer was downsizing, but I see it as a great opportunity to start something new."*

Sometimes a layoff or firing is a kick in the right direction. Don't badmouth your former employer. No one wants to hire or refer someone whose career path is "scorched earth."

Getting out does not mean you become a walking, talking resume. This is the time to do research. The best way to start and continue a conversation is to ask questions:

> *"What do you do for a living?"*
> *"How long have you been with that organization?"*
> *"How did you get started in that field?"*
> *"What do you like best about your organization?"*

This is not just job research, it's organizational research, because you learn which organizations have happy and satisfied employees and which ones don't. (One person badmouthing their organization might be a malcontent. Three is a pattern.) When you take an interest in others, others will take an interest in you.

Don't pounce on people with desperate pitches, look for inroads:

- *"I am trying to build more contacts in your line of work. Can I call and make an appointment to speak to you further?"*
- *"Do you have any advice for someone like me who is just getting started in your field?"*
- *"I know data analysis is not your area, but can you recommend a person at your organization to speak to?"*

If you are really a star, you will follow up with a note to a few of these people at their workplace. *"I enjoyed meeting you at..."*

Weathering Unsolicited Advice

There may be a lot of unsolicited and unwanted advice – especially from family members:

> *"You should have never majored in history. Go back and get an accounting degree."*
> *"I know an organization that is hiring telemarketers.*
> *"You should wear more make up."*
> *"So what if it's minimum wage? You're not making anything right now."*

Smile and say, "Thank you" (no matter what you are thinking.)

The Year End Job Search Blues

The holidays are especially tough, because a lot of organizations lay off people at the end of the year. Except for the retail sector, hiring and purchasing grinds to a halt in November and December. If you are job hunting at this time, it's easy to get discouraged, especially if you are around people who are in a good mood and buying lots of stuff. Don't be disheartened. Everyone has been there.

Organizations might recruit and do initial interviews in December for hiring in the new year. In January and February, commerce comes back to life. Hiring and purchasing heats up. Companies start fresh with new budgets. Don't take a month off, stick to your job search like a dog on a trail and soon enough you will be barking with the big dogs.

Referrals

Ask people you meet if they can refer you to others who might be willing to talk to you. If you email or call any of these referrals, there is a right way and a wrong way:

> Wrong: *"Here's my resume. Do you have a job for me?"*
> Right: *"I am interested in working in your industry, do you mind if I ask you a few questions about your organization and your career?"* Never forget you are representing the person who referred you. You have an obligation to represent that person well:

- Make sure your emails and letters have a salutation (Dear:) and closing (Sincerely,).
- Dress well. Your clothing should be professional, clean and pressed.
- Be early for appointments. Never be a no-show.
- Follow up with a thank you note to the referral, as well as the person who referred you.

If someone doesn't have time to talk to you, keep looking for the next person who will.

Online Referrals

Social media sites like *LinkedIn* are valuable for finding connections. To target a certain organization or city, plug that into *LinkedIn* and see if your connections match up with any other connections in your target. You can also sift through fellow university alumni on *LinkedIn* to find people to send invites to connect.

"I'm a fellow Hawkeye with a degree in economics, and I would like to learn more about your organization and area of expertise..."

Warming Up to the Cold Call

"Did you call the manager of the department that is hiring?"
"No, they said not to do that."
"Who's they?"
"Whoever wrote the online application. It's against the rules."
"Do you always follow the rules?"

Looking for a job is a job in itself. And part of that job, is making a few uncomfortable phone calls. Why do we have to cold call anyway? In Chapter 1.1: *Networking: The Basics,* I mentioned my friend, the realtor, who said, "We cold call, because we never know who needs us."

If you are looking for a job or an internship, you and your skill set might be exactly what that organization needs. How will you ever know if you don't make the call? Stop procrastinating and give yourself a goal.

"I am going to make five cold calls today."
"I am going to make ten cold calls this week."

Just do it. It begins with, *"Thank you for taking my call..."*

"You have an opening for a software engineer and I feel like my experience could be useful to your organization..."
"We have a mutual friend in Mack Ademia, and he suggested I call to ask about your experience in the restaurant association..."

You did it. How bad was that? Okay, it was awful. Really awful. Except for the one person who said, "Maybe." Keep going. It gets better. You could try "cold emailing" instead. But remember the "Hierarchy of No." It's easier to say, "No" to an email than a person's voice.

How we behave in the interview process is an indication of how we will behave in the job. Will you be the person who checks in with the client to see how the product or service is working? Or will you wait for the client to call you when there is a problem? Make the call. Is the person you are calling, not available? Gently coax information: "Is there a better time to reach him/her?" You do not have to make any calls, but you may lose the job to someone who did.

BE EXCEPTIONAL: Walk Your Resume In

After networking and cold calling, *The Exceptional Professional* pounds pavement.

I have a niece who is very shy. She had been out of college for year and was working, but looking for a better job. I convinced her to create a package with her resume and walk it into a few places. It made her more bold. She was really proud when she made it past the receptionist. A month later, she had a job.

Obviously, there are some places, like financial institutions, that have high security, where you won't be able to walk your resume in. But there are other places where you can.

A friend of mine was a single mother in college. When she graduated, she put on a suit and walked her resume into multiple marketing and advertising firms. One firm seemed indifferent at first, but when the manager thought about the moxie it took to walk in with her resume, he said, "That's the kind of person we're looking for." He called her up and offered her a job.

How you communicate with an employer during the interview process is a reflection of how you will communicate on the job. Who doesn't want someone professional, assertive and industrious?

Temp Agencies

Whenever I was in between jobs, I applied for temporary work through temp agencies, so I would still have income and I could pay my bills.

Organizations call on temp agencies to fill in people where they are short staffed. Usually, it's a clerical positions. But it could be manual labor, like factory work. Some temps have a specific skill, such as accounting or legal expertise. When you are interviewing, you can say, "I worked for temp agencies while in between jobs, to keep busy."

Temping can be a lonely job. Few people in a workplace talk to or even acknowledge the temp. Why? They know the temp might not be around next week or next month. Why bother?

Sometimes you land in awkward situations. I remember temping at a family-owned business where one of the owners was lunching out with attractive women who were not his wife, while I fielded calls from his angry wife demanding, "WHERE is that SONOFA- (bleep)?"

You have some control – you can reject an assignment if you like. But the more you reject assignments, the less the temp agency will call.

If you only sign up for one temp agency, you might not have work every day. Sign up for two or three agencies at once. That way, one of them will always be calling and you will stay busy. Clerical work may be well below your skill set, but sometimes, it gets your foot in the door and leads to bigger opportunities.

If the organization wants to hire you full time, they pay the temp agency a fee.

Career Fairs

A young woman told me she was late for a career fair at her university. Weighted down with a backpack, heavy with textbooks, she went running down a long flight of stairs in her pant suit and heels. You know how slippery marble steps can be? Her heel slipped, she stumbled forward. The backpack flipped over her head and the weight of it rolled her like a snowball down the steps, end over end.

No bones were broken, but she did end up with some scrapes and blood stains on the knees of her dress pants. She decided to muscle through. The blood stained knees became a topic of conversation with many of the recruiters.

Hopefully, if you go to a career fair, it won't involve a fall down the stairs. Here are some tips to having a successful career fair experience:

> **Dress appropriately.** Don't wear jeans and a sweatshirt. Dress like you would for an interview.
>
> **Shake hands coming and going.** Reach out and give a firm handshake when you approach a recruiter. Say, "Hello, I'm (first name, last name)." Shake the recruiter's hand again when you leave.
>
> **Ask questions.** Start a conversation, instead of an elevator speech.
>
> *"I am interested in learning more about the opportunities for liberal arts majors at your organization."*
> *"What skills are you looking for in your chemical engineering interns?"*
> *"What do you like best about working for this organization?"*
>
> Or ask any questions that came up in your research of the companies.
>
> **Close with an expression of enthusiasm.** *"Thank you for your time. I know I could help improve your customers' experience."*
> *"I appreciate your time. I will follow up by phone next week."*

Honor your commitments. An appointment for an interview at a career fair, is the same as a regular interview. Blowing off an interview, wastes the time of the interviewers, who could have scheduled someone else.

Employers at career fairs tell me some candidates have their mother in tow… or possibly, the other way around. If they get hired, do they plan to bring their mother to work with them? Sometimes Mom works the career fair without the candidate. "Maybe we should hire the mother," said one employer. If you go to a career fair, leave your significant mother at home.

Follow up. Get a business card or name from recruiter. Send an email and a typed thank you note with another copy of your resume.

Letters of Recommendation: A Team Effort

The first time I needed a letter of recommendation, I asked a favorite college professor. He said, "Write the letter you want and send it to me. I'll make any changes."

What? How could I write a letter in this brilliant professor's voice? He has a PhD – can't he generate these letters in no time at all?

But it made sense. He probably had dozens of recommendation requests from students. Imagine the time it would take. Anyone writing a recommendation is doing you a big favor. Help that person help you. Editing is easier than writing from scratch. When asking for a recommendation letter:

- Give the purpose for the recommendation: job, graduate school, etc.
- Include points you would like emphasized: excellent verbal and written skills, self-motivated, good team player. (It's the privilege of the recommender to agree or disagree.)
- Provide a suggested letter and include your resume or CV.
- Send a follow up note thanking the person for the recommendation.
- Don't say, "I need this tomorrow." Nobody is sitting around waiting to write your recommendation. Give at least a week or two lead time.

I agonized over my recommendation draft. What if it's too bold and he thinks, "Who is she kidding?" What if I undersell my skills and he just signs it? My fears were unfounded. If there were a Pulitzer Prize for recommendations, my professor's final edit would have won.

While in college, cultivate close professional relationships with your future recommendation writers. Be attentive to professors, prepare for class, participate in discussions and ask thoughtful questions. Write thank you notes for classes well taught.

Give your recommendation writer information, time and gratitude. The best recommendation letters are a team effort. Get your references in order. Ask people ahead of time if they would provide a reference. Be prepared to write your own reference letter and submit it for approval.

Research Before the Interview

One executive told me his first question for any interview is: "Tell me what you know about my organization." If a candidate has no information, he says, "Thank you very much, there is no reason to continue this interview, because you are obviously not prepared."

We're always reading about how you should research an organization before an interview. But what type of information should you look for? Even if you are not interviewing, review this list to see how much you know about your own organization.

Organization

Mission statement
Structure
Public or private?
Stock performance (if publicly-traded)
Action by shareholders or activists

Leadership

Background of your interviewer
Top management

Organization founder and the founder's story
Notable board members
Changes in leadership
Alumni from your school with that organization (find on *LinkedIn*)

Products
Products or services/product lines
Innovations
Target customer
Markets the products are sold in and emerging markets
Market share
Sales channels
Advertising campaigns

Industry
Competition: domestic and abroad
Market share of competitors
Recent mergers and acquisitions
Controversial issues in the industry

Sources for Research
Organization website, annual reports, press releases
Trade publications
Business publications: *Wall Street Journal, Bloomberg, Barron's, Forbes, Fortune,* etc.
Local newspaper business section
Internet searches
Twitter: #organizationname
LinkedIn: search by organization to see if you have related connections

Learning all of these elements about an organization may sound like a lot of work. But it could be the difference between you and another candidate, who didn't bother to do the homework. And it's never wasted information. If you do get the job, you will be that much more ahead.

Don't fill out online applications and wait for things to happen. If you want a certain job, go get it. The more proactive you are, the more you increase your chances of finding the opportunities that are the best fit. But it's never just about one job. The efforts you make to meet people will move you forward in life.

NOTES

1 Scott Stratten, *UnMarketing*, speaking at the National Speakers Association Conference in Phoenix, AZ, 7/24/2016, Available at: https://www.youtube.com / *watch?v=W7a8WiAmmo0*

2 Lee Rainie and Kathryn Zickuhr, "Americans Views on Mobile Etiquette," *Pew Research Center*, 8/26/2015.

3 Dale Carnegie, *How to Win Friends and Influence People,* Simon and Schuster, New York, 1964.

4 "Why You Should Consider Friending Your Boss On *Facebook*," *MONEY*, 7/7/2014, Available at: http://time.com/money/2963442/why-it-might-be-smart-to-friend-your-boss-on-facebook/

5 Tim Sohn, "Survey: Senior Managers Do Not Want You to Friend them on Facebook," *AdWeek*, 8/12/2013, Available at: http://www.adweek.com/socialtimes / survey-senior-managers-increasingly-dislike-friend-requests-on-facebook/ 135144

6 "Number of Employers Using Social Media to Screen Candidates Has Increased 500 Percent over the Last Decade," CareerBuilder.com survey, 8/26/2016, Available at: http://www.careerbuilder.com/share/aboutus/press releasesdetail.aspx?ed=12/31/2016&id=pr945&sd=4/28/2016

7 "Number of Employers Passing on Applicants Due to Social Media Posts Continues to Rise, According to New CareerBuilder Survey," CareerBuilder.com release, 6/26/2014: Available at: http://www.careerbuilder.com/share/aboutus/pressreleasesdetail.aspx?sd=6%2F26%2F2014&id=pr829&ed=12%2F31%2F2014)

8 "Number of Employers Using Social Media to Screen Candidates at All-Time High, Finds Latest CareerBuilder Study," CareerBuilder.com release, 6/15/2017: Available at: http://press.careerbuilder.com/2017-06-15-Number-of-Employers-Using-Social-Media-to-Screen-Candidates-at-All-Time-High-Finds-Latest-CareerBuilder-Study

9 Rod Serling,"To Serve Man," *The Twilight Zone*, Season 3, Episode 24, first aired 3/2/1962.

10 "31 Million U.S. Consumers Skip Breakfast Each Day, Reports NPD," The NPD Group, 10/11/2011.

11 Rachel Laneri, "Body Language Decoded," *Forbes*, 2009.

12 Letitia Baldrige, *New Manners for New Times*, Scribner, New York, 2003.

13 Judith Martin: *Miss Manners' Guide to Excruciatingly Correct Behavior*, W.W. Norton and Company, New York, 2005.

14 Maria Everding, *Panache that Pays: The Young Professional's Guide on How to Outclass Your Competition*, Maria Perniciaro Everding, 2007.

15 Elizabeth Post, *Emily Post's Etiquette, 15th Edition*, HarperCollins Publishers, New York, 1992.

16 Amy Vanderbilt, *Amy Vanderbilt's Complete Book of Etiquette: A Guide to Gracious Living*, Doubleday and Company, New York, 1954.

17 Suzanne von Drachnenfels, *The Art of the Table: A Complete Guide to Table Setting, Table Manners, and Tableware*, Simon and Schuster, New York, 2008.

18 Marjabelle Young (Stewart) and Ann Buchwald, *White Gloves and Party Manners*, Robert B. Luce, Inc., Washington, D.C., 1967.

19 *NCAA Football 2016 and 2017 Rules and Interpretations*, National Collegiate Athletic Association Publications, p. FR-93, 7/19/2017, Available at: http://www.ncaapublications.com/productdownloads/FR17updated.pdf

20 *Google's "Ten Things that we know to be true,"* Available at: https://www.google.com/about/philosophy.html

21 Ruchika Tulshyan, "Is Casual Dress Killing Your Productivity at Work?" *Forbes*, 10/17/2013.

22 "Survey Shows How Clothing Choices Affect Promotion Prospects," Survey by OfficeTeam, 5/16/2013. Available at: https://www.prnewswire.com/news-releases/survey-shows-how-clothing-choices-affect-promotion-prospects-207688301.html

23 "Tattoo Takeover: Three in Ten Americans Have Tattoos, and Most Don't Stop at Just One," Harris Poll, 2/10/2016. Available at: http://www.theharrispoll.com/health-and-life/Tattoo_Takeover.html

24 Maybelle Morgan, "An ex-lover's name, foreign misspellings and dolphins: The top 10 most removed tattoo designs... and the celebrities that had them inked on their bodies," *U.K Daily Mail*, 7/10/2015.

25 Cheryl Lu-Lien Tan, "Making Your Cashmere Last for Decades, Softer Over Time," *Wall Street Journal*, 12/1/2011.

26 Mortimer Levitt, *The Executive Look: How to Get It – How to Keep It*, Atheneum, New York, 1981.

27 Molloy, John T., *Dress for Success*, Warner Books, New York, 1976.
and *New Women's Dress for Success*, Warner Books, New York, 1996.

28 Tom Hopkins, *Selling for Dummies*, Wiley Publishing, Inc., 2001.

29 P.M. Forni, *The Civility Solution: What to Do When People Are Rude,* St. Martin's Press, New York, 2008.

30 P.M. Forni, Choosing Civility: The Twenty-five Rules of Considerate Conduct, St. Martin's Press, New York, 2002.

31 Thomas J. Stanley, Ph.D. and William D. Danko, Ph.D., *The Millionaire Next Door: The Surprising Secrets of America's Wealthy,* Pocket Books, New York, 1996.

32 Dale Carnegie, *How to Win Friends and Influence People,* Simon and Schuster, New York, 1964.

33 Christine Pearson and Christine Porath, *The Cost of Bad Behavior: How Incivility is Damaging Your Business and What to Do About It,*" Portfolio, New York, 2009.

34 "Sexual Harassment," U.S. Equal Employment Opportunity Commission, Available at: https://www1.eeoc.gov/laws/types/sexual_harassment.cfm

35 Gary Namie, Ph.D., Research Director "U.S. Hostile Workplace Survey," Workplace Bullying Institute, 2000, Available at: http://www.workplacebullying .org/ multi/pdf/N-N-2000.pdf, and "Who Gets Targeted," Workplace Bullying Institute, 2012, Available at: http://www.workplacebullying.org/individuals/ problem/who-gets-targeted/

36 Jeannie Gaffigan, @jeanniegaffigan tweet on Twitter: 9/5/2014.

37 Uber, "Can I tip the driver in cash?" Available at: https://help.uber.com /h/8459a496-5ed2-4f9d-b15c-d8afd9ccf34f)

38 Abraham H. Maslow, *Maslow on Management,* John Wiley and Sons, Inc, New York, 1998.

ABOUT THE AUTHOR

CALLISTA GOULD is a Certified Etiquette Instructor and Founder of the Culture and Manners Institute. Prior to this, she had 20 years of business experience working for global brands such as Sony Music (Columbia and Epic recording labels), Amana Appliances and InterTech Media. Born in Des Moines, Iowa, she has an MBA from Loyola University of Chicago and a BA in English and Medieval Studies from the University of Iowa. She lives in West Des Moines, Iowa. Her etiquette expertise has been featured in *The Wall Street Journal, The Chicago Tribune, The Dallas Morning News* and *The Baltimore Sun.* Her *Etiquette Tip of the Week* runs in *The Des Moines Register.* And sometimes... *she tweets.*

INDEX

Made in the USA
San Bernardino, CA
19 October 2018